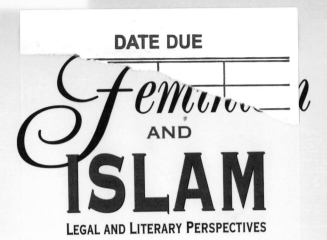

Feminism

AND

ISLAM

LEGAL AND LITERARY PERSPECTIVES

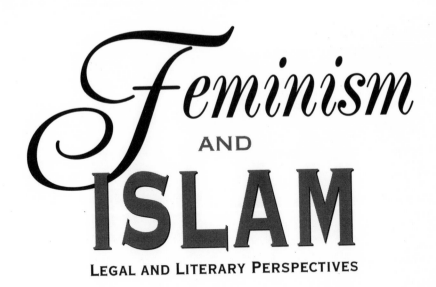

Feminism AND ISLAM

LEGAL AND LITERARY PERSPECTIVES

EDITED BY

MAI YAMANI

WITH
ADDITIONAL EDITORIAL ASSISTANCE
FROM

ANDREW ALLEN

NEW YORK UNIVERSITY PRESS

WASHINGTON SQUARE, NEW YORK

Copyright © Mai Yamani, 1996.

First published in the USA in 1996 by
New York University Press
Washington Square
New York, N.Y. 10003
by special arrangement with Ithaca Press, UK.

Jacket and book design by David Rose
Typeset by Samantha Abley

Printed in Lebanon

Library of Congress Cataloging-in-Publication Data
Feminism and Islam : legal and literary perspectives / edited by Mai Yamani with
additional editorial assistance from Andrew Allen.
     p.   cm.
Includes bibliographical references (p.   ) and index.
ISBN 0-8147-9680-X. – ISBN 0-8147-9681-8 (pbk.)
1. Muslim women.
2. Women – Legal status, laws, etc. (Islamic law)
3. Feminism – Religious aspects – Islam.
4. Women – Islamic countries – Social conditions.
I. Yamani, Mai.   II. Allen, Andrew.
HQ1170.F46 1996
305. 48'6971 – dc20

96-21420
CIP

CONTENTS

Contents

ACKNOWLEDGEMENTS

The Centre of Islamic and Middle Eastern Law (CIMEL) at the School of Oriental and African Studies (SOAS), University of London, is particularly indebted to Susan Faidi for her tireless effort in the preparation of this book, and also to Cathy Green and Rukhsana Kiani. CIMEL would also like to acknowledge its debt to Investcorp and to Mr Nemir Kirdar, who have supported its activities and made this book, *inter alia,* possible.

Special thanks are due to Dr Chibli Mallat, Director of CIMEL, for his continuous devotion to the cause and to His Honour Judge Eugene Cotran, Chairman, for his patience and forbearance.

NOTE ON TRANSLITERATION

The transliteration of Arabic words and names is largely based on the system used by the *International Journal of Middle Eastern Studies.* No diacritics are used; the *'ayn* and the *hamza* are indicated by a single opening and closing quotation mark respectively.

CONTRIBUTORS

Lama Abu-Odeh has a doctorate in law and works currently as Legal Counsellor at the World Bank.

Haleh Afshar is Senior Lecturer and Head of the Centre for Woman's Studies at the University of York and also teaches Islamic Law at the Faculté Internationale de Droit Comparé at Strasbourg. She was born and raised in Iran where she worked as a journalist and a civil servant before the revolution. She is the convenor of the Development Studies Association's Women's Group, and Development Study Group, and has edited several books produced by this group; the most recent include *Women in the Middle East* (Basingstoke: Macmillan, 1994); and jointly edited with Mary Maynard, *The Dynamics of Race and Gender* (London: Taylor & Francis, 1994). Haleh Afshar is also the convenor of the Political Studies Association's Women's Group. She remains active in feminist Iranian politics and has written extensively on the subject.

Maha Azzam is Senior Researcher at the Royal United Services Institute for Defence Studies, London, where she is running a programme on Security and Development in Muslim States. Her main area of research and writing has been on Islamist groups and politics in the Middle East. Her forthcoming publication is *Radical Islam in Egypt* (Cambridge: Cambridge University Press, 1996). She is currently working on a MacArthur-funded project (Programme on Peace and International Cooperation) on the connection between ideology, culture and development in the Middle East, Pakistan and South East Asia.

Jane Connors is an academic lawyer, educated in Australia. She moved to Britain ten years ago and has taught at the School of Oriental and African Studies for the past nine years. Her research and interests are in women's human rights and violence against women. Her publications, which have been mainly action-oriented, include *Violence Against Women in the Family*, which was written for the United Nations. She acts as a consultant for a number of international bodies, including the UN for whom she has worked on the UN Declaration on Violence Against Women in 1993. She is currently involved in the work towards the elaboration of a complaints mechanism for the Convention on the Elimination of All Forms of Discrimination against Women.

Munira Fakhro obtained her Master's degree in Social Services from Bryn Mawr College and her doctorate in Social Welfare from Columbia University. A member of the Bahrain High Council for Culture and Arts, she served as head of the Special Welfare Section of the Ministry of Labour and Social Affairs. As an expert on the role of women, she has participated in many regional and international conferences and has contributed to projects in the Gulf region sponsored by the United Nations Development Programme (UNFPA). She is currently Assistant Professor of Social Change and Social Development at Bahrain University.

Najla Hamadeh has worked as cultural editor, translator and researcher in a number of journals and magazines, before teaching at the Lebanese University, then at the American University of Beirut as full-time Assistant Professor, where she gives courses on modern philosophy and cultural studies. She has published several studies in Arabic and in English and is currently preparing a book on *Biographies of Women from Lebanon and Syria.*

Ghada Karmi is Senior Research Fellow at the Centre for Middle Eastern and Islamic Studies, Durham University. She is an expert on Islamic mediaeval medicine in which she holds a Ph.D. from University College, London, and has written widely on the subject. Her recent research includes several studies on Arab migrant communities in Britain. She is also a doctor of medicine and a specialist in public health.

Jean Said Makdisi is the author of *Beirut Fragments: A War Memoir* (New York: Persea Books, 1990). Her second book, *Inside History: Three Generations of Arab Women,* is nearing completion and will be published in 1996, also by Persea Books. She teaches English and Humanities at the Lebanese American University (formerly Beirut University College).

Afaf Lutfi al-Sayyid Marsot, D.Phil., Oxford, is Professor of Near and Middle Eastern History at the University of California, Los Angeles. Her publications include *Egypt in the Reign of Muhammad Ali* (Cambridge: Cambridge University Press, 1983); *A Short History of Modern Egypt*

(Cambridge: Cambridge University Press, 1985). Her present contribution draws heavily on her recent work, *Women and Men in Late Eighteenth-Century Egypt* (Austin: University of Texas Press, 1995).

Elizabeth McKee studied Arabic at the School of Oriental and African Studies (SOAS) and after graduating in 1991, spent several months as a volunteer aid worker in Jordan in the aftermath of the Gulf War, before returning to London and obtaining her Ph.D. in 1995. During her research she taught modern Arabic literature and literary theory at SOAS and is currently working as a freelance journalist and translator.

Ziba Mir-Hosseini obtained her first degree in Sociology from Tehran University and her Ph.D. in Social Anthropology from the University of Cambridge, where she is a Research Associate. She also works as a freelance consultant on gender and development, and is the author of *Marriage on Trial: A Study of Islamic Family Law in Iran and Morocco* (London: I.B. Tauris, 1993) and a forthcoming monograph on the Ahl-e Haqq sect of Kurdistan.

Souad Mokbel-Wensley has a degree in Lebanese law from the Université Saint Joseph, Faculté de Droit et des Sciences Economiques, Beirut, Lebanon. She has completed a Master's degree in French Public Law from the Université Jean Moulin, Faculté de Droit, Lyon, France. She has also obtained a Diplôme des Etudes Superieures (D.E.S.) in French Private Law from the Université Jean Moulin, Faculté de Droit, and is Avocat à la Cour-Barreau de Beyrouth. She is also registered as an overseas lawyer with the Law Society of London.

Raga' El-Nimr graduated in English Literature and Education from Assuit University, Egypt. She taught English as a foreign language (E.F.L.) in Egypt and Kuwait. In London, she worked in the field of translation and journalism for a number of years. Due to the religious diversity encountered in London, she pursued studies in Islamic law and obtained an MA from SOAS, University of London, in the subject. She then taught at the Muslim College for some time. At present she teaches Islamic Studies and Philosophy of Religion at the King Fahad Academy in London.

Mona Siddiqui is Lecturer and Consultant in Islamic Studies at the University of Glasgow, Faculty of Divinity. Her Ph.D. thesis examined the development of classical Islamic jurisprudence with specific reference to the marriage contract. Her publications include an article in the *Oxford Journal of Islamic Studies* entitled *'Mahr:* Legal Obligation or Rightful Demand?'. She is currently writing an article on aspects of Islamic personal law and its possible relevance in Britain.

Mai Yamani gratuated in anthropology from Bryn Mawr College and gained her MA and D.Phil. in Social Anthropology from Oxford University. She was a lecturer at King Abdul Aziz University, Saudi Arabia, and has also lectured widely in the Middle East, Europe and the United States on topics related to women in Middle Eastern society. She was a research fellow at the Centre for Cross Cultural Research on Women at Oxford, Academic Adviser to the Centre for Contemporary Arab Studies at Georgetown University, Washington DC, and is currently Research Associate at the Centre for Islamic and Middle Eastern Law (CIMEL) at SOAS, University of London. She is a regular columnist on social affairs for the newspaper *Al-Hayat* and the magazine *Al-Rajul*, both published in Arabic from London. Mai Yamani is also a contributing member of many of the cross-cultural Arab societies based in Britain and America, in addition to the Royal United Services Institute for Defence Studies, Whitehall, and the Royal Institute for International Affairs (Chatham House).

ONE

INTRODUCTION

Mai Yamani

This book brings together renowned women researchers and academics –
historians, political scientists, lawyers, sociologists, social anthropologists and literary critics – who examine the phenomenon of feminism
within the Islamic cultural framework.

There is already a wide range of theories and expressions of behaviour related to feminism worldwide: legal feminism, Marxist feminism,
cultural feminism, liberal feminism, post-modern feminism . . .
"Feminists do not all think the same way or even about the same kinds
of problems."[1]

This book adds yet another layer by introducing a feminism which is
"Islamic" in its form and content. With the typology now embracing
religion as a new complex of references, such feminism is unique in
conjuring up delicate and challenging issues for political and religious
authorities as well as for scholars in a world of a billion Muslims. Within
that new overarching background which deals with Islamic laws and
traditions, the category of "Islamic feminism" may stand its ground by
the sheer diversity it includes: contributors to the debate have been
considered "new feminist traditionalists", "pragmatists", "secular feminists", "neo-Islamists", and so forth. For all these thinkers, however,
there is a common concern with the empowerment of their gender within
a rethought Islam.[2]

The question of what is intrinsically Islamic with respect to ideas
about women and gender remains complicated by several clichés which
have been confused with Islam, e.g. female circumcision and the concept
of "crimes of honour". Here a return to history is required, looking
at religious texts and *fiqh* documents in a more critical and objective
manner.

The collection also identifies obstacles facing those women who aim
at equality in areas of family law and civil rights. Concepts of gender in
societies that preceded early Islamic society are examined in order to
better understand the foundation of Islamic discourses.[3] With the book
focusing on Islamic legal feminism, traditional interpretations of Islamic

I

law are confronted by women feminists and scholars with a determined, if not always easy, strategy renovating the field. In an increasingly rich and effective literature, this book features also studies which shed light on the treatment of women by the Islamic legal system and investigate factors that are preparing the ground for new reformed schools of Islamic jurisprudence.

Although the general concern over a broad definition of "Islamic feminism" offers the common underlying theme, the fight for increased rights for women is not always presented in traditional Islamic terms. In addition, not all Muslim states and societies should necessarily be termed "Islamic". Sizeable Christian communities also come under examination. Comparison between religious and secular laws concerning women are useful in that context, as are the complex legal areas where the traditions need to accompany mixed marriages and marriages contracted abroad.

With all their diversity and the different contexts in which they were written, several chapters highlight surrounding social and political conditions for the flourishing of organised feminist movements in Muslim countries, movements that aim at the amelioration of the status of women primarily by the utilisation of Islamic rights.

The societies studied by the authors in this volume are geographically, culturally and politically diverse. There is no uniformity in Islamic law across Muslim countries,[4] and the book does not try to cover the full scope of Muslim societies. It does seek however to offer a significant range of shared social problems covering women's economic activities, political power, domestic and social relations, and attempts to underline strategies and practical analyses that are current in the wide Muslim world.

Be the diversity of Muslim societies as it may, the collection was intended to contribute to the enrichment of the field, a better understanding of which must surely be a further step on the way of liberation and equality.[5] One hopes that this volume will show that in a dynamic and critical world, Islam cannot but be viewed critically and objectively. The reinterpretation of the Qur'an is not a new practice. The Qur'an has been interpreted and reinterpreted from the time of Revelation to the present, including by women. Whilst most interpretations have been products of the discourse of male *'ulama*, women's Islamic discourses are starting to provide significant counter-points, including in the rereading of Islamic religious texts with attention given to the female figures of the early Islamic polity.[6]

The papers have been accordingly grouped into four parts. The first, "Beginnings and History", contains the chapters dealing with the historical context. The second, on "The Language of Literature and Culture", covers the treatment of women's issues in recent Arabic literature and in social perceptions. The third part, "The Politics of Interpretations" examines the interface between politics and words as they shape the world of women – from Iran to Egypt. The fourth part defines "The Confines of Law" in which women are able to operate. Whilst the present Introduction does not aim to reduce the unusual richness of the contributions to bland summaries, it might be helpful to rapidly sketch some of the ideas which are forcefully emerging in the process of investigation.

Beginnings and History

Afaf Lutfi al-Sayyid Marsot bases her argument on the position of women in a historical survey of the eighteenth, nineteenth and twentieth centuries. She shows that woman's position is determined not so much by the principles of Islam as by social practices. Only against a well-studied historical context are feminists able to analyse the factors that favour women's equality and those that hinder their rise to prominence. These factors are related to the political structure. The chapter examines economic power ascribed to Muslim women and highlights the difference between the ideal and practice in Islamic societies. Although it is a fact that Islam offers economic capacity to women with regard to ownership and control of wealth, in practice there were periods where these rights could not be fully exercised. For example, while the Qur'an clearly lays down that women can inherit (usually half of the share of a man of equivalent connection to the praepositus), in some Muslim societies their share was cut, with properties transformed into trust, *waqf*.[7] The dowry, *mahr*, legally owing to the bride, has often been retained in practice by her family. Furthermore, since there is no concept of joint property in Islam, her wealth is, in some cases, unjustly used by her husband as his own.

Political, economic and social factors determined women's economic participation in the 18th century. The government in Egypt was then decentralised, with the Mamluks fighting each other in a struggle for supremacy. Their fear of death and of the confiscation of their properties led them to give it to their wives. Women as a result inherited substantial wealth from their fathers and husbands, and it was often the case that a woman was married more than once. On the religious side, the *'ulama* were powerful in the legal and commercial world and hence promoted business and dealt with and supported women in court. Women sued in court for divorce and although they needed agents in their business enterprises, they had full control over their property. During that period, entrepreneurial women mostly engaged in property-related activities – the buying and selling of land. The political and religious set-up and the economic circumstances clearly favoured women's entrepreneurial efforts in that epoch.

The chapter then shows how political authority can change the position of women in a Muslim society. In the nineteenth century the government was centralised and the marginalisation of the position of the *'ulama*,[8] together with the British presence caused a significant set-back to women's economic participation. Egyptian wealth became increasingly controlled by the state; Muhammad 'Ali, who governed Egypt over much of the first half of the century, rewarded people he favoured, but these were not women. Women lost their rights to participation in banks and they lost their links with the *'ulama*, who, in turn, had lost their judicial duties. The decline in women's status and loss of rights filtered down through society. Under the new order the women *fallahs* (peasants who worked as labourers) were paid half the wages of men. Native Egyptian women's economic rights based on Islam were diminished as Western influence took over. Victorian standards of women being "mere wives" or decorative appendages to their husbands took over. Rather than progress, this was clearly a step back following a departure from basic Islamic teachings.

The beginning of the twentieth century saw again radical changes in political rule. Egyptian independence offered women another opportunity to re-establish independent professional status. The route they took was gradual; at first they engaged in benevolent social work and eventually made it to paid professional jobs. Education for women and especially university education during the 1930s was their most important tool. Marsot also points out that once women had demonstrated in the streets, they crossed a point of no return. Once women become aware of their rights it was too late to go back.

Rather than merely copying the Western model, Egyptian women fought for rights. The tools women had was their knowledge of their rights within Islam generally and the exercise of their economic rights in particular. At the same time, it was necessary to take account of ambiguous popular concepts relating to such issues as the veil, which, according to Marsot, expresses both women's need of protection and subordination. It is against this peculiar history that, rather than through a mimicking of processes specific to Western feminism, women will be able to channel their efforts towards achieving greater gender equality.

In her study of the law of marriage, and in particular the Fatawa 'Alamgiri of the seventeenth century Hanafi Sunni school, Mona Siddiqui examines some rights granted to women in Islam and the measures taken by a male-dominated society to circumvent or restrict those rights. Historically, legal literature reflects the nature of Islamic society; the law of marriage in particular shows patterns of behaviour between people. The function of marriage, other than legitimising sexual intercourse, is tied to the distribution of wealth and the preservation of the social hierarchy.[9] This makes marriage choices restricted to particular juristic interpretation – rarely based on concepts of "love", rather on the Islamic principle of *kafa'a*, which is translated as equality or compatibility between the spouses. *Kafa'a* establishes six points of reference: (1) descent, (2) Islam, (3) freedom, (4) wealth, (5) piety, and (6) profession.

Siddiqui examines the tensions between "prescription" and "preference" within the theory of *kafa'a,* equality or compatibility in marriage. Women are generally not allowed enough leeway or choices within the principle of *kafa'a,* which offers "preferential" elements that are not fully enjoyed. So much in the principle of *kafa'a* is debatable, however, that social expectations of particular behaviour of women remain restrictive.

Women's rights are sometimes restricted because of social and religious norms. For example, the Hanafi Sunni school, unlike the other Sunni schools, gives women the legal capacity to be her own *wali*; in other words, to marry without the consent of her wali or male guardian. But society attaches to this a taint of shamelessness despite the legal parameters. This reflects society's reluctance to equate the observance of legal rights with approved behaviour. A woman's freedom is circumscribed by social conventions (such as the idea of shame) which are marginal to the legal system.

Siddiqui concludes that due to the increase in women's education and employment in most Muslim countries, gender boundaries or roles that still remain must be modified with the general social changes. As women work with men in less segregated atmospheres, women feel and acknowledge their own social and emotional needs. When choosing a husband the concept of love will play a significant role. However, Siddiqui observes that women on the whole still hold on to the rule of compatibility, they choose as husbands men from comparable socio-economic backgrounds. Legal principles of *kafa'a* are flexible enough to allow women more freedom of choice than they are actually taking. So far, laws were interpreted by men in their favour. With women's greater understanding of the concept of "preference" in *kafa'a*, the more rigid boundaries of this principle will eventually fade away.

Ghada Karmi attempts to examine the source of patriarchy within Islam and questions the role of religion in maintaining patriarchal structure. Karmi's approach can be classified as modernist or pragmatic; she is among those who see Islamic reform as necessary, but not as the only step required to change women's political and social situation. They advocate secular action and look at the interplay of practical factors in order to explain women's status. Karmi questions the conventional wisdom that Islam originally improved the status of women, previously accorded very few rights in a pre-Islamic world, and considers whether the patriarchal system[10] that promotes the superiority of men and demeans the status of women in Arab countries is derived from or legitimised by Islamic law itself. Based on the literature of the pre-Islamic period, Karmi posits that women were better off in terms of personal legal status and independence than after the advent of Islam when rules of subjugation of women were introduced.

She refers to some scholarly work on the period which shows that marriage customs were flexible, that matriarchal rule was prevalent and that polyandry existed alongside polygamy – hence a more equal, balanced order of relationships appears to have existed between the sexes. Karmi, as others who question or doubt the improvement in the status of women after the advent of Islam, gives the example of Khadija, the first wife of the Prophet who was a prominent trader before the advent of Islam. Looking at the matrimonial life of the Prophet Muhammad, and comparing the first part which was monogamous with Khadija as the Prophet's only wife, with the second part which was polygamous, she views a deterioration of the position of the wife. In the same vein, although 'A'isha's religious or political prominence was viewed as acceptable during the transitional phase from the *Jahiliyya* (period of ignorance) to early Islam,[11] the assessment of subsequent Islamic scholars made her role as an active and committed protagonist controversial.

Karmi expresses the conflict that some Muslim women experience. Despite their devotion to the spiritual text, they increasingly question their right to equality. In her opinion, women are transformed into non-adults in the Qur'an – to be provided for economically, their testimony not given the weight of men's. This can be seen clearly in the context of women's status with regard to divorce, custody and polygamy, all of which favour men.

In Karmi's opinion, it is useless to continue with standard pieties that some adherents to Islam repeat to justify inequalities. Instead, real reform is needed especially in the field of family law, such as that in Tunisia when polygamy was abolished. *Ijtihad* (independent reasoning) is called for and Karmi suggests that the solution to the conflicting issues on women could be found in a more objective study of the Qur'an in its historical and social context. The Qur'anic precepts must be seen as a function of social dynamics rather than used as a fixed text legitimising rigid patriarchal claims.

In contrast, it is the traditional Islamic position which is expounded by Raja' El-Nimr, who believes that because the Qur'an contains God's divine words, there is no need for interpretation if the correct meaning is acted upon. By examining the historical context in which Islam was revealed, she shows that compared to other societies at the time (the Indian and the French, for example, in the sixteenth century), Islam did provide women with significant rights, and from this point she argues that since women were better off under Islam during the Golden Age, they could still enjoy rights and privileges today. This is because for her, Islam is both "divine" and "evolutionary". In other words, the divine nature of the Qur'an incorporates an evolutionary quality making it appropriate at every point in history. El-Nimr goes a degree further in emphasising that women should not demand more rights or equality, except in the spiritual domain, since women are fundamentally different in nature from men. This is an expression of the divine will; women cannot choose for themselves better lives than God has prescribed for them.

On this basis she finds justifications for areas of apparent inequality that other writers consider challenging and degrading. These comprise the "degree" or advantage (*daraja*) men have over women, explained as man's natural gift for judging domestic matters, man's ability to put up with his wife's bad moods or the principle of male guardianship. Likewise, El-Nimr says that there is nothing demeaning in the evidence of a female witness being considered as having half the weight of a man's. This is justified by the nature of women: their fluctuating moods and mental incapacity during menstruation, pregnancy and postnatal depression. The same applies to polygamy which is, at times, acceptable, despite objections by some modernists.

El-Nimr contends that the constant preoccupation with the role and status of Muslim women is a Western obsession which should not distract Muslims from their duty to follow the direct commands of God, conveyed through the Qur'an and Prophet.

The Language of Literature and Culture

Elizabeth McKee's distinctive contribution looks at women in society as portrayed in works of Arab women writers. She takes issues with those critics who have characterised these works as being of a purely feminist nature. She feels that such an approach overlooks the political and social resonance of the works and suggests that these works are better viewed in the light of recent literary theory than through the narrow focus of Anglo-American feminist critical thought. McKee notes that women's writing is not fundamentally different from male fiction in regard to the socio-political issues. The difference is in the structural variation from male writing which is responsible for producing the change in emphasis within the female novel form.

She examines the work of seven Arab women novelists drawing attention to the strong political allegories and ideological debates as well as the articulation of female protest against social injustice. She uses as a framework of analysis, a modification of René Girard's model of triangular desire which refers to the conflicts of desire between a subject, his or her mediator and a shared object of desire. Using this model she examines Layla Ba'albakki's *Ana ahya,* Sahar Khalifah's *al-Sabbar*, Ghadah al-Samman's *Beirut 75* and *al-Watan fi al-'aynayn* by Hamidah Na'na'.

McKee notes the textual planes that lie in *Ana ahya*: an existential level, a political level and a sexual-gender level. In her argument against falling into a narrow definition or a rigid view of feminism she refers to Ghadah al-Samman's writing; specifically as to how critics focused on the writer's views on the emancipation of women and the sexual re-volution rather more than her commitment to political issues.

The novels address national and political ambiguities. A pure focus on feminist issues reduces important literary works to a marginal and unidimensional importance, and McKee calls for a revision of the fem-inist agenda by looking at the works of Arab women writers within their political context.

Lama Abu-Odeh takes on an urgent issue that concerns the position of women in Arab countries, that of the "crime of honour", a paradigmatic example of which is the killing of a woman by her father or brother for engaging in, or being suspected of engaging in, sexual practices before or outside marriage. She analyses the origins of the laws, tracing its origins from the Ottoman and French Penal Codes, and examines the effect of the intervention of the Arab nationalist elite in the social and legal fields.

Through the process of codification, this intervention has tried to modernise this traditional practice by defining certain limits and providing penalties for those who transgress these limits. The scope of this intervention has varied from country to country. Abu-Odeh notes that in Algeria the tendency is more towards crimes of passion, where both the husband and wife benefit, while in Jordan the code is more rigid with only men benefiting. She offers an anthropological survey of the societies where these crimes of honour occur, with special attention given to the preoccupation (to the point of obsession) with virginity as the regulatory practice of gender. This pre-occupation is not limited to the physical virginity of women and the physical hymen, but also with what she calls the social hymen, which is the symbol of virginity, publicised for the benefit of the social audience. The social hymen delimits borders, and prescribes a whole set of rules and regulations for women. Crimes of honour can occur when any of these borders are crossed.

Abu-Odeh points to the fact that the social function of crimes of honour changed from being merely the punishment of vice to becoming a means of constructing gender relations within society. Here, she examines a complex triangle of interaction between state violence, social violence and crimes of honour. She explains how the attempt of the nationalist elites to modernise institutions while wanting to preserve certain traditions, had an effect on the area of codification. Within their ideology, they did contribute to creating a "new woman" – educated and employed, unlike her mother, but at the same time not Westernised. The emergence of this "new woman" has changed the previous boundaries of the social hymen.

Within this dynamic situation, Lama Abu-Odeh examines new types of women ranging from the "sexy virgin" to the "virgin of love", the "coquette", the "GAP girl", the "slut" and the "tease". Then she goes on to describe their male counterparts such as the "virgin by default" the "predator", the "romantic virgin", the "virginal virgin by default" and the "predator *manqué*". She concludes that what was imposed by the nationalist elites in their attempt to modernise and crystallise social practice did not affect them. The victims of crimes of honour are generally poor peasant women whose murderers are excused by the judiciary whatever the legal provisions may be.

She argues for the abolition of the concept of crimes of honour and their replacement by gender unspecific crimes of passion. She also states that feminists in Arab countries have not taken this cause more seriously for fear of being branded as advocating Western-style promiscuity and licentiousness. She argues that this fear is unfounded as every society has means of controlling sexual behaviour short of execution.

The Politics of Interpretations

Haleh Afshar, Maha Azzam, Jean Makdisi, Munira Fakhro and myself, show how women, in countries where Islam is used to legitimise political, social and economic activities, have succeeded (or failed) to use the dynamism of the religious framework to win rights for themselves.

Haleh Afshar's paper illustrates how Iranian women located their political actions in the context of Islam. She examines this process, looking into how women who had a leading prominent role during the revolution found themselves marginalised after the Islamic government was installed. For example, women could not become judges; in *qisas* law a woman was viewed as half a man and the murder of a woman is not a capital offence while a man's is. However, by staying within the Islamic context and strongly arguing their position in every available form, Iranian feminists were able to make considerable progress in the political and educational fields following this initial setback.

Afshar argues that Islamic history offers modern feminist role models (instead of Western ones that are alien to them and generally viewed as a tool of patriarchal capitalism). These Islamic role models are used to accommodate present needs. This is the case of Khadija, known for her economic independence, 'A'isha, for her political skill and religious knowledge and Fatima, the daughter of the Prophet, who symbolises morality and strength. Afshar demonstrates how, through both religious arguments and compromises, including the acceptance of the veil, which they turned into a feminist tool, women in the beginning of the 1990s were confirmed as equals in parliament and regained some of their positions within the liberal professions.

Women also made wider gains in education and in terms of job opportunities. Afshar gives examples of a number of prominent Iranian feminists – some active members of the "Women's Society of the Islamic Revolution" and leading Islamic feminists who demanded "Islamic" rights. Education is prescribed for all Muslims and this enabled prominent women to fight against discrimination in medical education. The process naturally entailed setbacks and resistance; on the basis of "negative Islamic" interpretations, such as "it is not in the nature of women to become judges", women have still to invest some crucial legal bastions.

Introduction

The theme of Muslim women seeking their rights from within religious culture and not from outside it, that is from Western ideas and values, is clearly portrayed in Maha Azzam's paper with particular reference to the Islamist movement in Egypt. The view could be seen as representative of the "new feminist traditionalists". She notes the flexibility of Islamic thought and refers to the different interpretations of the Qur'an by modernists, secularists and traditionalists.

In societies such as Egypt where economic malaise has led to a fundamental political reassessment, the answer for many men and women lies in an Islamic orientation, a return to orthodoxy and a refusal of things "unIslamic". Azzam surveys some of the alternatives which the "orthodox discourse" offers women. She traces the fast and widely spread appeal of orthodox Islam at Islamic schools, at the universities and in politicised Islamic groups. The emergence of the latter marks a new stage for women from across the Middle East, who are increasingly taking part in Islamist political movements in their respective countries. All political participation in this context is presented under the Islamic umbrella.

The *hijab* is central to this Islamist movement. In general, women who choose to wear it are aware of its social and economic advantages. These range from more possibilities for getting married (since men "prefer" *muhajjabat*) to economic practicalities (low-cost dress). Despite this umbrella of acceptability that Islam offers and despite the fact that the role models such as Sheikha Nafisa Shuhda (an authority on *hadith*) remain inspirational to Muslim women, there are no immediate solutions or arguments proposed by Islamic women to some of the obvious areas of inequality in family law, divorce, custody, polygamy or inheritance. This is in marked contrast to their counterparts in Iran pointed out by Mir-Hosseini and Afshar. However, Egyptian women have obtained more prominent jobs because of a different economic and political past. Azzam's paper concludes that since the Islamic legal framework can "liberate" or "constrain" both men and women, Islam remains the alternative for the masses and a route to empowerment within an environment of increasing Islamisation.

Jean Said Makdisi focuses on women in Lebanon and examines a number of issues that are of vital importance to women generally (Christian and Muslim) in the Middle East and to women in Islamic countries. Women are visible in Lebanon working in banks, hospitals, shops and the media; however, their real influence in the country is severely restricted: women are rarely active in political positions and in senior posts of the public administration except in some cases through their ties to important men. Makdisi blames this on the lack of true democratic institutions. There are barriers between class, gender and religious sects that do not help the idea of equality in general nor the organised women's movement in the country.

By questioning basic concepts of what is "modern" versus what is "traditional", she gives contemporary and actual examples of how misleading such dichotomies can be and how they can become a barrier against a real understanding of issues concerning women and a hindrance to their advancement: advancement not only in terms of being visible in society but in moving into positions of power and decision-making in their country.

Makdisi blames the lack of movement partly on the tendency to judge "modernity" by sect, dress or language. She shows how the woman who is well-dressed in European modern clothes and tied to a consumer's life-style, whilst remaining subservient to her husband, is seen as modern because of her knowledge of Western languages and her dress. On the other hand, a poorer woman who is less fashionably dressed, wearing the traditional head cover and speaking only Arabic, but who works in the fields or factories and has perhaps joined an underground movement against the Israeli occupation – this woman with her independence, political awareness and economic competition even *vis-à-vis* her husband, is considered backward or traditional, because of her appearance, dress and ignorance of a Western language.

Makdisi goes back in time to examine the historical basis for such social classifications and dichotomies. She notes that the background to the historic misunderstandings which divide women lie in the educational system established since the early nineteenth century – European and American foreign schools brought new ideas, new clothes, new languages and new manners. In Lebanon, unlike other Arab countries, these still remained the socially admired models even after the colonial period was over.

Christian schools with Western curricula became the example of what is modern. Most importantly, Makdisi states that women's advancement or equality can only take place within a less divided society. Class barriers hinder true liberation. Unless there is more democracy in Lebanon and elsewhere in Arab countries there can be no effective organised movement that demands an end to political exclusion on the basis of democratic justice.

As a prerequisite for women's involvement in the political sphere, Makdisi states that governments must be more flexible, that is, they should be more democratic. To illustrate this she makes an interesting observation that during periods of anomaly and anarchy, women flourished in Lebanon. She gives the particular example of the civil war that started in 1975. During that period of chaos as the state and institutions were less powerful, women dominated the scene. Meanwhile old concepts of honour and respect for mothers protected women from the dangers of the war. When the war ended and the state resumed its influence women were marginalised again. Furthermore, the women's movement cannot be based on a Western feminist model. Arab women view the latter as defective because it ignores the role of motherhood and has been viewed as partly responsible for the disintegration of the Western family.

Munira Fakhro's paper sees the possibility of women's rights being advanced within an Islamic framework provided that governments in the region allow for a democratic system that would lead to reforms in various domains including women's rights. In order to illustrate this modernist pragmatist concept, she compares the approaches of two known scholars who believe that the door to interpretation of the *shari'a* is open and recommend new guidelines regarding women. The research of the first scholar, Muhammad Shahrur, specifically addresses the issue of polygamy, of *sadaq* (dowry), women's attire, women's rights to political activities, marriage contracts and divorce. The second, 'Abdul Halim Abu Shaqqa, examines women's Islamic personality and equality, the concept of "decency" in dress, women's participation in social life and the family, namely the choices women have in marriage and divorce. Fakhro surveys some of these issues in the Gulf States of Bahrain, Kuwait and Saudi Arabia. She calls for reformed family law in the Gulf region as others have done during the twentieth century (Tunisia's banning of polygamy and Syria's reforms of divorce laws). This can only be achieved if the ruling elites in the Gulf are prepared, or forced, to make concessions.

My paper describes women attempting to achieve social status and power through observing strict Islamic values. Women have turned to "Islamic" ways of social and economic empowerment and have gained a degree of freedom of movement that cannot be challenged by the authorities because they use the legitimate language of the nation. The paper describes how this movement is a result of the interlinked political and religious systems of Saudi Arabia. The socio-political mood in Saudi Arabia is currently heavily Islamic, as Islam serves to legitimise all activities.

Saudi women have become a symbol of Islamic ideals. The honour of the family at one level and the honour of the nation on another level rests on the shoulders of the women. Strict segregation of the sexes in all spheres restricts physical mobility. It is a matter of national policy that women wear the black veil in public and not drive cars. The paper notes that even after political reforms introduced in 1992 women remain excluded from any public role.

A disjunction is created in a country where large numbers of women are educated at universities and are exposed to the outside world, yet remain confined to traditional Islamic ideals requiring them to stay at home with very few jobs being "suitable" for them. This results in new internal pressures that express themselves in diverse ways. Under the present system, the more liberal, Westernised attempts at reforms by women are immediately undermined because they are not speaking the language of the nation and are easily suppressed by the authorities. However, those who adopt the newly developed, stricter veil, and arm themselves with knowledge of Islamic avenues to power (for example, with respect to their personal economic capacity), find themselves better able to confront local obstacles to the advancement of women.

Women have made headway in the area of segregated employment and segregated business enterprises such as the women's branches of banks and women's shops. In addition they are able to get out of the house in their strict veil and thus have gained greater physical mobility. These women have created their own social and religious space.

The Confines of Law

Ziba Mir-Hosseini focuses upon the contemporary feminist movements in Iran. She offers an in-depth analysis of the structure and shape that this movement is taking. The main legal issues under debate by these feminists are published in a revolutionary women's magazine, *Zanan*. The chapter examines a number of feminist issues such as obedience to one's husband, *tamkin*, disobedience towards one's husband, *nushuz*, maintenance, *nafaqa,* the law of retribution, *qisas*, and polygamy, from their initial analysis through the active debate conducted in the pages of *Zanan*, and presented by feminists and male jurists, to a final resolution of these issues at the level of the religious authorities in Qum and at the level of parliament. In dealing directly with these specifically Islamic issues, she creates a clearly defined Islamic agenda for reform.

Post-revolutionary Iranian feminists have challenged the hegemony of the orthodox interpretative process and succeeded in creating changes in divorce laws, making a complete U-turn for women's financial rights after divorce. Mir-Hosseini illustrates the process in which the arguments on a particular issue are developed in this literary magazine – a process of logical reasoning – and in surveys of jurists' opinions. For example, the concept of *tamkin* which is generally understood to involve the woman's obligation to sexual demands of her husband at all times and his right to physically beat her if she disobeys him, is examined by a male cleric from Qum[12] who refers to the original source – the Qur'anic verse (Surat al-Hujurat). Through analysis of the context and meaning of the verse, he presents his arguments that *tamkin* must be mutual between husband and wife and that there are several alternatives to each situation depending on the circumstances or natural inclination of the woman. Different Islamic scenarios are extracted; if a woman is economically independent she should not have to put up with an unjust *tamkin* for we can take the example of Khadija who was a secure wealthy woman but remained loyal to her husband the Prophet Muhammad. Likewise, the literature attempts to secure better financial situations for women in Iran regarding wives' maintenance during marriage, *nafaqa*. By going back to the basic sources the Qur'an and the *Sunna* and by arguing against some interpretations of *fiqh* – those who claim that *nafaqa* does not include medical expenses – they succeeded in forming an opinion that it does.

Another example of the appeal for equality discussed in the pages of *Zanan* concerns punishment qisas and the protest against gender biases in the courts. *Zanan* published several written appeals to the law-making authorities with thorough Islamic arguments for better rights for women. Mir-Hosseini points to the fact that although the discourses stay entirely within Shi'a Islam, they are not part of the establishment. In fact, they challenge the hegemony of the orthodox interpretative process. The success or even the acceptability of these feminist discourses is made possible by the Shi'a acceptance of *ijtihad* and the possibility of re-interpreting Qur'anic verses. These women do not take on a Western feminist language but one of Shi'a thought. Their issues, *tamkin, nafaqa,* etc., are those that pertain to the everyday life of Iranian Muslim women, but they are also universal issues dealing with power relations between men and women, such as marriage, divorce and custody. Among the "neo-Islamists", Iranian women themselves appear to be in a special group or category.

Souad Mokbel-Wensley highlights what she sees as a discrepancy between the tenets of the Lebanese Constitution and some aspects of the legal system concerning women. For example, according to the constitution women are equal to men, but Wensley points out that this "legal capacity" only exists unless the law provides otherwise. She substantiates this by outlining a number of outstanding areas in which the principles of equality are violated. These are in the areas of nationality law, commercial law, life insurance and criminal law with specific regard to adultery and crimes of honour. For example with regards to nationality, a Lebanese woman married to a non-Lebanese man cannot pass her nationality on to her children while a man can. With regard to the ability of the married woman to trade (until the reforms passed just recently), she loses her capacity to trade after marriage if not granted consent by her spouse. This consent can also be cancelled for "just motives" – all this despite the fact that "community of property" does not exist between husband and wife under Lebanese law. The worst discrimination, according to Wensley, is under what are classed as crimes of honour. Article 562 of the Penal Code allows legal exemption of any male committing unpremeditated homicide or injury upon surprising his spouse, a female forebear, daughter and other female descendant in flagrante delicto of adultery or illegitimate sexual act with a third person. Wensley identifies these as areas urgently in need of change not only because they conflict with internationally set standards of human rights, but also because they stand out as contradictory to the Lebanese Constitution. Wensley exposes these laws as not just unconstitutional but as patriarchy masquerading as law.

Najla Hamadeh examines the suppression of free expression – what she calls the "authoritarian discourse of silence" in Muslim countries with particular emphasis on Islamic family legislation. She argues that the religious and political powers conspire to impose silence on all dissenters and examines this thesis in the contexts of divorce and custody. The laws of divorce and custody according to Hamadeh, as they stand today, are based on weak arguments and little common sense. Although they are derived from the Qur'an and the *Sunna* they have been twisted by male legislators in directions that they see as favourable for them. Islamic legislators chose to interpret Islam in a way that diminishes the rights of women. She illustrates this in the case of divorce where under most family laws, among Sunni and Shi'a groups, there is no way out of a marriage for a woman whose husband refuses to let her go, thereby disregarding the Islamic command "Do not retain them (your wives) by force, to transgress (against their rights)". In contrast, Islamic family law makes divorce extremely easy for men, regardless of the Prophet's *hadith* that describes divorce as abhorrent to God, while making it difficult for women to find a way out of an intolerable marriage.

Hence, for a wife, the marriage contract becomes akin to a form of bondage to her husband that cannot be revoked by her will alone. As Hamadeh points out this is not in harmony with what is generally known about the life of the Prophet who considered a wife's disinclination to himself tantamount to breaking the marriage contract. The reasons given for the wife's disqualification from the right to divorce are generally based on women's emotional nature.

Hamadeh goes on to show that few of these arguments make any sense nor do they comply with reality. Furthermore, she explains that in order to justify treating women as owned objects, Islamic family law emphasises men's economic obligations towards their wives such as the *mahr*, bride-price. This results in treating the marital relationship as one between a buyer and his acquisition, and in connecting *nushuz* with the giving of sexual gratification to the husband as a material obligation.

Hamadeh further contrasts the rights attributed to motherhood prominent in the Qur'an, and the dictates of Islamic family law which gives custody to mothers for only the first few years of her children's lives. Once again economic explanations and justification have traditionally been made on the grounds that women are not capable of educating a child once it has been weaned. Hamadeh argues that even if this was the case in the past with mothers who had been refused access to education themselves, times have changed and women are now increasingly involved as educators themselves, at all levels of the school system. Social circumstances have changed, and Islam being a dynamic religion must meet these new situations.

Hamadeh concludes that by Islamic jurisprudence imposing silence on the multitudes and serving totalitarian rule it has deviated from true Islam and is consciously reserving more power for the male gender. She calls on Islamic communities to restore family law from stagnation. Continuous interpretation of the Qur'an is needed with more open discourse of its subjects as a prerequisite. Opposition to political totalitarian rule is essential to break the monologue that suffers from intellectual sterility.

Jane Connors studies the position of women in Muslim countries in the light of the Women's Convention (1979) drafted for the United Nations Decade for Women. By examining the reservations entered by participating Muslim states with reference to the *shari'a*, she arrives at the conclusion that there is a possible way forward to the easing of the tensions between some Islamic countries and certain Northern European and American States on the issue of the reservations unacceptable to the international community.

Connors' analysis reveals that a number of reservations entered by "Islamic" states to the Women's Convention are based not so much on the *shari'a* as on local practice and convention. For example, Turkey's reservations relating to article 29 and to parts of articles 15 and 16 on civil matters and the legal capacity of women which are considered incompatible with the provisions of the Turkish Civil Code. Likewise, the rules of succession in Morocco conflict with paragraphs in article 2 of the Covenant. Likewise, article 9 which grants women equal rights with respect to nationality was met by reservation by Egypt, Jordan, Iraq, Morocco and Tunisia on the basis of local nationality codes.

In general, she finds that in matters of personal law such as marriage, divorce and custody, the *shari'a* is quite specific and therefore it would be more difficult to persuade states such as Morocco or Egypt to provide for equality between men and women basically to comply with article 16 that addresses the private sphere and family life. The above "Islamic" countries strongly argue that Islamic law offers financial rights to the wife – the dower at marriage, her husband maintains her financially during marriage, meanwhile her property is always separate and all hers, etc. For these financial rights she is obliged to him and hence unequal in other areas or situations, for example, divorce. This is perceived as the balance of relationships. Strong arguments are used to maintain the patriarchal, patrilineal and patrilocal order of things, in an attempt to maintain distinctive Islamic laws.

In matters of public law, however, dealing with issues such as employment, political participation, education and economic rights, the *shari'a* is more vague and here Connors perceives the possibility to bring Islamic countries in line with the Women's Convention. To this end, she urges scholars to "discern norms of non-discrimination and equality in the Holy Qur'an, the *Sunna* and the early commentaries".

Juxtapositions

When we view these papers as a whole, a number of challenging questions and themes suggest themselves. Firstly, did Islam help the position of women? El-Nimr strongly feels that in comparison with other systems, it did, while Karmi seriously questions this. On the other hand, Siddiqui and Marsot believe that it is not so much Islam that determines the status of women but other political, economic and social issues that are merged with Islamic precepts. Hamadeh stresses that the basic sources (Qur'an and *Sunna*) did improve the status of women during the period of early Islam but provide the potential for a contemporary movement towards equality.

The debate still continues elsewhere. Most scholars conclude that the Qur'an did bring in some reforms including the outlawing of infanticide, the payment of dower to the bride, and female inheritance as well as women's control over property. However, free divorce remains an exclusively male preserve. It remains a matter of interpretation which Leila Ahmed noted: "The message of Islam as instituted by Muhammad's teachings and practice comprehended two tendencies that were in tension with each other, patriarchal marriage and male dominance and yet Islam preached ethical egalitarianism."[13] Here the question arises as to what is Islamic and what is not. Is the veil prescribed in the Qur'an? Several of the papers address the symbolic and practical uses of the veil and the results of their investigations have yielded a picture quite different to that in popular Western perception. Marsot considers that the veil expresses the female need to be protected. She also points out that it is too late for those high-profile working women whose grandmothers participated in the Egyptian nationalist movement to choose to veil. Furthermore, the veil cannot necessarily be considered Islamic as it is not known what Muslim women wore in the time of the Prophet. Afshar in her studies of women in contemporary Iran approaches the veil from a different angle. Under the Islamic government this garment has gained a liberating dimension, freeing women from the fashion industry as well as the freedom for the wearer to become an observer and not one of the observed, thus averting sexual harassment and gaining respect. Since it is compulsory in Iran, accepting it represents one of the compromises made to reach political and economic power but more than that, it has itself become a feminist tool. A similar opinion about the veil is presented by Azzam who looks at the economic practicalities and element of moral superiority that it offers young Egyptian women. The veil in Egypt is worn by women Islamists out of choice. It gives them membership of an Islamic club offering a framework of hope in times of political and economic decline.

Fakhro's examination of the works of Shahrur and Abu Shaqqa also addresses the issue of the veil. They both question the attire of women and the concept of "decency" in dress for women in Islam and believe it is a matter of social circumstance rather than Qur'anic injunctions.

According to Makdisi, the concept of the veil has been over simplified both in its ethnic context and its political or religious significance by Western media. She criticises the preconceived ideas of the veil that is classifying people as "modern" versus "traditional" on the basis of costume and argues that a woman who wears the veil out of choice is not necessarily submissive or less modern.

In my paper I discuss the reaction of the Saudi feminists to the compulsory wearing of the veil. One way that these feminists who use Islam to empower themselves in Saudi Society demanded more rights in the country, was by wearing a strict modification of the veil. Veiling in this manner (thereby symbolising Islamic piety), becomes a way of achieving their goals. It is worth noting that in Algeria, during the struggle for independence, the veil became synonymous with Algerian patriotism.[14]

Fatima Mernissi attacks the practice of women's segregation by the conservatives as the institutionalisation of male authoritarianism achieved by way of manipulating the sacred texts.[15] The question is not so much whether the veil is Islamic or not, as it is mentioned in the Qur'an, specifically in reference to the mothers of the believers and has been used by Muslims to distinguish believing women since the time of the Prophet. The relevant question for Muslim feminists today is the element of choice attached to the garment, and whether it is a woman's right to choose whether to veil or not.

From the outside, the *shari'a* is seen as an obstacle to progress in women's rights but a legal system totally based on *shari'a* might leave substantial room for improvement in those rights because non-*shari'a* practices, which themselves curtailed women's rights, would no longer have a firm basis. An urgent issue that has been a practice in Muslim countries but that is not necessarily Islamic is the continuing existence of crimes of honour. This theme occurs frequently in this collection, especially in papers dealing with those legal systems with the highest degree of "borrowing" from Western systems. Most prominently in Abu-Odeh's analysis of the legal, political and social causes for this aspect of inequality in society, it can be seen that the origins of these laws do not appear to have a direct Islamic base. She examines social perceptions of female behaviour and social obsessions with virginity and honour that have been perpetuated by the law. Likewise, Mokbel Wensley addresses the flaws that allow such crimes to go unpunished, and calls for at least equal punishment for men and women in what should be classed as crimes of passion and not honour.

The concept of honour and modesty has been addressed elsewhere by scholars. Abu Lughod[16] has noted the link between honour and stratification showing how this ideology serves to rationalise social inequality legitimising the control that some have over the lives of others. This leads to another dominant issue of concern to feminists world-wide, male dominance in society, patriarchy. Since patriarchalism as a model differs in form from society to society, this book addresses the general "Muslim" model of partriarchalism. What is distinctive about Islamic patriarchy and what are its implications for women's lives and search for power and influence? Karmi focuses directly on patriarchy. She believes the Qur'an confirms and legitimises patriarchal rule and that looking back at the emergence of Islam, it was a time when Arab tribal society was moving towards male dominance. This, she claims, has been exacerbated by biased interpretations of the Qur'an in favour of men's power to the exclusion of women.

As McKee points out, Arab women writers or novelists reproduce and subvert the rigidly patriarchal gender systems of their society. The subversion takes place by exposing political structure and ideology, thus making their heroines politically aware. Afshar's study of the changes within the Islamic political system in Iran points to the fight of Iranian women against rigid patriarchal structure.

Hamadeh approaches patriarchy on a different level by addressing the manner in which the *'ulama* have subverted the original message of the Qur'an and the practice of the Prophet in totalitarian regimes. Men exclusively dominated the legal and political scenes where the majority of women remained silent. The patriarchal system in family law offers justifications for custody. In her view, Islamic patriarchy could become milder than other models of male dominance, if understood better by women.

Mokbel-Wensley states that, in a partly Islamic context, patriarchal concepts remain a cause of inequality despite the Lebanese constitution and irrespective of religious precepts. The ideology of patriarchy is connected with deep-rooted ideas of "blood" especially in aspects of agnation and descent. The organisation of political life in the region takes form around this ideology. Patriarchy as a system is challenged by most of these papers primarily by questioning and often by offering an alternative mode of thought.

The concept of irrationality or emotionality of women as a justification for discrimination in employment, in political and economic participation is universal. Pregnancy, the menstrual cycle and post-natal depression serve as reasons to perpetuate patriarchy. These are used as obstacles against increased access to employment for women. "Emotionality" has been a key factor in excluding women historically across culture and across religions from the public sphere. In this volume El-Nimr, in her survey of Islamic law, sees the cycle as a justification for the exclusion of women from public life. She sees a logic to the idea that the cycle prescribes to women, a domestic and subservient role. She believes that this is the natural role for women and the roles of the men and women complement each other. Hamadeh shows in contrast that the idea of emotionality has been exploited by male *'ulama* in their interpretation of Islamic family law to disqualify the wife from asking for divorce even when the Qur'an appears to entitle her to do so. This is while leaving the full ability to divorce in the hands of the husband. Hamadeh takes issue with the stereotypes and demands a rethinking of women's roles both in family law (custody, divorce etc.) as well as in public roles. Mir-Hosseini deals with this issue of the inequality of women in the legal sphere that is obviously based on the concept of emotionality and its sometimes inadequate tracing back to the *shari'a*.

In most countries in the region, there is a well-defined system of job classifications concerning the "suitability" to the temperament of women. Mokbel-Wensley points this out in Lebanon and Afshar in Iran. However, the most rigidly defined classification exists in Saudi Arabia where most jobs are not suitable for women and they must remain at home to perform the duties of motherhood. Meanwhile, the debate on emotionality including the perceived physical emotional effects of maternity and womanhood continues to be an impediment to equality worldwide. Women are denied jobs and economic opportunities because of their child-bearing role, and national policies maintain by and large that the workplace and the home are incompatible.[17]

Equaiity

In the Qur'an, male and female Muslims are equal in faith and dignity: "Oh mankind we have created you of male and female, of nations and tribes so that you may know each other the most honoured in the eyes of God is the most pious amongst you." At the same time, the modes and arenas of their struggle are seen as different, validating for many the exclusion of women from the public sphere, whether in the interpretations of fundamentalists, conservatives or modernists.[18] Where does the issue of equality stand in this complex configuration of countries and themes and the apparent imbalance that exists in social, economic and political practice?

Siddiqui concentrates on the idea and practice of equality within Islamic marriage. While women under the Hanafi school of law may choose a partner who is equal or superior in status, social restrictions remain in her choice of a husband as well as in her direct participation in the marriage contract. Siddiqui feels that this can be remedied, both by women's participation in the public sphere as well as by their education in the meaning of equality and how to seize it.

Marsot shows the discrepancy, between theory and practice, in the economic power of women in Islam. In order to achieve equality, women themselves took hold of their rights in eighteenth century Egypt. Karmi says that there are very obvious areas of inequality inherent in the Qur'an and the only way to deal with them is to be more pragmatic. Finally, Hamadeh believes that we have to go back to the original message enshrined in the spirit of Islam, a message of basic equality and gender balance. She suggests we look beyond male-oriented Qur'anic exegesis and try to redefine a more balanced perspective that aims at a progressive society.

Azzam identifies areas of inequality in the Qur'an, for example divorce, custody and inheritance, but says that Egyptian Islamist women are doing nothing about these practices partly because they believe in them as the divine word of God and the social circumstances of these women are such that Islam has become more of an answer than a question in relation to these problems.

Mir-Hosseini believes that feminist discourses address basic issues of inequality in Islamic *fiqh* text and practice with the aim of attaining more equally balanced marital relationships, basic human rights, and personal civil and political rights.

Connors notes areas of inequality in the Qur'an mainly within family law. At the same time, women can achieve equality in areas of employment, economic and political participation. This warrants perhaps an emphasis on a more practical interpretation in those areas of law imprecisely laid out in the traditional *shari'a.*

Equality of the sexes is asserted in human rights law. "Human rights philosophy regards women as no less individually distinctive, unique and mentally capable than men."[19] To affirm this equality was the purpose of the 1979 Convention on the Elimination of All Forms of Discrimination Against Women, passed by the UN General Assembly, but again there were reservations by some countries.

A strong theme that runs through the book is the suggestion that women should be taking a much more prominent role in interpretation of the basic sources of Islam. Likewise, the idea that the role models for modern women must be the Islamic role models from the seventh century rather than Western role models stands out in many papers.

Makdisi points out that, despite the fact that Western feminism has laid the foundation for accomplishments in women's economic, legal and personal standing, it is criticised for its failure to acknowledge motherhood. Abu-Odeh offers specific advice to Arab feminists in dealing with the crimes of honour and these can only be solutions to a local problem.

Iranian feminists also appear to reject the Western feminist role models. Mir-Hosseini's defining of the feminist movement in Iran describes it as opposed to Western values and lifestyles. Given the present political situation in Iran, solutions to the problems of Iranian women cannot be in Western language and must be in an indigenous, more legitimate, form. Afshar is even stronger in her emphasis on Islamic feminism in Iran. Muslim women must rely on their sisters in Islam and, in particular, on the mothers of the believers.

The beginning of an indigenous women's movement in predominantly Muslim countries is clearly outlined in the book. It can be seen against the context of the democratic deficit in the political systems of those states, as well as the specific gender-based inequality. Many of the rights that women seek are the rights of citizens that are equally denied to men. Unless there is freedom of expression, less censorship, freedom of association and less intolerance of differences in opinion, there will be no effective women's movement. The allowing of a religious heterogeneous society to exist is more liberating even if a society is not conventionally democratic. The more the tolerance the more the liberty. The Prophet is reported to have said, "the best thing about my people is their differences."

Makdisi clearly explains that women must be allowed to participate more fully in the democratic process of their countries. Barriers between classes, religions and genders must be broken down. McKee points out the awareness of Arab women's writers to the political realities surrounding them. Abu-Odeh traces the cause for crimes of honour partly to the political structure. The judges tend to pass these crimes by justifications of laws connected with post-independence political systems.

Azzam relates Islam to the political circumstances in Egypt. With reference to how the reassessment of the political situation has led to the return to Orthodox Islam. Mir-Hosseini analyses another dimension of this phenomenon where Islam is in power. Thus, the regime must account for contradictions only in Islamic terms. This allows for legal manoeuvres by women for the first time. Afshar's argument is that it is perhaps only because of the type of government in place that women in Iran have achieved specific rights otherwise outside the reach of reform. Hamadeh condemns totalitarian regimes in their silencing of people especially of women in the public sphere.

For the debate on women's rights to succeed, reforms must be encouraged. Liberals and democrats must be included in the systems, and more periodicals on women must be freely published.[20]

The papers show that historically, women have been able to advance their cause most when central governments have been weakened in times of wars or other disorders. Chaos creates a certain degree of opportunity for women enabling them to take initiative. Wars have had liberating effects on women. In Iraq, during the first and second Gulf Wars, a remarkable number of women were drafted into the workforce, in factories, fields and government offices, to replace men who were sent to the front. The war with Iran in 1980 gave a drastic impetus to the integration of women in the modern sector because of the loss of male labour. By the second year of the war, there was a noticeable increase of women in government ministries. By the third year, more than a million women were employed in unskilled work in the public and private sectors.[21] The war of independence in Algeria has been known to have a liberating effect on women. In Egypt, during the militant national independence struggle in 1919–22, women played a very visible role.[22]

Marsot notes how women acquired more economic and legal rights under the decentralised political structure during the Mamluk period of the eighteenth century in Egypt as opposed to the time of the centralised government rule of Muhammad 'Ali during the nineteenth century. More recently, during the civil war in Lebanon 1975, Jean Makdisi shows that women acquired a more influential position in Lebanese society. In Saudi Arabia, the only forthright attempt at reforms by women occurred during the Gulf War in 1990. Women seized the opportunity, at the time of chaos, to gain rights to drive their cars. The grip of the system relaxes during war. Government agencies such as the Religious Committee (*mutawi'in*) were directed towards the crisis, which allowed a breathing space for minorities including women. During the revolution, women fought for their own rights, achieving what they did through their knowledge of Islam.

The debate as to whether the position of women actually improves in situations of political chaos is not a simple equation between the type of regime, the religious power in place, and more importantly the economic circumstances. As long as the legal framework is not dissolved, though the order of things is shaken up, women frequently benefit. However, under severe economic recession or a total breakdown of the system, women often become victims as seen in Bosnia and Rwanda. Women as seen in this volume and elsewhere, react or take initiative at times of chaos in the political system, because of their desire to participate in the national process and because it is easier to demand rights during periods of change. Although this is often followed by a set-back, such as in Iran at the outset of the clerical rule, or in Saudi Arabia after the driving demonstration by women, women gain in the long term an awareness and political consciousness which will not be easily lost.

Epilogue

This awareness and the demand for rights in an Islamic context was a unifying theme at the fourth world conference on women by the United Nations Development Programme (UNDP) held in September 1995. All Muslim states were represented at the conference (except for Saudi Arabia) and displayed the cultural diversity prevalent in the Islamic world. The majority of Muslim women representatives of their respective countries, leaders, politicians, lawyers, journalists and academics expressed their belief that Islam is a great unifying force and has the scope to allow for greater human rights and dignity to women

The Algerian representative, Hania Semichi, called for religious tolerance within the framework of Islam. The Kuwaiti woman representative, Su'ad al-Sabah, included the demand for the right to vote and an appeal to government to eliminate discrimination. She also stated the need for a goal of equality, changes in the legislation and a developmental goal including increased economic and political opportunities for women. The Pakistani premier, Benazir Bhutto, pointed out that there is a crisis of silence engulfing the Muslim world and she stressed the potential of economic freedom and independence offered to women by an Islamic structure. She added that women should get their liberation from a correct form of Islam, their objectives starting with the fight against illiteracy and general poverty in that part of the world. The Egyptian representative, Suzanne Mubarak, stressed the importance of democracy as the ideal environment for freedom and for the prosperity of movements of emancipation and liberation within the context of sound religious values.

The conference was attended by women who expressed traditionalist Islamic views that opposed and criticised practices such as abortion and the moral deterioration of the family. Although other countries sent eloquent Muslim women as representatives, some chose to send men, such as Morocco, Oman and Qatar. There is no lack of intelligent, learned and powerful Muslim women in our time but more space needs to be created in order for their voices to be heard in an Islamic context. The present book should be seen as another scholarly voice in the increasingly crucial debate of gender equality in the world.

NOTES

1   L. Bouder, 'A Lawyer's Primer on Feminist Theory and Tort' in Kelly Weiseberg (ed.), *Feminists Legal Theory Foundations* (Philadelphia: Temple University Press, 1993).

2   As put forward recently by Margot Badran, *Feminists, Islam and Nation: Gender and the Making of Modern Egypt* (Princeton: Princeton University Press, 1995).

3   See also for the historical approach Leila Ahmed, *Women and Gender in Islam: Historical Roots of a Modern Debate* (New Haven: Yale University Press, 1992) and by Fatima Mernissi, *Women and Islam: An Historical and Theological Enquiry* (Oxford: Blackwell, 1991).

4   Ziba Mir-Hosseini, *Marriage on Trial: A Study of Islamic Family Law* (London: I.B. Tauris, 1993), p. 15.

5   See Haleh Afshar (ed.), *Women in the Middle East: Perceptions, Realities, and Struggles for Liberation* (Basingstoke: Macmillan Series, 1993).

6   Barbara Stowasser, *Women in the Qur'an: Traditions and Interpretations* (New York: Oxford University Press, 1994).

7   M. Amin, *The Waqfs and Social Life in Egypt 648–923* AH/*1250–1517* AD [In Arabic] (Cairo: Dar al Nahda al-Arabiyya, 1980).

8   Muhammad 'Ali brought al-Azhar under his control, breaking its independence and limiting its jurisdiction. See Badran, *Feminists, Islam and Nation*.

9   See W. Robertson Smith, *Kinship and Marriage in Early Arabia* (London: Adam and Charles Black, 1903). Also see Van Gennep, *The Rites of Passage*, trans. by M. B. Vizedon and G. L. Caffe (Chicago: University of Chicago Press, 1960).

10 An analysis of patriarchy or expressions of male power or dominance in society marked the beginning of feminist consciousness in other societies, for example, in nineteenth-century Egypt; see Badran, *Feminists, Islam and Nation*, p. 3, Deniz Kandioti, 'Islam and Patriarchy' in Nikkie Keddie and Beth Baron (eds.), *Women in Middle Eastern History* (New Haven: Yale University Press, 1991).

11 See Denise A. Spellberg, 'Political Action and Public Example: 'A'isha and the Battle of the Camel' in Nikkie Keddie and Beth Baron (eds.), *Women in Middle Eastern History*. Also see Fatima Mernissi, Women and Islam: *A Historical and Theological Enquiry* (Oxford: Blackwell, 1991).

12 The phenomenon of men who adopt the task of defending women's rights is seen elsewhere in Muslim countries, for example Amin and Fahmi in Egypt. See Badran, *Feminists, Islam and Nation*.

13 See Leila Ahmed, *Women and Gender in Islam*.

14 Nora Benallegue, 'Algerian Women in the Struggle for Independence and Reconstruction', *Social Science Journal*, Vol. 35, No. 4 (1983), 703–17.

15 Fatima Mernissi, *The Veil and the Male Elites: A Feminist Interpretation of Women's Rights in Islam*, trans. by Mary Jo Lakeland (Massachusetts: Addison-Wesley, 1991).

16 L. Abu Lughod, *Veiled Sentiments, Honour and Poetry in a Bedouin Society* (Berkeley: University of California Press, 1986).

17 Lucinda Finley discusses this in her article 'Transcending Equality Theory: A Way Out of the Maternity and the Work Place Debate' in Joanne Conaghan and Anne Bottomley (eds.), *Feminist Theory and Legal Strategy* (Oxford: Blackwell, 1993), p. 190.
18 Stowasser, *Women in the Qur'an: Traditions and Interpretations.*
19 Geoffrey Best, 'Justice, International Relations and Human Rights', *International Affairs*, Vol. 71, No. 4 (October 1995), p. 790.
20 Tahire Kocturk in *A Matter of Honour: Experiences of Turkish Women Immigrants* (London: Zed Books, 1992), describes the emergence of a Turkish feminist gazette during the beginning of the century. See also *Zanan* as referred to in this volume.
21 See Nadia Hijab, *Womanpower: The Arab Debate on Women at Work* (Cambridge: Cambridge University Press, 1988).
22 See Badran, *Feminists, Islam and Nation*; also, A. L. S. Marsot in this volume.

PART ONE

BEGINNINGS AND HISTORY

Two

Entrepreneurial Women

Afaf Lutfi al-Sayyid Marsot

The social condition of Muslim women seems to preoccupy non-Muslims as much as Muslims themselves, although for totally different reasons. The West, especially the United States, may have found a new bogey to replace communism in the "rise of Islam" or the dangers facing the so-called civilised world by the rise of the so-called "Islamic" and "Confucian" civilisations as though either were a monolith or together a hydra-headed monster out to get the West. On the other hand, Muslims are preoccupied with the rising current of fundamentalism and its effect on the position of women in society. All of which is built on the assumption that religion is the prime determinant in the position of women in a Muslim society. I shall endeavour to show that other, just as powerful, determinants are operating and that religion is often used to bolster non-religious arguments and conflicts.

Qur'anic Background

In any discussion involving Muslim women, the Qur'an and the *shari'a* are invariably the point of departure. Both devout Muslims and non-Muslims produce Qur'anic passages: either to show that Islam gave women certain rights, or that it did not give women such rights. What is clearly specified in the Qur'an is that women are equal to men in religious duties, they have the same obligations and will earn the same rewards or punishments. Throughout the Qur'an the term *zawj*, a pair, is used to accentuate the equality of both genders. Women are also given the right to inherit property from nine different relatives such as father, mother, grandfather, grandmother, siblings, children, spouse, etc. although their share is half that of an equivalent male. Both women and men are enjoined to dress modestly, only the wives of the Prophet Muhammad are enjoined to talk to men from behind a curtain, or veil, *hijab*, because "they are not as other women." Their separateness from other women is underlined by the fact that they may not marry other men after having married the Prophet, whereas other women could remarry. One passage in the Qur'an, often adduced to show the inequality in the relationship between the sexes is the passage stating "men are caretakers, *qawwamun*, of women as they spend of their wealth". This passage has led to several translated terms varying from "protectors" to "guardians" of women. The rest of the passage clearly shows that men were financially responsible for women (since they inherited twice as much). Thus we can conclude that the passages in the Qur'an laid the groundwork either for a society where women are treated on a par with men, or to a society where women are treated differently from men, i.e. equal in some aspects and less equal in others. It is the leaders or judiciary in such societies that determine which interpretation to espouse. All interpretations of the Qur'an have been produced by men, who consistently held the politico-judicial positions in their society; the result was that different interpretations were underlined at different periods. What we need to focus on is that in all societies women have been treated as second-class citizens. To date no society treats men and women equally, save for some tribes in the Himalayas or in Africa, so it is not the norm of different gender treatment that we need to examine but the degree to which such different treatment exists, and the consciousness in that society that there is inequality, not just a difference due to gender.

Clearly men and women have different biological functions, we may even believe that they think differently, or so modern medicine tells us, because of brain structure, but from there to jump to the conclusion that the sole function of women is reproductive, as some males do, is little short of ridiculous, were it not tragic. Religion sets out guidelines for society to follow. How society applies and interprets these guidelines is a function of economics, politics, social behaviour, demographics and culture, for these elements determine religious interpretations, otherwise how would we explain the different treatment of women at different historical epochs? When we know that at different epochs women's role in society took on different dimensions, which is the reason why feminists call for women's history, then we need to ask in what form did such changes take place, and how do we get to know about them? The one element in Muslim societies that has been neglected and which tells us something concrete about women's roles throughout history is the participation of women in the economic and commercial aspects of their society, that is, in the market place. This is to use the term in its broadest sense, without necessarily meaning that women sold goods in public – although they did indeed do that in certain eras – but simply to point out that they had an active role in the economic and commercial society of their time, and not only as consumers. One of the reasons for such economic activity on the part of women has to do with the Qur'an and its dictates, which set the groundwork for the right of women to possess property and to work. But that right was brought forward at some periods and pushed into the background at others, as we shall see. The Qur'an states that Muslim women are legal heirs and must therefore inherit yet we find that in some Muslim countries when it comes to land women were cut out of such a share in the inheritance, belying the religious directives. One method of cutting out women was to turn property into a trust, or mortmain, known as *waqf*, and exclude females from a share in it. On the other hand, upon marriage, women receive a dowry, *mahr*, and generally fathers were supposed to add to it and outfit the bride; the trousseau then forming her personal property, not her spouse's. Furthermore, the husband was legally expected to defray the household expenses and the support of his family and children. A wife's property was hers to do with as she pleased. Yet often we see the husband using his wife's property as though it were his own and using it not only for expenses in common but for his own personal usage. Clearly not all religious injunctions have been followed religiously, since the human conscience is very elastic. Equally clearly other motivations operate in human actions. In some periods women were hidden from public view and segregated in a harem, but that only happened to elite women since the rank and file could not do without the contribution of the spouse to the conjugal well-being. A poor man could not afford to buy slaves to guard his wife, or to send out to the market in her place, so the majority of women were neither segregated nor indeed veiled. Let us not forget that the harem as an institution came with the 'Abbasids and the age of Harun al-Rashid who was aping Sassanian customs. The passage in the Qur'an that specified that men should talk to the wives of the Prophet from behind a *hijab*, a screen or a veil, even though that applied solely to the Prophet's wives, was used as an excuse for establishing the harem as an institution. The specious argument that what was good enough for the Prophet's wives was good enough for other women was used, the Prophet's wives acting as a role model, which seems to make the argument somewhat pretentious. Furthermore, the passages in the Qur'an that deal with clothing simply specify that women were to cover their cleavage, and that both men and women were to cover their pudenda and dress modestly. It is only in the *tafsir*, the interpretations written by male scholars, using Bukhari and Muslim's collections of the

Prophet's sayings as proof for their allegations that we find a saying attributed to the Prophet in which he silently approved the garb of a woman who covered everything except for her face and hands. Yet much as Bukhari and Muslim laboured to sift through quotes handed down by various people which were allegedly said by the Prophet, it is necessary to remember that these men wrote their works two centuries after the Prophet's death, and that human beings are capable of error. Anything of importance is repeated in the Qur'an, so should the clothing of women have been of the least importance the Qur'an would have clearly spelled it out in no uncertain terms. What we need to spell out, is that clothing is culture specific, although it does make a statement. More significant are the Qur'anic passages that state the equality of men and women, and that the work of both is recompensed and the religious duty of both is equal, for they are two parts of a whole, *zawj*. We should not fall into the error of treating the condition of women as pre-set, based on religious injunctions and interpretations, but must keep in mind that different roles operated at different times. It would be far too tedious to go back to the early days of Islam and trace such roles, so I will limit myself to examining the role of women in the eighteenth and the following centuries.

Eighteenth Century

The system of government in eighteenth-century Egypt was chaotic and decentralised. Fourteen grandees, known by the title of Bey, each owned a household of retainers, all of whom were former slaves, Mamluks, manumitted by the grandees, themselves former slaves, formed a military oligarchy that dominated the Ottoman administration of Egypt. The Ottomans had conquered Egypt in 1516 and had not destroyed the military slave oligarchy that had ruled over the country since 1250, but had used them as auxiliaries. Consequently the Mamluks eventually overcame the Ottoman military system of regiments, placed their own slaves in the regiments, and came to effectively rule the country. Throughout the eighteenth century it was rare for one grandee to dominate the rest, resulting in constant infighting between Mamluks in struggles for supremacy. The wives and female relatives of these grandees, themselves former slaves, were thus entrusted with the grandee's wealth when he was otherwise occupied in fighting his peers. Fearing death or confiscation should a Mamluk grandee join the losing party, property was turned over to the women to prevent it from being confiscated or simply taken over, should the grandee die. Women then acquired great wealth; wealth that was either handed over by a spouse or father, who was otherwise occupied perhaps in exile; or inherited. The lifespan of Mamluks in general was often not long. Once a grandee fell then his wife or wives were married off to his second in command, or to his victor, so that Mamluk women were much married, resulting in an accumulation of wealth. We then find that these women used their wealth to invest in tax-farms. For the first time in the eighteenth century, having been previously a monopoly in the hands of the Ottoman regiments, or the Mamluks, tax-farms came to be owned by women, '*ulama* and long-distance merchants. The Mamluks needed ready cash to import weapons from Europe to fight each other and so sold their tax-farms to anyone who could pay upfront. Furthermore, nearly 40 per cent of wills registered were in the names of women, a rise of some 10 per cent from past ages, and we find that the same forms of investment that attracted men also attracted women. Such a pattern was not limited to elite women, for we find that women of all strata owned property; bought, sold and exchanged property; and endowed it at will.

The favoured form of investment was to buy a house, either to live in or to rent, and then to buy another dwelling, or parts of a dwelling. All property was divisible, to allow for the Muslim law of inheritance, so all buildings were divided by the courts into liveable units, and women and men bought such units. Other investments for the super wealthy were to build *wikalas*, in modern parlance a shopping mall. The buildings had storage rooms and shops, with an upper layer of rooms for renting out to the merchants whose goods were displayed below. Women also bought storage areas, tenement houses, weaving establishments, coffee shops, mills, funeral parlours and bathhouses, in fact any money-making venue was bought or sold. Some of these women were veritable entrepreneurs.

One woman named Salun was married to a minor Mamluk who bought, manumitted and married her. He then died and she inherited two shops. She parlayed these shops into a tremendous fortune, using five men, including her second husband, as her agents. In one year she bought tax-farms in the same area to the tune of over half a million coins of the day, and subsequently over a period of time she bought some 35 other shops and pieces of property. Her poor second husband barely owned one-tenth of her wealth. Nafisa Khatun, wife to two of the most powerful Mamluks, Ali Bey al-Kabir and Murad Bey, was one of the most powerful women in the country. She was famous among all the *'ulama* for her acts of charity and her piety, and she married her female slaves to all the Mamluk leaders. Her networking techniques must have been tremendous. One of her co-wives built a large *wikala* in Bulaq, other women belonging to the strata of native elites, merchants or men of religion had tremendous wealth as well, some having inherited part of it from their spouses or fathers, others generating it themselves.

The important point is not that women owned property and endowed charities, for they had done so throughout Islamic history, but that they were free to dispose of that property, to increase it and become involved in trade and commerce as they pleased, even from within the harem. Other strata of women were not limited to the harem and had more freedom to circulate in the market place and see for themselves what they were buying and selling. The only hindrance was in the case of land. In theory all land was crown property. It was then divided into lots, *iltizam*, and tax-farmed. The tax-farmers bid for the lots, paid one year's taxes in advance, then collected the taxes from the peasantry, keeping a share for themselves and forwarding the rest to the Ottoman administration. As part of the tax-farm there was a piece of land, known as *usya*, which was farmed by corvée labour and its produce belonged to the tax-farmer.

As for the peasants, they could not be removed from their land unless they failed to pay the taxes for three consecutive years. Because they only had the right to till the land, and enjoy its usufruct, theoretically they did not own the land but neither did the tax-farmer, the owner being the sultan in Istanbul. However, sons inherited the right to till the land from their fathers, and naturally daughters were prevented from enjoying that right since they did not till the soil. There were rare exceptions where women proved that tilling the land was their only source of livelihood and could show that they had males willing to till it for them, e.g. a husband or a son.

During that period the *'ulama* of the day praised the accumulation of wealth as licit and a blessing from God, very much in the manner of the Protestant ethic that Weber proclaimed, thereby encouraging others to behave in similar fashion. The *'ulama* themselves were involved in trade and commerce and a close, almost symbiotic, relationship between the long-distance merchants and the *'ulama* existed then. They intermarried and both represented the native elite as opposed to the alien, Mamluk, elites. The *'ulama* and merchants in the eighteenth century had also become tax-farmers. Many of the high *'ulama* were extremely wealthy, much of that wealth derived from being appointed supervisors of trusts.

A leading Sufi, Shaikh al-Sadat, was supervisor over thirty-three *waqf*, and was said to be the richest man of his time.

What was also different is that the period was one where a close relationship operated between the *'ulama* and women of all classes. Women felt confident enough to go to the courts and sue, for divorce, for business deals, for unpaid loans, i.e. for exactly the same things as men (except that men could repudiate their wives and women had to sue for divorce). Here too we find a support system for women. According to the Maliki school of jurisprudence women could sue for divorce simply by pleading *darar* (prejudice).

In one remarkable case, a woman had been married to a man for a year, and her uncle had been her guardian, although she was beyond the age to need a guardian. A year later she appeared in court and asked to be divorced claiming that her uncle had had no authority to give her in marriage to that man since she had already reached the age of maturity prior to her marriage. The court granted her a divorce. According to the law books divorce is granted to a minor once she reaches the age of maturity if the marriage had not been consummated, but in this case the husband had been tried and clearly found wanting. *Darar* then was a convenient and often used reason for divorce, for it implied that the wife had been physically or mentally abused, or that her husband was not satisfactory and if she remained married then she might depart from the path of righteousness, which would then cause her *darar*, hence the need for divorce. Another cause for divorce was on the grounds of desertion for a year. On these grounds, divorce was liberally granted in the eighteenth century. The judges of the day did not only use the *shari'a* as their source for passing judgements but also used *'urf* and *'adat*, customs and mores. Thus we find that cases and sentences passed in Upper Egypt were different from cases in the Delta since the customs differed in both locales. In the twentieth century a woman pleading *darar* would have to prove that bodily harm was inflicted on her; and desertion is not accepted as valid ground for divorce if the husband had business commitments which accounted for his absence for over a year. Thus the same legal tenet has been interpreted differently at different times.

Not only was divorce easier to obtain in the eighteenth century, but women also sued husbands if they borrowed money and failed to return it, or they sued each other as well. One woman appeared in court carrying a large washing tub in which lay what she claimed was her aborted foetus. She said that her neighbour had beaten her and caused her to abort and here was the proof of her allegation. The record unfortunately does not give us the end of the story, but this gives us an idea that women of the working classes as well as the elite felt comfortable going to court, without benefit of lawyers, and pleading for justice, which they believed they could obtain, because they were cognisant of the customs and mores of their society and knew that justice would be based on them.

Just as interesting is the fact that these women were described physically in the registers, as a means of identification, and the register stated that she was dark or pale in colour, whether she had any distinguishing mark, such as a tattoo, or the shape of her eyes, which is clear proof that they appeared unveiled in court, which obviously implies that they were also unveiled in public.

When women controlled their property and also had recourse to justice we begin to gain a different image from that of the downtrodden harem woman who was at the mercy of her lord and master. In fact he could often be at her mercy. Jabarti, the historian of the period, gives us accounts of women who beat their husbands, women who played tricks on the Ottoman soldiers, and women who were wealthy and powerful. It is true these women did not sit in official positions of power, nor hold legislative functions, but they were close to those who did, and wielded influence as much as those office-holders. It was and is commonplace that wives of powerful men were used as conduits to their husbands even by other men; one good reason for the relationship of the *'ulama* with Mamluk women is that the *'ulama* protected women legally, and elite women probably helped the *'ulama* to achieve wealth, if only by making them supervisors of endowments and trusts. The best example of how women of the elite were protected by the *'ulama* was during the punitive expedition sent by the Ottomans against the duumvirs, who were ruling Egypt in 1786. The leader of that expedition, Jazairli Pasha, had sold the concubines of the Mamluk Beys, which was illegal since many of them were *umm walad*, that is they had borne their masters sons, which would entitle them to freedom once the master had died, or before if he so wished. The *'ulama* remonstrated against such acts, and Shaikh Sadat, head of a Sufi order, was so adamant in his disapproval of such acts that the Ottoman Jazairli Pasha said he had "burnt his heart", meaning that he had angered him thoroughly.

We can summarise the eighteenth century by remarking that it was a decentralised system of government, often verging on the chaotic, that the men of the elite were constantly fighting one another, leaving their wives to handle financial affairs, and allowing the experience of the rest of the population to range from periods of exploitation to other periods when they were more or less free to do as they wished because the rulers had other preoccupations. This was also a time when agriculture was changing from subsistence to agriculture for export and the "pull" of the European market was met by a "push" on the part of the wealthy and the elites. Trade with the Hijaz and the Ottoman Empire flourished, and while trade with Europe was only around 15 per cent of the total it was beginning to increase as a result of the Industrial Revolution.

Nineteenth Century

When we compare the free-wheeling eighteenth century with the nineteenth century, we find a change in the status of women. Muhammad 'Ali had come to power and introduced a centralised system of government, one where all sources of wealth were controlled by the state and given as livings to the retainers and relatives of the ruler, for services rendered. Thus all tax-farms were confiscated. It is amazing to note that whenever the French occupied Egypt or Muhammad 'Ali tried to exploit tax-farms it was the women who took to the streets in defence of their property and not the men. Because of the dual monopoly of land and trade, women lost out on the two venues they had previously used to make money. Muhammad 'Ali rewarded those who were useful to him, and that excluded women, save those of his family. When he allowed trade to go to private hands he had by then invited a number of European merchants, over six thousand in fact, to trade and all trade was redirected towards Europe. In the previous century the major trade routes were to and from the Hijaz, Syria and the rest of the Ottoman Empire. By the end of his reign, most trade was with Europe, going through European merchants to whom the Egyptian women had no access. That situation was further exacerbated when European merchants in Egypt by the last third of the century numbered over sixty-eight thousand. Furthermore, over the century new institutions were introduced from Europe: banks, insurance companies and the stock exchange. They did not recognise the legal existence of women, who therefore had to deal through a male. In the eighteenth century elite women also had to deal through a male but the difference was that the male then was merely the woman's agent, so specified in whatever document was being registered, the woman's legal existence being recognised and respected. In the nineteenth century the legal existence of the woman as a participant in banks and such was denied.

Thus, the centralised system of government mitigated the involvement of women in the economic life of the country by limiting access and also set up a hierarchy that was echoed in the patriarchal family for the following reasons. Once the male became a salaried official, instead of a man of independent means, then he was at the mercy of the bureaucratic hierarchy, but also became the main breadwinner in the family. Hence, women lost not only their power to make money, but also lost the power and leverage within a marriage that having wealth gave a woman. The same transformation operated on all strata of society, though to a lesser extent on the working-class woman who continued to bring money into the family. Whether it was a bourgeois, a petit bourgeois, or a peasant, the man, with few exceptions, became regarded as the sole breadwinner, and the woman, even when she also participated in work, as with the *fallah* women, was underpaid to begin with and her work regarded as unimportant. That was also because the new system of land tenure had turned the peasants into wage labourers, so that their earnings were the main support of the family, and when women were employed they were paid half the wages of a male doing the same job.

It is true that women continued to inherit wealth from their relatives, but we note that when they did so the wealth was turned over to the male in the family, whether it be a husband, a brother or a son. It was then easy, with time, and with the British occupation, for the Victorian image of woman as a silly, emotional and decorative appendage, limited to the home and to raising children, to be applied to Egyptian elite and bourgeois women.

In the first place women had lost their linkage with the *'ulama*, for the *'ulama* had lost their moral and political clout in society. Muhammad 'Ali had confiscated their trusts, thereby undermining their economic independence from the government, and turned them into salaried government officials. He had also taken away their judicial duties, leaving them solely in charge of the laws of personal status. The predominant law was that of the Hanafi school and *'urf* and *'adat* were laid aside as sources of law. The *'ulama*, therefore, could not defend women as they had done in the past, and women therefore did not seek the assistance of the *'ulama* or the courts as they had done in the past, for they realised that in a paternal system the courts would not be as sympathetic as they had been formerly. Furthermore, since most Egyptians belonged to either the Maliki or the Shafi'i school of jurisprudence they were not as aware of the Hanafi school and its clauses, which was the preferred school of the Ottomans and the Turco-Circassian elite that then ruled Egypt.

Secondly, the sources of wealth for the native Egyptians became limited to internal trade, trade with the Sudan, or to receiving land from the ruler, or even buying it as '*uhda* or some other form, when the ruler was in need of funds. Such lands were bought by men only. Foreign trade was solidly in the hands of European merchants, very occasionally in partnership with a native Egyptian. Women could continue to invest in real estate and shops but by the end of the century modernisation had introduced large department stores catering to new European inspired tastes, and these, without exception, were owned, manned and managed by either foreigners or members of the minority who spoke foreign languages. Women of the elite therefore bowed out of participating in the commercial life of the country. Women of the middle classes naturally aped the elites, while women of the working classes continued to do what they had always done, which is work to support their families. But where in the past they had had access to certain professions such as scarf and handkerchief makers, or as *ballanas*, women working in bath houses, or going from house to house to wash hair, dye it, depilate women, prepare brides for weddings and so on, these professions were slowly dying as changes occurred in plumbing and style of clothing. New professions arose, such as teaching women new musical instruments, teaching them languages, selling European-style clothing from house to house, but a new non-native woman was now performing these new professions, one who spoke foreign languages and could dicker with the owner of the department store, or who knew how to play the new instruments.

Only the life of peasant women was relatively untouched, although the modern methods of agriculture forced a new exploitation on the peasantry through longer working hours and wage labour resulting from the changeover from basin to perennial irrigation. The right of the peasantry to till the same piece of land unchallenged, so long as the land tax was paid, fell by the wayside when land became private property. This turned the peasant into a wage labourer, and made women surplus labour, to be paid a pittance for doing the same job as the man, and only to be used when needed.

When new technology was introduced, women were sent to the bottom of the line and told that they were incapable of learning it. This happened in every country where technology was introduced. Steam engines brought in by Muhammad 'Ali had foreign advisers teaching workers how to operate them, and the foreign workers decreed that women could not learn to operate steam engines, or work in textile mills where such engines were used.

Towards the end of the century the British occupiers realised that women formed a good portion of the consumers in the country and therefore began to point out the lack of education of Muslim women, education then meaning Western-style education, not religious education (many Muslim women were educated in religious learning). Thus the push to educate women was to turn them into consumers of European products. Schools for women were opened and the education of women was encouraged by men who wanted a new kind of wife, one who was more "modernised". Effectively that meant a wife who could be trusted to bring up educated sons and who spoke foreign languages. In the past women of the elites married men who were older, the same age, or even younger. In the nineteenth century women were married to men with an already established position so the men were generally much older than the women. The difference in age mitigated against an equality between the spouses, for the older husband could dominate his younger, less experienced wife. Furthermore if she had any wealth he now controlled it, since he was the one with access to economic and commercial institutions, lastly he was more educated in the new-style secular education introduced under Muhammad 'Ali. In short he could impose on his wife through wealth, age and education.

Twentieth Century

The twentieth century brought a different form of government and a different economic system. By then wealth was obtained for the Egyptians through land, and the entire fields of trade, commerce, finance etc. were in the hands of foreigners. Elite women were becoming educated. The nationalist movement in 1919 changed the government of the day, and when the nationalists were exiled and imprisoned, women took to the streets to protest against British rule. Once women had participated in the nationalist movement – having come out of their harems in order to do that, modesty taking second place to nationalist demands – it was difficult to shove them back into seclusion. It could have been done as was the case in Algeria, where women joined the nationalist effort and once independence was won were sent back into seclusion. But the women of Egypt refused to go back to the veil and the harem and, leaving politics to the men, they cleverly took over the social services. The country which was not wealthy and could not afford social services accepted such a role for women. It was a traditionally recognised role for the wealthy of both sexes and also provided relief that women had found something to do that was useful but was not in competition with the role of men. Benevolent organisations run by women sprang up. Among the most successful of these was the Mabarrat Muhammad Ali, which changed its name after 1952 to the Mabarrat. It built up to two million hospital beds in the country, and raised a hospital, clinic or dispensary in every town and village. All was achieved through private contributions and manned by and managed by women. Homes for the blind, Braille institutes, orphanages, etc. were all set up and organised by elite women. When epidemics of any kind hit the country, such as malaria during the Second World War or cholera a decade later, it was women belonging to these benevolent organisations who toured the countryside inoculating the population, taking the diseased to hospitals, supplying food and medicines to the needy and in general taking over from the government which had neither the organisational talents of these women nor their energy and efficiency. Beginning in the 1930s the daughters of that first generation of liberated women went into the universities and became professional women who believed in earning a salary for their work and who were not content with purely benevolent work. In time they competed with men in all fields. Today the only position closed to women in Egypt is that of president of the republic, but maybe that too will change with time.

The new current of *intégrisme* that has swept the Muslim world over the past two decades has also affected the women of Egypt. A great deal of the so-called religious movement in Egypt, as elsewhere, is motivated not so much by religious fervour as by opposition to the present-day government. I have no doubt that some of that movement is motivated by a genuine desire to learn more about one's religion and a need for spiritual comfort, but a great deal of it is also the use of religious idiom to talk politics and economics, both of which are in need of radical change.

The outward symbol of such a movement is the change in women's clothing, which is certainly more obvious than in men's clothing, although the shorter gellaba and the beard are a sign of the committed *intégristes*. Women's clothing has taken two different forms with gradations in between. The most severe is the *niqab* where women cover the face completely, sometimes even wearing dark sunglasses to hide the eyes and gloves to cover the hands. Needless to say that is not religious garb since neither glasses nor gloves were known in early Islam; however, if women wish to dress that way that is their prerogative. The less severe clothing is when women wear something over their hair, and loose clothing to hide their legs and the shape of their body. While that is known as Islamic garb it is no more Islamic than anything else since we have no idea what people wore at the time of the Prophet. Wearing such clothing is an excellent brake on consumerism, since it prevents any outlay over changing fashions, make-up or going to hairdressers, and is fine for a society which is poor and cannot afford consumerism while producing little. But it is also a means for women of the petite bourgeoisie to be able to work without incurring either sexual harassment or criticism from neighbours and relations in strata that have not previously allowed their women to work. Thus women take their private space with them into the public space and can go out and work because two salaries are necessary in any household today given the rising cost of living, and the greater demands in terms of labour-saving devices, and "toys for grown-ups" such as TVs, video recorders and so on. Of course one sometimes wonders if it would not be easier for women to teach their offspring not to harass women and to develop respect for them rather than have to change clothing styles, but I suppose that is more difficult since women are the very ones who help perpetuate the patriarchal system since as wives they have plugged into it and gain status from it.

Thus while professionally women can be found in all positions, by their clothing some of them seem to accept a secondary role as someone who needs protection from the males of their society. That role is introduced as a consequence of economic requirements, and political opposition even when it is wrapped in the clean linen of religious interpretations. For today women are told that they are to play a different but equal role in order to protect them and respect them, but if respect is equated with isolation and regarding the female body as a blemish, a '*awra*, that does not mean equality but a superior role for the man over the woman. Otherwise men too would be veiled and the male body also regarded as a blemish.

How such attitudes will work out in the future will depend on whether liberalisation in politics will gain ground, and whether corruption in government will end, for when a society is ruled in an authoritarian fashion and corruption in government is rampant then the only means left to the average citizen to complain and demand changes is the appeal to religion. The call for a return to a rule of law, not caprice, is translated into a demand for a return to the *shari'a*. The desire for the religious tax, *zakat*, is to make the new rich pay taxes and to redistribute wealth, and the call for a Muslim form of society is to prevent corruption. All of these are desires shared by the entire population but expressed differently by different groups with greater or lesser degrees of appeal to the public. Some do it through pleading for secular, liberal rule, others through pleading for a Muslim form of government but they seldom know what form that government will take. Others take a nihilistic stand and want to destroy everything and then build a brave new world in its place. Whoever gains the upper hand will, no doubt, make an impact on the role of women in society. The only difference being that women today have a greater awareness of their rights and a greater knowledge of what goes on in the rest of the world so it will not be easy to deprive them of whatever gains they have made during this century. In the final analysis women will gain absolute equality, if such a thing were possible, only through their own efforts in teaching future generations to respect women and not deny them their rights in society.

THREE

LAW AND THE DESIRE FOR SOCIAL CONTROL: AN INSIGHT INTO THE HANAFI CONCEPT OF *Kafa'a* WITH REFERENCE TO THE FATAWA 'ALAMGIRI (1664-1672)

Mona Siddiqui

One area of society in which language is used to express elements of cultural values is in the realm of written law, for example law which consists of a literary presentation of social norms. Written law uses language for the purpose of stamping conduct with approval or disapproval and with the intention of creating a desired social order. In this context it is generally useful to define law as a force regulating customs and the behaviour patterns of a society. It is therefore useful to assume that one of the functions of written law as we understand it today, is to reflect to a considerable extent the social standards and cultural ideals of the community in which it operates.

With Islamic legal texts, it is the symbiotic relationship that religion shares with the law which is its most distinguishing characteristic, making Islamic law a reflection of the religion. The texts reveal the interaction between Islamic religious values, how they determine legal principles and how these principles subsequently formulate their own life forms. Law articulates a way of looking at society and Islamic law is no exception. Its "essence" is its religion but its "expression" is a response to the formal exigencies of juristic style in language, logic and structure.

One of the most interesting examples of this is the law of marriage. In this chapter I propose to analyse a particular area of the law of marriage within the Hanafi school in order to discuss how far religious law is used to interpret the order of society. The principle of *kafa'a*, generally translated as equality or compatibility between husband and wife, has been given particular prominence in this school and has been developed extensively in the seventeenth century text, the Fatawa 'Alamgiri,[1] also known as the Fatawa Hindiyya. Although I focus primarily on the Fatawa, reference has also been made to select material from other Hanafi sources. The aim is to give an overall picture of how the classical jurists defined this legal principle and its social consequences.

The collection of the Fatawa 'Alamgiri was compiled during the years 1664–72 under the patronage of the Mughal emperor, Aurangzeb 'Alamgir, who appointed a team of scholars to put together a collection of legal opinions with the aim of achieving an authoritative body of Hanafi law. The existing material on the Fatawa does not discuss how the book was preserved or distributed, nor do we have sufficient details about the compilers themselves. Although the book bears the title *Fatawa*, it is not as the name suggests a book of legal responses to specific questions. It is a book of *fiqh* where the primary aim is to elucidate principles and rules of Hanafi law by presenting legal problems quoted verbatim from a wide selection of authorities within the Hanafi school on all the subjects generally covered within the *fiqh* tradition. In presenting the masa'il from the source books of the Hanafi school, the *zahir al-riwayah*,[2] the Fatawa has adopted a specific method of citing from various authorities and ending its quotes with the expression "according to" or "so in the . . ." followed by the name of the author or the title of the book. It occasionally has the phrase "and this is our preferred opinion" or "this is the better view" inserted into the problem although it is not clear whether this is a part of the actual citation that has been quoted or the Fatawa expressing its own view.

I have limited this study to the law only; it is not a sociological study nor would I claim that an exclusive study of textual law only can reflect marriage in the actual lives of Muslim men and women. My aim is to show that in as much as written law reflects social norms and uses language for the purpose of stamping conduct with approval or disapproval with an intention to create a desired social order, Islamic law is no exception. Furthermore, in Islam, the symbiotic relationship that religion shares with the law means that one of the methods of exploring the nature of Islamic society can be pursued through the dimension of its legal literature.

Marriage

No society has ever excluded marriage from its institutions, whether the basis was bride-seizure, payment, parental arrangement or the comparatively recent emergence of romantic love. In Islam, the laws of marriage form the nucleus of all family law and touch upon many of the most significant aspects of human relationships. In *fiqh*, marriage is discussed within the *Kitab al-nikah* where juristic debate is centred mainly upon a careful observation of legal principles and social realities. The legitimisation of sexual intercourse, the preservation of a system of social hierarchy, and the distribution of wealth are a few of the most basic concepts that structure these particular laws. The delicate balancing of individual rights and authorities within these laws has resulted in the formation of an extremely detailed labyrinth of rules, some of which appear bewildering for the modern reader. In these rules, however, the use of emotive language such as love or companionship to describe the relationship between husband and wife does not feature as a subject for juristic speculation. Their concern is mainly with defining marriage on the basis of sexual rights and financial obligations.

As an institution, ceremony, and male–female relationship, marriage is primarily described in all of these three aspects as a contract in law, *'aqd.* It is seen as a verbal agreement although any theoretical discussion of the word "contract" is actually absent from *fiqh* works as Chehata has pointed out:

> La notion générale de contrat n'a jamais fait l'objet dans les ouvrages de doctrine, d'une théorie générale.[3]

The Fath al-Qadir provides us with a definition of a verbal contract where the emphasis is on the completion of the agreement:

> The intention of a contract is completion whether it is marriage or otherwise comprising the offer of one of the two speakers followed by the acceptance of the other.[4]

This means that the marriage contract is primarily a verbal contract where the words spoken are in the nature of a "performative utterance"; i.e. by virtue of the words being spoken, the status of the man and woman changes to that of husband and wife. That the offer may be made explicitly by the woman implies a certain autonomy which she can exercise. Yet, this right to propose is a logical consequence of her status as a free and sane adult, who in Hanafi law may enter into any contract including the marriage contract. All contracts are concluded only once the proposal and acceptance of the two parties concerned has taken place. Marriage as a contract must follow this format. However, it will be seen from the brief outline of marriage below that for this simple format to be effective in concluding marriage, there are certain conditions preceding and ensuing that have to be in existence.

The following description of marriage is based in part on Quduri's *Mukhtasar*.[5] The Qur'an uses two terms to refer to marriage: *nikah* and *zawaj*. Most commonly used is the term *nikah*. The word *nikah* literally means "intercourse" but in the technical terminology of Islamic jurisprudence is used to denote "marriage" in its legal context.[6] *Nikah* is viewed as a bilateral contract or *'aqd* between two parties. The first speech, from whichever side it emanates, constitutes the offer and the second speech constitutes the acceptance.[7] The two parties to the contract, however, are not necessarily the two people bound by the contract since the groom may enter the contract with the girl's father or closest guardian. In this way, the woman may be viewed as a third party to the contract. As ward to her father or guardian, Islamic law regulates gender significance by giving a woman identity primarily through her relationship with a close male member of her family. This notion of "giving" a woman in marriage is a reflection of a society that accepts patriarchal rights as the norm. It is a system of agnation that is not based on the marriage of father and mother, but on the authority of the father. Women may be legally competent to act for themselves but social values place constraints on their behaviour so that acting in their own interests without male participation is basically seen as denying male authority.

It is generally held in Sunni law that the contract must be undertaken in the presence of two witnesses but there is disagreement as to whether this is a condition without which the marriage is rendered invalid. The witnesses are either two men or one man and two women, who must be of legal capacity, i.e. sane, free and adult. It is agreed amongst Muslim jurists that where the two parties to the marriage, *ghair 'adul*, have been subject to legal punishment, *mahdudin fi qadhf*, but can nevertheless satisfy the legal criteria, their testimony remains valid. There are however limitations to the capacity of a Muslim to marry any person of the opposite sex. Those who are prohibited are known as the maharim.[8] The prohibition may be on the grounds of (a) number, (b) religion, (c) relationship either through affinity or consanguinity, (d) foster-relationship, (e) unlawful conjunction and *'idda*.[9]

If the girl is a minor at the time her guardian enters her into marriage, on reaching maturity she has the option of rejecting the contract, known in legal terms as *khiyar al-bulugh*.[10] However, there is conflict within the

Hanafi tradition as to whether the woman retains this right if the guardian was her father or grandfather.[11] If the girl is a free adult of sound mind, then the marriage becomes operative only upon indication of her consent; she cannot be forced into marriage against her will. Consent however may simply be an absence of refusal on the woman's part. Nevertheless, since coercion invalidates any marriage contract, the adult woman remains in relative charge of her marital destiny. An adult woman may also give herself in a contract without the consent of her guardian or *wali*.[12] This is the tension running through the Hanafi arguments; family involvement in the arrangement of marriages is part of the social fabric and yet men and women, having reached legal majority, have the right to choose their own partners. Such a marriage is legally valid but subject to intervention by the girl's guardian if it is found wanting in any of the qualities required under the principle of *kafa'a*.[13] *Kafa'a* is the presence of equality or compatibility required between husband and wife and is measured according to the six considerations of descent, Islam, profession, freedom, good character, and wealth or means. In juristic terms when a woman marries one who is not her equal but is lower, her guardians reserve the right to oppose the marriage and may appeal to a *qadi* to set the marriage aside.

Again, the ultimate decision to accept or reject a marriage proposal lies with the woman. But the principle of *kafa'a* entails a sense of precaution that she must take if she were to choose her own partner. As we shall see throughout this discussion, although the right of objection that belongs to her father or guardian has to be justified on strict principles, it automatically subordinates the woman's choice to male approval. There is no concept of maternal rights being given any precedence on the basis of mother–daughter gender identification; the ties that bind a woman to her male relatives ensure both her protection and subjugation. This is in contrast with the position of the male who on attaining legal majority is no longer under the aegis of any guardians. Thus, gender difference with regard to marriage arrangement remains in spite of the juristic recognition of a woman's right to select her partner or refuse a partner chosen for her.

Although marriage is seen as a natural and desirable state for Muslim men and women, it is tempered in juristic discussions by the overriding objective of social harmony and stability. One of the more concrete ways of achieving this was to make the provision of nurture and material support fundamental to the legality of the contract. However, this support is strongly gendered so that the responsibility of providing maintenance, *nafaqa*, in the form of food, shelter and clothing lies entirely with the man. This is an obligation which devolves upon the husband once the marriage has been consummated. Consummation perfects the marriage contract and full legal consequences of the contract can only be realised once intercourse has taken place. In return for this maintenance, the wife's duty is to obey her husband. The wife's obedience is pivotal to the union working harmoniously, so much so that there is a specific term for a disobedient wife, *nashiz*. Even though there is some dispute over what constitutes disobedience, there is agreement on the consequence – which is that the wife forfeits her right to maintenance.

Defining specific gendered obligations and expectations distinguishes the male from the female in the marital unit. Usually, the man's obligations are financial whereas the woman's are sexual. This is best illustrated by the provision of *mahr*. The payment of *mahr* or dower to the wife is an obligation in every valid contract of marriage whether or not the dower is declared at the time of the contract.[14] Objects that are suitable for dower are money, land, buildings and payments in kind.[15] The dower which is specified at the time of the contract is the *mahr al-musamma* or the specified dower and may be divided into *mu'ajjal*, "prompt", or *mu'ajjal*, "deferred".[16] If no amount of dower has been fixed, the wife is entitled to the *mahr al-mithl*, the standard or proper dower, which is determined with regard to the social position and other qualities of the bride. The Islamic mahr is in actual fact a debt owed by the man to his wife

If, however, the woman is divorced before the marriage has been consummated or before husband and wife have engaged in *al-khalwa al-sahiha*, valid privacy, the wife is entitled to only half the dower.[17] The implication by the jurists is that the Islamic dower is a form of financial compensation paid for the sexual enjoyment of a woman; when sexual intercourse has not taken place, the woman loses her claim to the full amount. The dower belongs essentially to the woman as it is a financial recognition of her new sexual status. It is the woman who assumes a new status through sexual intercourse within marriage, not the man. Despite the inherent principle that husband and wife are mutually entitled to sexual enjoyment within the marriage contract, the payment of *mahr* is a confirmation of gendered roles in which the provision of material wealth for any privileges or rights within the contract is essentially the man's responsibility.

Any contract that is not valid can be dissolved through the *qadi*'s jurisdiction. The *qadi*'s role is imperative for the termination of such contracts.[18] His presence however is not a legal requirement for the marriage contract itself, nor is it required that a *qadi* register the marriage irrespective of social practice. He cannot pronounce divorce, *talaq*, for this is a right which belongs only to the husband, the consequence of which is that the wife must observe *'idda* or waiting period in order to confirm whether she is pregnant and thereby establish the child's paternity.

It will be seen from this skeletal framework that although marriage as a legitimate ceremony could quite simply be a free act of agreement between a man and woman, Islamic law ensures that freedom of choice is regulated. The hierarchical chain of authorities, paternal, legal or political reserve the right to contend, terminate or pressurise an undesirable marriage contract. This ensures that those who exercise some measure of social power can prevent radical changes in the existing social system which could possibly occur with random mate choice.

Kafa'a

In Islamic law, one of the legal principles that ensures the continuation of particular stratification systems is that of *kafa'a*. With a root meaning of "equality" "suitability" or "capability" in Islamic legal terminology, it has assumed a specific meaning whereby it is required that a Muslim husband must be equal to or superior to his wife; in other words, although a woman may choose her partner in marriage every effort is made to ensure that she does not marry beneath herself and more, importantly, beneath her family. The legal criteria by which this equality or superiority is measured are developed in detail in the principle of *kafa'a*. This particular principle seems to be relatively more prominent in the Hanafi school, a point which has been explained by Farhat Ziadeh:

> It would seem that Malik's denial of the social distinctions upon which *kafa'a* is built is due to the fact that his milieu of Medina and Hijaz had not developed such distinctions while that of Abu Hanifah in Kufa and Iraq, which was more cosmopolitan and socially complex, had. The admixture of ethnic groups, the long tradition of urbanisation, the existence side by side of Arab and "client", the resulting social differentiation, all these factors were highly conducive to the development of *kafa'a* in Iraq.[19]

In view of this comment, it would appear that a complex social structure led to a complex juristic tradition. Furthermore, pre-Islamic customs were incorporated into the legal fabric developed after the advent of Islam and commanded observance. Custom which does not contravene the principles of *shari'a* is generally regarded as valid and authoritative. This approach has continued in modern times. Thus we have the Majalla, the Ottoman Civil Code of 1877, which states in Article 43, "A thing acknowledged by custom is regarded as one agreed upon stipulation." In the Fatawa, the jurists give considerable and perhaps more than usual significance to the doctrine. The six qualities which form the points of comparison between the man and woman are (1) lineage (*nasab*), (2) Islam, (3) freedom (*hurriya*), (4) property (*mal*), (5) piety (*diyana*), (6) profession (*hirfa*). It must be pointed out that these qualities pertaining to *kafa'a* are legally significant only at the time of the marriage contract not during the continuation of the marriage.

Kafa'a is to be considered only at the commencement of marriage and subsequent inequality does not affect its permanence. So, if a man marries a woman and he is her equal then he becomes an adulterer or tyrant, this is no ground for cancelling the marriage.[20]

The Fatawa develops the point:

> *Kafa'a* is considered in men with regard to women as a requirement of marriage according to the *Muhit* of Sarakhsi. It is not considered in women with respect to men. So in the *Bidaya*.[21]

> And if the woman marries a man better than her then the guardian cannot separate her for the guardian is not shamed by being under a man to whom he is not an equal. So in the *Mabsut*.[22]

However, this is not a full citation and we have to turn to the *Mabsut* itself to understand the concept of shame in this:

> For *kafa'a* is not demanded in women and the guardian is not shamed by being under the man to whom the woman is not equal. For descent will be to the father and not the mother.[23]

It is the point of paternity and descent that is at issue. Since kinship transfers from the male line and a child's descent depends upon the lineage of the father, it is of no consequence what lineage the mother is;

the husband's superior lineage lifts the woman on to a higher social plane and thereby her own family and kin are at a social advantage. Furthermore, if *kafa'a* has been satisfied, or the woman has married better than her own status, the guardian no longer reserves the right of objection.

In fact, the issue of descent or *nasab* is probably the most important of the six considerations. In giving priority to this concept, the Fatawa like other Hanafi works emphasises the legal and social importance of birth and background. It is the view that social identity is transmitted through males and not females which provides the rationale for the Hanafi arguments. The Quraish are equal to each other but the non-Quraishites, i.e. the other Arabs, are equal amongst themselves and inferior to the Quraish. The *mawalis,* i.e. the non-Arabs, are not equal to the Arabs. It seems reasonable to deduce from this that family or tribal pride prevalent among the Arabs has contributed immensely to this element of *kafa'a*. However, the meticulous discussion of the various tribes in the juristic texts has led many scholars to conclude that this aspect of descent is of relevance only to the Arabs and is not applicable to the non-Arabs:

> Les auteurs classiques expliquent laborieusement cette discrimination en faisant valoir que les questions de lignage, de prééminence de clans, sont propres aux habitants de l'Arabie où existait une hiérarchie minutieusement établie depuis plus de treize siècles entre les diverses tribus . . .[24]

It would be reasonable to assume therefore that by the time of the Fatawa in seventeenth century India, this element of *kafa'a* served more as a juristic argument than a legal requirement.

The second consideration is that of Islam. What needs to be determined here is for how long a person's family has been Muslim. The criterion of Islam stops at the third generation, so that a third-generation Muslim is equal to the daughter of any non-Arab whose family has been Muslim for several generations. There is however a distinction between those places where Islam has been dominant for some time and where it is a recent religion. In the latter, recent conversions should not be looked upon as a defect:

> One who has embraced Islam is not the equal of a woman who has two or three ancestors in Islam; he is equal to one like himself. This is relevant to a place where Islam has been in existence for a long time. If Islam's existence is only recent, then there is no shame and such a marriage will incur no disgrace. So in the Siraj al-Wahaj.[25]

If this is a description of Indian society at that time when conversions from Hinduism to Islam were a predominant feature of the social structure, then one could interpret this requirement as a possible example of law directing social attitudes. Again what is significant is that belief in Islam is used as a measure of a person's lineage.

The third consideration is that of freedom which is discussed through the institution of slavery. In Islamic law, slavery can originate only through birth or through captivity, that is if a non-Muslim who is protected neither by treaty nor by a safe conduct falls into the hands of Muslims.[26] Within Islamic law, slavery is a defect in legal capacity. As A. Rahim comments:

> In its inception, it was a penalty for unbelief and non-acknow-
> ledgement of the authority of the Law-Giver, and therefore the
> creation of the condition of slavery is said to be a public right.[27]

Therefore, what is at issue is that the institution of slavery distinguished between the believer and the non-believer. The penalty the non-believer paid was that even when he became a free person, his status with respect to marriage did not equal that of a woman who had always been free:

> A freed slave is not equal to a woman who has always been
> free.[28]

It appears that the question of marriage between slaves and free women is a common point of discussion in law books. Just as the requirement of equality in point of tribe or family is peculiar to the Arabs, so the requirement of equality in point of freedom is peculiar to the Muslims of all other nations who pride themselves on these issues rather than lineage:

> For the Arabs it is not necessary that the father be a Muslim too.
> So that if an Arab man whose father is a *kafir* marries an Arab
> woman whose paternal ancestors were Muslims, he is her equal,
> for freedom is inevitable to an Arab; it is not permitted to enslave
> Arabs. So in the *Bahr al-Ra'iq*.[29]

Therefore, one's lineage determines the conditions that need to be satisfied for the purpose of *kafa'a*. Non-Arabs who have no claim to tribal pedigree need to fulfil a different set of religious and social criteria than their Arab counterparts.

On the point of wealth or property, there are two separate considerations: dower and maintenance. By dower is meant the payment of the prompt dower and on the issue of maintenance, a period of at least one month has been specified on the basis of the book, *Tajnis al-Mazid*, as the length of time during which a man must have sufficient means to support his wife:

> According to Abu Yusuf, if he is able to provide the dower and earns enough daily to support the woman, then he is her equal. This is correct according to the *Sharh al-Jami' al-Saghir* of Qadikhan.[30]

Two of the most juristically interesting qualities pertaining to *kafa'a* are piety, *diyana*, and profession, *hirfah*. The concept of piety is the most difficult to define since it is a fusion of religious behaviour with individual morality; the Hanafis needed to provide legal distinctions by which *diyana*, the area of morality and law proper could be more systematically assessed:

> The sinner is not equal to the pious (person), whether the sin is apparent or hidden according to the *Muhit*.[31]

This left the jurists with the problem of defining a particular social behaviour which would be possible to translate into a legal argument. Despite the equal gravity of both the apparent and the hidden sin, the problem remained of defining the overt act of wickedness, *fisq*, that would distinguish the sinner, *fasiq*, from the virtuous, *salih*. The act upon which most jurists are agreed as being evidence of sin is excessive and manifest drinking of alcohol. However, the difficulty of reconciling public and private morality created a point of *ikhtilaf* among Abu Hanifa and his two companions. Sarakhsi quotes Abu Yusuf in the *Mabsut*[32] as stating that if a person is discrete in his drinking habits and does not venture out in a state of inebriety, he is an "equal". Sarakhsi also claims that there is no tradition from Abu Hanifa on the issue of *fisq* bearing any relevance to *kafa'a*. It would seem that the Muslim jurists realised that the province of law is external behaviour and private inclinations cannot be legally assessed or established with enough certainty to incur legal consequences.

Profession or *hirfah* is the last of the six qualities that is given legal consideration. There is dispute within the Hanafi tradition over the relevance of considering profession but the reason is explained in the *Hidaya*:

Men assume to themselves a certain consequence from the
respectability of their callings, whereas a degree of contempt is
annexed to them on account of the meanness thereof.[33]

However, the Fatawa states that Abu Hanifa claims profession is
not to be considered; the example given is that one who is a doctor of
animals is thus equal to one who deals with perfumes. Later on in the
same section, but from a different tradition, Abu Hanifa is cited as agreeing with his two companions in distinguishing the low professions such
as doctor of animals, one who bleeds people, the weaver, the sweeper,
the tanner of skins from the higher profession of one who deals in per-
fumes, sells cloth or deals in coins. This careful listing of the professions
is taken from the Fatawa Qadikhan whereby for the purpose of *kafa'a*,
a member of the first category is not equal to a member of the second.

The categorisation of professions leads to a difference of opinion for
two reasons. Firstly, there are those professions which the jurists deem
intrinsically low because they are manual and "dirty", perhaps even
impure. Secondly, there is an inevitable shift in the importance and value
of some professions over others according to custom and place. Within
the field of marriage, a woman who marries into a profession or trade
lower than that of her own family immediately incurs disgrace upon her
guardians. From the discussion on profession emerges the complex
balancing of trades that reflects the varying categories of social hierarchy
available to society at that time.

What is developed from the theory of *kafa'a* is the tension between
"prescription" and "preference". Anthropologists and sociologists have
analysed these dual concepts in relation to a man's choice of partner but
a similar set of circumstances occur from the female perspective when
referring to the doctrine of *kafa'a*. *Kafa'a* in defining boundaries offers
"prescriptive" rules of marriage, that is, a woman ought to marry a person
from a particular social hierarchy. However, the "preferential" element
is also present since the woman is given a choice albeit within preset
boundaries. With the exception of Islam as the only religious criterion
and an absolute prerequisite in her husband, the observation of the other
five points reflect a respect for social expectations. Social expectations
and economic needs seem to mandate that marriage be controlled by the
parents of the bride. The elaboration of the separate points reveals a society that desires a particular type of behaviour and one where the legal
system may be functioning as first and foremost a literary expression
of these norms.

Therefore, what we are presented with is human relationships being analysed in terms of a system of laws; laws that provide a structure and guidelines in the decision to marry. One thing which is not considered as a crystallising element in this decision to marry is the notion of romantic love. As William Goode writes:

> Love may have a potentially disruptive effect on mate choice and stratification systems. Therefore, it is necessary for society to keep it in check.[34]

The emergence of romantic love playing a significant role in the decision to marry is relatively recent in many social systems. In Islamic law texts the abstractions of romantic love do not figure and thus, in the socio-structural patterns that are discussed, the potential importance of love as affecting mate choice is denied any juristic reckoning.

It is understood that if a woman marries a man of an equal or superior status to herself, there is no legal problem. The problems arise only when the woman has married one below her status or, more correctly, the status of her guardians. The relative significance of *kafa'a* in the Hanafi tradition and the multiplicity of problems that ensue from cases where equality has not been established are a consequence of the twin issues of legal capacity and guardianship (*wilaya*). Unlike the other Sunni schools, Hanafi legal logic made it imperative to accord a woman her legal capacity which rendered her eligible for entering a marriage contract without her guardian. In other words, she may act as her own *wali*:

> The marriage of a free, sane adult woman is operative without a guardian according to Abu Hanifa.[35]

Al-Bahr al-Ra'iq states:

> Everyone whom [the law] permits to dispose of their property by acting as their own guardian, it also permitted them to marry, acting as their own guardian.[36]

The *Hidaya* provides an explanation for this position:

> In marrying, the woman has acted with regard to a right that concerns her exclusively. For this, she is fully competent, being sane and capable of distinction. These very reasons which allow her to

act for herself in matters of property, permit her to choose a husband. She only requires a *wali* to marry her off so as not to be
associated with shamelessness.[37]

To contract herself in marriage without the consent of her guardian
may therefore be a legal right, but it allows her a freedom which has
nevertheless to be kept in check. Furthermore, the taint of shamelessness
that is associated with a woman who acts within the legal parameters
reflects a society reluctant to equate the observance of a legal right with
approved behaviour.

The second issue that comes into focus is that of the right of the
guardians:

> If a woman gives herself in marriage to one who is not her *kaf'*,
> then the marriage is valid according to the majority of the tradi-
> tions, so that before separation all rights of divorce, *ila'*, *zihar* and
> inheritance claims remain firm etc.; however, the guardians have
> the right of interference . . . so in the *Muhit*.[38]

The right of interference is not tantamount to the right of separation,
which belongs to the *qadi* alone. However, what it renders is control and
power in the hands of the guardians who would otherwise have no legal
say concerning the woman's marriage. Not only would she have the
absolute right to contract herself in marriage but also to marry whom-
soever she wished even if the man were beneath her social status. The
guardian's role would be limited to the marriage of minors. Thus, despite
recognising the validity of a marriage where *kafa'a* has not been established, the Hanafi tradition has conflicting views on this point. The
Fatawa cites a tradition in which Shaybani states on the authority of Abu
Hanifa that the "marriage is not put into effect". The original quote is
traced back to Sarakhsi's *Mabsut*:

> According to the tradition of Hasan, he says, if she marries some-
> one who is not her equal, the marriage is not permitted in essence
> and that is nearest to precaution. [This is because] not all the
> guardians have an equal right to take a case before the *qadi*, nor
> are all the *qadis* just. Therefore, it is a proper safeguard that mar-
> riage be barred to a woman where there is a difference of *kafa'a*.[39]

The rationale for this ruling from Sarakhsi is that if marriage is not permitted in the cases where equality is absent, it will avoid the complications that could subsequently arise as a result of conflicting interests between the *qadi* and the guardian. However, what this quote is actually implying is that a contract entered into by a woman which does not satisfy the requirements of *kafa'a* should be regarded as void from the beginning. This conflict is not resolved within the Hanafi tradition because, despite the desire to prohibit marriages that are concluded without the guardian, the jurists cannot deny a woman the right to act of her own accord nor can they deny the guardian the right to oppose an unsuitable marriage contract. What we have with *kafa'a* is in fact an example of how law attempts to compromise with social reality.

The legal authority that is invested in guardians is of such a nature that it ensures that a woman still remains subordinate to the wishes of the higher authorities around her. It is a capacity that does not lapse with time although there is some direct dispute as to whether this right ends if the guardian does not raise opposition and the woman has a child. The Fatawa Qadikhan conflicts with an earlier citation from the *Mabsut* in which it is stated that irrespective of how many children a woman may have, the guardian still retains the right to interfere in a marriage which he regards as unequal.

This is however refuted by the Fatawa Qadikhan:

> The failure of a *wali* to demand separation does not invalidate his rights in respect of *faskh*, however much time, unless the woman has a child. So in the Fatawa Qadikhan.[40]

The modification of this rule does in fact release the woman from what would otherwise be a perpetually precarious position. Any demand for separation must be based on reasons pertaining to absence of *kafa'a*, not on mere dislike of the groom. The guardian's objection may lose its validity for the following reasons:

(a) if the guardian takes the dower and sees the woman off to the groom's house, then this is a sign of consent to the marriage.
(b) if the guardian takes the dower but does not see her off, then there is dispute over this point.
(c) if the guardian does not take the dower but disputes the amount of maintenance, *nafaqa* and dower, then this is a sign of consent by the guardian.

This line of argument shows that acceptance of the dower is an acceptance of the marriage and that objections raised over financial discrepancies may not be sufficient in themselves to serve as grounds for judicial separation. What emerges is that dispute over the groom's financial position is in fact evidence of acceptance of the more important issue of his lineage and therefore ultimately, acceptance of the marriage.

This type of discussion on the nature and scope of the guardian's authority illustrates the contextual and structural balance of *fiqh* texts in general. From the general principle that the guardian has the right of interference, various rules elaborate not the contradiction of this principle but a careful cross-section of the rights of those whom this principle affects.

In Malinowski's words:

> The fundamental function of law is to curb natural propensities, to hem in and control human instincts . . . to ensure a type of co-operation which is based on mutual concessions and sacrifices for a common end.[41]

An interesting example of how this is achieved is demonstrated in the following example from the Fatawa where the emphasis shifts from the woman to the guardian, that is, a situation whereby a man contracts a woman to someone who is not her equal. The guardian has given the woman in marriage to someone who is not her equal and the husband has intercourse with her. She is then separated from him by a declaration of divorce. If the woman then marries the same man without the consent of the guardian, the guardian has the right to take the case to a *qadi*. If the divorce was a reversible divorce, that is, where the marriage still subsists and the woman returns to the man without the consent of her guardian he has no right of appeal for separation. It is again juristic logic that provides the explanation for this. In the first case, the second marriage is legally a marriage contracted by the woman herself so that even though it is to the same man to whom she was married by her guardian, he is still not her equal. This time it is not the guardian who is legally responsible for the marriage, and therefore he has the right to interfere in a marriage that has taken place without his consent and which is wanting in *kafa'a*. This means that neither the guardian nor the woman have the right to oppose a marriage which may be wanting in *kafa'a* but which has been contracted by the guardian. This right belongs to the guardian only if the woman is responsible for the contract. However, if the divorce was a reversible divorce, then in effect the marriage never came to an end and there is no question of a second marriage entered into by the woman; the marriage is in legal terms a marriage contracted by the guardian who therefore has no right to oppose it.[42]

The objectives underlying the institution of *kafa'a* go beyond the fear of "misalliance" whereby a woman may contract herself in marriage to someone who is not her equal. This could only occur in the Hanafi tradition which gives the woman the right to contract herself in marriage without a guardian. By citing this tradition, the Fatawa defends this important right belonging to the woman. However, choice of partners is socially important because both placement and choice link two kinship lines together. To permit, therefore, random mate choice could introduce radical changes in the existing social structure. Since individual selection of partners affects the social structure, *kafa'a* may be interpreted as a legal argument carefully elaborated by a juristic desire to ensure control of social stratification. The rules emphasise that it is desirable that individual groups should confine their choice of partners to particular categories of people. Within this choice the distribution of money and the preservation of particular descents are the most significant factors in determining the control necessary to keep marriage in check.

The Relevance of *Kafa'a* Today

Although the concept of equality as outlined in the classical theory of *kafa'a* forms an extremely interesting juristic debate, the social reality of such perceptions is very much an existing phenomenon of Muslim communities. Family background and wealth are still fundamental considerations in the choice of grooms, particularly within the arranged marriage system where the woman's entry into marriage is usually a consent to parental choice rather than personal choice. However, the changes in society today have shifted our values to some extent so that economic and social factors are compromised for the sake of mental compatibility and even love.

The most significant social change in many Muslim societies is that women are leaving their interior world. They are becoming more and more visible because of education and employment. The inevitable result has been the fragmentation of a social pattern based on segregation leading to greater social discourse and even intimacy between the two sexes. This has not only broadened women's perception of the outside world but also their own gender experience. Their involvement in public life has increased opportunities for making decisions about their lives. Within the field of marriage, it has meant that women are putting the legal rights of personal autonomy into practical experience. Outright patriarchal authority may be rejected as more and more women go beyond the traditional boundaries which determine choice of partners. It is reasonable to say nevertheless that the risks of women making unwelcome marriage choices is still limited because mate choice is not usually an exercise of random selectivity but is often achieved through an inner and sometimes unconscious attraction to those who are of similar social and material standing. Furthermore, these changes are more widespread in urban areas; in rural societies, the Islamic social system remains relatively intact with defined gender roles and expectations.

Although the guardian's right of intervention as implied in the principle of *kafa'a* remains a legal right, its significance has faded to some extent. As women have become more aware of rights accorded to them by Islamic law, the distinction between use and abuse of the law has become more manifest. It is not that women oppose a desired social order as implied through *kafa'a*; the problem is that too often safeguarding male authority is achieved only at the expense of a woman's emotional needs as well as her legal rights.

NOTES

1 I have used the Beirut, 1973 edition, hereafter referred to as *Fatawa* in the footnotes.

2 The *zahir al-riwayah* are the six Hanafi law books by Muhammad B. Hasan al-Shaybani (d.187 AH) which together form the source books of the Hanafi school. They are *al-Mabsut* (or *al-Asl*), *al-Jami' al-Saghir, al-Jami' al-Kabir, al-Ziyadat, al-Siyar al-Kabir* and *al-Siyar al-Saghir*.

3 C. Chehata, *Etudes de Droit Musulman* (Paris: Faculty of Law of the University of Paris, 1971), p. 157.

4 Ibn al-Humam, *Fath al-Qadir*, Vol. 3 (Cairo, 1970), p. 187.

5 All references to Quduri's *Mukhtasar* are from G. H. Bousquet and L. Bercher, *Le Statut Personnel en Droit Musulman Hanéfite* (Tunisia, 1950), pp. 974–1039.

6 *al-Bahr al-Ra'iq* defines *nikah* as both intercourse and contract, p. 82. See also C. Hamilton, *Hidaya* (India: Islamic Book Trust, 1982), p. 25: "In the language of the law it implies a particular contract used for the purpose of legalizing generation."

7 Quduri, *Mukhtasar*, p. 13. A. A. A. Fyzee, *Outlines of Muhammadan Law*, 3rd edn (London: Oxford University Press, 1964), p. 89: "The proposal and acceptance must both be expressed at one meeting; a proposal made at one meeting and an acceptance at another do not constitute a valid marriage."

8 cf. Quduri, *Mukhtasar*, pp.13 and 15.

9 I.e. the waiting period of a woman after the termination of a marriage through either divorce or death of her husband.

10 cf. Quduri, *Mukhtasar*, p. 21.

11 cf. *ibid.* See Muhammad b. Abi Sahl al-Sarakhsi, *Kitab al-Mabsut fi al-Furu'*, Vol. 5 (Beirut, 1986), "Where minors are contracted in marriage by a father or grandfather, they have no option on arriving at puberty; but when contracted by one other than a father or grandfather they may, according to Abu Hanifa or Muhammad, on arriving at puberty, if they wish it either abide by the marriage or cancel it."

12 cf. Quduri, *Mukhtasar*, p. 17. Hamilton, *Hidaya*, p. 34 "A woman who is an adult and of sound mind may be married by virtue of her own consent, although the contract may not have been made or acceded to by her guardians."

13 cf. Quduri, *Mukhtasar*, p. 23. The Arabic term for either intervention or objection is *i'tirad*.

14 cf. Quduri, *Mukhtasar*, p. 25. Ameer Ali, *Muhammadan Law*, Vol. 2 (Calcutta, 1917), p. 489, "The *mahr* of the Islamic legal system is similar in all its legal incidents to the *donatio propter nuptias* of the Romans. It is a settlement in favour of the bride made prior to the completion of the marriage contract in consideration of marriage. There is however this essential difference between the Roman *donatio propter nuptias* and the *mahr* of the Mussulmans, that whereas the former is purely voluntary on the part of the husband, the latter is absolutely obligatory."

15 S. V. Fitzgerald, *Muhammadan Law,* abridged edn (London: Oxford University Press, 1931), p. 64: "Objects must be such that are capable of sale in Muhammedan law, useful and ritually clean, not therefore things which are not subject to private ownership, e.g. pork, wine or instruments of gambling."

16 cf. Quduri, *Mukhtasar*, p. 25. The deferred portion of the dower is usually paid upon

the dissolution of the contract through either death or divorce.

17 cf. *ibid.*, *Mukhtasar*, p. 25. Valid privacy is a legal term which assumes that there was no impediment to a newly married couple having had intercourse.

18 The *qadi*'s judicial separation is a *tafriq* and amounts to a real dissolution of the contract.

19 F. J. Ziadeh, '"Equality" (kafa'a) in the Muslim law of Marriage', *American Journal of Comparative Law*, 6 (1957).

20 *Fatawa*, 291: 29–30.

21 *Ibid.*: 290: 10–11.

22 *Ibid.*: 290: 11–12.

23 Sarakhsi, *al-Mabsut*, Vol. 5, p. 29.

24 Linant Y. De Bellefonds, *Traité de Droit Musulman Comparé*, Vol. 2 (Paris: Mouton, 1965), p. 174.

25 *Fatawa*, 290: 21–3.

26 Joseph Schacht, *An Introduction to Islamic Law* (Oxford: Clarendon Press, 1964), p. 127.

27 Sir A. Rahim, *The Principles of Muhammadan Jurisprudence*, Tagore Law Lectures, 1907 (London, 1911), p. 246.

28 Fakhr al-Din al-Hasan b. Masur al-Uzjandi al-Farghani, *Fatawa Qadikhan*, Vol. 1 (Calcutta, 1835), pp. 71 ff.

29 *Fatawa*, 291: 4–5.

30 *Ibid.*, 291: 12–13.

31 *Ibid.*: 291: 22–3.

32 Sarakhsi, *al-Mabsut*, Vol. 5, p. 25.

33 *Hidaya*, pp. 40–1.

34 William J. Goode, 'Love: The Theoretical Importance of Love', *American Sociological Review*, 24 (1959).

35 *Fatawa*, 287: 13–14.

36 *al-Bahr al-Ra'iq*, Vol. 13, p. 117.

37 *Hidaya*, Vol. 1, p. 196.

38 *Fatawa*, 292: 9–13.

39 Sarakhsi, *al-Mabsut*, Vol. 5, p. 13.

40 *Fatawa*, 292–3: 30–1.

41 Bronislaw Malinowski, *Crime and Custom in Savage Society* (London: Kegan Paul, Trench Trübner 1926), p. 64.

42 This problem is discussed in *Fatawa*, 293: 5–7.

FOUR

WOMEN, ISLAM AND PATRIARCHALISM

Ghada Karmi

Islam and the patriarchal system, either singly or in combination, have had a profound effect on the status of women wherever they have been applied. I will focus in this chapter on the situation of women in the Arab world.

To set the scene, I should like to start with quotations from two well-known Arab feminist writers, each bemoaning in her own way the plight of Arab Muslim women today, and each summing up the effect of Islam and patriarchalism on women's lives. Fatima Mernissi says this of the situation in Morocco:

> What was and is still an issue in Morocco is not an ideology of female inferiority, but rather a set of laws and customs which ensure that women's status is one of subjugation. Prime among these are the family laws based on male authority. Although many institutions were withdrawn from the control of religious law (business contracts for example), the family never was . . . Morocco claims to be modern, Arab and Muslim . . . As a modern state, it is a signatory to the UN Declaration of Human Rights whose article 16 stipulates that "men and women, regardless of race, nationality or religion, having reached the age of puberty, have the right to marry and establish families. They have equal rights with regard to marriage, in the marriage, and in the event of its dissolution." However, as a Muslim society affirming its will to keep the family under traditional Muslim law, Morocco promulgated a modern code which respects dutifully, wherever possible, the seventh-century *shari'a*.
>
> The sexual *umma* is based on sexual segregation and the subordination of one sex to the other. Women, members of the domestic universe, are subject to the authority of men, members of the Umma universe. Separation and subordination are embodied in institutions

which enforce non-communication and non-interaction between the members of each universe.[1]

Admittedly, reforms of family law carried out in 1992 have ameliorated the picture, but the fundamental principles that Fatima Mernissi describes still hold. The same is true in Egypt. Nawal Sa'dawi, the prominent Egyptian doctor and campaigner for women's rights, reviewing the situation of Arab women in modern Egypt, concludes that:

> Arab men, and for that matter most men, cannot stand an experienced and intelligent woman. It would seem as though the man is afraid of her because . . . he knows very well that his masculinity is not real, not an essential truth, but only an external shell, built up and imposed on women by societies based on class and sexual discrimination. The experience and intelligence of women are a menace to this patriarchal class structure, and in turn, a menace to the false position in which man is placed, the position of king or demi-God in his relations with women. This is essentially why most men fear and even hate intelligent and experienced women. Arab men shy away from marrying them, since they are capable of exposing the exploitation inherent in the institution of marriage as practised to this day. An Arab man, when he decides to marry, will almost invariably choose a young virgin girl with no experience, imbued with a childish simplicity, naive, ignorant, a blind "pussy cat" who does not have an inkling of her rights, or of her sexual desires as a woman, or of the fact that her mind has its needs and should have its ambitions.
>
> Arab men look upon their women as bodies which must remain forever youthful. The value of women deteriorates with age. Attitudes towards the age of women, their youth and their beauty, can be easily understood against this background. Their youth extends in fact over the years during which they are capable of giving the husband sexual pleasure, bearing children for him, and serving the family. It usually extends from the beginning of puberty, that is from the first menstrual period, until the menopause. In other words, it encompasses the whole of her fertile age from roughly fifteen to forty-five years.[2]

One does not have to be either Muslim or Arab to recognise the truth inherent in these sentences. Few women (and men) will not acknowledge or empathise with these sentiments.

The dismal picture painted by these passages finds an echo in a women's conference held in Tunis in 1993. Representatives from the Arab world were there to highlight the violence which women are subjected to, both political and social. Algerian women have suffered much more than men at the hands of Islamic fundamentalists; many women had been murdered and their homes set on fire for the "crime" of living on their own. The expulsion of women from the matrimonial home after divorce was a special problem for which houses of refuge had had to be found. The Palestinian representatives indicated that their struggle was twofold: against Israeli occupation and for their rights in a patriarchal Arab society. The Tunisian Advice and Complaints Centre for Women reported that 77 per cent of the women they saw between the ages of 12 and 55 had been the victims of domestic violence.

The inequality between Arab men and women illustrated in these examples is reflected in some of the official statistics relating to women in the Arab world.

In education, women lag behind men in both primary and secondary education. In Egypt in 1990, for example, there were 76 females for every 100 males in secondary education. In Tunisia, this figure was 77; and in Morocco, it was 69. These inequalities can also be seen in primary education: 80 girls for every 100 boys in Egypt, 87 in Syria, and 66 in Morocco. In Saudi Arabia, the figure was 84. It should be pointed out in fairness that all these figures showed a marked improvement on what had been the case twenty years before. Nonetheless, the differences between male and female school attendance are striking.[3]

Women also suffer disproportionately from illiteracy. The adult illiteracy rate for females in 1990 in Kuwait was 33 per cent, and 51 per cent in Iraq and Libya. In Somalia, it was 86 per cent.[4]

Employment statistics for the Arab world in the late 1980s show a marked discrepancy between men and women, with the women being consistently and significantly less economically active. The proportion of women in the workplace, expressed as a percentage of the total workforce, was 4.4 per cent in Algeria, 6.2 per cent in Egypt, 5.3 per cent in Jordan, and 8.3 per cent in Syria. The highest percentages were to be found in Yemen, 16.4 per cent, Tunisia, 12.7 per cent, and Bahrain, 19.1 per cent, but none of these exceeded a fifth of the total. It should be pointed out that the proportion of economically active women is also lower than that of men in the more developed societies, but the average for the Arab countries is significantly towards the lower end of the scale.

The same discrepancy applies over child mortality. In a study of three Palestinian villages in the occupied West Bank published in 1988, Giacaman found that child mortality was higher among females. The rate of malnutrition among female children was double that of males, and female infants at all stages were more severely malnourished. She concluded that this was due to preferential treatment of male over female children, and suggested that no improvement in the situation would take place until there was a radical change in the nature of the division of labour within Palestinian society. It was not sufficient to establish nursery schools and literacy programmes; fundamental change was needed to "the institutions and relations in society which bring about and perpetuate a debasement in the status of women in general, and the health problems encountered in these villages in particular".[5]

In view of the facts and statistics related above, we need to ask how it is that the situation in which today's Arab woman finds herself unequal, abused and oppressed, has come about. On the one hand, the proponents of Islam have always argued that Islam supported and expanded the rights of women and rescued them from the oppression of pre-Islam, the *jahiliyya*, the time of ignorance. The Islamic resurgence today has also focused on the superior rights accorded to Muslim women when compared with their sexually exploited Western counterparts. In the opposite camp are those who impute every ill which afflicts women in Islamic society to Islam itself.

Indeed, few issues have excited as much debate and fascination as the subject of women and Islam, and few subjects have created such confusion. The sensitivity of this issue is such as to prevent most people from engaging in rational debate for fear that they will either be branded as Muslim fanatics or as enemies of Islam. The whole matter is so charged with emotion and paranoia that to attempt a cool evaluation of exactly what are the rights of women under Islam is no easy matter.

Nor has the situation been helped by the intrusion of the Western debate about feminism which has sought to apply itself and its own conclusions to the situation of Muslim women. Arab women writers have pointed to the inappropriateness of Western liberal ideas in Third World situations, where political and economic considerations play an important role.[6]

Adherents of Islam have complicated the picture further by providing apologist interpretations for those Qur'anic verses which would seem inescapably discriminatory against women. Likewise, opponents of Islam have found in these same verses a convenient stick with which to beat the backs of those Muslims and Arabs whom they despise for other reasons.

So, what is the truth? One approach would be to examine the supreme source of Islamic dogma, the Qur'an, and review the major passages which deal with the position of women. If these are studied for themselves and in isolation from the historical and social context of the Qur'an, one finds that they contain contradictions and generate mixed messages for the reader. On the one hand, there is an emphasis on the importance of women's issues and their equality with men before God, especially in matters of religious duty. Several verses call on men and women to adhere to God's law and emphasise repeatedly that both sexes are being equally addressed. The following verses are a good example of this:

> Muslim men and Muslim women, believing men and believing women, obedient men and obedient women, truthful men and truthful women, steadfast men and steadfast women, humble men and humble women, men and women who give alms, men who fast and women who fast, men and women who guard their modesty, men and women who remember God much, for them God has prepared forgiveness and a mighty reward. (Qur'an XXIII, 35)

This is also the case in the inheritance verses, which prescribe "to the men a share of what parents and kinsmen leave and to the women a share of what parents and kinsmen leave." (Qur'an IV, 7)

Likewise, punishment is meted out equally: "To the fornicatress and the fornicator, whip each one of them a hundred lashes and let not compassion for them seize you in the matter of God's religion if you believe in God and the Last Day." (Qur'an XXIV, 2)

Modesty is enjoined on both sexes: "Say to the male believers that they cast down their eyes and guard their modesty: that is purer for them. And say to the women believers that they cast down their eyes and guard their modesty." (Qur'an XXIV, 30-31)

On the other hand, there are observations and injunctions about women and their legal position which are hard to reconcile with the concept of equality. This is the case of the famous verse which states that "men are in charge of (*qawwamun*) women in so far as God has made the one to excel over the other and in so far as they spend of their property." (Qur'an IV, 34)

The apparent sentiments in this verse sit ill with another verse in the Qur'an which, to my mind, extols the virtues of male–female companionship in the most beautiful way:

> And one of His marvels is that He created mates for you from yourselves, that you may find rest in them. And he created love and compassion between you. (Qur'an XXX, 21)

Many translators and interpreters have bent over backwards trying to give the *qaymuma* verse a meaning which is less pejorative to women. Hence, Arberry translates it as: "Men are the managers of the affairs of women, for that God has preferred in bounty one of them over the other, and for that they have expended of their property."[7] He thus gives the verse an economic meaning, and indeed other translators go further and add an explanatory phrase in parenthesis which reinforces the fact that law requires men "to spend of their property (for the support of women)".[8] Indeed, the verse in question occurs in the midst of several verses concerned with financial details. It is not unreasonable, therefore, to see it only as a part of an economic arrangement suited to the time when it was written.

However, the verse continues in a manner which is more difficult to explain away:

> Righteous women are therefore obedient, guarding the secret for God's guarding. And those you fear may be rebellious, admonish them; banish them to their couches and beat them. If they obey you, look not for any way against them. God is all High, all Great.[9]

The *sura* goes on in the same vein:

> O believers, draw not near to prayer . . . until you have washed yourselves; but if you are sick, or on a journey, or if any of you comes from the privy, or you have touched women, and you can find no water, then have recourse to wholesome dust.[10]

The reference to cleanliness and women occurs again in other parts of the Qur'an:

> They will question thee concerning the monthly course, say: it is a pollution. So go apart from women during the monthly course and do not approach them until they are clean. (Qur'an II, 220)

The verse continues:

Your women are a tillage for you; so come unto your tillage when
and how you wish, but do some good act for your souls. (Qur'an
II, 223)

The Qur'anic regulations over the matters most important to
women: marriage, divorce, child custody, unquestionably discriminate
against women, when taken at face value. In essence, they permit men a
sexual licence completely forbidden to women: the right to marry up to
four wives, to have an unlimited number of concubines, and to divorce
with extraordinary ease. The classical jurist al-Suyuti cites in *Nuzhat
al-Muta'ammid* several instances of men in Islamic history who married
80 or more women in their lifetimes. Al-Ghazali, the famous Muslim
theo-logian, records that the Prophet's grandson, Hasan, married 200
times, sometimes marrying four women at one and the same time.[11]
Punishable fornication for men means intercourse with women who are
outside these categories, a prohibition which should not be too hard to
observe! For women, on the other hand, the only permissible sexual relationship is that within marriage to one husband. Divorce is permitted for
women only on limited grounds, unless the woman takes the precaution
of inserting her own right to divorce in the marriage contract.

Rights over child custody are again in favour of the man. When a
couple divorces, a male child stays with his mother until the age of seven,
and a female child until nine. Thereafter, they revert back to the father.
But if the divorced mother decides to remarry before the period of legal
custody is over, she loses her children immediately. Whatever the motivation or justification for this regulation, there can be no doubt of its
devastating effect on women. I remember in Aleppo coming across
women who had lost their children in this way. One woman in particular
used to stand outside the gates of her daughter's school every day in the
hope of catching a glimpse of her. And another who still had custody of
her children refused an offer of marriage with a man she loved for fear
of losing them. Yet a third woman had been brought up by an aunt
because her mother had remarried. This woman never forgave her mother
for "abandoning" her, never spoke to her or about her and behaved as if
she were dead.

There are standard explanations for these laws which attempt to tie
them in with the historical and social realities of the time. For example,
the laws on polygamy supposedly derive from the fact that there was

often a surplus of women in early Islamic society due to the frequent inter-tribal wars.[12] According to this approach, the laws on custody and unequal provisions for inheritance between men and women reflect the economic realities of the time which placed the financial onus on men.[13] Given this situation, it was only logical that children should be cared for by those who could provide for them. Likewise, it followed that men should have a larger share of the family inheritance, since they would carry the burden of financial responsibility for the women of the family.

Esposito argues that Muslim family law reflected the social mores of the time, the traditional roles of men and women and the functions of the extended family in a patriarchal society. It demonstrates, in his view, the interrelatedness of law and society.[14] This raises the question of how and why the society of the time was patriarchal. Was it always patriarchal and did Islam merely confirm or even attenuate a system already in place? Or did Islam have a more active role in overturning an earlier social organisation which was not patriarchal in nature?

There is a generally accepted view of the status of women in Islam that argues that their lives were significantly improved by the advent of Islam. It is said that women were in pre-Islamic times sold in marriage to men. The tribe's honour was linked to the woman's chastity and fidelity and therefore her behaviour was strictly controlled. She was subjugated by males, whether her father, brother or close male relative, and then by her husband. The man had a right of unrestricted polygamy; or, more correctly, of polygyny. The woman had no rights of divorce or inheritance.[15] Furthermore, female infants were commonly put to death in pre-Islamic times, as this Qur'anic verse clearly implies:

> When news is brought to one of them of a female child, his face darkens and he is filled with inward grief. With shame does he hide himself from his people because of the bad news he has had. Shall he retain it in contempt or bury it in the dust? Ah, what an evil choice they decide on. (Qur'an XVI, 58–59)

Or again:

> And when the buried female infant shall be asked for what sin she was slain. (Qur'an LXXXI, 8–9)

However, it may be that the situation for women in pre-Islam was not quite as bad as has been attested.[16] The problem is that we have little information available which has not come down via the censorship of ardent Muslim believers wishing to throw a bad light on everything which preceded Islam. But even with the evidence that does exist, it is possible to draw a picture, if only by inference, of a social structure before Islam in which women had independence and some prominence.

Not least in significance is the fact that we know of several female goddesses who were held in considerable esteem by the pre-Islamic Arabs. The three best-known of these, to whom many shrines existed, were al-'Uzza, Manat, and al-Lat. This suggests the existence, at some time before Islam, of ancient female-dominated religious cults. The existence of such cults, in turn, suggests that society was originally organised on a matriarchal and/or matrilineal basis.

It also seems to have been the case, as was also true in the ancient Greek world, that pre-Islamic marriage customs were flexible and some of them gave women considerable independence and control over their own lives. In such cases, women tended to remain within their kin family circles after marriage. The husband, if not related to the wife, visited her at her home. Sometimes there were several husbands at the same time, for polyandry existed. When the wife bore a child, she summoned her husbands and announced which of them she believed to be the father and her word was law.[17] In any case, exact paternity was not very important, since the child stayed within the mother's family. This should be contrasted with the situation under Islam where a man is legally permitted to deny paternity to a child, no matter what the mother says, and his testimony has precedence over hers.

The *hadith* compiler, al-Bukhari, describes different kinds of marriage custom during the *jahiliyya*.[18] In one of these, the husband invited the wife to cohabit with another man and refrained from having sexual relations with her in case there should be any doubt about the paternity of any child which resulted. It seems the husband did this in order to procure a child for his wife. In another kind of marriage custom, which was in effect a form of prostitution, a woman had sexual relations with whichever man visited her. When she bore a child, all the men involved gathered at her house and physiognomists were called in to decide which man the child resembled most. He was then designated the father.

It also appears to have been the case in pre-Islamic times that women frequently remarried as soon as they were divorced. If the woman was pregnant at the moment of remarriage by her first husband, the child would belong to the second husband. In short, physical paternity seems to have been unimportant, by contrast with the situation once Islam had been introduced.[19] Under Islamic doctrine, women are forbidden to re-marry for several months after they have been divorced, in case they are pregnant by their previous husband.

Gertrude Stern's study of marriage in early Islam reveals some other interesting facts.[20] She found no reliable evidence of the practice of polygyny in pre-Islamic times, either in Mecca or Medina. She raised the possibility that Meccan men might have contracted temporary marriages with tribal women who remained with their own people, and that this might explain the absence of any evidence to support the existence of polygyny in Mecca.

The fact that women enjoyed a more independent role in the pre-Islamic period, especially those in high positions, may be inferred from the number of outstanding women who feature in the early history of Islam. It is difficult to see how this could have happened unless there had been a prior tradition of female independence. This features in the Prophet's own life, for when he married Khadija she was a wealthy woman with her own business in which he was an employee. Further-more, when the Prophet's father, Abdullah, married his mother, Amina, he stayed with her for only three days because she remained with her own tribe. Abdullah died when she was pregnant with Muhammad, and after his birth, the child remained with her until her death. It was only then that he was taken in charge by his father's kin.[21]

It seems that there were two prevailing trends in the marriage customs of the sixth and seventh centuries which formed the historical backdrop against which Islam was born, one of which was matrilineal and the other patrilineal. These two systems were diametrically opposed to each other and also implied fundamental differences in the position of women and the structure of social relations.[22]

In the matrilineal case, marriage took place at the house of the woman, any offspring belonged to the mother's kin group who protected her, physical paternity and female chastity were unimportant, and the woman had the right to dismiss her husband. Traces of this matrilineal structure are to be seen in the feminine endings to many Arabic men's names in common use today (e.g. Mu'awiya, Umayya, Usama), and also in the special position which maternal uncles hold within the Arab family. There is a common saying in the Arab world to the effect that "two-thirds of a child belong to his (maternal) uncle", and most Arabs would acknow-ledge that they have a greater closeness to their maternal than their paternal uncles.

In patrilineal marriage, on the other hand, the woman followed her husband and her children belonged to his family. He had authority over her and he alone had the right of divorce. The man captured the woman or purchased her from her father, and thereafter he had total dominion over her. In yet another form of marriage, the *mut'a*, which was practised in early Islam and today by Shi'i Muslims, a temporary union took place between a man and a woman whose sole object was sexual pleasure.[23] Mernissi points to the fact that this form of marriage gave the women as much freedom as the man and also implied a different set of paternity rules to those on which Muslim marriage is otherwise based.[24] Robertson Smith in his study of marriage and kinship in early Arabia, came to the conclusion that Islam ensured the ascendance of patrilineal over matrilineal marriage by condemning all forms of the latter category as fornication, *zina*.[25] This shift would be in keeping with an overall transition from a society with matriarchal features to a wholly patriarchal system.

Islam can therefore be seen as an agent of change in an Arabian society which was already moving in the direction of patriarchy. In this sense, the Qur'an confirms and legitimises the patriarchal structure through a set of regulations which place man at the head of the family and at the head of society. This can be seen even in the linguistic form of the Qur'an which addresses men almost exclusively. Injunctions are given to men about women. Yet there is a legend that when the famous female warrior, Nusayba, asked the Prophet why in the Qur'an, God always addressed himself to men and never to women, God recognised the truth of her complaint and thereafter, revelation referred to the believers in both genders.[26]

This is not, however, to suggest that the Qur'an is a misogynist document. A much better description would be to suggest that women are infantilised in the Qur'an. They are to be protected and economically provided for by men, but admonished and punished if they are disobedient. Their testimony is only half as reliable as that of men. Their welfare is in the hands of their menfolk. But on the other hand, we have the paradox that they are equal to men in terms of religious duties and punishment for transgression.

Nonetheless, a hierarchical social structure which ensures male supremacy is fundamental to the Qur'anic view of society. A modern reading, therefore, of the corpus of Islamic laws which regulate the lives of women cannot but see them as inequitable, infantilising and unacceptable in today's world. And here is the nub of the problem. Muslim women have been caught in a conflict between their genuine admiration and devotion to Islam and their dismay at its apparent denial of their status as full human beings equal with men. Many an intelligent woman has wrestled with this contradiction and attempted to reinterpret Islamic tenets in a way less pejorative to women.

Some Muslim men sympathetic to women have even offered biological explanations for this paradox. Muhammad 'Abduh, the Egyptian theologian and legal authority, writing at the turn of the century, explained that man is charged with leadership as part of the natural order. He merits this leadership because his physical constitution is stronger, more beautiful and more complete, as is the case with all male species. This superior physical constitution is linked to a stronger mind and sounder judgement. Women's role in this natural order is to be in charge of domestic affairs, and this forms the exact equivalence of their spouses' duties.[27]

In my opinion, however, this conflict of interpretation may be an artificial one. It is created by the view that everything in the Qur'anic text is eternally applicable and therefore unchanging. If, however, one stands back and tries to see the Qur'an more in its historical and social context, then it is possible to draw different conclusions. After all, we cannot know fully what the social situation in seventh century Mecca was, nor to what social forces the Islamic revelation had to address itself. There are other factors to be taken into account as well.

The process by which the Qur'an was put together did not end until after the Prophet's death. The work is understood, by tradition, to have been completed at the time of the third caliph, 'Uthman (644–56 AD), although later dates have been suggested.[28]

The case has also been made that, at the time of Muhammad, tribal life was disintegrating as a result of the rise of a new mercantile class in the urban centres. Women and children were amongst those most affected by the insecurities engendered as a result of the disruption of the old tribal order, and provision therefore had to be made for their care.[29]

Furthermore, the Prophet was anxious to change personal concepts of allegiance away from the tribe and towards a new unit, the family. This would then form the basic unit of the new super-tribe, the Islamic *umma*. The patriarchal family thus became the engine which drove this major social transformation, and in this scheme there could be no place for a sexually independent female with children of uncertain paternity.

From this point of view, it is possible to discern that the Qur'an is really not one document but two.

The first deals with social and practical questions and may be understood as a specific response to the contemporary socio-political situation. It is legalistic and regulatory in content.

The second is concerned with universal spiritual, moral and philosophical issues. It is this which embodies the eternal message of Islam. As a result, undue emphasis on the legislative aspect of Islam is to lose sight of its spiritual content.

The modern Islamic judge Muhammad Sa'id al-'Ashmawi may well be right when he argues that Islam is basically a message of compassion and morals with legislation occupying a secondary place. Of the Qur'an's 6000 verses, less than 700 deal with legislation and only 200 of these are directly concerned with regulation of social matters. The remainder are devoted to regulation of worship.[30]

If this is the case, the argument can be taken further. In other words, the idea of adapting the social precepts of seventh-century Islam to a later age becomes feasible. *Ijtihad*, interpretation, is an Islamic concept which permits exactly this kind of activity, and there is in theory no objection to it. But the reality is that the major tenets of Qur'anic family law which govern the lives of Muslims were subjected to very little *ijtihad* – which could have led to reform – after the tenth century, largely because of the attitudes adopted by the great theologian al-Ghazali, although this has not been true for Islam's Shi'i minority.

This had serious consequences for the position of women in Muslim societies who, as we have already seen, are still to this very day subject to marriage, divorce and custody laws which discriminate against them. This is not to suggest that modern reforms have not been enacted in various Arab and Muslim countries. Indeed, Tunisia has gone so far as to abolish polygamy altogether. But in general the reforms of family law which have been permitted have only tinkered at the edges of the problem and have done little to change the basic principles on which such law is based.[31]

I have argued that Qur'anic precepts on the position of women should be seen as a function of the social dynamics and imperatives which obtained in the Arabia of the seventh century. They should therefore not have been used to determine the fate of women up to the present time. Ironically enough, however, whereas *shari'a* laws governing many aspects of life have been reformed or withdrawn altogether in many Muslim countries, for example, the *hadd* punishments of beheading and amputation of limbs, the laws which affect women have scarcely been altered at all. Why is that? And is it Islam itself which is responsible for the plight of Arab and Muslim women today, as some critics of Islam have tried to assert? The answer to this question is both yes and no, for one must agree with Nawal Sa'dawi when she says:

> We, the women in Arab countries, realise that we are still slaves, still oppressed, not because we belong to the East, not because we are Arab, or members of Islamic societies, but as a result of the patriarchal class system that has dominated the world since thousands of years.[32]
>
> Under the generalised patriarchal system now found throughout the world, and in whichever society they live, men have accorded themselves special privileges, particularly in the sexual sphere, which they simultaneously deny to women. It can even be argued that Arab men are at least honest in practising a system where promiscuity is openly admitted and legalised in the form of polygamy and concubinage. Other men do or desire to do the same, but in secret and behind a smoke-screen of puritan morality.[33]

In Arab society, the patriarchal structure has been enshrined and most effectively perpetuated through the Arab family. In its typical form, the Arab family is patriarchal and hierarchical in relation to age and sex, the old and the males having authority over the young and the females. The father holds a key position with regard to power and authority. He expects and exacts unquestioning obedience from his wife and children and may punish disobedience harshly. In this structure, the sexes become extremely polarised: the man is expected to be strong and dominant and the woman is weak, dependent and inferior. Thus the subordinate position of women in the traditional Arab family is underpinned by customs and laws to which the majority of the population still subscribes. Indeed, although the Arab family might be an extreme form of this phenomenon, it exists to a greater or lesser degree in most societies in the world. To that extent, Islam cannot be held responsible for patriarchalism in the Muslim world.

I sketched above the way Islam appeared within the social context of seventh-century Arabia, in which patriarchy was present within Arabian society. The question is whether Islam merely supported this social transformation, or whether it facilitated and legitimised it or, indeed, whether it was the agent of introduction itself. This question cannot be definitively answered, but it is clear that Islam has been exploited by patriarchal society to legitimise its discrimination against women. It is interesting to note that the majority of *suras* dealing with the status of women in Islam were revealed during the Prophet's Medinan period. At that time society in Medina was undergoing rapid social change, so it is hardly surprising that the Medinan *suras* should have dealt with such social legislation.

It seems to me that this factor underlines my earlier point: that the Qur'an is, in reality, two documents in one; one eternal and unchanging and the other conditional and adjusted to social circumstance. In this context, the actual role of the Qur'an in patriarchalism is of secondary importance, for the real problem for women is patriarchalism itself which will exploit any opportunity it perceives to legitimise its objectives. On this reading, the evolution and development of Islamic law in the wake of the original revelations contained in the Qur'an, particularly with respect to women, exemplifies to perfection this process of patriarchal legitimisation.

NOTES

1 Fatima Mernissi, *Beyond the Veil: Male–Female Dynamics in a Modern Muslim Society* (Cambridge, Mass.: Shenkman Publishing Company, 1975), pp. ix–x, 82.
2 Nawal Saadawi, *The Hidden Face of Eve: Women in the Arab World*, trans. S. Hetata (London: Zed Press, 1980), pp. 77–8.
3 World Bank, *World Development Report* (Oxford: Oxford University Press, 1993), pp. 300–1.
4 *Ibid.*, p. 304.
5 R. Giacaman, *Life and Health in Three Palestinian Villages* (London: Croom Helm, 1983), pp. 152–7.
6 See Soad Dajani, 'Palestinian Women under Israeli Occupation' in Judith E. Tucker (ed.), *Arab Women: Old Boundaries, New Frontiers* (Bloomington and Indianapolis: Indiana University Press, 1993), pp. 103–7; and F. Malti-Douglas, *Women's Body, Women's World: Gender and Discourse in Arabo-Islamic Writing* (Princeton: Princeton University Press, 1992), p. 7.
7 A. J. Arberry, *The Koran Interpreted*, Vol. 1 (2 Vols., London: Allen and Unwin, 1955) p. 105.
8 L. L. al-Faruqi in M. T. Taqi Mesbah, M. J. Bahour, L. L. al-Faruqi (eds.), *Status of Women in Islam* (Sangam Books, 1985).
9 Arberry, *The Koran Interpreted*, pp. 105–6.
10 *Ibid.*, 107.
11 al-Ghazali Abu Hamid, *Ihya' 'ulum al-din* (Cairo: al-Maktaba al-Tijariyya al-Kubra, n.d.), p. 30, cited in Mernissi, *Beyond the Veil*, p. 18.
12 Saadawi, *The Hidden Face of Eve*, p. 121.
13 M. Iqbal, *The Reconstruction of Religious Thought in Islam* (Lahore: Javid Iqbal, 1971), p. 170.
14 J. Esposito, *Women in Muslim Family Law* (Syracuse, N.Y.: Syracuse University Press, 1982), p. 48.
15 *Ibid.*, p. 48.
16 H. A. R. Gibb and J. H. Kramers (eds.), *Shorter Encyclopaedia of Islam* (Leiden: E. J. Brill, 1973), pp. 82–3.
17 N. Minai, *Women in Islam* (London: John Murray, 1981), p. 5.
18 al-Bukhari, *al-Sahih* (Beirut: Dar al-Ma'arif, 1978), cited in Fatima Mernissi, *Women and Islam: An Historical and Theological Enquiry* (Oxford: Blackwell, 1991), pp. 183–4.
19 Mernissi, *Beyond the Veil*, p. 27.
20 G. Stern, *Marriage in Early Islam* (London: Royal Asiatic Society, 1939), pp. 62, 66, 70, 73; cited in Mernissi, *Beyond the Veil*, pp. 29–31.
21 Ibn Saad, *Kitab al-tabaqat al-kubra* (Beirut: Dar Beyrouth, 1958), cited in Mernissi, *Beyond the Veil*, p. 31.
22 W. Robertson Smith, *Kinship and Marriage in Early Arabia* (London: Adam and Charles Black, 1907), pp. 77 ff, 156, 172.
23 S. Haeri, *Law of Desire: Temporary Marriage in Islam* (London: I. B. Tauris, 1989).
24 Mernissi, *Beyond the Veil*, p. 37.

25 Robertson Smith, *Kinship and Marriage*, p. 19.
26 A. Bouhdiba, *Sexuality in Islam*, English trans. (London: Routledge & Kegan Paul, 1975), p. 19.
27 Barbara Stowasser, 'Women's Issues in Modern Islamic Thought' in Tucker (ed.), *Arab Women*, p. 9.
28 Albert Hourani, *A History of the Arab Peoples* (London: Faber and Faber, 1991), pp. 20–1.
29 See W. Montgomery Watt, *Muhammad at Mecca* (Oxford: Clarendon Press, 1953) and *Muhammad at Medina* (Oxford: Clarendon Press, 1956).
30 al-'Ashmawi quoted in N. Ayubi, *Political Islam* (London: Routledge, 1991), pp. 203–4.
31 Esposito, *Women in Muslim Family Law*, pp. 91–4.
32 Stowasser, 'Women's Issues in Modern Islamic Thought', p. xv.
33 *Ibid.*, p. 98.

Five

Women in Islamic Law

Raga' El-Nimr

Much of the history of pre-Islamic Arabia is obscured by myth and legend and romantic notions have often been confused with factual elements. One feature, however, which seems to stand out as the most striking characteristic of Arabian society is its diversity. In southern Arabia, the language was different from that of the north and was written in a different alphabet. The southerners were sedentary people who subsisted largely on agriculture, which may have reached a high degree of development. The political organisation was at first monarchic, but the authority was limited by a council of notables.

The northern population, on the other hand, was itself diverse. The Hellenic influence in central and northern Arabia produced a series of semi-civilised border states. In addition, there were towns of the oases and more advanced towns established here and there by settled nomads, the most important being Makkah, though in Makkah the population was diverse.[1]

Diversity was probably most evident in the field of religion. Different forms of pagan idolatry, Judaism, Christianity, Zoroastrianism and Hanifism (those who believed in monotheism) were all embraced by various elements of the population.[2] This religious diversity has prompted a variety of speculations. Before Islam, Arabia's religion was either nominal, formal or superstitious.

According to the theory of Arab genealogists, the groups were all patriarchal tribes, formed by the subdivision of an original stock, on the system of kinship through male descent. At the time of Muhammad (PBUH) the tribal bond was conceived as one of kinship and tribesmen regarded themselves as one blood.[3]

During the ninth and tenth centuries, Islamic civilisation reached its climax of interaction between the material and spiritual elements. Yet, the penetration of Greek thought provoked a conflict which grew as the years went by. Nevertheless, the conflict did not result in intellectual stagnation but in rechannelling the flow of intellectual energies. The religious culture embraced other forms of activity, and by some minor accommodations converted them into its own instruments. The religious culture intrinsically provided sufficient opportunity and stimulus for intellectual creativity, and such creativity led to the growth of several new sciences and considerably improved the old ones, although the master science of the Muslims was, without doubt, law.

Islamic law was crucial to the development of Muslim society, not because of its intellectual pre-eminence but because of its social, moral and political role in Islamic history. Islamic law was the most far-reaching and effective agent in moulding the social order and the community life of the Muslim people.

By the end of the tenth century a great civilisation had built up, one which was brilliant, wealthy and enterprising. From that time on, the state gradually diverged more and more from the path of earlier generations. The result was political stagnation and internal strife. The decline of Muslim political power, however, did not mean a corresponding decline of the forces of Islamic society. In fact, it would almost seem that the decline of the former injected a new vitality into the latter.

The nature of law in Islam has been differently thought of: is it divinely revealed or socially grounded? Positive or supernatural, immutable or adaptive? Disagreements stem from uncritical use of two equivocal concepts, *Shari'a* and *fiqh. Shari'a* is defined as:

> those institutions which Allah has ordained in full or in essence
> to guide the individual in his relationship to God, his fellow
> Muslims, his fellow men and the rest of the Universe.[4]

It is the basis for moral judgement of actions as good or bad, thus it can come only from God. The term *fiqh* literally denotes intelligence or knowledge, and is the name given to jurisprudence in Islam.

Islamic law is "evolutionary" in that its full growth took centuries and passed through various phases. At first it dealt with simple, practical problems of everyday life, but as time went on it grew complex and inclusive. At any rate, the most characteristic feature of Islamic law may be stated in the following proposition: while Islamic law attempts to "moralise" legal actions and formalities by placing them in the context of religion and morality, it tends to discourage the formalisation or ritualisation of the religious and moral precepts.[5]

According to Islam there is a specific sex individuality in man and woman which they must preserve and cherish. It is this individuality which gives them honour and dignity and enables them to fulfil their specific roles in society in an effective way. The differences existing between man and woman are of a mere fundamental nature. Ignorance of these fundamental facts has led the promoters of feminism to believe that both sexes should have the same responsibilities.

The question of the relationship between man and woman and their respective rights and duties is really a part of the socio-economic problem of man. Its solution depends on the way in which this larger problem is dealt with by civilisation. It is wrong to study the question of women's rights and their place in society in isolation from the total context of human relationships in all their aspects.

Before dealing with the position of women in Islam, it would be right to examine how the question of women's rights and their claim for complete equality with men came to the forefront in modern times and what the underlying causes were which added strength to women's claim for freedom and equality.

The eighteenth century was a period of great social and intellectual unrest in Europe. The rising intelligentsia and the middle classes of Western countries found themselves encumbered with a host of social barriers, economic restrictions and intellectual fetters which were blocking the path of progress in every direction. They were legacies of an age of feudalism. The feudal landlords and the Catholic Church with its vast power had a vested interest in perpetuating age-old customs and artificial social restrictions which the new spirit was seeking to break through. In these circumstances, it was not unnatural that freedom and liberty should acquire a sanctity out of all proportion to their importance in the total scheme of human values.

In the eighteenth and nineteenth centuries, liberty and freedom became exclusive sovereign values in Europe. History bears witness to the fact that when a powerful idea takes root in a civilisation it permeates every sphere of human life and activity.[6]

This happened with the notion of liberty which, extending from the domain of politics, invaded the social sphere and expressed itself in a demand for the readjustment of sex relations. Powerful voices were raised on behalf of the female sex which had long suffered from innumerable legal and social disabilities. Freedom and equality of the sexes became accepted principles with the new social reformers.

The position of women under Islam has been the subject of repeated controversy among educated Muslims ever since they came under the impact of Western civilisation. The position of Islam on this issue has been among the subjects presented to the Western reader with the least objectivity. Here, we are trying to provide a brief and authentic exposition of what Islam stands for in this regard. We are also trying to provide a fair evaluation of what Islam contributed, or failed to contribute, to the restoration of women's dignity and rights. To achieve this objective, it may be useful to review briefly how women were treated in general in previous civilisations.

Describing the status of the Indian woman, *Encyclopaedia Britannica* states:

> In India subjection was a cardinal principle. The rule of inheritance was agnatic, that is descent traced through males to the exclusion of females.[7]

In Hindu scripture,

> A good wife is a woman whose mind, speech and body are kept in subjection in this world, and in the next, the same abode with her husband.[8]

The historian E. A. Allen in his book *History of Civilisation* says:

> Athenian women were always minors to their father, to their brother, or to some of their male kin. The woman was obliged to submit to the wishes of her parents, to receive from them her husband and her lord.[9]

A Roman wife was described by the same historian as

> . . . a babe, a minor, a ward, a person incapable of doing or acting upon anything.[10]

In France, they were debating the position of women and in 1586 they concluded that they were created to serve men. In 1938 the laws were amended to allow women to deal in property and operate a bank account.[11]

In England, it was only until the late nineteenth century that the situation improved, with a series of Acts starting with the Married Women's Property Act of 1870, amended in 1882 and 1887, through which married women gained the right to own property.[12]

So all civilisations, Greek, Roman, Chinese, Indian and Persian, at the height of their cultural prosperity, treated women as properties with no individual rights.

When Islam appeared in Arabia, women held a very low position in society. They were treated not only as social inferiors but like chattel. It was a mark of dishonour for a man to have a daughter and many buried their female children alive.

In the midst of the darkness that engulfed the world, the divine revelation echoed in the wide desert of Arabia with a noble and universal message to humanity:

O Mankind, keep your duty to your Lord who created you from a single soul and from it created its mate (of the same kind) and spread from these two many men and women. (Qur'an: IV, 1)

A scholar who pondered on this verse stated:

It is believed that there is no text, old or new, that deals with the humanity of the woman from all aspects with such amazing brevity, eloquence, depth and originality as this divine decree.[13]

The Qur'anic verse promulgates the doctrine of human equality, including sex equality and negates all inequalities due to sex, race, colour, nationality, caste or tribe; because all humans ultimately spring from a single source.

The Holy Qur'an has in more than one place made it clear that, in regard to moral and spiritual development, men and women stand on the same level of equality. In addressing the believers, the Qur'an often uses the expression "believing men and women" to emphasise the equality of men and women in regard to their respective duties, rights, virtues and merits. The Qur'an says:

For Muslim men and women, for believing men and women, for devout men and women, for true men and women . . . (Qur'an: XXXIII, 35)

In regard to religious duties the Qur'an recognises no distinction between men and women. Their obligations towards God and fellow men are similar in many respects, and therefore their position and status in the eyes of God are also similar. In the Qur'an we read:

Whosoever performs good deeds, whether male or female, and is a believer, we shall surely make them live a good life, and we will certainly reward them for the best of what they did. (Qur'an: XVI, 97)

If men and women have equal duties in regard to prayers, the payment of tax for the poor, *zakat*, and in the enjoining of good and the forbidding of evil, it is necessary that they should have equal educational opportunities. How can a woman raise her voice against ruinous economic policies or advocate beneficial economic reforms, enjoin the good in politics or forbid bad politics, if she is not mentally and spiritually well-equipped for the supreme religious duty?

It is also worth remembering that Islam makes no distinction between secular duties and religious duties. According to the teachings of Islam, all duties, whether they concern politics, economics or social well-being in general, are religious duties, in no way different from prayers, fasting and the organisation of social charities. It is a plain deduction from the above verses that men and women should be regarded as equal in the field of education.

Prophet Muhammad (PBUH) said:

Seeking knowledge is mandatory for every Muslim.

The Prophet not only enunciated this general doctrine of sex equality involving equal educational opportunities but also practised it. Innumerable are the traditions which show that women, like men, used to come forward freely in the presence of the Prophet, putting questions and addressing enquiries on all sorts of social, religious and economic matters. He used to answer their queries and enlighten his questioners on all current issues.

Arabia in particular, and the world in general was so backward in those days that there were no organised educational institutions even for boys. So the Islamic attitude towards female education can be studied only from the casual remarks of the Prophet and his permission to women to approach him freely for enquiries on matters of religious, economic and social importance.[14]

His wife 'A'isha was a very learned woman, and during the reign of the four Caliphs her advice, even on political matters, was sought by the rulers of Islam. On Islamic jurisprudence she was and is still regarded as a great authority. One of her pupils, 'Urwa ibn al-Zubair, testifies to her place in learning:

I did not see a greater scholar than 'A'isha in the learning of the Qur'an, obligatory duties, lawful and unlawful matters, poetry and literature, Arab history and genealogy.[15]

'Urwa himself was a great scholar of literature. When he was praised once, he said that he was nothing compared to 'A'isha.[16] She was among the great memorisers of *hadith*. She narrated as many as 2210 *hadith* in all.

Sayyida Nafisa, a descendant of 'Ali, the fourth Caliph, was also a great scholar. Imam al-Shafi'i, founder of the Shafi'i school of Islamic law, was one of her illustrious pupils and sat in her circle in al-Fustat when he was at the height of his fame.[17] Sheikha Shuhda who lectured publicly in one of the principal mosques of Baghdad to large audiences on literature, rhetoric and poetry, was one of the foremost scholars in Islam.

There are numerous other learned Muslim women who have been teachers, writers and poets, and were accorded the highest respect by Muslim society. There is, therefore, every encouragement for a Muslim woman to pursue studies in any field for her intellectual benefit and to make use of her academic or professional training for the good of the community.

Islam stressed the essential and fundamental equality of men and women and their equal rights in all matters of vital concern; but the Holy Qur'an does not believe in the concept of sex equality which ignores the natural difference and specific powers and faculties of men and women with the fitness of men for some kinds of work and the fitness of women for some other types of activities. The Qur'an regards men and women as complementary to each other.

We read in the Qur'an:

And they (women) have rights similar to those of men over them in a just manner and men are a degree above them. (Qur'an: II, 228)

The main points are that men and women excel each other in some respects and that in general affairs of life men are partially superior to women. The Qur'an first sets forth a general doctrine of sex equality and then qualifies and defines it with the assertion that this is not an undifferentiated equality but one involving special rights and duties both for men and women, within the framework of their special responsibilities.

Sheikh 'Abduh, a Muslim scholar and a social reformist, says that it does not imply that every man is better than every woman or vice versa, but it emphasises that each sex, in general, has some preferential advantage over the other, though men have a degree over women.[18]

What is this degree? There are different views about it. One view means the qualities of maintenance which are bestowed on men. Another view is that it signifies the tolerance with which men must treat their wives even when they are in an extremely bad mood. Another view is that it refers to man's natural gift for judging matters pertaining to his family and managing the problems affecting it. But the consensus of the scholars is that the "degree" comprises the principle of guardianship and nothing more.[19]

The conclusion is that the doctrine of equality must be qualified with due regard to natural facts.

Margaret Mead, says in her book *Male and Female*:

> But every adjustment that minimises a difference in one sex, diminishes the possibility of complementing each other. To seal off the constructive receptivity of the female and the vigorous out-going constructive activity of the male leads them both to the duller version of human life, in which each is denied the fullness of humanity that each might have had. We must protect and cherish both sexes through the crises that are sometimes harder for one sex than for the other.[20]

With regard to the woman's right to seek employment, Islam regards her role in society as a mother and wife as the most sacred and essential one. Such a noble and vital role, which largely shapes the future of nations, cannot be regarded as "idleness".

However, there is no decree in Islam which forbids women from seeking employment whenever there is a need for it, especially in positions which suit her nature and capability in which society needs her most. Moreover, there is no restriction on benefiting from woman's exceptional talent in any field. Even for the position of a judge, where there may be a tendency to doubt the woman's fitness for the post due to her more emotional nature, we find early Muslim scholars such as Abu Hanifa and al-Tabari saying, "Women can be appointed to judicial positions."[21]

Jurists differ in their opinion about giving women positions like ministership and leadership; since there are complicated issues to be handled, both religious and political. They refer to the *hadith* said by the Prophet (PBUH), "A nation will not prosper if it is led by a woman."

Imam Ghazali, a contemporary Muslim scholar, explains the context of the *hadith*:

> When Persia showed signs of imminent downfall because it was ruled by a despotic, corrupt queen and the people were lost and lacked guidance, the Prophet (PBUH) commented on this by the above-mentioned *hadith* and if the situation had been otherwise his words might also have been different.[22]

The Prophet (PBUH) himself told the people of Makkah what the Qur'an said about the Queen of Sheba, who led her country to success and prosperity because of her wisdom. The Prophet would never relate any *hadith* which contradicted the Qur'an.

The intellectual status of a Muslim woman is neither marred nor degraded by the commandment of the Qur'anic verse:

> And get two witnesses out of your men, And if there are not two men then a man and two women such as you choose for witnesses, so that if one of them errs the other can remind her. (Qur'an: II, 282)

It should be borne in mind that Allah, the creator, with his infinite wisdom gave the directives best suited to humankind. He is the creator, therefore, he knows man better than man himself.

In this age of science, we can explore the significance of this legislation. Women fall under psychological strains of the cycle that they have to endure, such as the symptoms during early pregnancy, antenatal and post-natal depression, the phenomenon of menopause and the psychological problems faced after miscarriage. It is under these circumstances that women can experience extraordinary psychological strains giving rise to depression, lack of concentration, slow-mindedness and short-term memory loss. We must also not overlook the fact that women are known to be more sensitive and emotional than men. It does not however render the woman inferior to man. Allah knows his creation best and has prescribed precise laws in keeping with the nature of man.

Islam considers marriage as one of the most virtuous institutions. The Qur'an says:

> And one of his signs is that he created mates for you from yourselves, so that you may find peace of mind in them and He ordained between you love and compassion. (Qur'an: XXX, 21)

As male and female are sources of comfort to each other, this can happen only when men and women are united in a bond of interests which are planned and based on some idea of the future. This also requires them to cooperate and not to compete, and integrates them in an ordered whole. This can only be achieved in a pattern of life which is marriage.

The importance of the institution of marriage receives its greatest emphasis from the following *hadith* of the Prophet (PBUH):

> Marriage is my *Sunna* (way), whoever keeps away from it is not of me.

The Qur'an has constantly used the word *muhsin* for chaste men and *muhsinat* for chaste women. The Arabic root of the word *hisn* means "fort". The underlying idea is that marriage safeguards and protects chastity in the same manner that a fort protects the garrison within from a besieging army.

The consent of both the man and the woman is an essential element of marriage, and the Qur'an gives women a substantial role in choosing their own life partner.

> Do not prevent them from marrying their husbands when they agree between themselves in a lawful manner. (Qur'an: II, 232)

Imam Bukhari emphasises in his *Sahih* that:

> If a man gives his daughter in marriage and she dislikes it, the marriage should be annulled. Once a girl came to the Prophet (PBUH) and told him that her father had married her to a man against her will. The Prophet gave her the right to repudiate it.[23]

The wife may not legally object to the husband's right of divorce. The marital contract establishes her implicit consent to these rights. However, if she wishes to restrict his freedom in this regard or to have similar rights, she is legally allowed to do so. She may stipulate in the marital agreement that she, too, will have the right to divorce or keep the marriage bond only as long as she remains the sole wife.

We read in the Qur'an:

Men are the protectors and maintainers of women with the boun-
ties God has bestowed . . . and because they spend out of their
possessions. (Qur'an: IV, 34)

The word *qawwamun* (which means protectors and maintainers)
refers to a person who takes the responsibility of safeguarding the interests of another. It does not mean that men are masters to be blindly
obeyed or a police force giving orders, as most men interpret it for their
benefit. They are protectors because of their physical strength and capacity for strenuous work. Moreover, it is necessary for the functioning
of the family that there should be a head who settles things among the
members of the family and ensures their compliance. It is for this reason
that the wife is asked to obey her husband and she should not obey him
if what he asks is against Allah's injunctions.

In order to safeguard the economic position of women after marriage, Islam has made it obligatory on the husband to pay her a reasonable amount as dower. The amount of dower can be as low or as high as
the parties may desire. The object is to strengthen the financial position of
the wife, so that she is not prevented, for lack of money, from defending
her rights. We read in the Qur'an:

And give women their dowries as free gift, but if they themselves
be pleased to give up to you a portion of it, take it and enjoy it
with right good cheer. (Qur'an: IV, 4)

The Prophet (PBUH) emphasised in his farewell speech on Mount
Arafat that Muslims should be good and kind to their wives. "O people!
you have rights over your wives as they have rights over you."[24] He
also reported in one of his *hadith*. "The best of you is he who is good to
his wife."[25] His wife 'Aisha reported that he said about women, "They
are like pleasing roses, that their grace and tenderness deserve special
regard from men."[26] It is also reported that he said, "No believer should
be angry with his wife. If some of her qualities are displeasing, there will
be many other qualities worth appreciation."[27]

With regard to domestic duties, Islam has relieved women of all
manual drudgery. According to strict Islamic injunctions, it is not obligatory for a woman to cook the food for her husband or children, or to wash
their clothes or even to suckle the infants. A woman can refuse to do any
of these things without this being made a ground of legal complaint
against her. If she undertakes these duties, it is an act of sheer grace.

It is reported that once a man came to 'Umar, the second Caliph, with the intention of complaining about his wife. When he reached the door of 'Umar he heard the Caliph's wife railing against him, so he turned back. 'Umar saw him, called him and enquired about the purpose which had brought him. The man answered that he came with some complaints about his wife but he found that the Caliph himself was subject to the same treatment. 'Umar said:

> She has certain rights over me. She cooks my food, washes my clothes and suckles my children although she is not in the slightest degree responsible for any of these duties. I enjoy peace of mind on her account and I am protected from committing the sin of adultery. In view of these advantages, I put up with her excesses.[28]

Bukhari reports in his *Sahih*:

> Man is the ruler in his home. He will be held responsible for the conduct of his dependants, and woman is the ruler in her home. She will also be held responsible for the conduct of her dependants.[29]

In Islamic law, a wife, even after having come into partnership with her husband, is a separate legal person capable of suing and being sued in her own individual capacity and entitled to sue her husband for any infringement of her just rights. This is a position which was not accorded to females in Europe and America until the nineteenth century and after a great deal of agitation against the existing legal disabilities of women.

In order to ensure a really stable family life, Islam has assigned to marriage the status of a contract, dissoluble if either party develops grievances against the other leading to a final and irrevocable breakdown in their mutual relations. This may appear a factor operating against family stability, but in fact it is designed to safeguard it. There is really no virtue in keeping two persons tied together to save appearances, when their relations have deteriorated beyond all hopes of reconciliation. The Qur'anic verse reads:

> O believers! It is not lawful for you that you should take women as heritage against their will and do not treat them with harshness in order to take from them a part of what you have given them unless they are guilty of open lewdness. (Qur'an: IV, 19)

As men have the legal right to divorce their wives, women also have legal permission to seek and obtain divorce through mutual agreement or the intervention of courts. Actual legal decisions by the Prophet (PBUH) show the spirit and principles which the law courts should apply to cases brought by women against their husbands. The famous case of Thabit ibn Qais, whose wife came to the Prophet complaining about his ugliness, and said, "O Messenger of God (as for) Ibn Qais, I do not blame him for his character and piety, but I dislike infidelity in Islam." (She meant that, as a Muslim, she did not want to go with another man whilst being married.) The Prophet asked if she was prepared to give back the orchard given to her by him (as her dowry). She agreed. The Prophet asked Qais to accept the orchard and divorce her.[30]

During the time of 'Umar, the second Caliph, a case of divorce was brought to him. 'Umar advised the women to put up with her husband. She refused. 'Umar put her in a room by herself for three days. On the fourth day he asked her how she had felt. She answered that she had real peace of mind only for those three days. 'Umar ordered the dissolution of the marriage.[31]

The Prophet (PBUH) felt sorry for Buraira's husband and appreciated his love for her. So he went to her and asked her to go back to her husband. She asked the Prophet, "Are you ordering or interceding?" He answered that he was interceding. She said, "Then I am not going back."[32]

These examples show that the mere fact of a woman becoming disgusted with her husband is sufficient ground for legal separation between them. This should be contrasted with all the laws applied in Muslim countries, where the police take the wife by force and compel her to go back to her husband's house or, as they call it, "The house of obedience."

In Islam, a woman has a completely independent personality. She can make any contract or bequest in her own name. She is entitled to inherit in her position as mother, as wife, as sister and as daughter. Qur'anic injunctions have made it clear that there is a share for men and a share for women in inheritance. Women and minor males were denied inheritance not only in pagan Arabia but also in biblical law and even as late as this century, as reported in Cheyne and Black's *Encyclopaedia Biblica*:

Women appear to have been universally and in every respect regarded as minors as far as rights of property.[33]

It was not until 1938 that the French Law was amended so as to recognise the eligibility of women to contract. A married woman was still required to secure her husband's permission before she could dispense with her private property.[34]

According to Islamic law, a woman's right to her money, real estate or other properties is fully acknowledged. The right undergoes no change whether she is single or married. She retains her full rights to buy, sell, mortgage or lease any or all of her properties.

The method of division of inheritance is clearly laid down in the Qur'an and the general rule is that women are entitled to inherit half the share given to a man. This was not determined because of any inferiority on her part, but in view of her economic situation, and the place she occupies in the social structure of which she is part and parcel. Islamic law has put greater economic responsibility on men while women's role is economically much lighter. The half share that a woman inherits may therefore be considered a generous one since it is for her alone. Any such money or property which a woman owns or any business which she runs is entirely her own and her husband has no right to any of it.

Polygamy is permissible in Islam under certain conditions and circumstances. Before the advent of Islam, polygamy was practised by the pagan Arabs without any limit. It was also practised through human history by prophets, kings and governors; by common people of the East and West in ancient and modern times alike.

The permission is an exception to the ordinary course. It has come to solve some social and moral problems. The verse concerning polygamy was revealed after the battle of Uhud in which many Muslims were killed, leaving widows and orphans. The verse reads:

> If you fear that you shall not be able to deal justly with orphans, marry women of your choice two or three or four. But if you fear that you will not be able to deal justly with them, then marry only one. (Qur'an: IV, 3)

Islam did not invent polygamy by introducing these regulations and it does not encourage it as a rule. It did not abolish it because if it were abolished that would have been in theory only and people would have continued the practice, as is happening today among other people whose constitutions and social standards do not approve of polygamy.

Islam cannot compromise on moral standards or tolerate hypocrisy, nor can Islam deny the existence of the problem or resort to condemnations and prohibitions. To save a man from his own self, to protect the woman involved, whether she is the wife or the secret friend, against unnecessary complications, and to maintain the moral integrity of the society, Islam has allowed polygamy with restrictions. Another stipulation in the Qur'an in the same chapter refers to the human weakness that men cannot be just. "You will never be able to be fair and just between women even if it is your ardent desire." (Qur'an: IV, 129)

Modernists consider this verse as a legal condition attached to polygamy. Since impartial treatment is impossible, one must restrict oneself to monogamy. What they overlook is that "impartial treatment" in the matter of residence, food and clothing is a relative term which will differ from person to person and from country to country according to the economic standards of the society.

Women as mothers command great respect in Islam. The Qur'an speaks of the rights of the mother in a number of verses. It enjoins Muslims to show respect to their mothers and treat them well even if they are unbelievers. The Prophet (PBUH) states emphatically that the rights of the mother are paramount.

Thus the Muslim mother has a great feeling of security about the type of care and consideration she can expect from her children when she reaches old age. Thankfulness to parents is linked with gratitude to God as the Qur'anic verse says, "Show gratitude to me and to your parents." (Qur'an: XXXI, 14)

Failure in either of these respects is indeed a major failure in one's religious duties.

Any fair investigation of the teaching of Islam or the history of Islamic civilisation will show clear evidence of woman's equality with man in what we call "political rights". This includes the right of selection as well as the nomination to political offices. It also includes woman's right to participate in public affairs. In both the Qur'an and Islamic history we find examples of women who participated in serious discussions and argued with the Prophet himself and the succeeding Caliphs.[35]

A woman once argued with the Caliph 'Umar in the Mosque, who on proving her point caused him to declare in the presence of the people, "this woman is right and 'Umar is wrong".

Muslim history is rich with women of great achievements in all fields of life. Throughout history the reputation, chastity and maternal role of Muslim women have been the object of admiration by outside observers.

NOTES

1 Hammudah Abdul Ati, *The Family Structure in Islam* (Indianapolis: American Trust Publications, 1977), p. 6.
2 *Ibid.*, p. 6.
3 *Ibid.*, p. 8.
4 *Ibid.*, p. 13.
5 *Ibid.*, p. 17.
6 Mazharuddin Siddiqui, *Women in Islam* (Delhi: Adam Publishers & Distributors, 1987), p. 2.
7 Jamal Badawi, *The Status of Women in Islam* (Birmingham: Islamic Propagation Centre), p. 7.
8 *Ibid.*, p. 8.
9 *Ibid.*
10 *Ibid.*
11 *Ibid.*, p. 5
12 *Ibid.*, p. 9.
13 *Ibid.*, p. 12.
14 Siddiqui, *Women in Islam*, p. 17.
15 Abdur Raman I. Doi, *Women in Shari'a* (London: Ta-Ha Publishers, 1989), p. 140.
16 *Ibid.*, p. 140.
17 Aisha Lemu and Fatima Hareen, *Woman in Islam* (Leicester: The Islamic Foundation, 1978), p. 16.
18 Doi, *Women in Shari'a*, p. 11.
19 *Ibid.*, p. 12.
20 See Siddiqui, *Women in Islam*, p. 22.
21 Doi, *Women in Shari'a*, p. 137.
22 Muhammad al-Ghazali, *al-Sunna al-nabawiyya bayn ahl al-fiqh wa ahl al-hadith* (Cairo: Dar al-Shuruq, 1992), p. 48.
23 Doi, *Women in Shari'a*, p. 35.
24 *Ibid.*, p. 42.
25 Siddiqui, *Women in Islam*, p. 56.
26 *Ibid.*
27 *Ibid.*
28 *Ibid.*
29 *Ibid.*
30 Ahmad Aziz, *Islamic Law in Theory and Practice* (Lahore: Punjab Educational Press, 1956), p. 236.
31 Afzular Rahman, *Role of Muslim Woman in Society* (London: Seerah Foundation, 1986), p. 153.
32 Muslim, *Sahih Muslim* (Sharh al-Nabawi) (Cairo: al-Matba'a al-Misriyyah, 1929), Vol. 10, pp. 144–8.
33 Doi, *Women in Shari'a*, p. 162.
34 Badawi, *Status of Women in Islam*, p. 20.
35 See *The Holy Qur'an* (LVIII, 1–4) and (LX, 10–12).

PART TWO

THE LANGUAGE OF LITERATURE AND CULTURE

SIX

THE POLITICAL AGENDAS AND TEXTUAL STRATEGIES OF LEVANTINE WOMEN WRITERS

Elizabeth McKee

No sexual revolution can take place without a total human revolution on all levels: economic, ideological, political and social. The "sexual revolution" in my opinion, is only part of the revolution of each individual Arab against the forces which have taken from him his basic human rights.[1]

The Cambridge History of Modern Arabic Literature contains an entry by Miriam Cooke in which she discusses the development of a specifically female writing tradition extending from the late-nineteenth-century achievements of intellectual women living in Egypt such as the Lebanese Wardah al-Yaziji (1838–1924) and Zaynab Fawwaz (1850–1914), the Egyptians Aishah al-Taymuriyyah (1840–1902) and Malak Hifni Nasif, better known as Bahithat al-Badiyah (1886–1918), and the Palestinian Mayy Ziyadah (1886–1941), to contemporary women writers of the latter part of the twentieth century onwards, several of whom appear in my own study,[2] such as the Lebanese authors Layla Ba'albakki, Emily Nasrallah and Hanan al-Shaykh, the Syrian writer Ghadah al-Samman and the Palestinian author Sahar Khalifah.[3] What interests me most about Cooke's article is her constant affirmation that women's works are first and foremost works of polemic feminist protest about the inequality between genders and that almost all of the women writers that she cites, "eschew political specificity [in order] to deal with its effect on personal life."[4] In her discussion of the Moroccan writer Khunathah Bannunah, Cooke even goes as far as to suggest that the writer's allusions to the 1967 debacle concerning Palestine are somewhat extraordinary:

> Bannunah is not so much concerned with gender rights and relations as she is about politics, particularly about global Arab politics.

There is certainly some exploration of mood and character, but the personal delving is subordinated to the political declaiming. It is the prioritization of the political over the social that makes her writing unusual for a woman.

I would argue to the contrary, that it is Cooke's prioritisation of "personal delving" that causes her to overlook the intensely political resonance of a great many works written by women.

Is it really possible to completely overlook the acute ideological dilemmas that threaten to tear Linah to pieces and undermine the stability of Lebanon and the Arab world in Ba'albakki's *Ana ahya*? Equally *Tuyur aylul*, Nasrallah's tale of migration and social change, is surely a lyrical "exposé" of the effect of urbanisation in a rapidly expanding industrial economy where *all* those who leave the village become ostracised from their roots, not only women like Muna. No one could possibly deny that Khalifah's work, *al-Sabbar*, is an intense political debate about resistance to occupation (or lack of it), and even al-Shaykh's victimised heroine, Zahrah in *Hikayat Zahrah*, may be seen as the pock-marked and abused embodiment of the ravages of war on Lebanon. Cooke also fails to acknowledge the numerous subtexts of the symbolic, sometimes distinctly allegorical, elements of al-Samman's *Beirut 75* which traces the events leading up to the outbreak of civil war in Lebanon, concentrating instead on the feminist content of many of the writer's earlier short story collections. To suggest that these works are not political is to ignore the supreme skill of these fiction writers who weave a rich and multi-textured fabric of meaning that may be understood on various levels be they humanist, feminist, nationalist, ideologically committed, politically biased or otherwise.

Having asserted my belief that the works that both Cooke and myself are dealing with may be either implicitly or explicitly political, I must also take issue with Cooke's claim[5] that a distinctly separate literary tradition of women has developed in isolation from male-authored Arabic literature. This is patently not true: not only do the majority of the women authors that I have spoken to during my research refuse to acknowledge that their work is representative of such a cleavage, but also, as far as I can see and without overlooking the originality and specificity of their contribution, the subject-matter of most of their novels may be said to correspond quite faithfully to the general tenets of *adab al-iltizam* (literature of commitment) eloquently described in Suhayl Idris's editorial note to *al-Adab*, the monthly periodical that he founded in 1953, and in which he stated that literature is, an intellectual activity directed to a great and noble end, which is that of effective literature that interacts within society: it influences society just as much as it is influenced by it. The present situation of Arab countries[6] makes it imperative for every citizen, each in his own field, to mobilise all his efforts for the express object of liberating the homeland, raising its political, social and intellectual level. In order that literature may be truthful it is essential that it should not be isolated from the society in which it exists. The main aim of this review is to provide a platform for those fully conscious writers who live the experience of their age and who can be regarded as its witness. In reflecting the needs of Arab society and in expressing its preoccupations they pave the way for reformers to put things right with all the effective means available.[7]

There seems to be little reason for us to presume that injustices perpetrated on account of a person's gender are any less worthy a social ill to be written about than other blatant denials of human rights. Even before this declaration of commitment appeared, many attempts had been made by writers, of both sexes, to highlight the impoverished position of women as one of a plethora of deprivations in Arab society.

It needs to be stressed that the objections raised here are in no way intended to appear anti-feminist *per se*, but rather to question Cooke's reading strategies and the methodological parameters that she and other feminist commentators on Arabic literature such as Evelyne Accad employ. Both *War's Other Voices* and Accad's *Sexuality and War: Literary Masks of the Middle East* make explicit some important connections between oppression and sexuality, in particular the link between violence and masculinity, but do so ostensibly by offering interpretive readings of the texts that owe more to the disciplines of sociology, anthropology and gender studies than they do to the field of literary criticism. In her introduction to *Sexuality and War*, Accad argues that creative works of literature are the only media capable of granting us the "total" picture of social and political realities not least because the "unconscious world of the author" is revealed through the text.[8] Here I find Accad's reasoning somewhat vague and her later comments concerning Lukács' concept of the novel's internal logic serve to undermine rather than strengthen her argument. It is evident that far from respecting the novel form in a Lukácsian sense as an "intensive totality" that corresponds to the "extensive totality" of the world, Accad sees the novels in her study as being directly representative of the reality from which they emanate. Lukács himself rejected the notion of the "photographic" representation of an external reality and insisted on the principle of an underlying order and structure which the novelist renders in an intensive form.[9] So whereas Cooke manages to neatly side-step the political resonance of women's writing, Accad glibly reduces all writing, both men's and women's, to mirror-image expressions of society and human behaviour. In the same introduction, Accad briefly discusses literary style and claims that there exists a "marked similarity between female and male authors" based on their use not only of a mixture of realism and symbolism but also surreal techniques and extreme irony.[10] It continues, however, to establish the central theme of her study as a contextual analysis of the authors' "view" of war and thereby opts out completely from any further serious discussion of the impact of textual strategies or formal techniques for the majority of the ensuing study.

It would seem then that neither of these prolific writers on Arab women novelists have addressed female-authored works from the perspective of recent literary theory beyond the recent, relatively narrow focus of Anglo-American Feminist critical thought. Their subsequent preoccupation with women's intensely personal experience of war and their sexuality to the exclusion of other less glamorous considerations, such as the poignant use of narrative strategies, is drastically reductive. Here, my argument runs parallel to Toril Moi's indignant complaint about Elaine Showalter's reading of Virginia Woolf's *A Room of One's Own* in which Showalter declares:

> If one can see *A Room of One's Own* as a document in the literary history of female aestheticism, and remain detached from its narrative strategies, the concepts of androgyny and the private room are neither as liberating nor as obvious as they first appear. They have a darker side that is the sphere of the exile and the eunuch.[11]

Showalter appears to have been exasperated by the shifting, multiple perspectives that Woolf creates using a variety of techniques: repetition, exaggeration, parody and multiple viewpoint. Moi views Showalter's desire for a more unitary vision as a manifestation of a traditional humanism firmly rooted in patriarchal ideology. Moi contends that remaining detached from the narrative strategies of *Room* is tantamount to not reading it at all and that Showalter's impatience with Woolf's essay stems from her inability to effectively decode its formal and stylistic features.

Moi continues her argument, saying that individual experience may only be understood through the study of the multiple determinants, conscious and unconscious, that make up the "unstable constellation" known by the liberal humanist term as "self" and that:

> It is in this sense that Showalter's recommendation to remain detached from the narrative strategies of the text is equivalent to not reading it at all. For it is only through an examination of the detailed strategies of the text on all its levels that we will be able to uncover some of the conflicting, contradictory elements that contribute to make it precisely this text, with precisely these words and this configuration. The humanist desire for a unity of vision or thought . . . is, in effect, a demand for a sharply reductive reading of literature – a reading that, not least in the case of an experimental writer like Woolf, can have little hope of grasping the central problems posed by pioneering modes of textual production.[12]

Moi's complaint against Showalter mirrors my own dissatisfaction with the theoretical framework of Cooke and Accad and Moi's subsequent reading of Woolf goes on to reveal the important difference between what Moi terms Anglo–American Feminist "criticism" and French Feminist "theory". It is precisely this contradiction between criticism and theory that has guided me in my study of Arab women's narrative discourse and has, I hope, helped me to develop a theoretical approach that will distinguish my work from that of my predecessors.

My main premise in this respect is that close attention to the narrative codes inscribed in the text help us form a more balanced view about the diverse elements at play and the inherent emphases of meaning. I contend that much has been written about what women writers say or, at least, what various commentators think they are saying, and alarmingly little has been produced within the field of Arabic literature concentrating on how they say it. I am not only interested in how women writing in Arabic create an impact on their audience, but in what way that "how" is significant to their status as women. Contextually, I would argue that women's writing is not fundamentally separate from male fiction in regard to the socio-political issues that they choose to tackle. The perceived difference between male and female works would seem to be more closely connected to the way in which some feminist critics have chosen to prioritise certain themes to the detriment of others, and, indeed, to focus attention on certain women authors over and above other lesser known, less clichéd writers.[13] I would argue that this apparent difference is actually first and foremost a structural variation from male writing which may be responsible, subsequently, for producing the change in emphasis within the female novel form.

The seven Arab women novelists whose works I have researched in some detail, Layla Ba'albakki, Emily Nasrallah, and Hanan al-Shaykh from Lebanon, Ghadah al-Samman and Hamidah Na'na' from Syria and the Palestinians Sahar Khalifah and Liyanah Badr (the former still resident in the West Bank and the latter part of the diaspora), have all produced literary works exhibiting complex structural patterns that at once reproduce and subvert the rigidly patriarchal gender systems of their societies. These patterns, despite their individual specificities, reveal certain structural homologies with each other as well as demonstrating strong homologous relations with external power structures.[14]

In this paper, I will attempt to draw the reader's attention not only to the potent political allegories and intense ideological debates contained within some of these narratives by Arab women, but also to the way in which the articulation of female protest against warped ideologies, social injustice and occupation is actually encoded in the narrative structure. I have used a modification of René Girard's paradigm of triangular desire as a framework for introductory readings of four novels, Layla Ba'albakki's Ana ahya (1958), Sahar Khalifah's *al-Sabbar* (1974), Ghadah al-Samman's *Beirut 75* (1976) and Hamidah Na'na''s *al-Watan fi al-'aynayn* (1979)[15] in order to demonstrate how the plot and narrative structure of each text revolves around political foci, whether explicitly or implicitly realised.[16] Triangular or mimetic desire is the term that Girard uses to describe the structuring elements of the novel form, especially those which deal with the differentiation between self and other. It particularly refers to conflicts of desire that take place between a subject, his or her mediator, and a shared object of desire. The subject never desires the object directly, only through the mediation of that essential third element, the mediator. The relationship between the subject and the mediator is usually one of intense rivalry which often escalates into a system of reciprocal violence that can only be stopped by eliminating one of the elements of the triangle. It is important to note that mediation may occur on both external and internal planes: external mediation occurs when the mediator of desire remains external to the immediate events of the novel, rarely or never actually coming into contact with the desiring subject, and internal mediation takes place when both subject and mediator are principal characters in the story. Throughout the following readings I also refer to the degraded or inauthentic nature of the fictional world and the ontological contagion by which I mean the contagion of mediated desire that pervades the novelistic structure.

Arab women's writing exhibits an essential awareness of the negative effect of dyadic mimetic rivalry between men or agents of male power on the fictional world and all its characters. In fact, women's narrative persistently subverts the triangular paradigm, not least through the inclusion of central female characters as desiring subjects, and in this way women writers parody the political structures external to the text. In addition, female protagonists are seldom caught up in the kind of intense rivalrous clashes characteristic of male desire and tend to nurture more ambivalent feelings towards their mediators, often culminating in some form of convergence or symbiotic union rather than separation and hatred. This is often closely related to the women's maternal status or, at least, their relationship to some kind of maternal figure. Women authors' preoccupation with such maternal images and the procreative process of birth are a clear refutation of Girard's claim that all novelistic conclusions and moments of transcendence must occur via the death of the principal character. In Arab women's narratives, the physical act of childbirth often becomes synonymous with the rebirth of the woman herself and a crucial means of coming to terms with her own subjectivity and autonomy of desire, enabling her to transcend the degraded structures of the fictional world.[17]

Ana Ahya! An Existential View of Lebanon's Political Divides, 1958[18]

In her book *al-Riwayah al-nisawiyah fi bilad al-sham 1950–1985*,[19] Iman al-Qadi places Layla Ba'albakki in the "first generation"[20] of Lebanese "feminist"[21] writers. Al-Qadi goes on, however, to assert that Ba'albakki's existentialist approach, like that of other women writers of this first generation, fails to relate the freedom of the individual with the concept of a free society and other "general freedoms".[22] It would seem that al-Qadi has not paid adequate attention to the novel's very definite subtext regarding the political identity of Lebanon and its contradictory nature in the light of the political turmoil of the Middle East in the 1950s. Indeed, al-Qadi and other writers such as Hanan 'Awwad base their analyses solely on the story existents[23] rather than on the plot structure and its metaphorical considerations. In their eagerness to emphasise the work's importance as a feminist protest, these critics manage to ignore explicit discussions of current ideological dilemmas as well as specific references to Lebanon's identity crises.

Existentialism, ideology and inauthentic values

Lina's struggle to define her existence becomes a metaphor for the nation's political ambiguities. In the novel, the central character, Lina, attempts to reconcile her individuality with the dominant ideologies of the day. The degraded search on which she embarks and her various encounters with mimetic rivalry and inauthentic desires are accentuated by the spirit of existentialism that pervades the work. Far from concentrating solely on family, parental control and the call for sexual freedom as al-Qadi suggests, Ba'albakki's novel utilises these images in order to establish the inextricable nature of the personal and the political, employing contemporary existentialist thought in order to emphasise the role of the individual and his/her responsibility towards society.

Lina's degraded search reflects Lukács' attitude towards the failure of Marxism to reaffirm the reality of men. He viewed existentialism as "the only concrete approach to reality" and believed that Marxism had left mankind stranded and without vision beyond the recognition of historical materialism and the liquidation of bourgeois categories of thought.[24] In the novel, Lina, who has already turned away from what she perceives as the capitalist treachery of her father, is ultimately disappointed by Baha's similar intolerance towards the specificity of human existence, its value and its potential compatibility with the principles of a socialist democracy. McElroy sums up Lina's dilemma when he says that,

> the individual has lost his identity. For proof of this we need only consider that the two conflicting ideologies which are engaged in a struggle to the death for the possession of man's future, both regard him as an object. [25]

The two ideologies to which McElroy refers are also those dealt with by Ba'albakki, namely Marxism and Western bourgeois democracies although, in the novel, they are generally dealt with under the broader terms of Communism and Imperialism. These ideologies play a direct role in manipulating the interactions of all the characters and may be regarded as external (or abstract) mediators of Lina's quest for truth. Consequently, Lina's degraded search leads her to recognise that the contradictions of these seemingly conflicting ideologies are illusory and thus inauthentic objects of desire. She comes to realise that their overwhelming similarity in excluding woman from the political equation poses the greatest threat to her attempts at establishing her own subjectivity and escaping the monotonous rhythm of mimetic rivalry.

Lina emphasises her distress at being objectified as a woman within the mimetic system and parodies the displacement of individuals by objects by referring to herself and other protagonists as items of furniture. The office workers are referred to as machines (p. 37) and in Uncle Sam's café Lina is terrified of becoming an empty chair that can be easily replaced (p. 105). The chair analogy is extended elsewhere, particularly in reference to her status as a woman (p. 112), and serves to emphasise the objectification of women in general terms as seen in Baha's worship of the one-dimensional, cinematic image of women (p. 165). Baha' himself also takes on a strange alternative presence in Lina's mind as an empty ashtray on her dressing-table.

Narrative structure and triangular desire

There seem to be three textual planes through which the novel unfolds: on the existential level it is the search for subjectivity and self-worth; on the political level the text concerns itself with a polyphonic[26] discussion of the dominant ideologies of the time and their relationship to the individual; and on the level of sexual and gender identity it provides some radical comments concerning the treatment of woman as man's private property. The coherent interaction of all three levels is regulated in accordance with the laws of mediated desire applied within the structure of the novel.

Like the tripartite division of the textual planes, the novel is structurally divided into three parts. Part One deals with Lina's initial stirrings of rebellion while still caught up in the conformity of her affluent background; Part Two sees the breakdown of Lina's relationship with the capitalist establishment when she recognises it as an extension of the domestic patriarchy she rejects; Part Three traces Lina's attempts to come to terms with Marxist idealism but this is ultimately rejected when it is revealed to endorse the same phallocratic power structures from which she had hoped to escape.

Narrative strategies delineating the presence of triangularly mediated relationships become increasingly significant in *Ana ahya*. Externally mediated desires take the form of abstract ideologies which find their way into Lina's internally mediated relations through the dictatorial philosophies of the male protagonists. As the desiring subject, Lina allows herself to be influenced by the desiring fervour of characters who have, in turn, been infected with the ontological contagion by external mediating powers. The false desires induced by the infection may be loosely categorised as extreme materialism, radical socialism and misplaced idealism. In her quest for individual significance, Lina's belief in the inauthentic search accentuates her state of existentialist self-deception (bad faith) and vice versa.

Metaphorically speaking, Lina's idolatrous search translates as Lebanon's fascination with Western modes of thinking and external foreign policies to which the government of the day willingly succumbed. It also represents the opposition's increasing empathy with leftist revolutions in neighbouring Arab countries such as Egypt and Iraq. Ba'albakki's novel seeks to undermine the reader's belief in the authenticity of any of the political mediating influences of the late 1940s–1950s with regard to Lebanon and the Arab world. The novelistic discourse effectively deconstructs the principles of opposing doctrines and exposes their surprising congruities and shocking capacity for self-deceit. Walid, for example, considers that as an individual he cannot be held responsible for the imperialist injustice that he helps to perpetuate while Baha' endorses the same view in his dismissal of individual significance in relation to the communist cause.

The mediation strategies at play within the work roughly correspond to three textual planes, sexuality, individualism and political conflict. These external mediating elements find parallels in the three internal mediators, the father, Baha' and the Jewish neighbour, who influence the desires of the main character and, hence, the events of the novel. The boundaries between external and internal mediations become somewhat indistinct as ideologies and personalities converge and separate within the degraded fictional world, but it is possible to outline the corresponding elements which combine to tempt Lina along the path of deviant transcendence. With regard to sexuality, the external mediation of traditional "ownership" of womankind manifests itself in the internal mediating relationship of the father and the hierarchy of the patriarchal family. It is also representative of the powerful grip of the ruling elites in Lebanon. Yet, defiance of the father–mediator is actually expressed as a rivalrous opposition where father and daughter vie with each other for rights of possession regarding Lina's future.

Similarly, the communist propaganda against which the censorship company strives, is embodied in the character of Baha' who gains prestige as an alternative mediator both to the father and to the imperialist bias of the company director. On the external level, Baha' (a radical, young Iraqi student) seems, at first, to be representative of the revolutionary spirit of the age which prompts Lina to substitute him as her new idol. Baha' and Lina's relationship, however, also becomes contaminated with meaningless rivalries and petty jealousies that render it worthless.

When Baha's position as mediator is threatened by Lina's increasing disillusionment she discovers a new and challenging mediator in the form of the pregnant Jewish woman who seems to hold the key to the future. On the external level, she symbolises the new-born, fertile and thriving Jewish state and Lina's ambivalent feelings towards her are indicative of the contagion of mimetic rivalry that Israel's existence has set in motion. In setting herself up in competition with the pregnant woman, however, Lina is unwittingly ensuring her continued sterility. During this third and final mimetic stage, Baha' loses the arbitrary prestige bestowed upon him and is renegaded to the position of object of (sexual) desire. The intensity of their mediator–subject relationship is shattered and with it Lina's fantasies of giving birth.

When Lina finally recognises the degraded reality of her relationship to Baha' which has greatly increased the distance between her and the possibility of transcendence,[27] the "idol" is shattered, quite literally, in a scene in which Baha' disintegrates before Lina's eyes. Realising that the route to transcendence can only be found from within, not mediated by the false values of others, Lina abandons her quest.

The novel points to the disparity between Lebanese tradition and Western modes of thought that seem to bear no relation to one another. The Suez crisis is commented upon as an example of true "Arabism" in the face of Western interference and the Baghdad Pact is criticised as a further act of Western coercion. The picture, however, remains bleak in regard to socialist ideals and the increasing popularity of Ba'thism in Syria and Iraq born out of the need to form a united opposition to pro-western regimes. The character of Baha' is the fictional world's representative of the potentially despotic nature of socialism. He is a victim of the ontological sickness propagated through the political dogma of the (communist) party to which he belongs. Lina is constantly aware of the insurmountable rupture between herself and the degraded world, a logocentric world where people are reduced to the status of objects and where individuality and difference are denied. Neither her father's corrupt materialism nor Baha's distorted idealism offer realistic altern- atives to Lina, who recognises that both will deny her subjectivity – that both seek to exclude her from their discourse. To the capitalist, she is private property; to the communist, she is objectified and rendered insignificant as an individual.

Palestine and the sterility of desire

The sterile nature of mediated rivalry as a metaphor for the political malaise of Lebanon is accentuated by the desire for fertility that over- comes Lina. In the third part of the novel, Lina has an unusual encounter with a young army officer who had fought in Palestine. She is aware of an invisible link between them – the link between Lebanon and the newly born state of Israel. The imagery of this strange passage is charged with both eroticism and violence. When Lina tries to pull away from the man's physical advances she accidentally aggravates a chest wound where a bullet remains painfully lodged. He tells her that he must endure the pain or risk almost certain death if he tries to remove it. In my reading of the novel, the painful scar is representative of the disastrous Arab–Israeli war of 1948. It is a scar that can never be removed and that threatens the stability of the entire Arab World. The soldier can only manage to soothe his pain using the cold metal of Lina's bracelet – or that of his gun, revealing Ba'albakki's fears of a violent future. Later, Lina traces the pattern of the veins on her bruised hand and sees them resembling:

> An officer's cap fixed onto a khaki-coloured staff and the boots of an ordinary soldier, lost in a marshy field of blood; and a torn flag buried in a rubbish tip of monstrous international betrayal! (p. 270)

After hearing the admiring comments of her mother and sisters describing the radiantly pregnant Jewish woman, Lina muses to herself:

> A living wound in the chest of an Arab officer. A yearning that moves and grows inside our filthy Jewish neighbour. A crushed bracelet on my wrist. An empty ashtray in front of me. (p. 276)

The staccato rhythm reflects the fragmented mosaic of Lebanese existence and the disjointed accumulation of factors that were gradually eroding the fabric of society: the failure of the liberation war, the fertile and thriving state of Israel, the distorted face of imperialist interference and an improbable vision of communism. Of these, it is the pregnant Jewish woman that has the most pervasive effect in mediating Lina's desires for the future through the creation of new life. Despite her sudden vehement hatred for the Jewish neighbour, Lina cannot resist comparing her own sterility with the other woman's beauty and evident fertility and a distinctly female rivalry establishes itself. Much of the interior monologue that follows her decision to give birth takes place whilst she is absorbed in studying herself in the mirror. Comparing her naked body with the massive proportions of the pregnant woman, Lina considers that:

> This Jewish woman carries a killer enemy while, in my head, I carry the tragedies of an isolated people, their ignorance and the feebleness of their insurrection. She is preparing a future for a banished nation, while I am preparing, in my head, illusions of a meeting. Every day she empties a drop of her foul blood into the veins of one who would deny humanity, while my days pass – monotonous, painful and sterile . . . And my thoughts became lost in imagining my figure swollen to the extent that it surpasses all others in its capacity to give. (p. 305)

Here, Ba'albakki emphasises the illusion of Baha's commitment to her in contrast to the perceived reality of this new mediating agent. This is the crucial turning-point for Lina who mourns her inability to be physically close to Baha' and their inability to express a deeper bond. Lina yearns for some kind of creative reciprocity to take the place of the lingering stagnancy of hatred that fuels Baha's revolution against the status quo. At this point, the text is surely alluding to Lebanon's inability to participate in satisfactory political intercourse with its Arab neighbours just as Lina and Baha' fail to communicate effectively. The novel is always aware of the mediating influence of external powers on both the personal and the political level. Lina's thoughts and actions have been mediated firstly by the existing regime, supported by the West and epitomised by her father's unscrupulous business dealings. In rejecting this, she is consequently influenced by Baha' whose actions are dictated by the Party, that seeks its inspiration from Arab nationalist movements,

who in turn have used the example of communism elsewhere as a yard-
stick by which to gauge their own endeavours. The Jewish woman, her
strong husband and her evident fecundity, representing Israel's Western-
backed, flourishing new nation, is the catalyst for Lina's rebirth. Ultimately, she turns away from all mediators in order to establish her own
subjectivity, signifying Lebanon's need to develop a new, autonomous
direction and not to succumb to the mediation of other nations with
regard to political objectives and ideologies.

Al-Sabbar: Political and Economic Crisis in the Occupied Territories[28]

In *al-Sabbar*, the plot and the interaction of the characters is composed
within a system of ideological binary oppositions that form the main thematic thread of the text upon which the webs of mimetic male rivalry are
spun. The central, ostensibly male, dynamism of the textual fabric is,
however, subtly subverted by interwoven strands of undeniably female
subtexts that persistently dispute the bilateral framework of the novel.
The triumph of *al-Sabbar*, however, is its extraordinary ability to articulate the political reality of Palestinian life under Israeli occupation.
Khalifah's skilful use of characterisation to emphasise the novel's political themes never appears unnecessarily contrived nor does it undermine
the credible reality of the novelistic world. On the contrary, Khalifah's
relatively short novel (176 pages) manages to combine a wealth of sociological, economic and demographic information without threatening the
coherence and intensity of the story. Indeed, the story is gripping enough
in itself to distract the reader from the specificity of the political subtexts
that abound within this richly textured work. Fundamentally, these subtexts exist on two mutually dependent levels: on the external level the
novel examines the bitter conflict between Arabs and Israelis in the occupied territories, while on an internal level Khalifah expertly delineates
the clash of interests between the two main class divisions of Palestinian
society, the bourgeois elite and the manual workers. In particular, *al-
Sabbar* charts the demise of the middle-class land and factory owners
whose properties and incomes became defunct in the face of Israeli policies that support Israeli industry and agriculture to the detriment of
Palestinian interests.

    We should pause for a moment to consider the historical reality of
Israel's occupation. Higher wages paid by Israeli companies have led

to the near abandonment of Palestinian agriculture and the Arab labour force is compelled to seek work abroad or inside Israel itself. The bourgeois classes were split into two groups: one section was affiliated to Jordan, thus gaining access to financial assistance from the oil states although often unfairly subjugated by the Jordanian system, while the other section accepted occupation as a *fait accompli* and cooperated with the Israelis in order to attain integration into the Israeli economy. Most of the bourgeoisie, however, found themselves demoted to the ranks of the working class, like 'Adil in *al-Sabbar*. Khalifah embodies the disintegration of the middle classes in the character of Sabir al-Karmi (Abu 'Adil) whose body is succumbing to a similar fate of decomposition represented by his kidney disease. Abu 'Adil proclaims a radically nationalist stance to everyone, unaware that he is being kept alive by money earned by 'Adil in Israel. Meanwhile, the working classes, represented in the novel by Zuhdi and Abu Sabir, are hardly able to support themselves due to lack of employment and/or low wages.

The predicament of the Palestinian struggle is put over clearly and sharply in *al-Sabbar* and Khalifah successfully binds the conflicting perspectives of armed struggle versus the daily struggle against starvation, reinforcing once more the binary divisions of the text. At times, Khalifah is openly critical of the PLO's lack of regard for the harsh reality of the working classes and she attacks the compradors, such as Hajj 'Abdallah, who channels foreign goods through his shop as a way of making an easy profit without caring about the welfare of the country. Within this criticism, Khalifah also alludes to the PLO's inability to unite the bourgeois and working-class elements under one strong leadership and points to the Palestinian people's increasing loss of faith in the elitist bureaucratic hierarchies of the PLO.

In an article dealing in far greater detail with the political aspects of *al-Sabbar*, Ghalib Halasa applauds the novel for dealing with these essential realities and the divisions caused by the lack of understanding between those living under occupation and those outside its vicious grasp; the bourgeoisie's betrayal of the people and the misplaced schemes of reactionary Arab countries which have hindered the Palestinian cause.[29] Halasa is anxious that Western readers of the novel should not be surprised by the way in which every character is politicised and he stresses that all aspects of a Palestinian's daily life are necessarily political, the buying of bread, choice of workplace, the decision to leave in order to study or work, what paper to read, what café to sit in, what friends to sit with and so on, all of which are examined by Khalifah's novel. He observes how the conflict between the old and the new generation also harbours political connotations, such as Umm Usamah's desire that her son marries his cousin, Nuwwar, a traditional arrangement which would, in fact, force Usamah to make a political decision by agreeing to settle down and raise a family in the occupied territories.

Most importantly, however, Halasa notices how Khalifah's technique of characterisation reflects the binary structure of the work. Each character suffers from split loyalties of one kind or another. Usamah is torn between the sensitive nature of his childhood, when he mourned the slaughter of a little lamb, and the blood-thirsty vengefulness he exhibits on returning to the West Bank. 'Adil must choose between his middle class loyalties and the practical need to feed his large extended family. Zuhdi is torn between his sympathy for the Jewish workers who are hardly better off than him and his instinctive allegiance to the struggle against the Israeli oppressors. Even Umm Sabir whose bitterness towards the Israeli officer and his family appears implacable, has a change of heart when she pauses to consider the consequences of Usamah's "heroic" deed on the injured officer's wife and child. In this way, each character relates his or her experience of the ontological dilemma that pervades the fictional universe. The textual strategies that Khalifah employs elucidate the contradictions inherent in the Palestinian "reality" depicted by *al-Sabbar*, and the principles of mimetic desire become an integral part of the novel's structural divisions.

Binary oppositions, mimetic desire and plot structure

The novelistic universe is split down the middle in order to incorporate the contradictory "realities" of the Palestinian people under Israeli occupation. One reality relates to Usamah's vision of armed struggle against the occupiers and even against his own countrymen when they succumb to better wage prospects in the enemy territories. This vision is enthusiastically taken up by eager adolescents, such as Basil, who is dazzled by the heroism of Usamah and Salih and the prestige brought by imprisonment. The other reality is the economic crisis battled against by 'Adil and his colleagues, Zuhdi and Abu Sabir. They are family men with burdensome debts and hungry mouths to feed who refuse to risk the welfare of their loved ones for the nationalistic cause.

'Adil's economic difficulties then, are the combined result of both the Occupation and the crippling expense of his father's kidney machine.

The false economy of the West Bank created by Occupation and the artificial dialysis machine become synonymous with one another to the point
that 'Adil can no longer distinguish between them. The kidney machine
is symbolic of the country's economic stagnation: the essential biological
function of the father's kidneys has been replaced by an artificial one,
just as the "natural" functioning of the Palestinian economy has broken
down and been replaced by the artificial respirator of the lucrative factory
jobs within Israel. Despite the father's patriotic ideals and the arrogant,
self-assured rhetoric that he delivers to the foreign journalists gathered
in his sitting room, his hypocrisy and the renal disease become synonymous with the ontological contagion creeping through West Bank society,
compelling them to look to the "other side", to the enemy mediator, in
order to realise the most basic of human desires.

'Adil's desperation and the desperate state of his country is summed
up as he ponders on the misfortune of Abu Sabir's accident and the loss
of the three fingers on his right hand:

> Left hand, right hand, 'Adil thought, anything in the world would be
> better than my father's renal colic. Blood poisoning, swelling of the tis-
> sues, skin lesions and slavery to a machine. What a life! What a death!
> A slow death, whose costs even the Arab Bank with all its branches
> couldn't cover, let alone a farm that lost its workers. Even Shahadah
> had left. Only the old man and the dog were left on the land. Soon the
> old man will die, and that will leave the dog. My father's blood will go
> on mixing with his urine. And me, I'm a slave to the mouths I feed, and
> to the kidney machine. And Usamah searches our eyes for a glimmer
> of shame. Sink in the mud, Palestine, and kiss the world goodbye.[30]

The pattern of binary symbolism is unmistakable: Father (the bourgeoisie or *al-wujaha'*) versus Israeli State; Kidney versus Kidney
Machine; Blood versus Urine. 'Adil's desire to escape the clutches of the
kidney machine may be translated as his desire to transcend the limits of
the restrictive equation that suspends him between the false values of
his bourgeois upbringing and the inauthenticity of desires mediated by
occupation.

An essential binary conflict, such as that between Usamah and 'Adil,
is present in all aspects of the plot structure. Even the convoluted machinations of internal mimetic desire are subjected to a bilateral cleavage
between opposing mediating forces and in this way the fundamental
framework of the novel is suspended between the two contradictory poles

of Israel and Palestine. Indeed, the two pivotal characters, 'Adil and Usamah, expose the contradictions of the political situation through their antagonistic relationship to one another. They represent the two opposite poles of the conflict and although the multiple levels of the argument are tacitly acknowledged by 'Adil, both characters are ruled by their individual experience of the situation:

> In exasperation, Usamah said, "The picture's perfectly clear, can't you see that?"
>
> Flicking the flies away from his face, 'Adil replied, "There's more than one dimension to the picture."
>
> They walked on together, each contemplating his own dimension, and his own sorrows.[31]

Usamah continually goads and attacks 'Adil who persistently avoids open confrontation with his cousin.[32] In one exchange, 'Adil's drunken state makes him an easy target for Usamah's provocation:

> Suddenly ['Adil] burst out sobbing. "Okay," he shouted, "convince me that what I'm doing isn't part of the struggle, that the fight has fixed ground rules." Usamah didn't answer. He turned his head to one side to avoid the foul smell. 'Adil vomited again as he walked along, tottering. "And who's going to fight the battle of the stomachs?" He was talking to himself. Then he went on: "You can have my life, Usamah, if you can only convince me that freedom means that people who can't defend themselves go hungry. And that there's happiness in hunger. Come on, convince me!"[33]

'Adil tries to explain the dubious logic behind Usamah's complaints by likening the West Bank's suffering to the agonies of childbirth. When Usamah declares that he is disgusted by 'Adil's drinking, the latter retorts:

> "Drunk! Which one of us isn't? Some of us get high on the resistance. Some of us on the glories of warfare. And we get high on kidney pains, yes they really hurt, even worse than birth pangs. But labour pains are at least followed by a birth. We have kidney pains while you go into labour and then blame us for not giving birth! What are we supposed to give birth to?"[34]

'Adil understands that he and Usamah are both victims of an ontological contagion that threatens the integrity of the novelistic universe
and he tries to avoid infection by refusing to enter the equation of triangular rivalry against his own cousin. Yet 'Adil is already a victim of the
contagion. Eventually, it is Usamah's martyrdom that indirectly forces
'Adil to reassess himself during the final chapters of the novel. 'Adil does
not aspire to emulate Usamah, nor Usamah to become like 'Adil. Their
oppositional stance in relation to each other is static and the distance
between them is always relatively fixed. 'Adil's feigned indifference
fuels Usamah's anger and also his determination to carry out his brutal
mission, while Usamah's hot-headed petulance seems only to increase
'Adil's resigned attitude to the hopelessness of the situation. This antag-
onism, based on the essential conflict between militant resistance and
peaceful compromise, exists on a fundamental level between all the
characters of *al-Sabbar* as it does later in the novel's sequel, *'Abbad
al-shams*. Both the external and internal mediations at play which determine the behaviour of the two cousins are also the essential mediating
elements for every Palestinian character in the novel.

Beirut 75: A Symbolic Articulation of Lebanon's Pre-War Tensions[35]

Ghadah al-Samman's writing has attracted much attention and critical
acclaim over the past thirty years. Two books have been published devoted
solely to her life and works and she remains a prominent figure in the
Arabic literary world today. Most of this attention has centred around her
outspoken views about the emancipation of women and sexual liberation
during the late sixties and early seventies in both her journalistic and
fictional works, especially her short stories. Critics of her work praise her
originality, her stalwart feminism and her commitment to political issues
but few of them, including two in-depth studies by 'Awwad and Shukri,
offer more than piecemeal accounts of al-Samman's writing and none
attempt a full-scale analysis of her novelistic works. Again, much of the
criticism applied to al-Samman's literature focuses on the author, her
intentions and political leanings, or it resorts to picking out individual
lines and paragraphs containing passionate universal "truths" about
sexual and economic inequalities or injustices without locating them
in the context of the literary text as a whole. In general, it is the glamorous allure of sexual issues that invariably succeed in seizing the critic's

imagination (see 'Awwad), or al-Samman's idiosyncratic use of language that critics such as Shukri find most appealing despite its inconsistencies. Others, such as Farraj, are more attentive to the author's attempts to inject political relevance into her fictional works. Farraj and Shukri both enthuse about al-Samman's skill in pinpointing the determinants of the Lebanese civil war and encapsulating them within the text of *Beirut 75* but beyond this they fail to establish a link between the novel's textuality and the socio-political content that they only partially define.[36]

Similarly, 'Awwad fails to appreciate the textual integrity of *Beirut 75* by dedicating the majority of her study of it to relentlessly expounding the sorry lot of Arab women as delineated by the character of Yasminah, whilst devoting disproportionately less attention to the experience of the seven or so other male characters. Indeed, it would appear that 'Awwad's reading of the text scarcely skims the surface of this work, completely ignoring the specificity of its underlying structure due to her preoccupation with addressing gender issues to the detriment of the novel's other socio-political dynamics. I would venture to suggest that quite apart from calling on women to "redefine their role" and "strive for equality"[37] as 'Awwad claims, the novel quite often presents a conversely negative picture of women, depicting, in the strongest terms, the futility of women's struggle against injustice and the patriarchal network. Throughout the novel women are constantly marginalised, their presence wholly negated at times, and the call for social equality and justice is uttered more urgently through the mouths of the five similarly oppressed male figures, Abu Mustafa, Mustafa, Abu al-Malla, Ti'an and Farah than through Yasminah's vague dissatisfaction. This structural imbalance parallels the way in which al-Samman herself views the situation:

> The Arab woman suffers from economic, intellectual and sexual deprivation. But who can say that the Arab man is free? Tradition is as insurmountable an obstacle to his emancipation of mind and spirit as it is to woman's. If we are to achieve anything worthwhile in the present posture of affairs, it must be at the expense of tradition. It is impossible for any woman or man to be free in a society which does not theoretically value the idea of liberty.[38]

In short, 'Awwad oversimplifies this complex work, disregarding its contradictory and ambiguous elements through a reductive reading of the novel's fabula. Any comprehensive analysis of *Beirut 75* must acknowledge the structural function of *all* the characters and their interlinked destinies, not least that of Yasminah and Farah, the two focal characters whose polarised, yet paradoxically overlapping, sexualities emphasise the desperate need for complimentarity between men and women on a specific local level as well as a universal one. The contradictions of the novel are reflected in the disturbing ambiguities of Yasminah and Farah's androgynous sexuality and the text's concentration on sexuality and gender identity (rather than "women's issues") seems in itself to be a protest against reductive readings that single out issues regarding one gender, to the detriment of the other.

Triangular desire in the novelistic structure

The presence of mediated desires which control the machinations of the plot and the entire novelistic structure may be observed on both internal and external levels. On the specific level of character interaction the mediators are all internal except in the case of Ti'an, the young chemist who has become the victim of a revenge-killing tradition, whose mediator and object are essentially unknown and yet constantly influence his actions and his ultimate fate. The irony of his position emphasises the mockery of triangular desire as well as its inescapable authority. Yasminah (a young convent teacher who has arrived in Beirut in pursuit of literary fame) quickly falls victim to the dandyish indifference of Namir al-Sukayni which arouses her passionate desire; Abu Mustafa (the fisherman) becomes locked in a fierce battle with the ruthless business elite that control his fishing rights and his destiny; Abu Malla (the keeper of antiquities) is similarly engaged in a detrimental mediating relationship with the landowners in control of his heritage and his means of income; and finally Farah becomes the desiring victim of Nishan's despotic influence and sexual persuasion in pursuit of a singing career.

The external mediators are, necessarily, less specific and include a vast array of sociological pressures that bring about each character's ruin in one form or the other. Ti'an seeks to escape the awful burden that strict adherence to tradition has heaped on his shoulders; Yasminah is a victim of her economic dependence on men as well as her sexually oppressive conditioning as a woman; Abu Mustafa and his son are fighting the overwhelming mediations of poverty, social inequality, political injustice and exploitation; Abu al-Malla contends with poverty and exploitation in a similar manner; Farah is penniless, lost and lonely, which helps to push him into the tenacious grip of Nishan. It is Farah, however, who comes

the closest to a realisation of his mediated desire of fame and glory –
something he fleetingly achieves in order to recognise that the object of
desire, once possessed, loses its value and instead becomes one of the
catalysts of his downfall.

Spatial dimensions

The illusion of Lebanon's unity on an external level and of the characters' actual unity on an internal level are incorporated into the structure of
the text through the creation of spatial environments that confine and
direct the actions of the fictional characters. The journey in the cramped,
stuffy service taxi from Damascus into the focal arena of action, Beirut,
draws a vivid analogy with realities external to the textual world. The
uncomfortable conditions in the car reflect the country's sectarian discomfort – diverse communities finding themselves drawn together under
one government and supposedly one national identity, despite their cultural differences. Al-Samman hints the significance of the city in relation
to the occupants of the vehicle when she pauses to comment as the taxi
draws closer to Beirut:

> None of the five passengers in the car exchanged a word. Yasminah,
> Farah, Abu al-Malla, Abu Mustafa the fisherman, Ti'an: each one
> submerged in his own silence. Each one of them was a planet,
> alone and isolated, even though they revolved within the same
> galaxy. Everybody's eyes were fixed upon the brightly lit, con-
> crete jungle that sprawled in front of them called Beirut . . . and
> each one considered it with a different eye. There was no
> single Beirut . . . there were "five Beiruts". Only the taxi driver
> appeared indifferent like the grim reaper of death.[39]

On the internal level the taxi's physical limitations accentuate the
individualism of each character despite the fact that their destinies will
remain strangely linked from that moment on. In particular, the fate of
Farah, Yasminah and Abu Mustafa will depend upon their separate
triangular relationships with the al-Sukayni family and its unscrupulous
dealings.

The initial move from the external diversity of Damascus, Syria into
the intense, restrictive confines of Lebanon's capital, Beirut, echoes the
intensification of desire as the desiring victims draw nearer to their

mediators. The atmospheric tension that builds up between the travellers illustrates the beginning of the feverish tensions of triangularly mediated desires. Beirut itself becomes an object of desire that loses its concrete value once obtained. Beirut becomes a spatially restricted "unreal" world – a degraded world – where relational structures are intensified and exaggerated to display behavioural extremes. The use of spatial confinement as a metaphor for personal repression also appears in the depiction of Yasminah who is always portrayed alone in physically restricting space: in Namir al-Sukayni's flat; in his yacht in the middle of the bay; in her brother's flat as she awaits execution. The encapsulated tortoise with whom she shares her innermost thoughts during the long hours waiting for Namir in his flat, is an ideal reflection of her imprisonment. The only time that we see her walking freely in the street is from a taxi to her brother's flat (p. 87) when she witnesses a small boy run down by a speeding sports car and recognises the similarity of their fates – both of them destroyed by the fast and powerful elite in whose eyes they remain insignificant and expendable. It is important to stress here that Yasminah is not oppressed simply through being a woman but, more specifically, through being a working-class woman who sees her opportunity for privilege in the cold embrace of Namir al-Sukayni.

Politics and prophecies

The three weeping women who occupy the back seat of the car and who mysteriously disappear at the Lebanese border, predict not only the mediated demise of the five desiring victims with whom they are travelling, but also the catastrophic downfall of Lebanon itself in the years of civil strife lurking just around the corner at the time when al-Samman wrote the novel. Ghali Shukri refers to the novel as an example of "visionary narrative" in regard to the political conflict of the time. Again the metaphorical quality of the text exists on two levels: internal, that is specific to Lebanon, and external, that is of wider reference to both the Middle East and the rest of the world.

On the external level, the stranglehold of tradition, cultural (particularly sexual) taboos and aspects of class consciousness illustrate the universal relevance of the text concerning power, corruption and hypocrisy. On the more specific internal level, however, the references become immediately identifiable with particular issues of the day, the most outstanding of which concerns the Sidon fishermen's dispute which is commonly accepted to mark the beginning of the long and bitter civil war that afflicted the country from 1975 until recently. Al-Samman devotes a lot of attention to the unenviable plight of the fishermen in her novel, exploring the hardships of this dangerous occupation, the misery of the fishermen's extreme poverty and their lack of political support concerning the right to form co-operatives, the provision of pensions and benefits and the monopolisation of prices by business conglomerates serving their own interests, regardless of the unbearable conditions of those undertaking the thankless task.

Such detail would probably remain fairly unextraordinary if it were not for the violent suicide of the character of Abu Mustafa in the novel. Driven to desperation by bad weather, half-crazed by an obsessional hope that he will find a lamp with a genie to save him from his and his family's severe deprivation, Abu Mustafa hurls himself into the sea clutching a stick of dynamite and is blown to pieces. The ripples of this fictional death were to re-emerge in Lebanon five months after the book was written when, during a demonstration against the creation of a new fishing consortium under the chairmanship of ex-president Camille Chamoun, Ma'ruf Sa'd, a popular local deputy and leader of the fishermen, was shot dead by an unknown gunman – an incident that is usually accepted as the catalyst of the subsequent civil war in Lebanon. Al-Samman seems to have sensed the air of impending doom in Lebanon and the significance of seemingly small-scale disputes in the "tinderbox" of Lebanon, emphasising the gap between the affluent and indigent classes.[40] Indeed, Farah's slide into insanity and the nightmare sequences that he experiences towards the end of the novel are uncanny premonitions of the sheer madness and the nightmare reality that was to overwhelm Beirut the following year.

Al-Watan fi al-'Aynayn: Régis Debray and the Palestinian Revolution[41]

The immense structural complexity of Hamidah Na'na''s first novel displays a marked awareness of its own textuality in the creation of numerous layers of meaning, all elements of which are dependent on a tripartite novelistic framework. Written in 1979, the work represents a courageous attempt to make sense of the ideological and theoretical tensions, identity crises and political conflicts that were to plague the Arab world following the disastrous defeat of June 1967 after the Six Day

War with Israel. Its essential thematic outline immediately belies its adherence to triangular structure moving as it does between three fundamental poles of reference – the June defeat, the formation of the Palestinian resistance movement (*al-muqawamah al-filistiniyyah*) and the Jordanian authorities' attempt in 1970 to contain its militant activities known as Black September[42] and, finally, the outbreak of civil war in Lebanon (in which the Palestinian guerrillas were to play a significant part) a few years later.

Textual strategies

The author employs a varied array of literary techniques and includes a wealth of intertextual references throughout the work, such as the use of fictional place-names taken from the Qur'an,[43] Biblical references regarding the Song of Songs[44] and allusion to the betrayal of Jesus by Judas Escariot,[45] as well as references to the Greek myth of the Medusa.[46] There is a richly woven texture of narrative strategies including: metaphor and metonymic associations, such as the frequent reference to the *Palais de Justice* in Paris[47] clearly meant to highlight the lack of justice in the case of Palestine; historical and political allegory, such as the heroine's miscarriage representative of the death of Arab unity and her Kurdish background alluding to the forgotten issue of the Middle East's first Palestine;[48] symbolic representation, such as Nadiyah's chaotic state of mind symbolising the destabilising events of civil war and the use of women's bodies and the act of childbirth as symbols of future progress; prophetic announcements, such as Abu Mashhur's assertion that Nadiyah will marry no other;[49] and ironic contradictions, such as the inversion of the mediating relationship of the two main protagonists. The intricately patterned arrangement of these and other techniques, involving, for instance, the narrative focus and temporal dimensions, creates an elaborately layered text and reveals a plethora of hidden meanings and allusions.

These effects are further heightened by the careful arrangement of the textual materials to bring about numerous inversions (such as the change of mediators), reversals of direction, mirroring and merging of characters (Frank and Abu Mashhur sometimes seem to be two sides of the same coin and Nadiyah's complex character is torn between the two), and unsettling combinations of fiction and reality that seem to generate a third plane of existence: there seems to be a tacit acknowledgement of a political reality external to the text, the internal fictional reality of the plot and a third point where the two merge until the former division is no longer distinguishable (see p. 203, for instance, where Régis Debray and Frank become one, or the clear correspondence of the fictional cities to real Middle Eastern capitals as well as the use of real events within this fictional framework, such as the Palestinian issue which, in a deliberately paradoxical fashion, retains its real name and identity).

Formal structure

The text is separated into three uneven parts – a short, stream of consciousness style introduction (two pages); an extended monologue from the point of view of the main protagonist, Nadiyah, which takes the form of a letter addressed in the second person to her lover and fallen idol, Frank (one hundred and sixty-seven pages); and an epilogue mainly divided between an external narrator and Frank's interior monologue (thirty-five pages).[50] This structural imbalance is also to be found in the work of political theory upon which the novel appears to have drawn not only for its subject-matter, its inspirational, revolutionary dialogue and its philosophical debates, but for at least two of its major characters and also its distinctive preoccupation with specific temporal dimensions. Régis Debray's *Revolution in the Revolution?*[51] is the driving force behind Na'na''s novel and at times the two works seem to converge, while at others their relationship to each other is almost dialectical. It is often difficult to separate the voices of the various revolutionary characters in the novel from that of Debray whose persona is reflected in the character of Frank but whose message is echoed in the voices of the freedom fighter, Abu Mashhur, Nadiyah and others throughout the novel. This confusion is heightened by more than one specific reference either to the theoretical work itself or to the Cuban revolutionary, Ernest "Che" Guevara, and various insurrections that Debray uses as theoretical paradigms including Vietnam, Cuba and Bolivia.[52]

The most fascinating connection between Debray's essay and the fictional work of *al-Watan fi al-'aynayn* is the imitation of the former's structure employed by the latter. In *Revolution*, we find a short preface (two pages) then three main parts: chapter one – the historical background of the argument entitled "To Free the Present from the Past" (seventy-one pages); chapter two, the main suggestion for decisive action entitled "The Principal Lesson for the Present" (twenty-two pages); and chapter three, brief comments on "Some Consequences for the Future" (eight pages). Bearing in mind the temporal distinctions explicit in the titles of chapters two and three, and their embodiment of the main text of Debray's theoretical argument, we can see how Na'na''s novel has developed an almost identical technical and temporal structure. After a "preface" of two pages, the main text of the novel concerns itself quite precisely with Nadiyah's attempt to free her own present from the inescapable reality of her past and this part of the novel oscillates continuously between past events and the present-time narrating moment in reflecting this fundamental conflict of time within the life of the main protagonist. The novelistic resolution that takes place in the third part of the novel, the epilogue, is where narrative time ceases to regress and, at last, begins to move forward towards Nadiyah's return and her future hopes in resuming the search for meaning (whereas Frank returns to the past in his quest for authenticity).

The striking composition and distinctive asymmetrical arrangement of both works casts doubt on the possibility that this has occurred coincidentally and it seems that the principal aim of Na'na' was to somehow personify Debray's theoretical paradigm in the form of a novel that would investigate the specificity of the Palestinian attempt at armed insurrection. In achieving this aim, the author seems to have had two firm directives in mind: to challenge the theory's universal relevance outside the Far Eastern and Latin American contexts (in comparison to the particular dilemma of displaced peoples and nations such as the Kurds and the Palestinians) and, beyond the theory, to investigate the personal dynamics of the struggle and the human face of the revolutionary cause from an unusual female perspective – that of the woman fighter. It is interesting to note that Na'na' has, like the other authors in this study, illustrated specific phenomena of female desire within the novel form. These differences in the mimetic system concern the lack of intensive rivalry between female protagonists and the idiosyncrasy of female desire in tending towards the convergence and/or absorption of the mediator's personality in a kind of symbiotic union. The concept of unity and union is a frequent element of the text and the elusive nature of most of the characters coupled with their apparent interchangeability at times suggests a new overtly textual, rather than psychological, dimension to this mimetic expression of symbiosis.[53] In this way, *al-Watan fi al-'aynayn* establishes further alternative criteria for the redefinition of the Girardian paradigm of triangular desire and a further acknowledgement of women writers' firm commitment to the production of politically charged fiction based on fact.

Revising the Feminist Agenda

At least three of the above novels have been dealt with by one or more of the feminist critics that I take to task elsewhere in this paper. As far as I am aware, not one of them expresses more than a vague understanding of either the wider political context in which the works were written, or of the political issues and world events that have played a major part in structuring of the text itself. Many of these critics exhibit an extraordinary tendency to discuss women's lives and their writing as though they have occurred in some kind of political vacuum. I suppose, in all fairness to the critics, if feminist protest happens to be the focal point of a particular reading strategy, then other non-feminist elements might easily become marginalised, but Cooke, Accad and even al-Qadi go one step further by actually denying that works like *Ana ahya* have any political resonance at all. Accad simply ignores the abundant political analogies in *Ana ahya* and reduces all the events of the novel to symbolic portrayals of the principal character's self-centredness. In a fairly recent article, Accad's reading of Lina's encounter with the Palestinian guerrilla fighter and his chest wound (see above) leads her to surmise that:

> Lina fails to recognise the significance of the Palestinian's disappearance which is a symbol of her own inability to make meaningful contact with other human beings. With a little forcing, she can go so far as to soothe the guerrilla's wound, or provide an uncritical audience for Baha's political ramblings but she cannot give either of them the moral strength and understanding that proceed from unselfish participation in another person's world.[54]

I am somewhat surprised, not to say suspicious, that a self-respecting feminist like Accad appears to be suggesting that Lina has neither been understanding nor supportive enough of Baha'. In my reading of the text, Baha' appears to be an arrogant, hypocritical bore whose egocentric, chauvinistic behaviour regarding Lina and other women is acutely apparent. Indeed, I believe that Baha' is deliberately depicted as such by Ba'albakki to emphasise the inherent hypocrisies of the political dogma he expounds. If Accad had paid more attention to Baha's narrative function in this respect within the overall structure of the novel, she might have drawn quite different conclusions about Lina's character. Indeed, the self-centredness that Accad criticises in Lina is, ironically, a reflection of Accad's own feminist egocentrism in assuming that the main female character is also the principal focus of any female-authored narrative. I hope that my paradigmatic reading of the text has highlighted the need to pay attention to all the functional characters and the way in which different elements interact with each other to maintain the formal balance of the narrative. A reading that draws upon all these interconnected parts not only avoids the trap of focusing on one textual actor whilst actively reducing the significance of others, but also obliges the reader to consider, somewhat more thoughtfully, the exact purpose and function of each character and his/her position within the textual landscape. This means that we need to search beyond a surface reading of the text; to delve into the novel's ideological psyche in order to understand *what* the text is really trying to represent on a deeper level and, perhaps more importantly, *why*. Only then does *Ana ahya* cease to appear solely concerned with one woman's search for selfhood, and begin to reveal its complex ideological debates on the nature of Lebanon's national identity which are discussed via Lina's own quest for identity, hence forming the fundamental structural framework of the narrative.

Khalifah's *al-Sabbar* is a far more explicit exploration of the politics of occupation, offering less than a handful of interesting women characters, and as such has managed to escape the attention of the feminist critics. The policy appears to be, "no feminist protest, no criticism", which excludes an excellent novel from the arena of feminist critical discourse, while earlier, less competent works which revolve more directly around Khalifah's awakening feminist consciousness are, in general, afforded much more attention. Similarly, *Beirut 75's* distinctly allegorical subtexts constantly play second fiddle to al-Samman's feminist comment, while Hamidah Na'na''s *al-Watan fi al-'aynayn* has been almost totally ignored in Western studies, possibly because its uncompromising intellectualism, continual analysis of ideological discourses and fascination with theoretical concerns does not easily fit in with the usual definition of feminist rebellion.

Several Arab women writers that I know (including Layla Ba'albakki, Hanan al-Shaykh and Emily Nasrallah), have expressed their irritation at the way in which Western feminist critics have appropriated their works and manipulated their contents to serve a feminist agenda that is largely alien to the authors themselves. They are disturbed not only by what they perceive as the antagonistic, overtly anti-male stance of some feminist critics, but also by a sense of frustration that their writing is somehow being marginalised, almost ghettoised, into a female literary enclosure in which they are disenfranchised from mainstream literature.

They complain of not wanting to be known as "feminist" writers, but just as writers; not wanting to be renowned for their stance on women, but for their general outlook on life as well as the calibre of their prose; not wanting to receive critical acclaim for their abilities to highlight inequalities between the sexes, but for their skill in depicting a broad spectrum of inequities, injustices and contradictions in the Arab world and beyond. It is sadly paradoxical that some critics who seek to centralise Arab women's discourse have simultaneously marginalised, ostracised and alienated both the producers of that discourse and their works. It seems doubly ironic to me also, that the Western critics who persistently expose and condemn the omnipotent influence of patriarchy on Arab women's lives, should be caught so entirely off their guard when contemporary patriarchal politics emerge as a structural component in Arab women's writing. Surely the time has come for us to *really* listen to what Arab women writers are saying and to acknowledge, like the long-suffering 'Adil in *al-Sabbar*, that there is always more than one dimension to the picture.

NOTES

1 Taken from an interview with Ghadah al-Samman entitled '*al-Thawrah wa al-jinsiyyah wa al-thawrah al-shamilah* (The Sexual Revolution and the Total Revolution) in *Mawaqif*, 2, 12 (1970), pp. 68–73. The English translation appears in Elizabeth Warnock Fernea and Basima Qattan Bezirgan (eds.), *Middle Eastern Muslim Women Speak* (Austin: University of Texas Press, 1977), pp. 391–9. The extract quoted above appears on p. 392.

2 Elizabeth Mckee, *Narrative Structure and Triangular Desire in the Novels of Levantine Women Writers, 1958–1991*, unpublished Ph.D. dissertation, School of Oriental and African Studies, University of London, 1995. Most of the material in this article, particularly the abbreviated readings of the novels, have been extracted and/or adapted from my thesis.

3 Cooke neglects to mention other important women writers of the nineteenth century and early twentieth century such as Hind Nawfal (1859–1920), Labibah Hashim (1880–1947), Julia Tu'mah Dimashqiyyah (1880–1954), 'Afifah Karam (1883–1925), Salma Sayigh (1889–1953) and Hana Kasbani Kurani (1870–98). Similarly Cooke does not seem to be familiar with the works of two contemporary writers who are included in my study, the Palestinian Liyanah Badr and the Syrian Hamidah Na'na'.

4 Miriam Cooke, 'Arab Women Writers' in M. M. Badawi (ed.), *The Cambridge History of Arabic Literature: Modern Arabic Literature* (Cambridge: Cambridge University Press, 1992), p. 453. Cooke has overlooked a long tradition of fictional works with political overtones written by women. In his book *The Genesis of Arabic Narrative Discourse*, Sabry Hafez refers to three novels about the 1908 Ottoman *coup d'état*, two of which were written by women: *Hasna' Salunik* (The Belle of Salonica) (1909) by Labibah Mikha'il Sawaya and *Bayn 'arshayn* (Between Two Thrones (1911) by Faridah 'Afliyyah. Hafez comments that: "Although these three novels are of secondary literary merit, they were of considerable political signific-ance, and the fact that two out of the three authors are female indicates women's involvement in political life." See his *The Genesis of Arabic Narrative Discourse: A Study in the Sociology of Modern Arabic Literature* (London: Saqi, 1993), p. 76.

5 In Cooke's 'Arab Women Writers' and in *War's Other Voices: Women Writers on the Lebanese Civil War* (Cambridge: Cambridge University Press, 1988). A similar tone is adopted in the introduction to Miriam Cooke and Margot Badran (eds.), *Opening the Gates: A Century of Arab Feminist Writing* (London: Virago, 1990), which is, admittedly, an anthology dedicated to the feminist cause but nevertheless seems to imply that women writers have always adopted an ardently feminist stance in their writing and deal solely with personal gender issues.

6 Here Idris is referring to the turmoil caused by the creation of the State of Israel in 1948 and the 1952 *coup d'état* in Egypt.

7 Suhayl Idris, *al-Adab*, No. 1 (Beirut: Dar al-Adab, 1953) p. 1. This translation is taken from M. M. Badawi's 'Commitment in Arabic Literature' in his book *Modern Arabic Literature and the West* (London: Ithaca Press, 1985), pp. 12–13. Also in the *Journal of World History*, 14 (1972).

8 Evelyne Accad, *Sexuality and War: Literary Masks of the Middle East* (New York: New York University Press, 1990), p. 7.

9 See Raman Selden and Peter Widdowson, *A Reader's Guide to Contemporary Literary Theory*, 3rd edn (London: Harvester Wheatsheaf, 1993), pp. 76–7.

10 Accad, *Sexuality and War*, p. 7.

11 Elaine Showalter, *A Literature of Their Own* (London: Virago, 1978), p. 285.

12 Toril Moi, *Sexual/Textual Politics: Feminist Literary Theory* (London: Methuen, 1985), pp. 10–11.

13 One wonders for instance if Hamidah Na'na' has been left out of the majority of these studies because of her explicitly militant, pro-resistance message in her first novel, *al-Watan fi al-'aynayn*.

14 See generally Lucien Goldmann, *Towards a Sociology of the Novel*, translated from the French by Alan Sheridan (London: Tavistock Publications, 1975). For a summarised discussion of Goldmann's work, see Selden, *A Reader's Guide*, pp. 86–8.

15 These may be roughly translated as *I Live!*, *Wild Thorns*, *Beirut 75* and *A Homeland in the Heart*.

16 I use the term 'introductory' in order to emphasise that the following readings are far from exhaustive analyses of the novels. They are extracts from much longer and more comprehensive readings submitted as part of my Ph.D. dissertation (see above, footnote 2).

17 For a full explanation of triangular desire see René Girard, *Deceit, Desire and the Novel: Self and Other in Literary Structure* (Baltimore: John Hopkins, 1965).

18 Layla Ba'albakki, *Ana ahya* (Beirut: Dar Majallat Shi'r, 1963). First published in 1958.

19 Iman al-Qadi, *al-Riwayah al-nisawiyah fi bilad al-sham* (Beirut: Dar al-Ahali, 1992), pp. 209–17.

20 We may safely presume that al-Qadi is referring to the first generation in regard to the thirty-five-year period covered by her study rather than the entire history of women's writing in Greater Syria.

21 I am using the term "feminist" to emphasise my understanding of the Arabic concept of *al-Riwayah al-nisawiyah* as meaning "feminist novels" rather than "women's novels" which does not seem to capture the essence of the adjectival usage in regard to the content of the book. I regretfully acknowledge the conceptual limitations and the potential reductiveness of the term "feminist" in this respect also.

22 al-Qadi, *al-Riwayah al-nisawiyah*, pp. 209–10.

23 Seymour Chatman, *Story and Discourse* (Ithaca, N.Y.: Cornell University Press, 1980), p. 107.

24 Kaufmann, *Existentialism*, pp. 372–3.

25 D. D. McElroy, *Existentialism and Modern Literature* (New York: Citadel Press, 1963), p. 20.

26 Two important concerns of Bakhtinian dialogism are authority as authorship and authority as power. Michael Holquist states that, "The author of a novel . . . can manipulate the other not only as an other, but as a *self*. This is, in fact, what the very greatest writers have always done, but the paradigmatic example is provided by Dostoevsky, who so successfully permits his characters to have the status of an 'I' standing over against the claims of his own authorial other that Bakhtin felt

compelled to coin the special term 'polyphony' to describe it." *Dialogism: Bakhtin and his World* (London: Routledge, 1990), p. 34. I have employed Bakhtin's term here in order to emphasise the way in which Ba'albakki allows Lina to establish her own subjectivity and to underline how this subjectivity, conflicting with that of other characters, becomes a textual embodiment of the ideological clashes at play. Ba'albakki's technique in eschewing authorial totalitarianism is highlighted by, and contrasted with, her characters' apparent disdain for the other. Lina regards her fellow characters as having the otherness of mere things, lacking any subjectivity, and Baha' does likewise in his objectification of womankind. It is through recognition of her own monologic tyranny and Baha's pseudo-Marxist extremism that Lina is able to achieve conversion.

27 See Lucien Goldmann's discussion of parallels between the theories of Lukács and René Girard in *Towards a Sociology of the Novel* (London: Tavistock, 1975).

28 Sahar Khalifah, *al-Sabbar* (Beirut: Dar al-Adab, 1976). Translated by Trevor LeGassick and Elizabeth Fernea as *Wild Thorns* (London: Saqi, 1985). First published in English as *al-Subar* (Jerusalem: Galileo Limited, 1976).

29 Ghalib Halasa, '*al-Sabbar:* riwayat al-waqi' al-filistini', *Mawaqif*, 72 (Summer 1993), 72–83.

30 *al-Sabbar*, pp. 53–4; *Wild Thorns*, pp. 56–7.

31 *al-Sabbar*, p. 28; *Wild Thorns*, p. 29.

32 Here we can see the significance of the double meaning in the work's title since *al-Sabbar* might also be translated as either "cactus" or "the patient one".

33 *al-Sabbar*, p. 58; *Wild Thorns*, p. 63.

34 *al-Sabbar*, p. 60; *Wild Thorns*, p. 65.

35 Ghadah al-Samman, *Beirut 75*, 5th edn (Beirut: Manshurat Ghadah al-Samman, 1987), first published in 1975.

36 See Ghali Shukri, *Ghadah al-Samman bila ajnihah*, 2nd edn (Beirut: Dar al-Tali'ah, 1977). Hanan 'Awwad, *Arab Causes in the Fiction of Ghadah al-Samman, 1961–1975* (Quebec: Editions Naaman, 1983) and 'Afif Farraj, *al-Hurriyyah fi adab al-mar'ah* (Beirut: Mu'assaset al-Abhath, 1985).

37 'Awwad, *Arab Causes*, p. 115.

38 Ghadah al-Samman, '*al-Matlub tahrir al-mar'ah min al-taharrur*' (The necessity to liberate woman from liberation); *al-A'mal ghayr al-kamilah: Saffarat indhar dakhil ra'si* (Beirut: Manshurat Ghadah al-Samman, 1980), p. 83. Translation from 'Awwad, *Arab Causes*, p. 114.

39 *Beirut 75*, p. 12, my translation. All translations are mine unless otherwise stated.

40 See David Gilmour, *Lebanon: The Fractured Country* (London: Sphere Books, 1987).

41 Hamidah Na'na', *al-Watan fi al-'aynayn* (Beirut: Dar al-Adab, 1986). First published in 1979 and recently translated into English by Martin Asser and published as *The Homeland* (Reading: Garnet Publishing, 1995).

42 The Palestinian military strongholds in Amman were considered a threat to Jordanian sovereignty.

43 Such as the use of the names of two cities, Iram and Harran, which seem to be representative of the modern-day cities of Damascus and Amman. The name Iram comes from a reference made in verse seven of Surat al-Fajr in the Qur'an to "Iram of the Pillars" (*Iram dhat al-'imad*). Netton's *Popular Dictionary of Islam* says that,

"Although most probably the name of a town, commentators have differed widely over its precise identification. Suggestions include the town of 'Ad, Damascus and the early site of Alexandria," p. 124. Similarly, Harran has been identified as the Roman Carrhae which was a city in Northern Syria that played an important role in the development of mediaeval philosophy. Netton informs us that, "It was the home of the Sabaeans whose theology was much influenced by Neoplatonism; among a variety of distinguished scholars produced by the Sabaeans was the great 3rd/9th century Thabit b. Qurra. Harran also became home for the Alexandrian philosophers from the middle of the 3rd/9th century," p. 97. From Ian Richard Netton's *A Popular Dictionary of Islam* (London: Curzon Press Ltd, 1992).

44 "Why is the Song of Songs not written for the absent Nadiyah?", *al-Watan*, p. 204.

45 "You told them everything and your friend was killed as a result of your confession and after that you tried, tried in vain, to love yourself . . . You fell to your knees and called out to your murdered companion: Oh, All forgiving Messiah! I kneel before you not really knowing what has driven me here . . .", *ibid.*, p. 202.

46 "After the fifth of June, the men fell into the depths of the valley of fire where Medusa transformed them into black rocks unable to move or to love," *ibid.*, p. 156.

47 "The building was still in the same place but no doubt they would be searching for a long time for some justice to occupy it." *Ibid.*, p. 180. Alluding to the eternal search for authentic value on all levels of existence and not only a reference to the injustice of the Palestinian plight.

48 "From that spot, where the sea lives in silence and the nearby mountains are waiting, I learnt to draw the world starting from the Gulf of al-Iskandarun . . . the world doesn't start anywhere else . . . and at school I learnt that Palestine was quite near and it was possible to reach it by boat. As I got older, I discovered the whole truth – that the road to Palestine passes through the heart of the Arab cities. My father is so proud of his grandfathers who liberated Jerusalem. He's proud of his affiliation to the other Kurdish chieftains . . . the story of my noble origins spun repeatedly around my ears," *ibid.*, pp. 28–9.

49 She does, in fact, marry again but the marriage is a charade. She says, "I was only with him while I waited for Abu Mashhur," *ibid.*, p. 143.

50 See Iman al-Qadi, *al-Riwayah al-nisawiyah fi bilad al-sham: al-Simat al-nafsiyah wa al-fanniyah, 1950–1985* (Damascus: Dar al-Ahali, 1992) for a detailed structural breakdown and diagrammatic account of the novel's layout, pp. 366–88.

51 Régis Debray, *Revolution in the Revolution? Armed Struggle and Political Struggle in Latin America*, trans. Bobbye Ortiz (Harmondsworth: Penguin Books, 1967). First published in France by François Maspéro in 1967 as *Révolution dans la Révolution?*

52 Iman al-Qadi also points out instances of plagiarism of words from Debray's autobiographical work entitled *Memoirs of a Petit Bourgeois*; see *al-Riwayah al-nisawiyah*, pp. 386–7. Unfortunately the limitations of time, space and the theoretical framework of this article prevent me from a more detailed investigation of the parallels between the two.

53 The convergence and interchangeability to which I refer are complex narrative phenomena which are never explicitly stated but are always made implicit by the blurred character distinctions between, for instance, Frank and Debray; Frank's friend, Abu Mashhur and Che Guevara; Nadiyah and Frank when they swap roles; Khalid and Frank when the latter allows his principles to slide; Nadiyah and Frank's

murdered comrade – she seems to be the replacement mediator after his untimely death. Similarly, oppositional combinations occur such as Abu Mashhur and Frank, the fighter and the theorist, the combination of whom would amount to the type of intellectual and practical revolutionary portrayed in the character of Nadiyah. This constant fluctuation, mirroring and contrastive opposition heightens the intensity of the plot where ideals and idealised images are frequently stripped of their prestigious veneer to reveal their worthlessness and vice versa. Again, the author appears to be parodying the use of generalisations by creating a deliberately unspecific atmosphere within the text. Also, the guerrilla combatants' names are *noms de guerre* and so their identities are never really fixed or certain.

54 Evelyne Accad, 'Rebellion, Maturity, and the Social Context: Arab Women's Special Contribution to Literature' in Judith E. Tucker (ed.), *Arab Women: Old Boundaries, New Frontiers* (Bloomington and Indianapolis: Indiana University Press, 1993) pp. 224–53.

SEVEN

CRIMES OF HONOUR AND THE CONSTRUCTION OF GENDER IN ARAB SOCIETIES

Lama Abu-Odeh

This article is a discussion of crimes of honour in the Arab world. A paradigmatic example of a crime of honour is the killing of a woman by her father or brother for engaging in, or being suspected of engaging in, sexual practices before or outside marriage. On a simple and immediate level, this article calls for an end to these crimes for their obvious cruelty. All Arab laws or judicial practices that legitimise or sanction these crimes should be abolished.

On a more complicated level, an attempt is made here to identify the role that these crimes play in the production and reproduction of gender relations in contemporary Arab life. It contends that these relations are the outcome of a complex triangular interaction between social violence, the crime of honour itself, state violence, the attempt to regulate this crime, and the response by contemporary men and women to the balance between these two types of violence.

The argument of this article is that in the past, the crime has gone largely unregulated, practised as a means of controlling the violators, punishing them for vice and deviancy from the prescribed sexual rules. However, despite the fact that crimes of honour continue to exist to this day and do so on a significant scale, the article argues that their social function has become different.

The intervention of the Arab nationalist elite in the social field, by desegregating gendered social space, has rendered the concept of sexual honour ambiguous. Their intervention in the legal field, through codification, had the purpose of "modernising" a traditional practice, crimes of honour, by defining the limits of its practice: sanctioning it by penalising the violators in certain cases. The legal move that they made could be seen as a means of "containing" the practice of crimes of honour.

The mushrooming of diverse sexual types, for example, the sexy virgin, the virgin of love and the slut (see below) and of sexual practices among women and men are a response to the interaction between social violence and its regulation by means of state violence. There is an added complexity resulting from the fact that the judicial practice through the Arab world of judging incidents of honour has served a double function: trying to contain the practice of the crimes, whilst attempting to co-opt the emergence of new subversive sexual types.

The end picture has the complicated appearance of the crimes being a response to the new sexual practices, their contemporary function, the state regulation and judicial practice being a response to the violence and the sexual practices, and the resistant sexual types being a response to the balance between the two types of violence, social and official.

If indeed the demand to completely abolish crimes of honour is unrealistic, this article argues that these crimes, in so far as their legal sanction is concerned, should be reduced to those of passion. This is a viable move because the spectrum of codification of crimes of honour already existing within the Arab world has, within its parameters, the legal construct of a crime of passion (see the cases of Algeria and Egypt below). What has seemed to prevent the full development of the concept of a crime of passion in these two respective countries is judicial practice which has used alternative legal means to reintroduce the idea of a crime of honour.

I. What is a Crime of Honour?

"Where were you, bitch?" Maria Isa snapped as her daughter, Tina, 16, entered the family apartment.

"Working," Tina shot back.

"We do not accept that you go to work," interrupted Tina's father, Zein.

"Why are you doing this to us?" asked Maria angrily.

"I am not doing anything to you," Tina bristled.

"You are a she-devil," hissed Zein, "and what about the boy who walked you home? He wants to sleep with you in bed, don't you have any shame? Don't you have a conscience? It's fornication."

With that her parents threatened to throw Tina out of the apartment; rebelliously she challenged them to do it.

"Listen, my dear daughter," her father finally replied, "do you know that this is the last day? Tonight you're going to die?"

"Huh?" said Tina bewildered.

"Do you know that you are going to die tonight?"

Suddenly, realising he was serious, Tina let out a long scream. Then there was a crash, and the girl's shrieks became muffled, as if someone were trying to cover her mouth. "Keep still, Tina," her father shouted.

"Mother, please help me," Tina cried.

But her mother would not help. Instead, she held her struggling daughter down as Zein began stabbing Tina in the chest with a seven inch boning knife. "No, please!" Tina cried.

"Shut up!" Her mother shouted.

"No! No!" Tina shrieked.

"Die! Die quickly! Die quickly!" Her father shouted.

Tina managed to scream again.

"Quiet, little one," her father said, stabbing her the last of six times.

"Die, my daughter, die!"[1]

The Legal Codification of Crimes of Honour

The locus of crimes of honour in the Jordanian Penal Code (no. 16, 1960) is Article 340. The first Article of three in a section entitled, "Excuse in Murder", Article 340 states:

i) He who catches his wife, or one of his female unlawfuls committing adultery with another, and he kills, wounds, or injures one or both of them, is exempt from any penalty.

ii) He who catches his wife, or one of his female ascendants or descendants or sisters with another in an unlawful bed, and he kills or wounds or injures one or both of them, benefits from a reduction of penalty.

This Article owes its historical origin to two legal sources, that are not unharmonious when it comes to the issue of "crimes of honour". These two sources are the Ottoman Penal Code of 1858 and the French Penal Code of 1810.[2]

Article 324 in the French Penal Code[3] (which was abolished by Article 17, Law no. 617/75 issued on 7 November 1975) reads:

Pourra bénéficier d'une excuse absolutoire quiconque, ayant surpris son conjoint, son ascendante, sa descendante ou sa sœur en
flagrant délit d'adultère ou de rapports sexuels illégitimes avec un
tiers se sera rendu coupable sur la personne de l'un ou l'autre de
ces derniers, d'homicide ou de lésion non prémédités.

L'auteur de l'homicide ou de la lésion pourra bénéficier d'une
excuse atténuante s'il a surpris son conjoint, son ascendante, sa
descendante ou sa sœur avec un tiers dans une attitude équivoque.

Article 188 in the Ottoman Code reads:

He who has seen his wife or any of his female unlawfuls with
another in a state of "ugly" adultery[4] and then beat, injured, or
killed one or both of them will be exempt from penalty. And he
who has seen his wife or one of his female unlawfuls with another
in an unlawful bed and then beat, injured or killed one or both of
them, will be excused.

From the Ottoman Code, we notice that Article 340 of the Jordanian
Penal Code adopts the expression "female unlawfuls" and that of the
"unlawful bed". From the French Code, the Article borrows the expression "ascendante, descendante", and the idea of a reduction of penalty
stated in the second section of the Article as "une excuse atténuante".

Not only does a provision similar to that of Article 340 of the Jordanian
Penal Code exist in almost every Arab penal code, but this is also the case
in the Turkish and many European codes as well: Spanish, Portuguese,
Italian (abolished in 1979) and as we have seen above, the French until
as late as 1975 (abolished by Article 17 of the law no. 617/75 of 1975).[5]

Arab penal codes differ among themselves on two issues. Some limit
the application of the Article to situations of adultery; the Egyptian,
Tunisian, Libyan and the Kuwaiti, and the only excuse they use is that of
reduction, not exemption. While others expand the application of the
article to situations of the "unlawful bed" (Jordanian) or "*attitude équivoque*" (Syrian, Lebanese) and use for them the excuse of reduction and
exemption for the cases of adultery. The Iraqi Code is unique in that it
covers both the situation of adultery and what it calls "her presence in
one bed with her lover" but it gives them both the same excuse namely
that of reduction – three years.

The other issue on which Arab penal codes differ is that of "who
benefits from the excuse". The Syrian and Lebanese Codes adopt the

French terminology (wife, female ascendants, descendants and sister) so that the husband, the son, the father and the brother benefit. The Jordanian Code used this terminology in the second section of the Article and used the Ottoman expression in the first section (wife or female unlawfuls). This expands the beneficiaries to a considerable degree since a female unlawful includes every woman that the man cannot marry either for blood, marriage (in-law) or nursing reasons, which makes the disparity between the first and second section of the article quite significant and almost mysterious. The Iraqi Code used an expression similar to that of the first section of the Jordanian Article, "his wife or one of his female unlawfuls" to cover both cases of adultery and "one bed". The Egyptian, Kuwaiti and Tunisian Codes limit the beneficiaries to that of the husband, and the Libyan Code to that of the husband, father and brother. The Algerian Code is unique in that it treats both husband and *wife* as beneficiaries of the excuse, which it limits to situations of adultery.[6]

Structurally speaking, the codes seem to be distributed on a spectrum with two opposite poles. The first is best exemplified by the Algerian Code in which both husband and wife benefit from a reduction of penalty when she catches the other committing adultery. The other pole is best exemplified by the Jordanian Code which allows men to benefit from both a reduction and an exemption of penalty if they catch one of their female unlawfuls committing adultery or in an unlawful bed with her lover. The difference between these two ends could very well be the difference between the idea of a crime of passion, the former, and a crime of honour, the latter.

Arab Criminal Jurisprudence

Reading Arab criminal jurisprudence that comments on these provisions is an exercise in monotony. Almost all Arab jurists "borrow" the bulk of what they have to say from Egyptian jurisprudence, reproducing what it says, sometimes word for word, and barely commenting on the differences between the code of their own country and that of Egypt.[7] Not only that, but Arab jurists often use cases decided in Egypt as tools for explaining basic legal concepts, and rarely does one find a given jurist engaging in a discussion of cases decided in his own country.[8] And if the legal decisions made in the jurists' country are at all engaged with, it is only for the purposes of either confirming what the Egyptian commentators have said about their own code, showing the similarity or illustrating the difference between the Egyptian and the given country's code. In all of these writings the Egyptian Code/jurisprudence stands as the model/focal point, from which the commentator then sees his task as either to repeat, adapt, or show commonalities with, or differences from, the Egyptian jurisprudence. I have not seen in any of these publications a concerted effort to take the mass of court decisions pertaining to this given topic and treat them as an independent historical structure that is ridden with conflicts and contradictions peculiar to itself, thus lending the reader a unique insight into how crimes of honour have been judicially addressed in the particular country.

The classical jurisprudential treatment of crimes of honour

The Arab commentator typically starts with stating the provision in his country's penal code. Then he proceeds to briefly give us the "wisdom" behind this provision. It usually runs as follows:

> The legislature has taken into account the psychological state of mind that hits the husband whose honour had been violated, the most precious thing that he possesses. At the moment that he catches his wife committing adultery he will no doubt lose his reason and kill his wife and her partner.[9]

No commentator bothers to attack or even examine this rationalisation. The only exception is Laure Mughayzil, a Lebanese lawyer, who bases her critique on the argument that implementing provisions like this has the effect of continuously reproducing a tribal mentality that is inconsistent with "intellectual and social development in Lebanon".[10] She also argues that these provisions violate the principles of freedom and equality provided for in both the International Charter of Human Rights and the Lebanese Constitution.[11] The call for equality between men and women indeed is what some Arab (male) commentators propose, after giving us the benefit of their explanation of the "wisdom" of these provisions. This demand for equality between men and women is, in their view, met, if women are given equal benefit of the exemptory or reductive excuse. This results in a moving rhetorical argument made for the sake of women:

For isn't this the biggest shock she would have in her life? Isn't that the biggest betrayal by her husband that would injure her pride, integrity and honour? And isn't she, after all, human of flesh and blood with feelings that could get hurt too?[12]

After that we are provided with the commentator's elucidation of the three conditions that have to be present for the Article to apply: firstly, the relationship of the accused to the victim (husband, brother, son). Secondly, "Catching the woman committing adultery" which means that two elements are necessary, the surprise element, and the necessity for the woman to be caught red-handed, in flagrante delicto. Lastly, the act of killing has to be immediate and impulsive.

The commentator then proceeds to cite Egyptian decisions on the interpretation of the second condition. For instance, the Egyptian Court of Cassation has decided that if the husband suspected, but was not sure, that his wife was having sex with another man, and so pretending to go to the market, he hid in the house until the other man came and then killed him when the latter started to touch the wife, then there is still an element of surprise, and the husband can benefit from the excuse. The same Court also decided that a wife is caught red-handed when caught by her husband with her underwear placed next to that of her partner, despite the fact that the husband has not witnessed the actual sexual act between them.[13]

About the third condition the commentator tells us that if enough time has passed for the accused to have calmed down then he clearly does not benefit from the excuse. The Egyptian Court of Cassation has decided that if a man catches his wife and her partner committing adultery and he kills him but the wife escapes to her family, and if two hours later he finds her and kills her, then he does not benefit from the excuse. But if, as the court decided in another case, he goes to the kitchen to bring a knife as soon as he sees them, and then uses it to kill them both, then the husband benefits from the excuse.[14]

Having done all of the above, the commentator proceeds to discuss the penalty for the crime once the three conditions are met, and the dispute between criminal jurists, usually French, as to whether the reduction of the penalty affects its classification, from felony to misdemeanour.

The practice of different Arab treatise writers of simply repeating the Egyptian commentary, has effectively "fetishised" the Egyptian style of regulating the crime. As a matter of fact, and as we will see later, the Egyptian provision adheres more closely to the idea of passion rather than that of honour; it limits the beneficiaries to that of husband and only in cases of adultery, granting him merely a reduction. This could hardly be said of all the other codes. The difference is not simply an issue of detail, which seems to be the way the commentators have dealt with it. For instance, the commentator might note that while the beneficiary in the Egyptian Code is only the husband, in his own national code, it is the husband and the father. Being formalists, the commentators fail to see these differences as choices by the different countries that reflect policy conflicts.

Why is it that the Egyptian Code chooses the husband as beneficiary, while the Libyan one chooses father, brother and husband? How are these varied choices inspired? Clearly every choice is an act of "picking": adopting some elements, dropping others, a simultaneous act of inclusion and exclusion. Let us imagine that the choices in the codes are taken from a spectrum that has on its two poles, as I suggested earlier, the idea of pure honour on the one end and of pure passion on the other. Then we come to realise that every code that is situated in between the poles is some compromise on either idea (honour/passion) in its pure form. This compromise reflects an attempt to strike a balance between two conflicting ideas, each pulling in an opposite direction.

In order to understand the variations in the codes we have to get to grips with the ideas of honour and passion. We will take up the idea of honour first. And we will do so by looking at it from an anthropological perspective. The purpose of the discussion is to understand the honour/ shame social system that produces the crime of honour. The codes can be seen as a legal intervention in this universe of honour killings. We will see that their intervention takes the form of legitimising certain killings and de-legitimising others. For instance, all codes seem to make the radical move of de-legitimising the paradigmatic model of honour killings: the killing of a woman by her father or brother when she is discovered not to be a virgin on her wedding night. We notice that not one of these codes grants an excuse, exemption or reduction, for such a case. When we understand the prominence of this kind of killing in an honour-dominated world, then we get a sense of the seriousness of the codes' intervention.

The following section will consider honour relations in what I will call the "traditional text": a description of a society in which honour relations prevail with clarity and predictability. In this society, the transgression of boundaries almost immediately results in a crime of honour. Having identified what this society is like, I will, by way of contrasting with the social system of honour, reconstruct one that is based on passion. The point of the exercise is to understand the two conflictual ideals between which each code tries to strike some balance.

An Anthropological Discussion of Honour in Arab Societies

Virginity as the regulatory practice of gender

Writings about the importance of women's virginity before marriage in the Arab world are not lacking.[15] Arab women, according to the ideal model, are expected to abstain from any kind of sexual practice before they get married. The hymen, in this context, becomes the socio-physical sign that both assures, guarantees virginity and gives the woman a stamp of respectability and virtue. The wedding night, therefore, bears phenomenal importance for Arab women, since it is that crucial time when society is about to make a judgment on their propriety.[16] Some honour crimes are known to occur precisely then, when a woman's failing to bleed as a result of penetration to break her hymen, is taken as a failure of the social test. In the scenario that follows she is "taken back" by the groom and his family to her own family, who in turn might kill her for having shamed them. Only her bleeding in death can erase the shame brought about by her failure to bleed during sex on her wedding night.

The discourse on gender and the discourse on virginity in Arab culture criss-cross so intricately that they are hardly distinguishable. To be an Arab woman is to engage in daily practices, an important part of which is to be a virgin. A heterosexuality that is honour/shame-based such as the Arab one, demands, under the sanction of social penalty, that the performance of femaleness be "in conjunction with", "inseparable from", "part of" the performance of virginity. Put another way, the disciplinary production of femaleness in Arab culture stylises the body that is called female as virginal. The hymen, in this context, comes to have the double function of being a mark of virginity and of delineating the boundaries of the body that is called female. This, indeed, is what distinguishes it from the male body, since the latter can bear no such mark of virginity. When I say, "can bear no such mark", I do not mean biologically, because men do not have a hymen, but culturally, because the culture does not go out of its way to find means of marking the male body as virginal.

It is almost impossible to list the daily practices that are necessary for the construction of the virgin/female body in Arab culture. One way of doing it would be to look at it in a "regressive" fashion: women need to abstain from any sexual activity before marriage, and from any act that might lead to sexual activity, and from any act that might lead to an act that might lead to sexual activity. The further back we are in the regression, the more fuzzy the list of actions involved is. Every prohibitive demand she complies with constructs her simultaneously as female and as virgin.

> If you want me to count the do's and the don'ts, the list would go on forever. It seems that everything is *aib* (shame) for girls.[17]

The function of these prohibitive demands is not only the preservation of actual virginity but the production of the public effect of virginity. In other words, the physical attachment of the hymen to the body, needs to be evidenced and publicised through an elaborate performance for the benefit of the social audience.[18] Thus, the hymen becomes displaced from its biological vessel, the vagina, onto the body as a whole, "hymenising" it and producing it as a body called female. But then it is displaced again onto the social space where the female body is allowed to move/be, encircling it as a social hymen that delimits its borders. Gender female performance covers all three meanings together, so that Arab women are supposed to bleed on their wedding night as a result of the breaking of the hymen, and they are supposed to perform a "public" virginity with a certain body "style", the body moving within a defined and delimited social space. Each one of the above borders, the vaginal, the bodily, and the social is enforced through a set of regulations and prohibitions that the woman is not supposed to violate.

> I am always being told, you can't smoke because you are an Arab woman, or you can't dress that way because you are an Arab woman, and if I sit in a café with a male friend people immediately begin to gossip about me.[19]

A crime of honour can occur when any of the above borders are crossed. Killing a woman because she fails to bleed on her wedding night is only one possible scenario for an honour crime. Honour/shame-based heterosexuality usually requires "less" as evidence of failure in performance. In certain rural localities, a woman might suffer the violence of honour if she is spotted conversing with a man behind a fence, or, in lower-class urban neighbourhoods, if she is seen leaving the car of a strange man. In both these instances, the woman is seen as having "jeopardised" not her vaginal hymen, but her physical and social one. She moved with a body and in a space where she is not supposed to be.[20]

There are, however, sanctions that support this kind of heterosexuality and that precede the moment of the honour crime to preclude its happening. Through an elaborate system of commands and prohibitions, girls "learn" their performance at a very young age. The culture guards itself against possible violations by devising sanctions less violent than death that are meant to preclude it, such as physical abuse, spacial entrapment, segregation, the institution of gossip and reputation. "Because you are a girl, and people will talk if you do this", is rhetorically how women come to acquire their gendered subjectivity.

> From the time we were very small, my brother and I shared the same friends, nearly all boys, most of whom were the children of our neighbours. The boys remained my companions until I grew up – that is until I was about eleven when suddenly I was required to restrict myself to the company of girls and women . . . Being separated from the companions of my childhood was a painful experience.[21]

Marriage circumvents the performance of biological virginity. Since the absolute majority of women get married, and most at a relatively young age, 15 to 18, the poorer the woman the younger she is likely to be when she marries; this means that they are released early in their lives from the burden of the performance of biological virginity. This, however, leaves intact the social demand for their performance of bodily and social virginity.

What it is to be an Arab man

The man who kills his sister to defend his honour, epitomises in a dramatic way, through his act, the performance of his gender. Virginity, in its expanded sense (the vaginal/the bodily/the social) is also the locus of his gender in that he needs to guard, supervise, and defend against incursions, his women's virginity. In other words to be a man is to engage in daily practices, an important part of which is to assure the virginity of the women in your family. In Arab culture, a man is that person whose sister's virginity is a social question for him.

Ideologically, this is presented for "women's own good" since they are thought vulnerable to a predatory male sexuality. Thus, they are seen to be in need of male protection and tutelage.[22]

Male performance is equally sanctioned by penalties. If a man doesn't intervene by killing his sister once she has shamed him, he suffers a loss of his gender: he is no longer a man (therefore, a wimp, a woman). His performance has suffered a serious failure:[23]

> The husband (brother, father . . .) is expected to control his wife. To control means being aware of all her activities, knowing when she goes out and comes back, where she goes, and who she meets. The relationship between the husband's masculinity and his control over his wife is made clear by the following . . . The husband who does not control his wife is not respected; he is not considered a real man, for his wife rules him.[24]

But even before the situation is such that he has to intervene in a dramatic way, he gives licence, supervises, disciplines "his" women's behaviour so that he experiences his gender rhetorically through statements like, "I will not have my sister do this", or more magnanimously, "I don't mind if my sister does this."

A male university graduate narrated this incident: "I wanted to propose to a neighbour of mine of whom I was very fond. But I changed my mind when I saw a photo of her and a male neighbour. I wouldn't permit my sister to do this, and I would expect my fiancée to be similarly conservative."[25]

But inasmuch as the man is the censor of "his" own women, he is also censored in relation to other men's women. As he is busy cementing the blocks of "his" women's walls (hymens, in the expanded sense), he is also, simultaneously, bumping into similar walls elsewhere (that is, those cemented by other men). As women have internalised the censoring look of men, so have men internalised the censoring look of other men. This has the effect of stylising the space that men, in general, occupy.

One way of representing this is to think of it graphically. Men throw their arms in their women's faces, asking them to stay away, and looking at other men warningly, they say "Don't you dare." But that's not all that's going on: as they send their warning looks to each other, they are also trying to steal a look, a touch, a rub of other men's women.[26]

This being the case, it's always safer therefore, for men to talk to, look at, hold hands with, dance with and to, other men. Gender peace is thus preserved: male space is in that vein stylised.[27]

However, men quite frequently make implicit deals with each other which have the double effect of, on the one hand, nurturing their brotherly bonds, and, on the other, creating a certain *camaraderie* between them in their hunt for women. The male bond is nurtured when men promise each other, through their behaviour, that their friends' sisters are as *haram* (forbidden) to them as their own sisters. In other words, men make deals with each other that they will not try to "sneak" inside the walls cemented by their friends around their own sisters. Having made those deals, always implicitly, with each other, men are allowed to feel trust for each other and a certain *camaraderie* between them is thus created. This *camaraderie* is then exploited for the purposes of trying to "sneak" into the walls cemented by other men, for example men who are not their friends or relatives, or neighbours, or countrymen, depending on the context, and gain some sort of access to their women.

What this means is that Arab men are virgins by default. The culture does not actively seek, stress or demand their virginity. However, it makes it very hard for them not to be, given its stress, demand and invocation of women's virginity. Nothing befalls a man if he is not a virgin, and yet most men find themselves to be so. If they are not, it is only erraticall and infrequently (that is they have sexual experiences in an erratic form, infrequently, and as a result of a constant and difficult negotiation within the economy of space in which they live. So much so, that they often experience themselves as virgins).

Contrasting Honour with Passion

The discussion above reveals that there is a "relatively uniform value system based on complementary codes of honour and shame"[28] that unites Arab societies in the traditional text. The system has roots in the primordial idea of the integration of the individual in the group, where one becomes deeply sensitive to and threatened by public opinion. The index of masculine reputation in this moral universe is women's virginity. Throughout the Arab world, male honour derives from the struggle to retain intact the chastity of the women in the family, and this makes male reputation insecurely dependent upon female sexual conduct. When a man is shamed in this context, through female misbehaviour, he suffers a negation of his masculinity: he becomes reduced to a female, a castrated man. So that honour is not only what women must keep intact to remain alive, but what men should defend fiercely so as not to be reduced to women.

The men who are connected to women in this honour bond are many: father, brother, son, husband. The first two are probably the most prominent, since female misbehaviour could be remedied by husband through divorce, whereas father and brother are forced to behave in a more dramatic way once the occasion arises. The intervention is necessary for them to avoid being perceived as wimps or women by the public.

We have seen how many Arab Codes reconstruct this relationship by showing sympathy for the father, brother, husband: allowing them exemptions from or reductions in penalty. And we have also seen how some of these Codes have reflected the social intolerance for any female sexual behaviour, seeing it as deeply threatening to men's masculinity, by incorporating the idea of the triple hymenisation, unlawful bed, *attitude équivoque*.

However, the codes in fact fall short of legitimating honour killings as they existed in the traditional text. This they do in two ways: first, by excluding from excuse, whether that of exemption or reduction, two types of honour killings prevalent in the traditional text. The killing of a woman because she is found not to be a virgin on her wedding night, and the killing of a woman when she is discovered to be pregnant, are honour crimes that the construction of the codes simply excludes. The exclusion itself is a very radical move by the codifiers that attempts to hit at the heart of the traditional text by barring such cruel acts.[29] Second, the internal construction of the excuse in these codes is inconsistent with the idea of an honour killing. As we have seen above, looking at the commentaries, all codes require "surprise", *flagrante delicto*, and that the woman be killed immediately. Presumably, in a purely honour-dominated world none of these considerations would hold. A woman can commit a dishonourable act, that is reported through gossip to her family male members, who then meet to deliberate and decide to kill her. The killing would still be seen as one of honour. The bifurcation between reduction and exemption in the codes that adopt a distinction between adultery and unlawful bed, *attitude équivoque*, is foreign to the traditional world of honour. In that world, both cases would be excused; and the parties made beneficiaries in the codes fall short of those included by the traditional honour killings. If we take the "unlawfuls" as the paradigmatic model of the beneficiaries in this case, then we find that all codes exclude some or other members of the unlawfuls from their list, including even the Jordanian, which excludes them from the case of "unlawful bed", using instead the expression of ascendants and descendants. Even more, the Algerian code includes wife as beneficiary, which would never be permitted in the traditional honour world. To what, then, can we attribute these departures in the codes from the idea of traditional honour, this exercise of partial de-legitimisation? There appears to be, as indicated above, a rival conception also inherent in the codes, which also determines when it is legitimate for men to kill women. This rival conception is that of "passion".

To the idea of honour, we can now contrast that of passion. We come to see it, accordingly, as a private relationship between a man and a woman, as opposed to a collective one that involves several men related to the woman, who are deeply engaged in defending the public image of their masculinity. In the model of passion, female sexuality is not "fetishised" as the locus of reputation, but seen more as a libidinal goal and the locus of complicated human emotions. Thus the passion relationship is reduced to two people who are sexually involved with each other (man and wife), for whom the sexual misbehaviour of one is an assault on the other's feelings rather than public reputation. The passion model excludes all those other men who are not or cannot be sexually involved with the woman (father, brother, son), and the issue becomes less a matter of castrated masculinity and more of passionate jealousy. When a crime of passion is committed, it is the act of one spouse against his/her adulterous spouse arising from feelings of hurt, jealousy and passion. We have seen how the Egyptian and Algerian Codes reflect this kind of relationship: it is only the injured husband (or wife) who will benefit from a reduction when they catch the other *flagrante delicto* committing adultery. Under this model the concept of triple hymenisation is irrelevant.

But even here, the passion model is not allowed to dominate. Each of these two codes makes its own compromises on the idea of passion. The Egyptian Code, for instance, excludes the wife as beneficiary. The Algerian, on the other hand, includes only spouses, excluding lovers from its list of beneficiaries (lovers are, after all, the paradigmatic parties to a relationship of passion).

Up to this point, this has been a discussion concerning the Codes that lie closest to the passion ideal. But even those that are found at the other end of the spectrum, say the Jordanian Code which is the closest to the concept of honour, are influenced by the ideal of passion. The Jordanian code demands the "passion" requirements of in *flagrante delicto*, surprise, and immediacy in killing, requirements that are not part of the traditional conceptualising of honour.

Conclusion

The different Arab codes that regulate honour killings constitute attempts by the different countries to respond to the private violence of traditional honour. However, this legal intervention effectively promotes a different kind of violence. The form of this violence has inherent in it both the ideas of passion and honour in variable "degrees". For while the intervention seeks to de-legitimise certain honour killings, the most paradigmatic model of non-virginity and pregnancy, it however stops short of substituting honour for passion. By the same token, the codes have incorporated many elements of the crime of passion, namely flagrante delicto and immediacy, but they have stopped short of fully adopting the model of passion. What all the codes seem to have in common is a rejection of both pure honour and pure passion.

II. The Nationalist Project

The question that this section attempts to address is the following: where did the spectrum of honour/passion originate from? Is there an explanation for the variety of ways in which the question of honour killing was resolved in the various codes? In other words, why does the Libyan Code, for instance, have a list of beneficiaries (husband, father, brother) that differs from that of the Egyptian (husband only), when they apply to countries that are adjacent to each other and are, generally speaking, not culturally dissimilar? What is the nature of this legislative activity of selection from a pool of different and confiictual elements? Is it peculiar to the issue of crimes of honour or is it symptomatic of the modern phenomenon of codification in the Arab world? Who were the codifiers, and what ideological motivation did they have when they engaged in the activity of legislative selection? What is it that they were trying to do?

I shall argue that the structure of honour-crime regulation in the different codes, based on the idea of selectivity between various conflictual elements, is symptomatic of the modern exercise of wholesale codification in the newly independent Arab states. In the first and second halves of this century, as different Arab countries gained independence, nationalist elites took over.[30]

These elites were preoccupied with modernising the institutions of the new states, an important part of which was establishing "the rule of law". To that end, they became engaged in the attempt to pass modern codes regulating different areas of life: commercial codes, criminal codes, civil codes, personal status codes. But being nationalist, they also sought to reproduce "tradition" as the locus of the identity of the new "nation". Striking a balance between "tradition" and "modernity" the multiple activities of state building thus became the mark of the government of the nationalist elites. I will first explain how this was the case in the area of codification. After that, I will talk about the nationalists' policies relating to women and the family, in which similar activities of "balancing" were involved.

Any discussion of codification in the Arab world must refer to Sanhuri, the nationalist jurist *par excellence*. His style of codification gives us a clue as to the reason that various Arab codes chose different solutions to the crimes of honour issue. Sanhuri attempted to modernise the civil laws of different Arab countries while at the same time incorporating the *shari'a*.[31] This must be distinguished from the various choices made by the judiciary.

The Judicial Treatment of Crimes of Honour in the Arab World

The Jordanian Court of Cassation

The locus of the discussion of crimes of honour by Arab jurists is the applicable provision of their criminal code, which they comment upon by borrowing the structure of their ideas from Egyptian jurisprudence. But what is striking about all of this, is that by looking at the actual cases decided in Jordan, for instance, between 1953 and 1982, none of this seems to be relevant to the actual treatment of honour killings, or barely so. (This is also true of the Egyptian and Syrian judicial treatment of crimes of honour, see below.) In the case of Jordan the provision that seems to be actually applied to honour killings is not that of Article 340 with its two sections, but a totally different one (Article 98) provided for under the general provisions of the penal code (as opposed to the particular ones which deal with specific crimes such as murder, robbery and rape). Article 98 states:

> He who commits a crime in a fit of fury caused by an unrightful
> and dangerous act on the part of the victim benefits from a reduction
> of penalty.

The Jordanian Court of Cassation (JCC) did not always apply Article 98 to killings of honour. In fact, between 1953 and 1965 (perhaps even before then, but there is no way of knowing for certain because of the lack of criminal case reporting until then) the JCC resisted this idea strongly. During this period, while there is not a single case in which Article 340 was applied, we find many cases in which the JCC is arguing against the application of Article 98. The JCC's resistance took two strands of argumentation.

Primarily, it denied that the female victim's behaviour, seen by the accused as violating his honour, amounted to the commission of an "unrightful and dangerous act" within the terms of Article 98. In fact, the court chose to lay down a very rigorous and precise meaning for this Article by arguing that nothing less than "a minor case of self-defence" would justify applying Article 98. The JCC clearly thought that any dishonourable act that the woman might have committed hardly amounted to a case of "minor self-defence". Thus in a radical decision in 1953 (its radicalness will become shiningly apparent when compared with later cases) the Court decided that a woman's illegitimate pregnancy did not constitute an "unrightful act" within the meaning of Article 98, and accordingly refused to grant the accused a reduction of penalty.[32] In another decision, reported in a vague and ambiguous way, the Court decided:

> The shameless behaviour of the victim is not considered an
> unrightful act for the purposes of Article 93 [the historical origin
> of Article 98 before the Penal Code of 1960 was passed], and can-
> not be seen as calling for a reduction of the penalty, unless the act
> of killing occurred while the defendant was in a state of surprise
> at seeing one of his female unlawfuls in an unlawful bed.[33]

The other strand of argumentation that the JCC used (which starts to become visible in the above decision of 1954) was to treat Article 93 (now 98) as a general provision and Article 333 (now 340) as specific. In other words, the Court argued that killings of honour are specific crimes and consequently only the specific criminal provisions dealing with issues of honour can be applied to them. When there is a specific provision, the Court argued, you cannot apply a general one, because the specific constricts the general.

In 1964, however, the Court's resistance seems to have suffered a backlash. In that year it arrived at a decision that overturned its previous position by conceding the applicability of Article 98 to killings of honour, thus paving the way to a body of Court decisions that have defined the parameters of the crime of honour until our present day. In one case the Court argued that:

> Article 340/2 of the Penal Code provides for a reduction of penalty in a specific case which is that of the defendant catching one of his ascendants, descendants or sisters in an unlawful bed. While Article 98 is more general, the defendant benefits from a reduction if he has committed his crime in a fit of fury caused by the victim's unrightful and somewhat dangerous act.[34]

Contrary to its previous position the JCC now decided that Article 98 applied to killings of honour as complementary to Article 340, so that if the rigorous conditions laid down by the latter did not apply to a certain case, then the court may go ahead and apply Article 98 by latching on to the element of fury always present in honour crimes. Moreover, the Court decided that what dishonourable act the victim had committed did actually amount to an unrightful act against the defendant (or his honour, the defendant and his honour now being seen by the Court as inseparable).

> If the defendant learnt that his daughter had committed adultery at the moment that he killed her, then he is considered to have killed her in a fit of fury caused by the act that she had committed. Her act constitutes an unrightful attack on the defendant's honour and it is dangerous within the meaning of Article 98 of the Penal Code.[35]

The JCC's clear rejection of what were previously its two most prominent arguments against applying Article 98 is best exemplified in its decision of 1975:

The fact that the law has provided for a reduction of penalty in a specific case does not mean that the court cannot apply the general rules provided for in Articles 97, 98, as well. The general rules are applied when the provisions dealing with the specific cases do not. The victim's act of adultery is a material act that touches the defendant's honour and that is why it is not a violation of the law to grant him a reduction of penalty.[36]

Now that the Court has decided to apply Article 98 to crimes of honour, we find that the decisions are preoccupied with addressing three issues: Firstly, the nature of the act committed by the woman: does it amount to an unrightful act against the honour of the family?

The victim's illegitimate pregnancy constitutes an unrightful aggression on the family's honour, and of a dangerous nature according to our society's traditions. Therefore, the defendant benefits from a reduction of the penalty if he killed his daughter in a fit of fury according to Article 98.[37]

Secondly, the passage of time between the defendant's knowledge of the victim's unrightful act and the killing.

If the defendant killed his sister the minute he found her, two days after he had learnt that she was caught committing adultery with another, then the killing was done in a fit of fury caused by the victim's unrightful and dangerous act.[38]

The fact that the defendant killed his sister one day after he became certain that the rumours surrounding her illegitimate pregnancy were true, is not sufficient evidence that he committed premeditated murder, since this period is not enough for him to regain his sensibilities and calm down.[39]

Thirdly, the defendant's knowledge of the victim's act.

The fact that the defendant killed the victim after hearing rumours that she had committed adultery, does not allow him to benefit from a reduction of penalty according to Article 98, because the victim cannot be said to have committed an unrightful and dangerous act.[40]

If the defendant heard of a rumour that his sister had committed adultery and consequently asked her and was confirmed, then killed her immediately, Article 98 applies to him.[41]

The Jordanian case shows how Article 340, under which one would expect to find crimes of honour treated, is marginalised in the judicial process and made irrelevant by the application of the general provision under Article 98 which deals with crimes committed in a fit of fury. The historical moment in which Article 340 was marginalised to the benefit of Article 98 can be seen as the JCC's adoption of an attitude that tolerates honour killings by expanding the pool of the beneficiaries of the excuse. Determining the exact boundaries of this tolerance hinges on the way the Court has tended to address the three issues enumerated above in its application of Article 98. In so far as I can see, there is no pattern in its decisions which can provide a clear sense of the boundaries between what is tolerated and what is not. How the Court will address a certain issue at any given time is up for grabs.[42]

I will now move on to review the decisions of the Egyptian Court of Cassation from 1960 till 1987, and the decisions of the Syrian Court of Cassation from 1957 till 1982, and see how they compare with the situation in Jordan.

The Egyptian Court of Cassation

As I indicated previously, Egypt has one of the more "liberal" provisions dealing with honour killings. What I mean by "liberal" is that the beneficiaries of the excuse (reduction not exemption) are limited to the husband, and the excuse is available to him only in the situation of finding his wife committing adultery *flagrante delicto*. In other words, it is a strict provision that limits severely the pool of beneficiaries and the occasion that warrants such an excuse. Its strictness is reminiscent of the concept of a crime of "passion" rather than of "honour".

Article 237 of the Egyptian Penal Code No. 58, 1937 states:

He who catches his wife committing adultery and kills her instantly and her partner, is punished by prison instead of the penalties provided for in Articles 234, 236.[43]

The limited application of the Egyptian provision is appreciated when compared with the Jordanian one dealing with honour killings (see above Article 340/1/2). But what is more unique about the Egyptian case is that it does not have a "provocation rule", for example what is equivalent to Article 98 in the Jordanian Penal Code.

> Excuses are two kinds: general and specific. The general covers all crimes or most of them, and their example in the Egyptian Penal Code is the case of being a minor (between the ages of 12 and 15) which is considered an excuse for a reduction of penalty (Article 66). It is noteworthy to mention that the Egyptian legislature did not consider "provocation" as a general excuse. And there are specific excuses limited to a specific number of crimes such as the excuse granted to the husband who catches his wife committing adultery *flagrante delicto* under Article 237. This excuse is only a specific kind of provocation rule.[44]

Because the Egyptian Code doesn't have its own general rule of provocation, we do not find the Egyptian courts interpreting honour killings as existing somewhere between the rule of provocation and Article 237, as is the case in the Jordanian situation. Rather, the residue of cases of honour killings that Article 237, with its strict conditions, does not cover are dealt with by the courts as cases inviting the judge's "mercy", for instance, as cases of "extenuating circumstances" provided for in Article 17:

> In crimes requiring the sympathy of the court, the judge can replace the penalty in the following way, in place of capital punishment, permanent or temporary hard labour.
>
> The issue of the extenuating circumstances is one that is left totally to the discretion of the court of fact, and it is up to this court to take it into account for the benefit of the accused even if he didn't plead for it . . . and the Court of Cassation has no jurisdiction over the matter so that an appeal for considering the extenuating circumstances cannot be a cause for an action before the Court of Cassation.[45]

In one case[46] the Court decided that since the defendant did not kill his wife upon catching her *flagrante delicto* committing adultery (rather he had heard rumours and when he went home, after he returned to his village, and found a strange man's clothes in his house, he became furious and killed both his wife and mother-in-law), Article 237 did not apply because "legal excuses are an exception that cannot be analogised to". And then the Court rejected the defendant's appeal for "mercy" holding that mercy was solely within the jurisdiction of the lower court of fact.

In another case[47] a man, who had discovered that his unmarried daughter was not a virgin and killed her instantly in a fit of fury, attempted to argue that he was suffering from a temporary loss of sanity according to Article 62 of the Penal Code when at the time of the crime. The defendant was trying to use this Article in place of the rule of provocation that was unavailable to him. The Court rejected this argument on the basis that according to Article 62 the excuse of exemption "is granted only to he who loses . . . choice due to loss of sanity or a defect in his thinking . . . and since the defendant was merely in a state of excitement and was provoked to commit the act then he could not be said to have been suffering from insanity". The Court went on to say that "in cases of provocation only a discretionary judicial excuse of reduction is available to the defendant which is totally up to the court of fact over which the Court of Cassation has no jurisdiction whatsoever".

The above cases reveal that honour killings that cannot be accommodated within the strict sphere of application of Article 237 are being relegated to the discretion of the lower courts of fact as cases requiring the sympathy of the judge under Article 17 (extenuating circumstances). As we have no access to the decisions made by these courts (they are not published) it is hard to tell which cases win adequate sympathy and which do not and therefore at a loss as to how the boundaries of these crimes are being delimited in these decisions.

The Syrian Court of Cassation

The Syrian Penal Code no. 148 of 1949 has in its Article 548 (as modified in the Legislative Decree No. 85 on 28 September 1953) the locus of crimes of honour. The Article states:

> 1. He who catches his wife or one of his ascendants, descendants or sister committing adultery (*flagrante delicto*) or illegitimate sexual acts with another and he killed or injured one or both of them benefits from an exemption of penalty (an absolute excuse).

2. He who catches his wife or one of his ascendants, descendants or sister in a "suspicious" state with another (*attitude équivoque*) benefits from a reduction of penalty.

Article 548 has its historical legal source in the Lebanese Penal Code (Article 562) which it adopts almost word for word. As such, both articles, the Lebanese and the Syrian ones, are in fact adaptations of the French Article (see above) since it is the historical legal source of the Lebanese Penal Code (Law No. 340, 1943).

The Syrian Code has its own provocation rule, Article 242 (unlike the Egyptian one), which is almost the same as that of the Jordanian Code (Article 98, see above). But what is peculiar about the Syrian Code (a peculiarity that it shares with the Lebanese one) is that it makes provision for what is called the "honourable motive rule". Article 192 states:

Lorsque le juge reconnait que le motif était honorable, il appliquera les peines suivantes: au lieu de la peine de mort, la détention perpétuelle; au lieu des travaux forcés à perpétuité, la détention perpétuelle ou à temps pour quinze ans . . .

This is not the "extenuating circumstances" rule that exists in the Egyptian and the Jordanian codes and which the Syrian Code itself has in Article 243. The Syrian Article 243 starts with, "S'il se trouve en la cause des circonstances atténuantes, la cour appliquera au lieu de la peine de mort, la détention à perpétuité ou à temps de douze à vingt ans, au lieu des travaux forcés a perpétuité, les travaux forcés à temps non inférieurs à dix ans . . ." and when seen in comparison with the penalties provided for in the "honourable motive" rule it is hard to tell which is actually more beneficial to the defendant.

Thus we see that an accused charged with committing a crime of honour has a pool of rules that could be applied to him under the Syrian Penal Code: (a) Article 548 and (b) Article 192 (the honourable motive rule), (c) Article 243 (the extenuating circumstances rule) and (d) Article 242 (the provocation rule).

If we look at the Syrian cases closely,[48] we see that, similar to the Jordanian experience, a story unfolds of resistance and withdrawal by the Syrian judiciary. Except that in the Syrian situation the locus of the struggle is not the relationship between the provision that directly regulates the crime of honour and the provocation rule. This issue does not seem to arise in the Syrian cases; as if it has been taken for granted that if the requirements of the direct provision do not prevail the judge should look to other provisions. Syrian judges have before them a pool of alternative provisions (the provocation rule, the honourable motive rule, and the extenuating circumstances rule). Because the issue of direct provision versus provocation rule does not come up, the struggle has been displaced to the relationship between the provocation rule and the honourable motive rule. It is an important struggle given the difference in the reduction of penalty between the two: under the provocation rule the reduction is much more significant. In the cases decided in 1957, 1958, 1965, 1966 and 1982 we see the Court insisting on applying the honourable motive rule and refusing to apply the provocation one. In effect it insisted on the harsher penalty. These were all cases where the requirements of Article 548 were not satisfied. However, in a case decided in 1964, and one decided in 1970, the Court seems to have applied the provocation rule instead of the honourable motive one. In contrast to the Jordanian development, there is no historical moment at which the Syrian shift from one side to the other occurred. The Court vacillates from one position to the other, though ultimately leaning, in the majority of the cases, in the direction of the honourable motive rule.

One can characterise the Syrian courts as manifesting a stronger desire than the Jordanian ones to penalise the offenders, since the punishment attached by the honourable motive rule is greater than that of the provocation rule. Nonetheless, they do share with the Jordanian courts the desire to "reconstitute" the crime of honour in the traditional sense, by circumventing Article 548. In other words, if the rigid requirements of Article 548 were intended by the codifiers to de-legitimise certain honour killings (for instance, those based on the pregnancy of the victim), the Syrian courts have chosen to thwart that attempt by invoking other readily available provisions to partially legitimise them. So the "story" of the Syrian judiciary is one of an attempt to re-legitimise traditional honour, but only in a relative sense since in cases where censure is found deserving they tend to choose the harshest penalties available in the pool of alternative provisions.

After considering the judicial treatment of honour killings, I have come to the conclusion that the thing that unites the practice of the judiciary in the three countries of Jordan, Egypt and Syria is the tendency to introduce other criminal provisions when presented with a killing of honour. In doing so, they seem to mock the nationalist codifiers, pretension that a balance between passion and honour had been struck via the particular formulation of the direct provision. The ability of the judiciary to create alternative interpretations is a statement on the instability of the nationalist regulatory system based on the idea of balancing acts. But what is even more noteworthy is that this subversive practice by the judiciary is going in one direction rather than the other. In other words, they seem to be using their ingenuity to reintroduce the idea of traditional honour, rather than pushing the system to be passion-based. As we have seen, both ideas are inherent in the nationalist compromise. The fact that the judiciary seems to be pushing one way rather than the other, highlights its relative conservatism. One must, however, at the same time note its own ambivalence and attempt to strike yet another balance of its own. Though the Syrian judiciary, for instance, opts to apply the honourable motive rule in lieu of the direct provision, it nevertheless resists applying the provocation rule which would provide significant reductions of penalty. And while the Egyptian Court of Cassation insists on adhering to the strict requirements of the direct provision, it nevertheless permits the lower courts the power to introduce the extenuating circumstances rule. In other words, though the judiciary reintroduces the idea of traditional honour, it does not do it completely or wholeheartedly. Its practice remains constrained and limited. The nationalist balance has been displaced, through judicial practice, by another balance, equally vulnerable and unstable. This should not surprise us, since the judiciary shares with the codifiers the essential nationalist ideology of striking a balance between tradition and modernity.

Women and the Family in the Ideology of the Nationalist Elite

The post-colonial nationalist Arab elites have sought to produce a new (national, post-independence) woman: she is literate and educated in the nationalist curriculum designed by the respective Arab governments once her country has attained independence.[49] She is even, in many cases, employed. Education, and to a lesser degree, employment, have become not only respectable undertakings for this woman, but expected of her as well. Education is meant to groom her by refining her with modernity. At any cost, she must not be like her mother: illiterate, ignorant of the external world and secluded. But just as she is not to resemble her mother, she must also shy away from being anything like Western women. Education is supposed to help her to become a better wife and mother, for example it is meant to enhance (modernise?) her femininity, not jeopardise it. There must not be, at any point, a confusion over her essential difference from men. Though educated, the new woman must not lose sight of the fact that her education is not meant to rob her of her true place, the home. Work and the external world is for men, family and the spiritual world of the home is for her. Through education she raises happier and healthier children, and she is refined in order to be socially presentable with her husband. If and when she is employed, she should relegate her employment to a secondary position. What comes first is family, everything else is marginal to that.

Through this arrangement, nationalist ideology accomplishes a double feat: on the one hand the new Arab woman is modernised, on the other the family, the main asset of the nation and the vessel of its national/cultural spirit, is preserved.

What does all this have to do with our earlier analysis of the performance of gender? The construction of the new woman had the effect of displacing the previous boundaries of the physical and the social hymens that women used to perform. Women can now look and behave differently, wear Western clothes in contrast to the veiled/ "scarfed" look of their mothers, mix with their husbands' friends, and they can leave the confines of the home and gain a noticeable presence on the streets of the cities. The new boundaries, however, are no less culturally determinate than the previous ones. The boundaries may have changed, but "fixed" boundaries they remain, or so the nationalists hoped.

The post-independence moment requires, then, of men and women, new gender performances. A new list of licences and prohibitions has been slowly, painfully produced to accommodate the emergence of the new woman. (The new middle-class man does not experience a diminution of his maleness if his sister discusses her course work with a male university colleague.) One could argue that from the "bosom" of traditional patriarchy, a nationalist patriarchy was created.

The move is not a totally peaceful one. Indeed, men often recall traditional patriarchy with wistful nostalgia. It is generational, of course, with the younger having a more tenuous connection with the ancient than the preceding one. However, these moments of nostalgia sometimes produce erratic and unpredictable incidents of violence, the same new man who does not object to his sister discussing her course work with a university male colleague, might kill her for honour if he saw them having coffee alone together in a public place. One might say that these occasional incidents of violence are the way nationalist patriarchy keeps its new list of licences and prohibitions well-recited and precise. The moment the balance of the "modern Arab woman" is pushed too hard in the direction of "Westernised sexuality", it is met with violence. This type of violence, the Arab judiciary seems to condone.

Conclusion

While in general the different nationalist codifiers in the Arab world were engaged in striking a balance between passion and honour, the specific compromise that each country chose is, in all likelihood, simply the function of the eclecticism of the nationalist codifier. The different solutions are to a great extent superficial ones. The nationalist balancing system has proved to be unstable. Through its attempts to reconstitute traditional honour by effectively dismissing the internal structure of the codified excuse and by creatively attempting to legitimise certain crimes, the judiciary highlights the superficiality of the nationalist choice.

The nationalist state policies aimed at producing the "modern Arab woman" proved equally to be based on an inherently unstable structure. To modernise women in the nationalist manner in no way protects them from the wiles of Westernisation.

The question that arises now is why is it that the judiciary tends to react conservatively by reconstituting a more traditional version of honour? What is it that they are attempting to address? In the following section I will argue that although the members of the judiciary are themselves nationalists and concede to the nationalist project of modernising women and the family, they are nevertheless faced with the task of remedying the tendency of the nationalist policies to run amuck. The nationalist project, I will argue, has had the effect of producing new sexual types and sexual practices that are both products of the system but also resistant actors to and within it. These sexual types and practices are the nationalists' nightmare: they are the products of the nationalists' own policies, yet ones that nationalist ideology consciously rejects. Unleashing periodic private violence against these types, through the condonement of the Arab judiciary, is essential to keep these types and practices in check. This then appears to be the new social function of crimes of honour. Rather than representing an attempt to reconstitute traditional society, they are a response to emergent sexual types and practices. This, in turn, explains the judiciary's attempt to reintroduce traditional honour but only in a limited way. Limited, because judges consciously reject the reinstitution of traditional society. Rather, they are simply engaged in sending cultural messages that subversive sexual practices are not to be tolerated.

III. A Sexual Typology of Arab Women under Nationalist Patriarchy

In this section I attempt the task of developing a (sexual) typology of Arab women under nationalist patriarchy. I will do so by fleshing out the different relationships that different women have come to have with the most popular Arab female dance, the belly-dance, otherwise known in the Arab world as *sharqi, baladi*, or *raqs 'arabi*. In many ways this dance is one of very few venues, if not the sole one, through which modern Arab women express themselves sexually in public. Belly-dancing is widely viewed as a very erotic art especially when performed by professional dancers. However, when performed by Arab women across the classes, the eroticism associated with the dance is continuously re-negotiated, teased out, or, in rare occasions, even flaunted.

There are two sides to the belly-dance that one must bear in mind. First, that it is a social activity, particularly among women in their own segregated social gatherings (parties, weddings, celebrations). Second, it is an artistic activity, performed by professional dancers in nightclubs, restaurants, theatres and films. The costume that the belly-dancer wears is very sexy, reinforcing the dance's eroticism, heavy shaking of the hips and the breasts.

Historically, only professional dancers performed the belly-dance in public (before a male audience). These women came from the marginalised groups in society: gypsies, minorities, and the poor.[50] Though their performance was sought after, notably by men of all classes, they were nevertheless seen as disreputable and loose – whorish. Very few of them achieved a high and respectable social status in their art, or had patrons and providers in rich men, merchants, pashas, kings and sultans.

The situation remains very much the same today: most dancers are seen as loose and only a few are regarded as artists. Instead of performing on the streets and at the doors of coffee shops and hotels as they did in the past, they now perform in theatres, nightclubs and restaurants. The dance has come to bear a nationalist mark, seen as an Arab dance, and sought after by foreigners and tourists visiting the Arab world.[51]

But as a social activity Arab women have always danced and continue to do so. In the past it was always a private activity performed only in the company of other women, where every woman stepped into the middle of the circle and took her turn at dancing, while other women surrounded her clapping their hands and ululating in encouragement. In that setting there was no distinction between performer and spectator: everybody danced, often two or more women danced together, or to each other. Frequently, these occasions turned into a "bride-choosing" activity, where one woman would report to her son the dancing of a girl that she liked, soliciting his desire for a partner.[52]

An important historical moment took place when these very women started performing before a male audience. The change is virtually simultaneous with the intervention of the nationalist text. The public space progressively ceased to be segregated, with women's education and employment, and social gatherings (mostly familial in the extended sense) coming to include men and women seated in the same room. I contend that this was an important moment in the history of Arab women's sexuality, that has allowed women, through the belly-dance, to communicate erotically with their male voyeurs. There is no longer a mediator (the mother) who describes the dancing girl to the son; the son himself is now there getting his firsthand visual experience. The girl now seduces through her dance, and is often consequently approached and wooed by the man without a third party. Here, the girl parodies the belly-dancer as the publicly seductive female. By assuming some of the dancer's sexual powers, she captures the heart of her male spectators and solicits their requests to the respectable end of marriage. These mixed celebratory gatherings remain to this day bride-choosing occasions.

Even with the intervention of the nationalist text, women still needed to do a public performance of virginity. But what the nationalist change achieved was an alteration of the parameters of this performance. During the time of the traditional text one of the important statements of virginity was the segregation of the female space from the male space. Women were simply kept out of men's way, and on the streets they were clad from top to bottom. There was hardly any legitimised public interaction between the sexes, and if any exchange occurred between a man and a woman, and the community got wind of it, it was treated as a scandal.

Granting women education on a mass level, and then later on employment, constituted a serious bombardment of male space. Verbal daily exchange between the sexes came to be tolerated and seen (often grudgingly) as inevitable. Virginity had to "catch up", so to speak, and the gendered actors started to develop a new code of behaviour (and dress) that could accommodate interaction between them, and yet also provide a convincing (and necessarily novel) statement of women's virginity. This new code of behaviour was very difficult for its actors to carry out without an unconscious sense of the ambiguity and complexity of the new situation. Some women wore very conservative clothes, were very serious and brief in their exchanges with men, made sure not to be seen alone with them outside of the work context, and developed elaborate techniques of fending off potential "behavioural trespasses" by men. Others were a bit more relaxed, allowing a certain shy sexiness in their attire, were slightly flirtatious, friendly, and even playful with men. The ambiguity of the new code of behaviour and the constant negotiation of its rules by its gendered actors has generated a rich and "confused" institution of gossip. Determining the rules of the sexual code governing behaviour between men and women in the workplace remains to this day a mystifying task that escapes the grasp of the people involved.[53]

In belly-dancing, there is also the ambiguity and the confusion. Women's performance of belly-dancing in the desegregated public space of social gatherings and celebrations resembles to a large degree women's work in a desegregated workplace. As I indicated above, through belly-dancing women have come to communicate with men sexually without the mediation of a third party as was the case in the past, usually the man's mother. Determining a code of dancing that allows a performance of virginity, given the erotic "stuff" that belly-dancing is made of, is by no means an easy task. And yet, if anything, it testifies to the deep change that the performance of virginity has undergone: from the almost complete shunning of any sexual expression within the confines of the traditional text, to an ambivalent cultural acceptance of such expression in the nationalist text.

Repeating the old rituals of belly-dancing within women's gatherings, women still dance with and to each other in the new desegregated public place. However, now their consciousness is besieged with an awareness of the male gaze. It is a gaze that itself is very ambivalent. It appreciates and condemns. It wants to be seduced, yet is harshly judgmental of the propriety of the dancer. Whereas the appreciative gaze of the male voyeur drives women to be more seductive, the judgmental one pushes them to be reserved in their movements. Keeping the balance might be a hard thing to do, but most women have mastered, unconsciously, the act of "walking a tightrope". Women's success in this "acrobatic" act is evidenced by the fact that these party/wedding gatherings are today rich match-making occasions.[54] Let us call these women the "sexy virgin(s)".[55] One indication of their lurking virginity is that these women seem to be quite unaware of their sexiness. Virginal sexuality is a unique sexuality that colours the woman's fantasies, relationship to her body and erotic responses in general. There is a certain sexual girlishness and naïveté associated with the state of being a virgin, that precludes the woman from fully understanding the extent and nature of her sexualisation by the male voyeur. Men's sexual fantasies about the dancing, sexy virgin, if revealed to her, would be met by embarrassment, shock and shame. Her virginal understanding of men's appreciative gaze is otherwise interpreted by her as an appreciation of her "beauty", "attractiveness" and "cuteness". In no way is she capable of indulging herself in the complex, "terrifying" world of the male, virgin-by-default sexuality.

The other striking thing about virginal sexuality is that it has a tendency to turn inward. In other words, the sexual desire for the other seems to transcend itself, in the sexy virgins, into deep narcissism. These same women, who appear not to be fully aware of their sexual powers over men, are at the same time simply in love with their looks. Always adorned with nice clothes, jewellery and heavy make-up, and deeply conscious of how they look, these women continuously exchange admiring looks with each other and have the tendency to develop an obsessive relationship with their mirror. They are much more at home with their reflection in the mirror than with the male gaze, an experience that resonates from the old days of the traditional text where the male space and the female space were segregated.[56]

The violence of the honour universe has serious disciplinary effects on the sexy virgin. She is unwilling to take risks that would make her a potential victim of a crime of honour. She is the virgin of the traditional text who is utilising the sexual space opened up by the nationalist project.

At this point, I wish to introduce the class factor into my analysis in an attempt to explain the second sexual type in my typology, that of the "virgin of love". In the upper classes of Arab society, belly-dancing as a collective dance has suffered somewhat a diminution of value. Though upper-class folks still invite belly-dancers to celebrate their sons' weddings, the actual practice of belly-dancing among upper-class women has decreased dramatically. So much so that most of these women harbour a certain feeling of contempt for the dance and the people who perform it. The reason for this seems to be, partly, the progressive Westernisation of this class, a process which has been accompanied by a devaluation of Arab cultural arts such as Arabic music and belly-dancing. Belly-dancing has come to be seen by these women as a dance performed professionally by vulgar women, and socially by "common" women.

The contempt these women hold for belly-dancing seems to deprive them of the pleasure of publicly communicating in a sexual way with men at weddings and social gatherings. As they sit in their seats watching other women dance, they experience mixed feelings best described as "envious contempt". Often, these women are what I have previously referred to as the virgins of love. They believe in love and might even commit the revolutionary act of engaging in underground sex with their lovers (mostly precluding coitus, and mostly with lovers who had spent a long time courting them first), but they remain contemptuous of any public expression of sexuality. Their virginity manifests itself not in their private lives but in their public ones. Whereas the sexy virgin engages in acts of seduction in her belly-dance to attract a potential suitor and is afraid of engaging in the underground secret life of "sexual love", the virgin of love rejects public acts of sexual attraction and remains glued to her seat: pure, awaiting the fall of love from the sky. The first engages in public sexy acts that she does not have a full comprehension of, a statement on her virginal sexual consciousness, while the second engages in secret subversive acts of sex with the man she is madly in love with and dismisses public sexual expression as vulgar, a statement on her own virginal sexual consciousness. The sexy virgin and the virgin of love both reveal the ways in which virginity survives in the nationalist text.[57]

The virgin of love takes more risks than the sexy virgin. Utilising the mobility and social space that her upper-class environment allows her, she is able to conduct a sexual life, limited though it might be to the underground. Armed with a rhetorical arsenal on love and romance that she has developed for herself to justify her conduct, this woman is willing to relatively challenge the codes of conduct of the universe of honour. This is further reinforced by a sense of distance from the practice of the crime of honour which women of the upper classes have. Only women of lower social backgrounds are subjected to the threat of this practice.

The third sexual type in my typology is the "coquette". In a way this woman is an anomaly in Arab culture, and somewhat unexplainable. But she is there, and she has been allowed to exist. Usually this woman is married or divorced. She is flirtatious to various degrees, consciously sexy with men, and appears to the male gaze to be most skilful in exploiting the eroticism inherent in the belly-dance. In fact, this woman, upper-class or not, is invariably enamoured with this dance. She performs it most artistically, is freer in shaking her hips, and keeps a seductive, inviting look on her face as she dances. Most of the time she dances in the company of her husband (or brother) which gives her a certain social protection from the label of "slut". This woman is unusually friendly, free, dynamic, and very funny. She cracks jokes continuously, particularly sexual ones, often in the company of men. She is tolerated by her audience because she is married, a fact that explains her sexual savvy. The coquette is deeply desired by men; adored, envied and hated by women, often at the same time. Sexy virgins watch her with shock and glittering eyes. Virgins of love watch her with contempt and resentment. She is a figure both to be instructed by and to avoid. Women's ambivalence towards her is explained by their desire to learn from her, since she seems to enact a style of behaviour they have been forced to taboo, but at the same time she seems to smack so much of the slut they have so much repressed in themselves. That is why they both want her company and run away from her. Her ability to rescue herself socially, as the flirtatious wife of so-and-so (and not the slut) has always deeply impressed them. Her coquettishness does not seem to particularly doom her socially, but does doom her husband. He is seen as a wimp, unable to satisfy or contain his wife's sexuality.

The coquette usually plays the role of matchmaker. Her easy access to male company, through flirtation, and women's deep desire to emulate her, gives her leeway in the worlds of both men and women. She matches men and women up for marriage and is considered because of her sexiness and flirtation, as most sophisticated in her understanding of both sexes. Men's sexual desire for her is transferred, in instances of matchmaking, to the woman she introduces to them. If they can't have her, well then, they will have the woman she recommends, secretly hoping of course that this woman has received some sexual tips from the coquette.

The subversiveness of the presence of the coquette in any social setting is not to be underestimated. You see her on the dance floor freely shaking her body, trying to teach other women "how to do it". Her friendly and flirtatious behaviour with men can become contagious, giving courage to the women in her company to cross boundaries they never considered crossing before. She is the closest to the artistic figure of the belly-dancer: sexy, flirtatious, sought-after, admired, but secretly suspected of being loose. But as with the belly-dancer, she gives virginal women glimpses of the uncensored world of sex.

The coquette is, relatively speaking, a risk taker. Her sexual conduct is allowed to exist because of her rather "hung" status. Her family sees her as the responsibility of her husband, in most cases a man who either behaves like or is perceived as a "cuckold". Her hung status, however, is sometimes resolved unpredictably, when the husband/cuckold decides, all of a sudden, to redeem his honour. The coquette then becomes the victim of a crime of honour.

The fourth sexual type that I would like to introduce at this point is what I call the "GAP girl".[58] This girl is an interesting combination of the coquette and the sexy virgin. She shares with the latter some aspects of her virginal sexuality and with the former her easy and comfortable access to the world of men. I call her the GAP girl because she comes to the dancing floor dressed in jeans, or slacks, T-shirt and sneakers, or low-heeled shoes. She is the die-hard child whose virginity is the product of a prolonged childhood, one she appears to be determined not to relinquish. The GAP girl looks asexual. She is unlike the sexy virgin in that she is not conscious of sexuality, even in the virginal sense, which would entail a great deal of effort in negotiating one's sexual desires out of fear and shame. However, she is similar to the sexy virgin in that she is totally ignorant of the sexual world of men. Her childish look and body, typically has short hair and wears no make-up, which allows her to have a comfortable and friendly interaction with men that could include a great deal of physical contact. She gets away with this because it's all done in "innocence". They are all her "friends". This girl seems to be the product of the desegregated institutions of leisure, as opposed to educational and vocational ones, such as youth clubs, sports clubs and the like. In fact, she is often the sporty type.[59]

When this girl goes to the dance floor to dance she is usually with a group of male and female friends. She dances with men with the same ease that she dances with women, treating the dance more as a sporty, fun activity than an erotic, aesthetic one. When this girl grows older, if and when she decides to, she usually develops into the virgin of love. Her intense familiarity with men makes it difficult for her to become the sexy virgin, given the latter's usual estrangement and distance from the world of men. And her delayed sexuality makes it almost impossible for her to become the sexually sophisticated coquette.

The GAP girl does not have to deal with the idea of a crime of honour. The innocence that she displays and that permeates her consciousness, dismisses in the minds of the public and those related to her the prospect of illicit sexual behaviour.

The fifth type in my sexual typology I call the "autonomous virgin". This woman is "brainy", serious, and career-oriented. She has spent a great amount of time trying to prove to everybody, especially men, that she is both intelligent and competent. She is contemptuous of any sexual expression on the part of women, fearing that it would reinforce the idea that women are sexy dolls and empty-headed. She is formal and proper in her dealings with male colleagues, dresses very conservatively and wears no make-up. She avoids casual and non-substantive conversations with men, and is rarely caught laughing or having a light and fun exchange with them. This woman is interested in attracting a marriage partner, but only through the traditional venue of the family. That is why she banks a great deal on a reputation for respectability.[60]

The autonomous virgin does not even consider approaching the dance floor. Not out of contempt for the belly-dance, but out of the belief that the desegregation of the social space between men and women should only include the respectable institutions of the workplace and education. Erotic communication between the sexes is, to her, outrageous and ought to be banned. In many ways this woman is the old traditional virgin who once lived in the segregated female space, but who is now wearing a suit and going out to work or to get a degree. Though she shares with the virgin of love the contempt for sexual expression, she is similar to the sexy virgin in her refusal to engage in underground love and in seeking a marriage partner through the traditional means of the family. The autonomous virgin is not at risk of a crime of honour simply because she is one of its advocates. Believing in the propriety of the honour ethics, she avoids to the best of her ability all kinds of shameless behaviour. For her, honourableness in sexual conduct is a moral good.

The sixth type in my typology is that of the "slut". This woman has the sexual history of the virgin of love. She is one who has engaged in underground sexual practices with one or two men she was madly in love with, but has since dropped the romantic consciousness associated with that type. Her underground life seems to have taught her two precious lessons: one concerning her own sexuality, the other concerning that of men. She has come to like, savour and appreciate sex; she has become nuanced and sophisticated in her understanding of her own sexuality. She has also come to know a great deal about men, shrugging off in the process her fear and apprehension of their sexual world. She is very much like the coquette, except that she is not married and is consciously out there to seduce a potential sexual partner. She is consciously sexy, seductive, and has a knack for sexual experimentation. Her shameless burgeoning sexuality blurs the concept of sexual ethics for her, unlike the sexy virgin (traditional ethics: sex within marriage), or the virgin in love (romantic ethics: sex with the loved one). She could be polygamous, involved with married men, other women, and so on. When this woman takes to the dance floor she is as sexually sophisticated in her dance as the coquette, doing all the "right" moves and body gestures. She is often much more inviting in her dance than the coquette, utilising to the best of her ability the erotic "stuff" that the belly-dance is made of.[61]

The slut is a big risk-taker in the world of honour. Her behaviour exposes her to the dangers of a crime of honour; she is continuously pushing herself to the edge. Though mocking of the honour system, and daringly challenging it, she conducts herself with a combination of risk and caution. Most of her sluttishness is, after all, largely lived in the underground.

The last type in my typology is the "tease". This woman is an odd combination of the slut and the sexy virgin. She shares with the slut her sexual savvy, but only through hearsay. In other words this woman is sexually sophisticated, though she has not engaged in underground sexuality. She is usually upper-class and Westernised, which explains the richness and diversity of her sources of sexual knowledge (a temporary life in the West as a student, movies, books, magazines, parties). All this knowledge she uses to seduce, play, flirt and tease men. But like the sexy virgin she insists on remaining a virgin, holding to the social wisdom that preserving her virginity will get her a good marriage and a reputation for respectability. She is hardly naive or estranged from the world of men (and in that respect she departs radically from the sexy virgin). Her knowledge of the art of sexual seduction is sophisticated and learned. Her interaction with men is erotic, suggestive, inviting and playful. But it stops there. The exact opposite of the virgin of love, who keeps the public rituals of virginity, but in private engages in underground sexuality, the tease behaves publicly like a slut, but remains privately a virgin. She is the virgin slut who is attempting to be loyal to the last vestiges of virginity: the actual physical hymen.[62]

The sexual types that I have explored above are ideal types. The same woman can shift from one type to the other given the context, or have a combination of features associated with different types. Most women have a sexual history that covers more than one type. It is also important to state that women are not necessarily self-conscious about the type of sexuality they embody, and I suspect that many women would strongly resist my typology, preferring to understand themselves in much more reductive and simplistic terms than the types allow.

For the most part, the above sexual types are unmarried (except for the coquette). A very significant thing happens to Arab women when they marry, they almost always immediately become mothers. Motherhood seems to have a serious transformative effect on the different sexual types of women, so that, for instance, the narcissism of the sexy virgin is seriously curbed and she starts to develop a more careless dishevelled look. The GAP girl loses her lithe girlish body and starts to look more like an older, asexual woman. Whereas the autonomous virgin sustains her asexuality through balancing her double burdens of working and motherhood, the virgin of love, usually upper-class, joins the cult of motherhood and drops all her girlish romantic baggage.[63]

In general, after marriage, Arab women seem to become more relaxed in the company of men, less self-conscious, and feeling less estranged. Some develop, secretly and among themselves, a cynical attitude about men, as if in experiencing sex they came to comprehend the sexual power they hold over men, which in turn, seemed to undermine the social power that men have always held over them. And some come to participate in a sexual sub-culture that is verbally shared between married women who are either friends or neighbours, one rich with exchanged experiences, jokes, shared tips and mutual advice. It is through the medium of this secretive underground sub-culture that many women come to develop and learn about sexuality. It seems, however, to be open only to married women.

IV. A Sexual Typology of Arab Men
Under Nationalist Patriarchy

In this section I would like to develop a sexual typology of Arab men in the nationalist text. When I refer to Arab men as virgins by default, I mean that the system of honour does not command them to be virginal, rather, it made it very hard for them to be otherwise. This, of course, was due to the inaccessibility of women, who themselves are commanded to be virginal.

The first thing that should be acknowledged here is that while being a virgin by command is different from being a virgin by default, the two have a great deal in common. Though the literature is rife with discussions of the virginity of Arab women, the virginity of Arab men is hardly mentioned. I would like to stress this point because I believe that both men and women suffer under the yoke of the structure of honour, and that it is experienced as hardship by men no less than by women. Of course there is no threat to the life of the man if he violates the code of honour. However, that might not prove to be such a great consolation to him as he proceeds to negotiate his sexuality within the not-so-peaceful and often violent structure of honour.

With the intervention of the nationalist text and the desegregation of the gendered social space, the state of being a virgin by default has undergone a certain transformation, without being totally abolished. The basic elements that constitute this state still survive today in a very complex and novel way, shaping the various sexual types of Arab men.

The sexuality of being a virgin by default, as was the case in the traditional text, included a subset of social and sexual practices, that could look at first glance paradoxical.[64] A virgin by default usually engages in all kinds of underground sexual practices that were open to him socially, accepted but not openly condoned. This man attains a great deal of his sexual pleasures on the streets (harassment), visiting prostitutes, watching belly-dancers, practising masturbation, homosexuality and so on. And yet this same man was very much a virgin (in fact the majority of men seem to have been virgins when they were married) sharing with the virgin woman certain aspects of virginal sexuality. These aspects include a sense of estrangement from the other sex, shyness and embarrassment in their presence. Arabic literature and cinema are full of stories of men who could not have sex with their wives on their wedding night, this being their first sexual experience conducted in the context of a hyped-up social celebration with a great deal of expectations put on the man.[65]

The sexuality of being a virgin by default includes two other aspects that might, at first, look paradoxical. On the one hand, there is a strong predatory impulse in the virgin by default. Seeing himself as deprived of sexual pleasures due to the fierce patriarchal fences that surround his objects of desire (in his world women are guarded and threatened with violence by their fathers and brothers for veering from the honour code), this man behaves like a predator whose biggest challenge is to secretly break those fences and obtain access to other men's women. The predator sees women as conquests he can congratulate himself on: they are hard-won victories as far as he is concerned.

But on the other hand, paradoxically enough, this man is also deeply interested in (and feels strongly about) preserving other women's virginity. It is not that he has been terrorised into this position, though that might also be true, but that he very much feels that he has an investment in the institution of virginity. The virgin/whore dichotomy is something he strongly believes in. These contradictory impulses that the predator virgin by default experiences could conceivably put him in a situation where, having with hard work attained access to his object of desire, he chooses not to "blemish" her by having sex with her. In other words, he might very well voluntarily choose not to consummate his predatory project.

The desegregation of the gendered social space and the arrival of romantic love on the scene in the nationalist text have created new sexual types of men who look like the natural "children" of the virgin by default. These types have retained aspects of the sexuality of the virgin by default, but those aspects are present in a more loose and disintegrated way. These aspects no longer coexist in a tight embrace producing only one type (the virgin by default), rather, they have decomposed from their source of origin, each aspect producing a type in itself.

The first type in my sexual typology, and the one that is most prevalent in the nationalist text, is that of the "predator".[66] This new predator looks very much like the old one. His life is a sexual pursuit of the new nationalist virgin (recall that according to the above analysis women are now ambivalently virginal as opposed to unequivocally so as in the traditionalist text). However, the modern predator has a much more exciting life than his predecessor, his pool of potential conquests infinitely bigger. This man is out actively pursuing sexy virgins in the hope of turning them into virgins of love, as well as already converted virgins of love. He sweet-talks them into joining him in some sort of underground sexual practice in the name of love, leading them to imagine this might ultimately take them to marriage. Life has never been so good for the predator, his list of conquests never so long. He seduces and runs away. He tends to be charming, seductive, slick and a great romance conversationalist.

Usually his successes in seduction make him very suspicious of women and leery of their claim of an honourable sexual past. When this man marries, it is almost never out of love. He seeks the sexy virgin or the autonomous virgin through the traditional venue of the family when he marries, imagining to himself that he has secured a "clean and safe woman who had no experience with sophisticated deceitful predators like himself". This man usually continues his predatory pursuits shortly after marriage.

The second type is that of the "romantic virgin by default". This man is deeply unconventional in Arab culture in that he insists on establishing an intimate romantic relationship with the woman he intends to marry. In his more extreme forms he holds deep contempt for the predator whom he sees as an abuser of women's feelings. For him, love and sex are intertwined and inseparable whether as an underground practice or within the institution of marriage. Equally, he has deep contempt for the traditional familiar ways of marriage, seeing them as backward. He varies in his attitude towards women's virginity. He could either feel strongly about his loved one's virginity, seeing it as a sign of her honourability, or be totally nihilistic about it. His romanticism could push him to put his loved one on a pedestal, treating her as a romantic object of his fantasies rather than a sexual one. He could also choose to preserve his loved one's virginity out of a feeling of protection: he does not want to be the cause of something that might well result in her social damnation. There is always a project of marriage in the romantic life of this type of man, as the "natural" culmination of his love.

This is the new "feminised" Arab man. The cultural production of this type of man is creating a kind of crisis in the social understanding of masculinity. He tends to be gentle, soft-spoken, and fastidious in his looks, clothes and haircut. The fact that he allows himself to be vulnerable to the agonies, anguish and yearnings of love, greatly challenges the macho image that a man should project: heartless, purposeful, conquering, and a triumphant survivor of the lures of women. Both he and the predator are narcissistic and conscious of their looks, except that the latter uses it for the purpose of his conquests, lending him the look of the new modern macho man. The narcissism of the romantic, on the other hand, makes him look more like a castrated man.[67]

It is important to point out that a great many men lead a sexual life balanced on the border between the life of the predator and that of the romantic virgin by default. Though they see themselves as occasionally vulnerable to the woes of love, they nevertheless, at different points in their lives, lead the life of the predator. In doing so they seize the opportunity of sexual practice which would otherwise be difficult to attain, given the fact that they are living in a world that is full of virgins. For them, predation is sexual opportunity.

The third type in my typology is that of the "virginal virgin by default". This man is the inheritor of the virginal sexuality associated with the old traditional virgin by default. He is very much like a female virgin. His "proper" traditional upbringing has precluded him from pursuing underground sexual practices, or any predatory behaviour, only to leave him in the uncomfortable position of being an absolute male virgin (that is, he has had no sexual experience with women whatsoever). As much as he might prefer it, he finds himself, due to his virginal sexuality, simply unqualified to become either the predator or the romantic virgin by default.

Like a female virgin, he is shy, embarrassed and totally estranged from the world of the opposite sex. His intense discomfort in their presence and his sense of deep insecurity paralyse him and make it imposs ible for him to communicate with women erotically. He has neither the sense of comfort and ease that the romantic seems to have in the company of women, nor the self-confident conquering approach of the predator. This man senses himself stuck and unqualified for the new modern desegregated life of the nationalist text.

He shares with the old virgin by default the romantic culture of segregated love. He tends to suffer continuous crushes on women, most of whom he has never even spoken to. Love for him is a fantastical fixation on an object of desire that he experiences as unattainable. The predator and the romantic, sometimes his own friends, feel pity for him and they continuously offer him advice on how to summon his courage and his approach to his object of fixation. This man entertains mixed feelings towards women. They are mysterious to him, confusing, puzzling, desirable, but equally feared. They frustrate him, and he feels hatred and resentment towards them for making him feel so helpless.

But he also resents the predator and the romantic, not only for their success with women, but because they make it increasingly difficult for the likes of him to approach women. Their existence is a continuous reminder to him that women are as a matter of fact "wooable" and therefore attainable, but only in accordance with rituals and practices that these men themselves have created: rituals that he feels incapable of enacting. He is ashamed to resort to the familial venue to procure himself a wife (which he ultimately in desperation and frustration does) because it is an indication to his more skilful peers that he has failed to romantically seduce a woman.

His resentment is further increased by the fact that he feels that women themselves are rather contemptuous of him for his sexual and social inadequacies. To them, he is not a particularly attractive man or type to be associated with: he is shy, embarrassed, immature, a child. Though they might be impressed with his propriety, they do not find it a particularly inviting trait.

The fourth type in my typology is that of the "teaser virgin by default". This man has inherited the traditional virgin by default's deep respect for women's virginity, a state which he regards as necessary and before which he stands with a sense of awe that he cannot help. But he is neither virginal nor particularly romantic. In fact, he is quite predatory in his sexuality. Oddly and paradoxically enough, this man loves to attract women, and the more the better. He behaves very much like the predator: he dresses nicely, sweet-talks women into his trap, he is gentle, charming, slick and very seductive. But he is not interested in enjoying the potential pleasures made accessible by his successful conquests, and in this he is different from the predator. Having gained the satisfaction of knowing that the woman has fallen into his trap (she is in love with him or interested in having an underground relationship with him), he swiftly disappears and refuses to pursue the sexual opportunities presented to him. He refuses, because he simply believes that women should be kept respectable and virginal, and their willingness to have a relationship with him would inevitably tarnish them. The erotic pleasures of the teaser are derived from his own acts of seduction and conquests, consisting merely of making women cling and be attached to him.

This man is a predator *manqué*, with a sexuality that lies somewhere between that of the predator and that of the romantic. He could easily become a romantic because his interest in women's respectability makes him very susceptible to their feelings. In other words, for him women are not merely objects to be seduced as for the predator, they are also people with feelings, a view that he shares with the romantic. The teaser might easily, therefore, fall in love with one of his conquests and end up marrying her. Or, it is equally plausible that he might use the traditional venue of the family to get for himself a sexy virgin, or an autonomous virgin to marry.

The fifth type in my typology is the "self-interested virgin by default". This man is a combination of the traditional virgin by default and the new nationalist one. On the one hand, he believes strongly that women should remain virginal and feels secure in a world where he is assured of this fact. Yet, on the other hand, he feels seduced by the nationalist modern image of a man coupled with a woman who is educated, employed and looks modern. In many ways, he is like the autonomous virgin, in that he also approves of the desegregation of gendered space only in education and employment, and not in the erotic sexual arena. His attraction to modernity also pushes him to participate in the culture of love because it is more modern.

The contradictory aspects of his sexuality (traditional and modern) are not particularly hard to reconcile. What he does in the end to attain a modern "nationalist" marriage, is to allow himself to fall in love with a suitable (socially and economically), sexy or autonomous virgin in his family: a cousin (near or distant), a neighbour, a daughter of friends of his family, a childhood companion. He usually chooses an educated, rather socially sophisticated, and perhaps even employed woman.

This man may very well have the sexual history of a predator, seeing this as a continuation of the underground sexual practice that the traditional virgin by default has always carried out. But he sees his past as only a sexual phase to which he was entitled and which has given him an insight on who is a whore and who is a virgin in his community; those who have responded to his or his friends' seduction are the whores, and those who haven't are the virgins.

I call him self-interested because he appropriates the best of both worlds, the traditional and the modern: predation, romance, virginity, and a modern wife. By successfully achieving this combination, the nationalist virgin by default spares himself the pits of sexual ambiguity that have inevitably resulted from the intervention of the nationalist text. Being romantically involved with a modern-looking, but socially monitored female cousin, is an assurance to him that virginity and modernity are not particularly irreconcilable. Boundaries for him, as they were for the traditional virgin by default, remain clear and identifiable.

Having said all of the above, I feel I can still assert that the desire for regular sex, rather than romance and love, is the primary reason that most Arab men resort to marriage. This is the case because virginity still survives strongly in Arab culture. The ambiguity that has befallen virginity has made the sexual history of many Arab men much more diverse and complicated than that of their predecessors. But the ultimate need to resort to marriage as a means for obtaining frequent and easily accessed sex remains very much the case today.

Conclusion

In this section, I have discussed the ways in which nationalist patriarchy constructs a new modern sexuality. I have argued that the nationalist policies have allowed the proliferation of new and elaborate sexual types and practices. While the autonomous virgin represents the nationalist project in its most secure and balanced state, the other different sexual types express the inherent instability of this project. Some of these new practices give the nationalists a glimpse of what happens to their scheme when it is pushed to its logical end. The existence of an underground sexuality, practised by some of these new types, is a harbinger of the fact that the nationalist project of modernisation may be running amuck. These practices push men but, even more importantly, women in the direction of being more Westernised. In their underground behaviour, they touch the tip of that evil that must at all costs be avoided – Western sexuality. This is why the types are forms of resistance to nationalist patriarchy, even as they are, at the same time, products of it.

In this light, we can perhaps better understand the behaviour of the Arab judiciary with its tendency to tolerate certain forms of traditional honour killings. This tendency appears targeted to pre-empt subversive sexual practices. Unless a certain violence is unleashed against them, then they will flourish beyond control and Arab society will slide into the dark pit of Western sexual life, something to be avoided at all costs. Far from attempting to reconstitute traditional society, these judges are simply interested in maintaining the precarious balance struck by the nationalists between tradition and modernity. The cases presented to these judges confront them directly with the inherent instability of a faltering system that needs to be supported. Now we are able to understand that the forms of resistance engaged in by the sexual types are themselves a response to the balance being struck between two types of violence, the private and the official.

We are, however, thus far presented with an empirical situation that undermines this analysis. According to an informal study I have undertaken regarding crimes of honour in Jordan, it transpires that almost all the victims of these crimes are women who belong to tribal, peasant or urban working class backgrounds.[68] So how then, do we explain the behaviour of the judges when it is not exactly the "slut" who is getting killed, but more likely a peasant woman who has lost her virginity or got pregnant in the context of a sexual act in which she may well have been victimised? How are the judges, if our analysis is correct, pre-empting the emergence of new sexual types, by condoning the killing of poor traditional women?

There are many possible answers to this question, all speculative. First, that judges are simply delivering the cultural message that there is a limit as to what the system will tolerate. The reminder that private violence is still sanctioned in some forms, holds in check sexualities that might otherwise go overboard; secondly, that judges, as members of the ruling male elite, are making a concession to men in the lower classes, so as not to incur the wrath and resentment that will result if the system is pushed toward a liberalisation that the conservative working class will not tolerate; thirdly, this second generation of judges is in fact more conservative in sensibility than the early nationalists. Belonging for the greater part to the middle or lower middle classes, products of mass education who obtained law degrees in Arab countries, these judges share many of the conservative views of working-class men about the proper place of women. They are less interested in modernity than the earlier generation for whom it was a priority.

V: Concluding Notes

The writing of this paper was driven by the feminist impulse that crimes of honour should be abolished in the Arab world through a withdrawal of all forms of legal sanctions available for them. As a first step, the construct of crime of passion, already present in Arab criminal codes, should be reinforced in order to undermine that of honour. I have argued that the move made in some Arab codes (Egyptian, Algerian) to incorporate the legal construct of passion, as opposed to that of honour (Jordan, Syria, Lebanon), is a "progressive" one. The sphere of passion appears to be much narrower than that of honour: its range of female victims is narrower (wife only); its potential beneficiaries are fewer (husband only); its tolerance for violence is lower (acceptable only as a result of the passionate heat of jealousy); and its penalties are more severe (permitting only reduction rather than exemption).

Arab feminist activists have rarely treated the issue of honour crimes as political, and it has therefore been considered unworthy of collective mobilisation. These activists have always found themselves in the impossible situation of having to avoid discussing issues that give the impression that they are advocating sex before marriage. Dogged in their pursuit for an audience in their societies, and feeling already marginalised as feminists, Arab feminists tend to shy away from discussing the issue of honour crimes precisely to avoid giving that impression. Not to mention, of course, the vicious social censorship that precludes discussion of this issue, even in the face of a headstrong attempt. The published programme of a Palestinian feminist group, al-Fanar, unique in its attempt to openly call for the abolition of honour crimes, tries to respond to this attack by arguing as follows:

> The deliberate misrepresentations of feminism employed by enemies
> of the women's liberation, such as accusing it of being in favour of

immorality and permissiveness, is nothing other than an attempt at malicious deceit, the purpose of which is to perpetuate the oppression of women and the suppression of women's liberation movement. Our feminism is for freeing society from this kind of deceit, hypocrisy, and collective fraud, which amounts to moral bankruptcy of the existing Arab society.[69]

While this might be true, I do not believe that this approach offers a successful rhetorical argument. "If you abolish crimes of honour, Arab women will become promiscuous", is, I believe, a heartfelt argument, to which Arab feminists need to develop their own rhetorical response.

It seems to me that there is more than one discursive avenue open to Arab feminists as a response. First, it is empirically verifiable that almost all victims are poor urban working-class women or peasant women from communities that are very conservative and traditional. To imagine that condoning the murder of these women albeit half-heartedly, as the Arab judiciary tends to do, will change or control the sexual mores of women, is illusory. Even as these women are being killed, the map of sexual relations between men and women in the Arab world, appears, as a result of the nationalist project, to continue a course of irreversible change, unaffected by these deaths. It is tantamount to sacrificing the lives of poor women in a vain attempt to prop up a rhetorical argument about morality that has no basis in reality.

Second, to argue that Arab women will become sluttish like Western women if these crimes are totally abolished is ridiculous, no such promiscuous world really exists.

Third, feminists can use the "schizophrenic" structure of nationalist discourse to argue that the society will never be modernised as long as it continues to engage in prehistoric, primitive social practices such as crimes of honour. Besides, "it just does not look good abroad; it simply promotes the idea that we are savage and primitive."

Fourth, feminists can argue that Arab society should be pushed to make the move from shame culture to guilt culture. The argument would be that "proper" sexual behaviour should be promoted through ethical teachings rather than prohibitive violence; that society achieves its goals more successfully by leaving it to the "conscience" of the individual rather than instilling it through fear. The culture of shame is based on the idea that "if I can get away with it in private and nobody catches me, then that's fine." Guilt culture, on the other hand, assumes that one's internalised sanctions work even when no one is watching.

Fifth, feminists can argue that the desegregation of gendered space has created a sub-culture of romance between the sexes which is eradicable. They could then stress the idea that love is not sex; that it is pure, innocent and based on care, and that it requires an interaction between the sexes that the paranoid idea of honour refuses to accommodate. The argument is that there is nothing sexually dishonouring about romance.

The most powerful argument, I believe, is the initial one: the empirical fact that most of the murdered women are poor women, whose deaths are irrelevant to the sexual mores of a society that is changing irreversibly. The only powerful response to this argument, it seems to me, is the present fundamentalist push for a complete re-segregation of the gendered space. The fundamentalist agenda is an answer to all the complexities, ambiguities, and instabilities of the nationalist project. But as I had argued in a previous article,[70] the fundamentalist agenda itself is not devoid of its own ambiguities. An important question for the Arab world today is: "what is the meaning of gender when the traditional, nationalist and fundamentalist texts intersect?"

NOTES

1 *People Weekly*, 20 January 1992. On 6 November 1989, Zein Isa, an Arab immigrant in the US, stabbed his daughter Tina to death "to defend his honour". We have a record of the events that took place the evening of Tina's death, because the FBI, unknown to the Isas, was bugging the apartment, under the pretext that Zein was suspected of being a member of a "terrorist" organisation. Unfortunately for Tina, no one was listening to the tape at the time of her death.

2 The Lebanese Penal Code no. 340 of 1943 is considered the most immediate legal historical source of the Jordanian Penal Code of 1960. See Kamel Said, *The General Principles of Crime in the Jordanian Penal Code* (Amman: Naqabat al-Muhamin, 1981). The Lebanese Code itself has its historical origins in the Ottoman Penal Codes of 1840, 1851, 1858, a series of codes promulgated by the Ottomans in the nineteenth century in an effort to "modernise" their empire. While the first two were primarily based on Islamic Law and local custom, the third was deeply influenced by the French Code of 1810. See Mahmoud Nagib Husni, *Treatise on the Lebanese Code* (Beirut: Matba'at al-Naqari, 1968).

3 Emile Garçon, *Code pénal annoté* (Paris: Recueil Sirey, 1952) p. 151.

4 The word 'adultery' in this context is a translation of the word *zina*' which in Islamic Law refers to illicit sexual relations between men and women whether they were married or not.

5 Laure Mughayzil, *al-Mar'a fi al-tashri' al-lubnani* (Women in Lebanese Legislation) (Beirut: Mu'assaset Nawfal, 1985).

6 Article 562 of the Lebanese Penal Code, Article 548 of the Syrian Penal Code, Article 237 of the Egyptian Penal Code, Article 153 of the Kuwaiti Penal Code, Article 409 of the Iraqi Penal Code, Article 279 of the Algerian Penal Code, Article 375 of the Libyan Penal Code, Article 207 of the Tunisian Penal Code.

7 One possible reason for this phenomenon is that most of these jurists have studied in Egypt which they see as the birthplace of Arab jurisprudence and the place where it was most developed. These Arab jurists seem to have the attitude of the child towards the patriarch (the Egyptian jurist) who should be followed and imitated, rather than critiqued and challenged.

8 Indeed, one gets the impression that most of these books were produced for the benefit of the nationals of the author's country. A typical writer does that by the sheer act of copying Egyptian criminal commentaries, a practice that would obtain the national author a Ph.D. in law, thereby qualifying him to become a respectable law professor in his own country.

9 See Abdul-Hamid Shawarbi, *On Aggravating and Extenuating Circumstances* (Alexandria: Dar al-Matbu'at al-Jami'yya, 1986), p. 36.

10 Mughayzil, *al-Mara'a*, p. 191.

11 Her two arguments can, on one reading, be seen as contradictory: For if what concerns her is equality and freedom, then it could be argued that positioning "wives" as equal beneficiaries of these provisions satisfies the requirements of equality. This runs contrary to the spirit of her first argument which calls for abolishing these kinds of provisions for their adverse effects of "reproducing a tribal mentality".

12 Shawarbi, *On Aggravating*, p. 37.

13 Edward Ghali, *Treatise on the Libyan Penal Code* (Tripoli: Manshourat al-Jam'a al-Libiya, 1971), p. 85, citing the Egyptian Court of Cassation Decision No. 409, 1935.

14 Said, *The General Principles*, p. 196.

15 See in general Nawal Saadawi, *The Hidden Face of Eve*, trans. and ed. by Sherif Hetata (London: Zed Press, 1980); Leila Abu-Lughod, *Veiled Sentiments: Honor and Piety in a Bedouin Society* (Berkeley: University of California Press, 1986); M. E. Combs-Schilling, *Sacred Performances: Islam, Sexuality and Sacrifice* (New York: Columbia University Press, 1989); David Gilmore (ed.), *Honor and Shame and the Unity of the Mediterranean,* (Washington, D.C.: American Anthropological Association, 1987).

16 "If they find blood on the bride's *sarwal* (drawers) they make a quivering noise and dance in the room, the bride's sister dances in the room with the trousers on her head. It is then hung up in the yard so that all people should see the marks of virginity. Should there be no such blood, the bridegroom's family would exclaim, "go away from me, you bitch;" and the bride's father, or in his absence, her brother, would shoot her dead in the room or in the yard, besides which, all the money and presents given would be returned." Combs-Schilling, *Sacred Performances.*

17 Sana al-Khayyat, *Honour and Shame: Women in Modern Iraq* (London: Saqi, 1990) p. 33.

18 I borrow my construction of virginity as performance from the idea that gender itself is performance in Judith Butler, *Gender Trouble: Feminism and the Subversion of Identity* (New York: Routledge, 1990).

19 An interview with a Palestinian woman living in Israel published in *Kol Hair*, 28 June 1991. The performance of public virginity through a stylised body and space also covers the woman's speech. Not only is the woman not supposed to smoke in public or wear a short dress (acts associated with "whorish" behaviour), but she is also expected not to engage in talk that transgresses the code of virginity. Talk about sex in general (except between women in their own private space) is considered to be such a transgression. A woman who talks, hints, insinuates, or jokes about sex in public is seen as having committed a disgraceful act that often invites violent reactions from males in her family. Flirtatious behaviour on the part of the woman is perceived similarly.

20 Zein Isa killed his daughter Tina simply because she had been walked home by a male friend a number of times before the night of her death. Isa was an American immigrant who had originally come from a Palestinian village where he grew up most of his life. See the *People Weekly,* 20 January 1992.

21 Badran and Cook (eds.), *Opening the Gates: A Century of Arab Feminist Writing* (London: Virago, 1990), p. 4.

22 Gilmore, *Honour and Shame*, p. 5.

23 "When a man is shamed through an erotic defeat or an equivalent social submission he is symbolically emasculated: his physical integrity is dissolved and he succumbs to the ever-present danger of sexual reversal, or feminization. In a sense, he surrenders his own masculine identity and becomes a woman who is victimized and penetrated." *Ibid.*, p. 6.

24 Sawsan el-Messiri, 'Bint el-Balad: Self-Images of Traditional Urban Women in Cairo' in Lois Beck and Nikki Keddie (eds.), Women in the Muslim World (Cambridge, Mass.: Harvard University Press, 1978).

25 *Ibid.*, p. 721.

26 "Successful claims on a woman entail domination of other men, both from the point of view of the husband who jealously guards his wife, and of the adulterer who shows himself to be more powerful than the husband." Gilmore, *Honour and Shame*, p. 5.

27 One of the most powerful instances of the stylisation of Arab male space, that I have been privy to, happened one day as I was watching a group of men dancing in a Middle Eastern restaurant. Though both men and women occupied the dancing floor, it was immediately clear to any onlooker that women danced with women, mostly in couples, and so did the men. A group of five men danced in a circle. A man occupied the centre of the circle and was shaking his hips doing the belly-dance. Other men were clapping for him and cheering. The men's eyes met frequently, and they would dance to each other, now and then, subverting the attention from the man in the middle. A woman tried to enter the centre of the circle and replace the man shaking his hips and do the belly-dance herself. Every time she did, the circle broke down leaving her dancing alone, as the men recircled again repeating what they had been doing before, without her. She repeated her attempt twice and the same thing happened.

The men in the circle looked self-satisfied. By having a man in the middle belly-dancing, they already had in him the woman that they needed (in a world where women dance with women and men with men). When a real woman intervened and tried to occupy his space, the men instinctively rejected her, since the way in which their public space has been stylised leaves no place for her. Thus, the circle broke down and the men recircled without her.

28 Gilmore, *Honour and Shame*, p. 2.

29 This is supported in Jordan by the practice of the police who instruct gynaecologists to inform them if they are presented with a case in which the family of a woman wants to verify whether she is a virgin (this was communicated to me in an interview with the Criminal D.A. in Amman). The police in this case arrive at the scene and try to marry the woman to the man who she claims has caused her loss of virginity. Similarly, gynaecologists perform operations called 'hymenorrhophy' in which they reconstruct the hymen after it is broken (I have arrived at this knowledge through a series of interviews with Jordanian gynaecologists who prefer to remain unnamed). These practices support the intention of the codes in that they seek to delegitimise traditional honour killings.

30 What I mean by the nationalist elites or the nationalists, is the ruling group with whatever pronounced political label, be it FLN, Ba'th, Arab Nationalist, Royalist, Marxist, who took over the government of the nearly-independent states of the Arab world. I call them "nationalists" in the broad sense, for two reasons: first, they all shared "the sentiment/ideology" that Arabs constitute one nation, and the ideal that the Arab world should be united. Second, they were nationalist in the sense that the task they undertook of modernising the institutions of the state, started the historically irreversible process of imprinting on the consciousness of the population of their own particular state a sentiment/ ideology of local nationalism. Through government curricula, media, institutional indoctrination, the people of Algeria started to see themselves as Algerians, of Jordan as Jordanians, of Lebanon as Lebanese . . . etc. This is despite the simultaneously running belief that "we are all Arab" that everybody seemed to share.

31 Unfortunately space does not allow a full treatment of Sanhuri here.

32 Cassation Criminal 53/53, p. 578, 1953.

33 Cassation Criminal 8/53, p. 263, 1954.
34 Cassation Criminal 59/64, p. 1036, 1964.
35 Cassation Criminal 5/67, p. 221, 1967.
36 Cassation Criminal 30/75, p. 1021, 1975.
37 Cassation Criminal 11/78, p. 458, 1978.
38 Cassation Criminal 19/68, p. 494, 1968.
39 Cassation Criminal 58/73, p. 849, 1973.
40 Cassation Criminal 90/81, p. 1770, 1981.
41 Cassation Criminal 88/70, p. 962, 1970.
42 The ratio of honour crimes to all other killings committed in Jordan (according to Jordanian police records) was 33.3% in 1986, 26.5% in 1987, 30.3% in 1988, 32.2% in 1989, 26.2% in 1990, 31.5% in 1991.
43 Article 234 deals with the crime of killing somebody "with intent but without premeditation", punishable by permanent or temporary hard labour. Article 236 deals with the crime of unintentionally killing somebody by intending to "only harm or injure them", punishable by temporary hard labour or imprisonment from three to seven years.
44 Rauf Ubaid, *The General Rules of the Egyptian Penal Legislation* (Cairo: Matba'at al-Nahda, 1964), p. 863.
45 *Ibid.*, p. 864.
46 Appeal No. 615 of the Judicial year 46, 1967.
47 Appeal No. 71 of the Judicial year 42, 1972.
48 Due to lack of space I will not be able to provide a detailed exposition of the Syrian cases I had looked into (from 1957 to 1982). I will, therefore, limit myself to a commentary on the following cases: Cassation Criminal 264, dec. 408, 1957; Cassation Criminal 144, dec. 158, 1958; Cassation Criminal 358, 1963; Cassation Criminal 487, 1964; Cassation Criminal 291, 1965; Cassation Criminal 402, 1965; Cassation Criminal 443, 1966; Cassation Criminal dec. 6, 1970; Cassation 451, December 627, 1982.
49 The nationalists borrow their construction of the "modern woman" from writings by Arab renaissance writers and their disciples who believed in some form of Arab nationalism or even Islamic nationalism. Some of those who wrote on women were Butros al-Bustani, 'The Education of Women' [Arabic] in Fuad Afram al-Bustani (ed.), *The Teacher Butros al-Bustani* (Beirut, 1929); Rifa'a Tahtawi, *Guiding Truths for Girls and Youths* [Arabic] (Cairo, 1873); Qasim Amin, *The Liberation of Women* [Arabic] (Cairo, 1899) and *The New Woman* [Arabic] (Cairo, 1901); Tahir Haddad, *Our Woman in Religion and Society* [Arabic] (Tunis, 1930); Salama Musa, *The Woman is not a Man's Toy* [Arabic] (Cairo: Salama Musa lil-Nashr wal-Tawzi', 1953). The general idea in these writings was that women should be educated since this will turn them into an asset for the nation, through their roles as mothers who bring up good sons.
50 For my discussion of belly-dancing I have relied on Wendy Buonaventura, *Serpent of the Nile: Women and dance in the Arab world* (London: Saqi, 1989), a unique text that attempts to provide a history of belly-dancing and to theorize it both as an art form and as a social practice. On pp. 39–53, the writer discusses the role played by gypsy, minority and poor women in the Middle East in preserving and developing the dance throughout the ages. This, they did in a social enviroment that was fiercely ambivalent towards their art, and at certain times openly hostile and violently censoring.

51 Under the title 'Cabarets and Clubs', Buonaventura shows that despite the lurking cultural ambivalence towards the dance, belly-dancers have succeeded in turning their dance into an art performed in respectable and sought-after places. Dancers have even become, as in the case of Egypt, a nationalist feature of the country in which they perform, so that the Egyptian government frequently sends dancers as its representatives to perform in other countries and attract tourists.

52 *Ibid.*, p. 159.

53 For an excellent discussion of the confusion in the code of sexual behaviour that had accompanied the desegregation of the workplace, see Elizabeth Warnock Fernea, *Women and the Family in the Middle East* (Austin: University of Texas, 1985).

54 I must say that the sight of these women dancing has often made me feel very nervous. The belly-dancer's "shameless" shaking of the hips and breasts, her lewd immodest erotic movements turn, at the hands of these women, into girlish bashful embarrassed gestures that invite boredom, impatience and restlessness in me as a female voyeur who is enamored with the belly-dance.

55 For my sexual typology of Arab women I have relied on several modern Arab novels, interviews I have personally conducted, as well as my own observations of men and women in my life. The novels include: Sahar Khalifah, *Memoirs of an Unrealistic Woman* (Beirut: Dar al-Adab, 1986) and *The Sunflower*, Jabra Ibrahim Jabra, *In Search of Walid Massoud* (Beirut: Dar al-Adab, 1978.) and *The Ship* (Washington DC: Three Continents Press, 1985); Hoda Barakat, *The Stone of Laughter* (Reading: Garnet Publishing, 1995); Ghadah Samman, *Beirut 75* (Beirut: Manshourat Ghada Samman, 1975); Rachid Boujadra, *al-Inkar* (Algiers: al-Mou'assasa al-Wataniyya lil-Kitab, 1984); Ibrahim Aslan, *Malek al-hazin* (Cairo: Cairo Publications, 1993); and Ghassan Kanafani, *And What is Left to You?* (Beirut: Dar Tali'at al–Tiba'ah wal-Nashr, 1977) I have also found very helpful a number of interviews with Lebanese women talking about their sexual lives published in Bouthaina Shaaban, *Both Right- and Left-Handed: Arab Women Talk about their Lives* (London: Women's Press, 1988).

56 This situation produces a particular anomaly which is that the consumption by the "sexy virgin" of Western fashion does not necessarily mean that she is aware of the sexual messages that are delivered with this kind of garb, themselves a cultural creation of Western sexuality.

57 The virgin of love, often upper class, has the self-image of being a modern woman, which in her mind means belief in romantic love as the only legitimate basis for partnership between the sexes. Her belief, in a social environment that stresses to various degrees the importance of the traditional venues of marriage, could be very radical and subversive.

58 This is a reference to the GAP chain store, which sells clothes that are signified by their yuppie practicality (that is, fancy jeans and T-shirts).

59 It is important to bear in mind that the sexuality associated with virginity has its deep infantilising effect on its subjects, the GAP girl being a sexual type that is the natural product of this aspect.

60 Women who work as civil servants best exemplify this kind of sexuality. Also professional women: lawyers, engineers, doctors, and women who work in academia.

61 The slut, as exemplary of fully conscious sexuality is a unique and highly subversive type in Arab culture. Her equivalent in the West should be the thirty-year-old woman who preserved her virginity in protestation against the sexual culture of her own society.

62 This type exists in the younger generation (presently in their teens and early twenties) of the upper and upper-middle classes. They could be called the post-colonial, post-modern Madonna generation.

63 For an excellent representation of the life of the sexy virgin turn virgin of love turn mother, see an interview with a Lebanese woman in Shaaban, *Both Right- and Left-Handed*, pp. 116–22.

64 For a brilliant literary representation of male sexuality in the traditional text, see the novel entitled *al-Inkar* by the Algerian writer Rachid Boujadra, 1969.

65 This is best captured in a film entitled 'Wedding in Galilee' by the Palestinian director Michel Khalifeh, 1987.

66 For an interesting discussion of the modern predator, see an interview with Egyptian college students published in *Hurriyyati*, an Egyptian weekly, 1 November 1992. The title of the interview is 'This Man I Reject, and the Reason: His Superficiality'.

67 See (in Arabic) *The Letters of Ghassan Kanafani to Ghadah Samman* (Beirut: Dar al-Tali'ah, 1992). The publication of the love letters sent by the late Palestinian writer Kanafani to the Syrian writer Samman caused a furore in the Arab world among writers and non-writers alike. Kanafani, a much admired nationalist writer, came out in these letters as the "castrated" romantic who suffered greatly from Samman's rejection of his love; a shock to most of his faithful admirers.

68 According to the Jordanian police archives on crimes of honour committed between the years 1986 and 1991, almost all of the men charged with these crimes came from working-class or lower-middle-class backgrounds. They included those who worked as butchers, farmers, soldiers, bus drivers, civil servants, and the unemployed.

69 *Kol Hair*, 28 June 1991.

70 See 'Post-Colonial Feminism and the Veil: Thinking the Difference', *New England Law Review*, Vol. 26, No. 4 (1992).

PART THREE

THE POLITICS OF
INTERPRETATION

EIGHT

ISLAM AND FEMINISM: AN ANALYSIS OF POLITICAL STRATEGIES

Haleh Afshar

This chapter presents a brief outline of the succinct points made by Islamic women in defence of their faith which they define as a dynamic system that has offered much to women; in their view even more than Western-style feminism. The ways in which these arguments have been used politically to advance the cause of women in Iran will be used as an illustration of these strategies. It will be argued that elite women in Iran have succeeded in curtailing in this way some of the least enlightened measures that had been imposed on them in the early days of the post-revolutionary state.

For the past fifteen years Iranian women have become the standard-bearers of Islamism in Iran and have been obliged, by law, to present a veiled, and often serene and silent, face to the world media. Yet in practice, despite the continuous efforts of the State to control and curtail them and their activities, Iranian women have fought a long and successful battle and regained much of the ground that they had lost in the early days. This chapter seeks both to celebrate their success and analyse the strategies that they have used in this struggle.

Although different women's groups have fought on different fronts and taken up different issues, without doubt the most successful have been those who have located their political action in the context of Islam and its teachings. Since the Iranian State has, albeit nominally, prided itself in its Islamic adherence and has chosen to present itself as the defender of the faith, the believers have been better able to engage in positive discussion and extract "Islamic" measures which are liberating.

Islamic Fundamentalism

Islamic fundamentalism has for long been associated with greater or lesser degrees of oppression of women. Given the rise of fundamentalism and the decision of many women to consciously reject feminism of various kinds and adopt the creed, it is important for some of us to consider what it is and why so many have chosen it?

Part of the problem of understanding fundamentalism has been in terms of definitions and terminology. Muslims themselves do not use the term fundamentalist at all; the twentieth-century Islamists argue that they are revivalists, and are returning to the sources of Islam to regain a purified vision, long since lost in the mire of worldly governments. Shi'is, who are a minority school of Islam, but form 98 per cent of the Iranian population, have for long seen themselves as the guardians of the poor, the dispossessed and those trampled on by unjust governments.[1] Fundamentalism for them is a return to the roots and a recapturing of both the purity and the vitality of Islam as it was at its inception.

In this pursuit of the past, Muslims, like all those glorifying their histories, are returning to an imaginary golden episode to lighten the difficulties of their current-day existence.[2] The golden age for the Shi'is is the short rule of the Prophet, about a decade long, and the even shorter one of his nephew and son-in-law, 'Ali, who ruled for less than five years. The Sunnis, who accept the first four caliphs of Islam as being pure and worthy of emulation, can lay claim to about 40 years of just rule; from the hijra, the Prophet's move to Medina in 622, to 'Ali's death in 661 AD. In addition, all Muslims claim to adhere absolutely to Qur'anic laws and accept the Qur'an as representing the very words of God as revealed to his Prophet Muhammad.

The Qur'an, which is divided into 114 suras, contains expressly or impliedly, all the divine commands. These commands are contained in about 500 verses and of these about 80 may be regarded by *Western* lawyers as articles of a code[3] (my italics).

Thus in their pursuit of the golden age, Muslims are equipped with fifty years of history and 114 verses of a Holy Book. This is perhaps as good a resource as those offered by any other ideology or utopian vision. But, like all utopias, the past and the Holy Book have difficulties adjusting to the present. It is in the domain of interpretation and adjustments to history that Islam is deemed to have become degraded. Yet without such adjustments, it would find it hard to survive as a creed. Thus the notions of return and revivalism frame the processes of the new, puritanical interpretations that are to counter centuries of misdeed and hardship and pave the way for the future.

Women and Revivalism

In the twentieth-century domain of interpretations, women have been active in their own right. Although the bulk of Islamic theology has been adapted and interpreted by male theologians who have claimed exclusive rights to instituting the *shari'a*, women have always maintained a presence, albeit a small one.[4] They have consistently and convincingly argued that Islam as a religion has always had to accommodate women's specific needs. The first convert to Islam was the Prophet's redoubtable and wealthy wife Khadija; no religion which she accepted could discriminate against women. Khadija, who was nearly twenty years older than the Prophet, had first employed him as her trade representative and subsequently commanded him to marry her; overcoming his reserve and reluctance by informing his uncle that she was the very best wife that he could ever have. Their marriage was a happy one and the Prophet did not take another wife in her lifetime.

Thus some fourteen centuries ago Islam recognised women's legal and economic independence as existing and remaining separate from that of their fathers, brothers, husbands and sons. Islamic marriage was conceived as a matter of contract between consenting partners (Qur'an IV, 4; IV, 24), and one that stipulated a specific price, *mahr*, payable to the bride before the consummation of marriage. Women must be maintained in the style to which they have been accustomed (II, 238; IV, 34) and paid for suckling their babies (II, 233).

Besides personal and economic independence, women were also close confidantes and advisers to the Prophet. Khadija supported him in the early years and undoubtedly her influence protected the Prophet against the various Meccan nobles who wished to destroy Islam at its inception. After her death Muhammad's favourite wife 'A'isha, who married him as a child and grew up in his household became not only his spouse, but also his closest ally and confidante. She is known as one of the most reliable interpreters of Islamic law.

Besides being a renowned source for the interpretation and extension of Islamic law, 'A'isha was also an effective politician and a remarkable warrior. Like many of the Prophet's wives, she accompanied him on his campaigns. After his death she ensured that her father Abu Bakr and not Muhammad's nephew, 'Ali, succeeded to the caliphate, and led the Muslim community. Subsequently, when 'Ali became the Caliph 'A'isha raised an army and went to battle against him, taking to the field herself. Although she was defeated 'Ali treated her with respect, but beseeched her not to interfere in politics.

Thus, if fundamentalism is about returning to the golden age of Islam, Muslim women argue that they have much reason for optimism and much room for manoeuvre. Furthermore, many highly educated and articulate Muslim women regard Western feminism as a poor example and have no wish to follow it. Not only do they dismiss Western feminism for being one of the many instrument of colonialism, but also they despise the kinds of freedom offered to women in the West.[5] Using much of the criticism provided by Western women themselves, Islamist women argue that by concentrating on labour market analysis and offering the experiences of a minority of white affluent middle class women as a norm, Western feminists have developed an analysis which is all but irrelevant to the lives of the majority of women the world over. They are of the view that Western-style feminist struggles have only liberated women to the extent that they are prepared to become sex objects and market their sexuality as an advertising tool to benefit patriarchal capitalism.[6] They are particularly critical of the failure of Western feminism to carve an appropriate, recognised and enumerated space for marriage and motherhood. They argue that by locating the discussion in the domain of production and attempting to gain equality for women, Western feminists have sought and failed to make women into quasi men. They have failed to alter the labour market to accommodate women's needs and at the same time have lost the recognition, respect and honour that women had once obtained in matrimony. Thus Western feminists have made women into permanent second-class citizens, not a model that most women, in the West as elsewhere, choose to follow.[7]

By contrast, Islamist women argue that they can benefit by returning to the sources of Islam. They are of the view that Islamic dicta bestow complementarity on women, as human beings, as partners to men and as mothers and daughters. They argue that Islam demands respect for women and offers them opportunities, to be learned, educated and trained, while at the same time providing an honoured space for them to become mothers, wives and home-makers. They argue that unlike capitalism and much of feminist discourse, Islam recognises the importance of women's life-cycles, they have been given different roles and responsibilities at different times of their lives and at each and every stage they are honoured and respected for that which they do. They argue that Islam at its inception has provided them with exemplary female role models and has delineated a path that can be honourably followed at each stage. Muhammad's daughter Fatima, for the Shi'is in particular, provides an idealised and idolised role model, as daughter to the Prophet and wife to the imam, 'Ali. For all Muslims, Khadija represents a powerful representative of independence as well as being a supportive wife. The Sunnis admire 'A'isha for her renowned intellect as well as her political leadership. Thus, revivalist content Muslim women have no need of Western examples, which are in any case alien and exploitative. They have their own path to liberation which they wish to pursue.

Islamist women are particularly defensive of the veil. The actual imposition of the veil and the form that it has taken is a contested domain.[8] Nevertheless, many Muslim women have chosen the veil as the symbol of Islamisation and have accepted it as the public face of their revivalist position. For them the veil is a liberating, and not an oppressive force. They maintain that the veil enables them to become the observers and not the observed; that it liberates them from the dictates of the fashion industry and the demands of the beauty myth. In the context of the patriarchal structures that shape women's lives, the veil is a means of bypassing sexual harassment and "gaining respect".[9] In Iran it is seen as a means of liberation from the plight of being the unveiled, exploited "slaves of imperialism" and facilitating their full participation in the public domain.[10]

As post-modernism takes hold and feminists deconstruct their views and allow more room for specifics and differing needs, demands and priorities of women of different creeds and colours,[11] it is no longer easy to offer pat denials of the Islamic women's positions.

Iran and the Practical Politics of Islamist Women

Like all political theories, the Islamist women's has had difficulties in standing the test of time. Although Islam does provide a space for women, it has been as difficult for Muslim women, as for their Western counterparts, to obtain and maintain their rights. The throng of women who supported the Islamic revolution in Iran were no exception to this rule. On its inception the Islamic Republic embarked on a series of misogynist laws, decrees and directives which rapidly curtailed the access of women to much of the public domain. Female judges were sacked, the faculty of law closed its door to female applicants and article 163 of the Islamic constitution declared that women could not become judges.

Subsequently the Islamic laws of retribution, the *qisas* laws, severely eroded women's legal rights. Not only was the evidence of two women equated with that of one man, as required by the Qur'an (II, 82), but women's evidence, if uncorroborated by men, was no longer accepted by the courts. Women who insisted on giving uncorroborated evidence are judged to be lying and subject to punishment for slander (Article 92 of the *qisas* laws).

Murder is now punished by retribution; but the murderer can opt for the payment of *diyya*, blood money, to the descendants of the murdered in lieu of punishment (Article 1 of the *qisas* laws.) Whereas killing a man is a capital offence, murdering a women is a lesser crime:

> Should a Muslim man wilfully murder a Muslim woman, he must be killed, the murder can be punished only after the woman's guardian has paid half of his *diyya* [blood money, or the sum that the man would be worth if he were to live a normal life; this is negotiated with and paid to the man's family] (Article 5 of the *qisas* laws).

By contrast, women murderers have no blood money and must be executed (Article 6). Similarly, violent attacks against women, resulting in maiming or severe injuries, can only be punished after payment of mutilation money to the male assailant before retribution can be administered. The reverse does not apply (Article 60).

What is worse, fathers, who are recognised as the automatic guardians of the household, have the right of life and death over their children. Fathers who murder their children are "excused" from punishment, provided they pay blood money to the inheritors (Article 16); however, there is no specific blood money stipulated for children. If they murder one or more of their children, all fathers have to do is to pay themselves the blood money! Khumaini decided to return to all fathers their Islamic automatic right of custody of children on divorce, which they had lost under the 1976 Family laws in Iran. By doing so and legislating the *qisas* laws, the post-revolutionary state endowed fathers with the undisputed right of life and death over their children.

Men were now entitled to kill anyone who "violates their harem". Men who murdered their wives, sisters, or mothers on the charge of adultery, were not subject to any punishment. But women were not given similar rights. Nor do they have the right of life and death over their children.

In addition, in the early post-revolutionary years the access of women to almost half of University departments was barred and they were encouraged to abandon paid employment.[12] They could not be employed without the formal consent of their husbands, a rule that after much struggle was extended to apply to both marriage partners before the revolution, but was revised in favour of men afterwards.

Politically, too, women were marginalised. Article 115 of the Islamic constitution follows Ayatollah Khumeini's instructions in insisting that the leader of the nation, *velayat-e faqih*, must be a man, and so should the President. Since its inception the Islamic Republic has never had a female member of the cabinet and the numbers of female Majlis representatives had been less than five in all but the last Majlis, where they reached nine.

Thus with the arrival of the Islamic Republic, with the notable exception of the vote, Iranian women lost all they had struggled for over a century. The situation seemed grim indeed.

The Politics of Feminist Fundamentalism

Yet, to despair of the plight of women is to fail to recognise the formidable resilience of Iranian women. They refused to be daunted by this onslaught of patriarchy, as they had been for the past hundred years or more. Although some bowed to the pressures of the Islamic Republic, many remained firm, both as women and as believers in the faith. It was only the devout Muslim women who could counter the demands made of them by the Islamic Republic. Given the Islamic nature of the national political discourse, which posits the government as the defender of the faith, women were able to take the Republic to task for failing to deliver on its Islamic duties. For Iranian women revivalism has almost literally been God-sent. They have fought against their political, legal and economic marginalisation and although victory is yet to come, they have won considerable ground and are continuing to do so. Throughout, their arguments have been anchored in the teachings of Islam, the Qur'anic laws and the traditions and practices of the Prophet of Islam.

Using the Qur'anic instruction that all Muslims must become learned, women have finally succeeded in removing many of the bars placed on their education. At its inception, the Islamic Republic excluded women from 54 per cent of the subjects taught at the tertiary level[13] and were reduced to 10 per cent of the total student population in 1983.[14] Slowly and painfully women fought their way back. Even though by 1991 women were still barred from 97 academic areas,[15] they have been able to insist on specific quotas for women in some subjects. They were most successful in the field of medicine where a special all women faculty was set up at Qum and in 1994 the government instituted a nation-wide 25 per cent quota for women for the intake in certain medical fields.[16] Women who trained in the pre-revolutionary days of equality now command high salaries and many run their own successful businesses in the private sector.[17] Private sector schools have simply defied the laws of gender segregation and employed male science and mathematics teachers to teach girls. As a result Iranian girls regularly come top in the University entrance examinations in most subjects!

Women in Public and Politics

Although they fought shoulder to shoulder with men, women were not given high office by the revolutionary government. It has never appointed a woman to a ministerial post. This point was made by Zahra Rahnavard in 1990 when she complained:

> Women have been and continue to be present, at times in larger numbers than men, in our public demonstrations for the revolution and in its support. But when it comes to public appointments, they are pushed aside . . .
>
> Women like myself have continuously campaigned for better conditions. We have made our demands in the press and in the public domain. But no one has taken any notice and our voices are not heard.[18]

But getting elected is only the first step and women members of the Majlis are severely constrained by the ideological views that designate them as inferior, demands of them to be modest, silent and invisible[19] and defines them as interlopers in the public domain. Maryam Behruzi, a veteran representative who had served a prison sentence before the revolution and whose 16-year old son was martyred, during the Iran–Iraq war, still found herself firmly discriminated against in Majlis. She pointed out that women are never elected to high-powered committees. Nor do they become chair or officers of other parliamentary committees.[20] Azam Taleqani, who gained a seat in the first post-revolutionary Majlis, explained that women were expected to be "naturally modest" and this prevented them from "saying too much in the Majlis".[21]

In April 1991, as the country was preparing for the Parliamentary elections, Maryam Behruzi demanded that bills allowing an earlier retirement age for women, reforming some of the more Draconian divorce laws[22] and provision of national insurance for women and children, be put before the next session of the Majlis. Behruzi also asked for the laws to be reformed to allow single women to travel abroad to continue their studies. The request was not endorsed by the Presidential adviser on women's issues, Shahla Habibi. She stated that such an act would devalue Iranian women and knock them off their perch of purity:

> Since women are the public face of our society and the guardians of our honour, we must not intentionally dispatch them to a corrupt environment (i.e. the West).[23]

In the subsequent Majlis, twelve women were elected. Representatives Behruzi, Nafiseh Fiazbakhsh, Fatemeh Homayun Moqadam, Monireh Nobakht, Bib Qodsieh Seyedi Nabavi and Marzieh Vahid Dastgerdi, did their best to revise this law. But they failed.

But Behruzi did succeed in pushing through a bill which allowed women to retire after twenty years of active service, while the men still have to serve twenty-five years. Her success was in part achieved because it was framed in the accepted context that women belong to the home and should return there as soon as possible.

Nevertheless, for those who were actively campaigning for women, this bill was a remarkable success, since the path of women's liberation has been less than smooth. In 1991 the Women's Cultural-Social Council, despite its conservative membership, submitted 13 women's projects to the High Council of Cultural Revolution; but only one of these was considered and ratified by the Council. It was a proposal to eliminate the prejudicial treatment of women in higher education and in the selection for degree courses. This was no mean feat since there were discriminatory measures against women in 119 academic subject areas.[24]

Women and the Judiciary

At its inception, the Islamic government sought to remove women from the legal domain altogether. Within a year of his arrival, Khomeini had sacked all women judges, declared their judicial ranks, earned through years of service, to be null and void and excluded women from the faculty of law. Officially he discontinued legal practices by women. Yet, in an exemplary fashion, Iranian women lawyers refused to be marginalised.

Women had had access to the Faculty of Law since it was set up in 1932 and they formed an important part of the legal system before the revolution. After the revolution some continued to practice, under their husband, son or brothers' name; others worked as legal advisers to companies and all continued to fight for re-entry to the formal judicial domain.

Thus, even though Article 1 of the 1982 "Selection of the Judiciary" Bill *qanuneh sharayeteh entekhabeh qozateh dadgostary*, expressly stated that "judges will be selected from suitably qualified men", the critical shortage of lawyers and women's agitation resulted in the addition of a revisionary note, clause 5. It permitted women lawyers to act as "advisers" in Family Courts and on matters relating to care and responsibility for children and minors.[25]

Two years later clause 5 was revised and the Head of Judiciary was empowered to appoint women (who fulfil the qualifications stated in the 1982 Selection of the Judiciary Bill) to judicial functions as advisers to the administrative justice courts, to family courts, and to the posts of: Assistant to the Public Prosecutor; Examining Magistrate and offices concerned with legal research and preparation of laws; personal law and taking charge of custody of minors and legal adviser in government departments that have a legal affairs department.

But in the years that followed, the heads of the Judiciary remained reluctant to use these powers to any great extent. As Ayatollah Muhammad Yazdi explained in 1990:

> There are very few women working in the judiciary and most them are doing secretarial and clerical jobs; they hardly ever reach the higher levels. So you cannot expect us to hand over to such women the problems of family laws at a national level.[26]

Nevertheless, the law allowed access to a few newcomers and in particular helped to keep in their posts some of the women who were already employed by the Ministry of Justice.

In part this was the result of the hasty Islamisation of the courts in Iran. Overnight the courts were expected to implement the Islamic laws and be run by judges trained in *shari'a*. Since, until the mid-1980s, women had not been deemed as suitable material for training in Islamic law all the available women lawyers were graduates of Teheran University and therefore, strictly speaking, not suitable. But in the early days, there simply were not enough Islamic judges of any kind and so the government permitted the attendance of secularly trained "advisers" to assist the courts. As a result many women lawyers, though stripped of their formal rank, continued to do the work they had been doing.

At the same time leading religious figures such as Ayatollah Muhammad Hosein Beheshti, the first post-revolutionary Head of the Judiciary, Ayatollah Musavi Ardabili and Ayatollah Mohaqeq Damad, set up informal classes for postgraduate law students, male and female, to teach them Islamic law. This enabled many of the women who had graduated just before the revolution to acquire the necessary Islamic training. Given the shortage of male lawyers and the closure of the faculty of law for about three years, those women who were both edu-cated and had good revolutionary credentials found themselves propelled into relatively powerful positions in no time at all. For example, Azam Nuri, the Director-General of the Legal Department of the Ministry of National Guidance (*Ershadeh Meli*) was appointed to her post in 1979, when she was 24 years old.

But many of the more conservative *'ulama* remained wary of the presence of women in the judiciary and feared that women would gradu-ally progress through the ranks to become judges. To prevent such an eventuality by the end of the decade, the *'ulama* sought to remove women from the legal domain by cutting these posts. In September 1992 the post of adviser to judges was eliminated. In April 1994 the Committee on the Judiciary decided to gradually discontinue the posts of Assistant to the Public Prosecutor and examining magistrate and to reject clause 5 altogether. Their decision was brought to the Majlis for ratification in May 1994.

The Commission had decided to eliminate women from the domain of law on three grounds: first and foremost was the assertion that Islam excluded women from the judiciary and that the state should ensure that women in no way diluted this stipulation. In addition many were of the view that by their very nature women were not suited to act in this domain and that they would be both dangerous and vulnerable to con-tamination and corruption if they insisted on pursuing their activities in courts. Furthermore, some members of the Committee felt that given the high levels of male unemployment women should not usurp men's places and should move out.

Many of the *'ulama* remained convinced throughout that once allowed in, women would retain the potential of becoming judges. This would counter the very core of the faith that only men could make legal judgements. Eventually these views prevailed and in May 1994 the Majlis Legal and Judicial Affairs Committee decided to reject clause 5.

As the committee's Secretary Mir-Taqi Qazipur explained:

> One of the certainties in Islamic law is that the judge is a repres-
> entative and a part of *velayat-e faqih*, Islamic government, and
> this God-given duty has been imposed exclusively on men.[27]

Majlis representative 'Abbas 'Abbasi underlined the prevailing view of many of the *'ulama* that it was not in the nature of women to become judges:

> Judicial posts are not emotional posts and we all know, as every-
> body knows, that women's very nature has been created with an
> enhanced emotionalism; this shows the love and wisdom of God.
> Men have their own particular hard-headedness and fierceness
> which is known the world over, and women have their sensibil-
> ities. These posts need more than sensibility. We have to deal with
> cases concerned with fostering, with custody of minors. Even
> drafting of laws has been included in this clause 5, that is *hudud*,
> criminal law, penal codes . . . [T]hese are not domains where we
> should allow sensibilities to rule. These are domains which are
> suited to the nature of men and to allow women in would under-
> mine the stability of the family.[28]

This view was shared by Majlis representative Razavi Ardakani:

> God almighty in his wisdom has created women with particular
> souls and ideas. In some cases where the problems are more a
> matter of sound judgement and wisdom and prudence then women
> in their formation have not been granted an abundance of these
> characteristics . . . From the point of view of creation the fragility
> that we see in women indicates a natural weakness in them . . .
> Women are tender-hearted, their emotions rule over their intellect.
> In critical cases they are likely to be swayed by the accused or the
> defence lawyer and, God forbid, their tender nature would lead
> them to the wrong judgement . . . Law is a critical issue. Therefore
> the penetration of women in this domain, albeit step by step, is
> dangerous.[29]

The Committee's rapporteur Hasan Soleimani elaborated the point that to give women a judicial post of any kind would erode the basic requirement that the judiciary should be male:

> ... the necessary qualification for becoming a judge in the Islamic system is to have had a firm grounding in and long experience of the judicial system. These appointments may have paved the way for women by enabling them to have both firm grounding and long experience ... So the committee decided to halt this process which enabled women to hold formal posts within the judiciary.[30]

The chair of the Committee, 'Ali Asghar Baghbani, told the Majlis that the first Imam of Shi'ism had expressly forbidden the use of women as advisers:

> The leader of Muslims and the first imam of Shi'ism, 'Ali, said to his son "Dear Hasan do not consult with women. Do not take their advice. They are weak-willed and often their resolutions are temporary. If you ask for their advice they may change your mind, make you doubt your own mind and undermine your resolve."[31]

Razavi Ardakani suggested that women should chose to serve the country by becoming doctors and gynaecologists instead.

There were however some Committee members, such as Mas'ud Karimpur Natanzi, who were willing to admit that women had over the past decade and a half proved themselves to have been good lawyers:

> I myself have been working as an inspector in the past twelve years and must admit that, in the domain of law, our sisters have been remarkably successful in accomplishing all the tasks that we have given them. Particularly in the posts of legal advisers and assistants in the administration of justice and supervision of family courts. They have been remarkably thorough, serious, caring and more systematic than their male colleagues and must be congratulated for this. When we did a survey we found that the most learned and thorough doctoral theses were submitted by our sisters who graduated from law schools. So I have no doubt that they are capable of doing the job.

Nevertheless, Karimpur felt that as they stood the laws were inconsistent and if women wanted to work in the domain of law they should find ways other than clause 5 to gain access.

There were also members of religious institutions and the Majlis such as 'Abbas 'Abbasi who opposed the employment of women in any job so long as male unemployment existed:

> Men and women are equal before the law but have different rights . . . Furthermore, as my respected colleagues are aware we have plenty of unemployed males who have the appropriate training and we all know that if the male sector of the society has an income it will be easier to form families and reduce societal problems.[32]

Some Majlis representatives were categorical that women should on no account even enter the domain of mixed employment because of the "danger" to their honour. Baghbani painstakingly elaborated this point:

> Imam [Khomeini] instructed us to be extremely firm about imposing and maintaining and not permitting contact between women and strangers. You know how wary he was about the vulnerability of women and the protection of their honour. Yet in our offices we are employing female typists, female secretaries, female computer operators. I don't want to elaborate the seditious consequences, you are all more or less familiar with the issues. How often we find that a ministry disregards the dozens of unemployed young war returnees who put their lives on the line for this country and employs a female telephonist instead. Of course it is not shaming for women to work. But why do we insist on exposing women to danger. Why make them work in places where they have to be in contact with men from dawn to dusk?[33]

In seeking to reject the committee's proposal, women members of Majlis and their supporters had a difficult task. They had to disclaim any wish to aspire to equality or to take charge of the Islamic government or its judiciary, while maintaining their toe-hold in both. They had to remain centrally within the teachings of Islam and justify their demands in the name of faith rather than equality. They chose to highlight the exemplary path set out by the Iranian government as a beacon of light for Muslim women everywhere. They stressed the differences between the sexes and the specific needs of women and at the same time emphasised their acceptance of the different parts played by women within the judiciary. Very intelligently they extended the arguments about complementarity, which is usually used to justify domesticity[34] to support their claim for participation in the domain of law. Men were to be judges and women their "advisers".

The Speaker of Majlis 'Ali Akbar Nateq-Nuri offered categorical assurances on this point:

We have a series of basic religious principles which are immutable and we will not dilute them on any account. This includes the issue of judges in Islamic law . . . An Islamic judge must have certain qualifications which religious scholars have stipulated and which has been confirmed by the Imam. A judge must be mature, must possess reason, faith, justice, the ability to interpret Islamic laws independently, be pure in mind and body and to be male. I have no doubt that no one, including our sisters who are present and who share our Islamic faith and commitment, would wish to take any step that would erode it. But we must separate out advisory functions from exercising judgement.[35]

To make this point clear, Majlis representative Nafiseh Faizbakhsh chose to denounce Westernisation and accept the differences between the sexes and emphasise the "natural modesty" of women. She declared:

Many of the women who have to resort to law and go to the courts have told me personally that feminine modesty and honour prevents them from talking about many of their personal problems in front of men. As a result they are treated unjustly and cannot get a fair judgement. I am sorry to report that a heavily veiled woman told me how difficult she found it to talk about things that she should not have mentioned in front of male judges. So what I want to know is where is the male honour which was to defend women's modesty? . . . Should we not instruct women advisers to hear the personal problems and then present them in court using legal language and protecting our modest women and not shaming them in front of men?[36]

In this she was supported by the Majlis Speaker who noted that over 80 per cent of the applicants to the custody courts are women. The point was elaborated by deputy 'Abbasi who argued that the only way that justice could be done, and could be seen to be done, was by appropriate experts in the field of women and law dealing with the needs of women demanding custody or going to courts for other reasons.

Nafiseh Faizbakhsh developed the argument noting that her demands facilitated the recognition of the "difference" that existed between men and women going to the judiciary and in no way did her position reflect a Westernised stance:

> The Western media choose to misrepresent us . . . As the representative of my Iranian Islamic sisters I categorically state that Islamic Iran has the most advanced pro-women laws and we have no need whatsoever to resort to the West, its laws and its shortcomings which have resulted in uncertainty, injustice, problems and sufferings. We are at the forefront of the best and most forward looking laws for women. Our only hope is that our legal study centres and universities will be able to pull out these laws from the text of Islamic teachings and codes which, God willing and with the help of Majlis, they will do so very soon.[37]

The exemplary part played by Iran in giving women their rightful Islamic position was another argument offered by women and their supporters in defence of clause 5. Veteran representative Maryam Behruzi endorsed these points and noted the "great achievements" of women under the Islamic government:

> Under the Shah women's participation in the public sphere could only occur if the women adopted the loose and shameful dependent character of Western women. But our learned, committed and intellectual women were ousted. Our revolution has allocated a major part to women and has removed the barrier of Westernisation which viewed the veil as an impediment to participation in the public sphere. Women's active and remarkable contributions to this revolution which have been part of its very formation has clearly proved that Islam is a means of attaining success and fulfilment for women in the Islamic society . . . We are the very cornerstone of the future civilisation which will be rooted in Islam and the standard-bearers of victorious Islam in the world.[38]

In this Behruzi was supported by the Majlis Speaker 'Ali Akbar Nateq-Nuri who noted that Iran was setting an example to world:

> We say that Islam can rule over people, can run societies, that it offers the very best and most valuable and lively legal structures.

On the question of women we emphasise that we rely on Islamic values and honour the rights that it has granted to women. We cannot just say that this is what we are and how we act and these are our values and then fail in practice and be so narrow-minded as to even question the issue of women acting as advisers and councils, which we know has no religious impediment whatsoever.

Maryam Behruzi underlined this view by referring both to Khomeini and to the creed. Quoting extensively from Khomeini, Behruzi argued that the Imam had always supported women's participation in all domains:

The Imam used to say repeatedly that Islam has made women equal to men, but heaven knows that the services it rendered to women and the entitlements given to them were much greater than those of men.[39]

Behruzi was careful to defend the hard-won right of women to return to the faculty of law. But she went much further and contested the view that they should be excluded from any level of the judiciary. In this she chose to refer to the Islamic dictum that God alone is the lawmaker and human beings must submit to the laws of God:

If anyone, a representative using his personal inane judgement, says that "Islam has made men the governors of women", then he would be going against the faith and its laws and against what is practised in Iran. Islam does not permit anyone to rule over another. No power other than God Almighty can rule over human beings. Men are not permitted to rule over women nor women over men . . . when a judge issues a judgement all he is doing is implementing God's laws.[40]

Eventually women managed to retain their foothold in the courts and clause 5 was not rejected.

Conclusion

The rule of Islam in Iran has not been easy on women. They lost much of the ground that they had won over the previous century and the way to recapturing some of those rights has been slow and barred by pre-judice and patriarchal power. Undaunted, Iranian women have struggled on. For the moment they have had to concede the veil and its imposition in the name of Islam, though they have done so reluctantly and have continued the discussions about its validity, relevance and the extent to which it should be imposed. But the bargain that they have struck[41] has enabled them to negotiate better terms. They have managed to reverse the discriminatory policies on education, they are attacking the inequal-ities in the labour market and demanding better care and welfare pro-visions for working mothers. Although the road to liberty is one that is strewn with difficulties, Iranian women, as ever, have come out fighting and have proved difficult to dominate.

NOTES

1 M. Momen, *An Introduction to Islam: The History and doctrines of Twelver Shi'ism* (New Haven: Yale University Press, 1985).

2 A. Chhachhi, 'Forced Identities: The State, Communalism, Fundamentalism and Women in India' in D. Kandiyoti (ed.), *Women, Islam and the State* (London: Macmillan, 1991).

3 H. Afshar, 'The Muslim Concept of Law', *The International Encyclopedia of Comparative Law* (The Hague and Paris: J.C.B. Mohr Tubingen, 1986).

4 See Nadia Abbott, '*A'ishah the Beloved of Mohamad* (Chicago: University of Chicago Press, 1942); Leila Ahmed, *Women and Gender in Islam* (New Haven: Yale University Press, 1992); R. Keddie and B. Baron (eds.), *Women in Middle Eastern History: Shifting Boundaries in Sex and Gender* (New Haven and London: Yale University Press, 1991); Fatima Mernissi, *Women and Islam: An Historical and Theological Enquiry* (Oxford: Blackwell, 1991).

5 See Zeinab al-Ghazali, *Ayam min hayati* (Cairo: Dar al-Shurua, 1988), quoted by Valeri J. Hoffman, 'An Islamic Activist: Zeinab al-Ghazali' in Elizabeth Warnok Fernea (ed.), *Women and the Family in the Middle East* (Austin: University of Texas Press, 1985), and Ahmed, *Women and Gender in Islam*, and Z. Rahnavard, *Toloueh Zaneh Mosalman* (Tehran: Mahboubeh Publication, n.d.).

6 See note 5 above.

7 Rahnavard, *Toloueh Zaneh Mosalman*.

8 Mernissi, *Women and Islam*.

9 This statement, one of many examples, was made by a woman interviewee in Algeria for the *Today* programme, BBC Radio 4, 21 September 1993.

10 Majlis Representative for Tabriz Fatemeh Homayun Moqadam, interviewed by *Zaneh Ruz*, 30 April 1994.

11 See Haleh Afshar, *The Needs of Muslim Women and the Dominant Legal Order in the UK*, forthcoming, and K. Mirza, 'The Silent Cry: Second-Generation Bradford Women Speak', *Muslims in Europe*, 43 (Centre for the Study of Islam and Christian–Muslim Relations, 1989).

12 For detailed discussion see A. Tabari and N. Yeganeh (compilers), *In the Shadow of Islam* (London: Zed Press, 1982), and H. Afshar, 'Khomeini's Teachings and their Implications for Women' in the same volume, pp. 79–90, and H. Afshar, 'Women and Work: Ideology not Adjustment at Work in Iran' in H. Afshar and C. Dennis (eds.), *Women and Adjustment Policies in the Third World* (London: Macmillan Women's Studies at York Series, 1992).

13 See S. Qahraman, '*Siyasateh hokumateh Eslami piramuneh dastressi zanan beh amouzesheh ali va assarateh an bar moqeyiyateh ejtemayi va eqtessadi zanan*' (The Islamic Republic's policies on women's access to higher education and its impact on the socio-economic position of women), *Nimeyeh Digar*, No. 7, Summer 1367 (1989), and H. Afshar, 'Women and Work'.

14 H. Omid, *Islam and the Post-Revolutionary State in Iran* (Basingstoke: Macmillan, 1994), p. 162.

15 *Zaneh Ruz*, 31 August 1991.

16 Quoted by Fatemeh Homayun Moqadam, *Majlis* Representative for Tabriz, at a press conference 30 April 1994.

17 H. Afshar, 'Women and Work'.

18 *Zaneh Ruz*, 10 February 1990.

19 Farzaneh Milani, *Veils and Words, the Emerging Voices of Iranian Women Writers* (London: I. B. Tauris, 1992).

20 *Zaneh Ruz*, 30 January 1988.

21 *Ibid.*, 20 January 1991.

22 For detailed discussion see Ziba Mir-Hosseini, 'Women, Marriage and the Law in Post-Revolutionary Iran' in Haleh Afshar (ed.), *Women in the Middle East: Perceptions, Realities and Struggles for Liberation* (London: Macmillan, 1993), and Ziba Mir-Hosseini, *Marriage on Trial: A Study of Islamic Family Law* (London and New York: I. B. Tauris, 1993).

23 *Zaneh Ruz*, 29 October 1990.

24 *Ibid.*, 31 August 1991.

25 Article 5 of the 'Five additional notes to the Bill', *qanuneh elhaqeh panj tabsareh beh qanuneh sharayeteh entekhabeh qozateh dadgostary.*

26 *Zaneh Ruz*, 10 January 1990.

27 *Zaneh Ruz*, 7 May 1994.

28 *Ibid.*

29 *Ibid.*

30 *Ibid.*

31 *Ibid.*

32 *Ibid.*

33 *Ibid.*

34 See Haleh Afshar, *Why Fundamentalism? Iranian Women and their Support for Islam* (York: University of York, Department of Politics, Working paper no 2, 1994).

35 *Zaneh Ruz*, 7 May 1994.

36 *Ibid.*

37 *Ibid.*

38 *Ibid.*

39 *Ibid.*

40 *Ibid.*

41 D. Kandiyoti, 'Bargaining with Patriarchy', *Gender and Society*, Vol. 2, No. 3, September 1988.

NINE

GENDER AND THE POLITICS OF RELIGION IN THE MIDDLE EAST

Maha Azzam

General Context and Background

The rise of Islamist politics has highlighted an interest in the position and role of women in Muslim societies. This interest is, however, not altogether new, since the very mention of the word "Islam" has tended, in the West, to give rise to particular concern over the place of women, minorities and the issue of punishments, *hudud*, all of which cannot be easily reconciled with present-day Western liberal attitudes. What I intend to present here is primarily an approach to understanding the position of women in relation to the contemporary Islamist assertion, in the context of some of the main developments in the region, which have implications on society as a whole and from which women are not immune.

The different readings of Islam by traditionalists, modernists and secularists, based on claims and counter-claims derived from the Qur'an and the *hadith*, present problems that arise partly from remaining within an Islamic framework of reference. Alternatively, to attempt to understand the role of women in Islam from a non-Muslim perspective and reading secular Western liberal principles into Islam, is also an exercise fraught with problems. In Islam, as with other long-established and highly articulated religions, the questions of gender and the role of women are integral to its value-system and world-view, in which the major changes are set in motion by push factors operating in wider society.[1] It is important to keep in mind the differential nature and impact of these factors in the diverse social and economic arenas of the Middle East.[2] In order to understand the relationship of women with the current Islamist movement, it is crucial to take into account something of the experience faced by the majority of societies in the Middle East during this century. There are those states, particularly those of the Maghreb, which suffered from the harsh experience and legacy of colonialism. Furthermore, all states of the region have experienced one form of authoritarian regime or another, be it military or monarchical. The promise of unity among Arab states, the military defeat of Israel and economic progress remained part of many unrealised expectations for the peoples of the region. This has resulted in widespread disillusionment with present regimes and their ideologies, which have failed to deliver and which are perceived as corrupt. Rural to urban migration, demographic growth, pressure in finding accommodation – to the extent that in Algeria some families have to sleep in shifts because there is not enough space – have had a negative impact on the basic family unit. All of these factors have affected the different societies of the region which have experienced strains in their social fabric and an increase in crime and drug addiction. The strains have been evident on the family unit and individuals within it, be they men or women.

The general political malaise and economic underdevelopment that has characterised the majority of the states of the Middle East for much of this century, has given rise to a reassessment of the political, cultural and moral direction of society by an increasing number of people from different socio-economic strata. The main trend that has emerged has clearly been one of an Islamic orientation which, in its various manifestations, holds that Islam should constitute the basis of law and identity. Since the 1970s the region has witnessed, beginning with Egypt, the emergence of Islamic political groups and the revival of old ones. These have been determined to establish an Islamic system of government and became engaged at various levels, depending on the country and group involved, in power struggles with the ruling regimes. Whether because of secularisation, a failure to apply the *shari'a*, a disregard for the rule of law, or corruption, those in power are perceived by Islamists as violating the basic precepts of Islam.

The more decisive the attacks and violations on what is considered part of Islam and its tradition, the more urgent becomes the necessity for demanding a return to what is seen as orthodoxy and conformity and the greater the intolerance for all things considered not to conform with Islam. In the political field every new attempt to manipulate, utilise and establish a programme for women is expressed through a new reading of the "orthodox discourse" as the source and guarantor of legitimacy. It is this that makes the discourse relating to Islam interesting for us, not only in terms of it being based on a holy text that is believed by a vast number of men and women as providing a way of life and of being of great relevance in the contemporary world, but as the focus of interpretative strategies that one confronts every day in Muslim countries. An

awareness of the contradictions and underlying reasons for interpretation might allow us to understand policies concerning women as being
imposed by herself as well as by others and by a societal situation that has
caused the actual *tafsir* – exegesis or interpretation – to be re-actualised.

An important guiding criterion is the question of authenticity, asala,
and how it remains operational in society. Authenticity assumes a fundamental importance in this historical juncture where there is political,
economic and cultural dependence on the West and where there has been
recent Western military interference and aggression in the region. This
process began with, and was embodied in European colonisation and
control in the region. According to this schema, what is pre-colonial is
often believed to be authentic, and what is not is probably adulterated and
corrupted by Western influence, which was being exerted at a time when
the weakened Muslim societies did not have the power to defend and
assert their cultural identity from encroachment and attack.

"Turning to Islam": The Reformulation of Boundaries

Beyond these overarching considerations there are the specific problems
faced by women on a daily basis which include, for example, those that
arise from the attitudes and behaviour of male family members, who,
through a socially accepted role of authority attempt to control women
through different levels of manipulation and abuse. A woman will often
find it difficult to bring charges against her husband to court and if
she does, she will frequently arouse social condemnation and not receive
justice in the courts. The application of laws vary within each country
and of course within the region as a whole, depending on the way in
which governments prosecute, how the justice system allows for defence,
and the way in which individuals exercise their rights.[3] Although the
severity of cases of discrimination and abuse differ, they are nevertheless related overall to the absence of a reliable and just system that would
allow for recourse to the law whether it be secular or Islamic.

The impact of Westernisation on the laws and culture of the different
societies of the region has contributed to a breakdown of traditional definitions and understandings of what is "right and wrong". There has been
a perceived shift away from particular expressions of respect for women
and the elderly which were on the whole shared by those of different political and religious affiliations within society. The absence of an alternative
value-system on which to manage social relations, has left room open for

the distortion of traditional modes of behaviour. As a reaction, there has been a growing emphasis on tradition as the guarantor of what is good and just rather than an assessment of the laws themselves. This is not to imply that traditional attitudes are ideal or are immune from abuse. However, confusion over old and new values and what constitutes them has contributed to the appeal of a more strict and puritanical reading of Islam.

As with all societies men and women on the whole share a common set of values which are relevant to them, with differences in values often being greater between social strata than between men and women. This is not to overlook that women across classes and in different societies face some degree of discrimination and are denied rights that their own society often claims to uphold. In Muslim societies today, women mainly from the lower-middle and middle classes, are contributing to the Islamisation process that is underway, whether officially, for example in Iran and Sudan, or unofficially, in Egypt and Turkey. This has taken the form, among both men and women, of an increased interest in Islamic subjects either through following religious-related topics in the media, or an increase in the religious literature being read, and in the creation of informal groups and circles to discuss different aspects of Islam relating to *tafsir* of the Qur'an. For example, it has become common in Egypt for women from the professional classes and middle-class housewives to form groups and invite a speaker to discuss religious subjects.

In the 1970s and 1980s the appeal of Islam appeared to be most prominent among younger women, mainly university students, and there was much reference to the fact that their mothers were often reluctant to see them take up the *hijab* which, they themselves did not wear. However, since the late 1980s the appeal of religion and the wearing of the *hijab* is being increasingly taken up by older women as well. An increasing number of middle-class women in Egypt are keen to wear the *hijab* and go on the hajj, fulfilling one of the main pillars of Islam and signifying status and prestige. In Egypt and Jordan there has been a growing keenness to send daughters to newly founded private Islamic schools for girls. These schools stress an Islamic value-system and emphasise the teaching of the Qur'an and Arabic and Islamic history, while continuing to be part of the national curriculum which is otherwise considered to have failed to provide enough emphasis on Islamic teaching. Pupils at these schools wear the *hijab* as part of a school uniform, the language that teachers use contains increased religious references, while the songs that the girls learn express religious values as opposed to nationalist ones. There is an emphasis that Islam encourages rather than prohibits women's education. Girls in these schools are imbued with the knowledge that in the early history of Islam, women became famous as religious scholars, writers, poets and teachers. Nafisa, a descendant of Imam 'Ali, is cited as such a great authority on *hadith* that Imam al-Shafi'i sat in her circle in Fustat when he was at the height of his fame; they are told that Sheikha Shuhda lectured publicly in one of the principal mosques in Baghdad to large audiences on literature, rhetoric and poetry, and was one of the foremost scholars of Islam. Such is the type of heritage to which women are increasingly turning for inspiration to excel.[4] The rich and complex tradition offers contemporary women a wide range of examples that inspire intellectually and culturally as well as politically.[5] All this contributes to an emphasis on women's right to education and public participation, and boosts her sense of dignity and pride in being a Muslim. This is part of an overall struggle to improve her status, but which is not radical or far-reaching enough to satisfy feminists and secularists active in Muslim societies.

The general interest and commitment to Islam has been happening in parallel to, but generally separate from, women's involvement in more politicised Islamist groups, such as the *Jama'at al-Islamiyya* in higher educational institutions in Egypt. It is important to note that much of the activities of these groups have been seriously curtailed by regimes in Algeria, Tunisia and Egypt, because of government policy of clamping down on Islamist opposition groups. The goals of the Islamist groups include an educational aim that seeks to inform women about Islam while providing them with psychological support in their shift towards their, so-called, new identity, as well as providing where possible a degree of health care, transport and clothing. The welfare aspect of the Islamist groups is one of the most important channels through which they have managed to attract admiration and support from ordinary people, who see them as providing much needed help where the government has failed to.

Some increased official political participation by women can be seen in countries that have opted for an Islamic system of government, namely Iran and Sudan, which is an interesting phenomenon, despite the fact that these women are formally part of the government apparatus. It contrasts with other strictly Islamic countries such as Saudi Arabia, where women are not visible on an official level, but wield social influence and where, among the wealthy, there are an increasing number who are involved in business enterprises.[6] In Iran, there are active women's groups in the universities and women in parliament, the civil service and the foreign service; they are present in delegations to international conferences, such as the Islamic Conference Organisation meetings for foreign ministers. In the universities and in parliament women represent- atives tend to articulate their women supporters and constituents' concerns as regards the government's thinking and practice over a range of issues related to family law, punishments, education and employment. They act mainly as pressure groups with limited political clout to significantly change policy. In Sudan, women receive military training and participate in military parades. This participation is of course not exclusively part of the new Islamist ideology, but it has featured under other non-Islamist "revolutionary" regimes, such as that of Qadhdhafi's in Libya. This kind of participation, whether under secular or Islamist regimes, does not amount to a radical shift in the legal rights of women. However, it does make them more visible in society, even though it may be a society where segregation is officially institutionalised, and it does afford them greater opportunity and participation in public life. Therefore, it is questionable whether an Islamist system altogether denies women a public role or whether, under the umbrella of Islam, women may find it easier to demand a role, even though it may not be that of a judge or head of state, so long as they are functioning within strict rules both on the level of appearance and in voicing Islamic principles.

There is a seemingly contradictory attitude towards the education and participation of women in the public sphere among Islamist groups, although this is not altogether surprising given the vast number of different groups. On a general level, there is acceptance that women have a right to be educated and that it is necessary so that they can teach other women, and provide them with female doctors and nurses. On another level, in Algeria for example, where the unemployed are in large num- bers, women graduates are perceived by some as taking up employment that could otherwise go to men, while a woman would then fulfil an essential role of bringing up her children. The whole issue of women at work in countries such as Algeria and Egypt, which are over-populated and suffer from serious economic problems, is that employment of women is a necessary means of making ends meet, and an increasing number would prefer not to have to work.[7] Employment in most cases lacks any form of job satisfaction and involves harsh conditions to and from work and often humiliation and boredom in the workplace.

Women's perceptions of their right to education and employment have been shaped by the provision of mass education, which was part of the socialist agenda of the leading states of the region during the 1950s and 1960s. These have co-existed with notions of woman's primary role as mother and wife. Unrealised expectations of full emancipation and equality, in addition to economic demands, have pushed women into the work space and its concurrent strains on the family, have combined to make the idea of a woman's place in the home appear increasingly attractive. Nevertheless, the appeal and demand for education remains strong and is perceived by Muslim women as a right enshrined in tradition which, unlike employment, cannot be compromised. The changing political, economic and social situation over much of this century in Muslim states has offered women opportunities as well as creating new pressures and demands, which an increasing number believe they can alleviate through an Islamic code of reference and conduct. Women, like men, are increasingly seeking to manage their condition in relation to society as a whole and towards the opposite sex, through a revival, as well as a reformulation of religion.

Symbols of Community and Separateness

There are two obvious manifestations of the new religiosity and Islamist assertion, namely those of segregation and a particular mode of dress. "Islamic dress", *ziyy Islami* or *ziyy shar'i* involves the wearing of the *hijab*, I use this as a generic term to include the different types of veiling including the *niqab* which covers the face. The entry of women into economic spaces such as factories and offices during this century has involved a restructuring of space, and undermined the separation of men and women. Accommodation of these changes throughout much of the urban centres of the Middle East has been an uneasy one given the degree to which a reversal to segregation in some areas has not been altogether rejected.

Women frequently confront some form of sexual harassment in public space, for example on the overcrowded public transport system, which has meant that the idea of separate seating arrangements on transport is generally considered by women as a necessity. The provision of separate transport facilities by the *Jama'at al-Islamiyya* for female students in some colleges in Egypt during the early 1980s was greatly welcomed by many such students. Segregation in the universities, that is separate seating areas for men and women and the ending of combined social activities, is due to the policy of Islamist student societies, who in their commitment to an Islamic political system view the enforcement of these social aspects as an essential part of their goal. The particular definition of space and appearance, to which women are inextricably linked, constitutes part of the strategies of both Islamists and secularists for control of the political domain.

The governments in both Tunisia and Egypt have clashed with Islamist societies in the universities, over among other things, the issue of women students wearing the *hijab*, whereby both these governments have, at certain political junctures prohibited the wearing of the *hijab* (in the case of Egypt, the *niqab*) in the midst of a demand by the Islamists that no female students should be allowed onto the campus without a *hijab*. In both cases, particularly in Egypt, this sort of government policy proved unsustainable because of both the control of students unions by the Islamists and because what could be generally perceived as an infringement by government on an area where tradition still remains strong.

When women are asked why they wear the *hijab*, they frequently respond by simply saying that they are merely complying with a Qur'anic injunction. The verses that are being referred to are the following:

O Prophet, tell your wives and daughters and the women of the believers to draw upon them their over-garments. This is more appropriate so that they may be recognised and not molested. (XXXIII, 59)

Another verse states:

O wives of the Prophet you are not like any other women. If you would keep your duty, be not soft in speech, lest he whose heart contains malice may thereby be encouraged. Employ suitable speech. Stay in your homes and do not dress to display your finery in the way they dressed during the Jahiliyya; and keep up prayer, and give welfare due and obey God and His messenger; for God desires only to remove from you abomination of vanity since you are the household of the Prophet and to purify you by a perfect purification. (XXXIII, 32–3)

Literally, these verses are directed to the wives of the Prophet, and liberal Muslims maintain that it applies only to them. Traditionalists in this case have decided not to interpret the Qur'an literally and argue that, what better example can one follow than that of the Prophet's wives.[8] There is also the argument that to abide by the injunction to the Prophet's wives fits in more comfortably with the spirit of Islam that stresses modesty. The injunction for modesty is directed to both men and women and reflects the emphasis on equality in the spiritual sphere, although there is some differentiation in the duties that are incumbent on men as opposed to women. In a Muslim society, the man is seen as being responsible for the maintenance of his family; this is not only a moral but also a legal obligation while anything a wife earns is her own. The wife herself is responsible for the care and welfare of her children and is seen as having a crucial role to play in their character building.

> Tell believers to ward their glances and to cover their private parts; this is purer for them. God is all-knowing of everything they do, tell women to avert their glances and guard their private parts and not to display their charms except what normally appears of them. They should draw their coverings over their breasts and not show their charms except to their husbands . . .
> (XXIV, 30–1)

Most women who wear the *hijab* believe they are fulfilling a religious duty while some, mainly university students, believe it is partly a statement that they are not Westernised. Being Westernised in this context reflects sexual promiscuity and decadence, *fasad*, which is perceived as being partly symbolised by Western fashions that constantly try to reveal a different part of a woman's body. Some will also say that the *hijab* allows a woman not to be considered only in terms of appearance and promotes their search for more equal treatment. Furthermore, it conveys a signal to men that discourages them from approaching or molesting women and consequently makes them less visible in mixed public areas. These attitudes also serve to strengthen the commonly accepted view that a woman's behaviour is linked to the upholding of the honour of the family in general.

As the wearing of the *hijab* becomes more commonplace and popular, so attitudes become more relaxed as to the underlying meaning of dress, whereby it is less of a primary consideration in dictating a particular type of behaviour, for example one that is more distant or deferential between the sexes. In this respect, a woman's appearance loses a large part of its uniqueness and become much more "matter-of-fact". The *hijab* as well as being a symbol of cultural separateness from the West, also represents a strategy of accommodation by women to the political and social environment of their societies and a means by which they can function more easily and increasingly more successfully within them.[9]

For some women the wearing of the *hijab* is seen as a way of helping them get married since an increasing number of men will only marry a woman who is a *muhajjaba*. It has been argued that for the less well off, the *hijab* has been something of an answer to the problems of keeping up with the latest fashion and the expenditure this involves. The *Jama'at al-Islamiyya* in the universities of Cairo and Alexandria, who controlled the student unions in the 1970s and 1980s, encouraged women to wear the *hijab*, especially the less well off by providing fabric for this particular form of dress at low prices. While this may have encouraged the wearing of the *hijab*, particularly in the early stages, when Islamist societies were establishing their hold on university campuses, this does not explain the increase in the phenomenon beyond the universities and among well off women from higher income brackets. In addition, *al-ziyy al-Islami* has become a fashion unto itself that is varied and ranges from the cheap to the expensive, while styles include the simple and puritanical as well as the lavish and colourful, depending on the wearer and the degree of con- formity that is imposed from above as to what can and cannot be worn in public, as is the case in Saudi Arabia and Iran. There is obviously the psychological pressure whereby, if an increasing number of women begin wearing the *hijab*, which carries the message of being a better Muslim than those who do not wear the *hijab*, it becomes more comfortable and more secure to follow suit. Another possible explanation for a stricter adherence to Islam by women is that among the urban population relationships are undergoing change and conflict. Couples face tensions in integrat- ing Western attitudes, partly presented via the media, and traditional mores. Islam appears to many as providing a stable framework of refer- ence which limits the uncertainties related to the rights and wrongs of a woman's right to work, relations with the opposite sex and mode of dress.

Despite these explanations, it is important not to overlook the fact that the *hijab* is worn by women out of sincere religious conviction and it is primarily meant to convey piety and respect for religious values rather than political radicalism and anti-Westernism, but the potential for it to symbolise a political stand is very powerful. As is the case with a commitment to an Islamist system, mode of dress is also a step towards membership of a community that defines itself as Islamic in precedence over, or even to the exclusion of, other allegiances. This development has occurred in the contemporary Muslim states where religious practice and symbols are becoming increasingly charged with political meaning.

The protest of the Islamists against what are seen as Western sym- bols of decadence involve among other things attacks on nightclubs, free mixing of the sexes and the media. These attitudes have a resonance in society as a whole and should not be understood in terms of only what is permitted, *halal*, or prohibited, *haram*, by Islam.[10] In its different guises concern with what is permitted and what is prohibited is part of popular morality and beliefs, a change which would entail as much, or more, control and re-definition as the process of Islamisation itself.

Another distinctive feature of the Islamisation process and of the Islamist groups is not only the *hijab* for women, but also the beard for men, which is part of the call for the return to the Sunna and a commitment to a strict moral code. In addition, there may be rejection and defiance of the appearance patterns of a particular generation and a mode of life. What is often being challenged whether directly or indirectly are certain aspects of Westernisation and not modernisation itself. A particular mode of dress represents for the Islamists a degree of political commitment to the idea of a different type of society, while for the majority of the religiously inclined, it symbolises an aspect of faith. Hair symbolism implies that men and women at specific periods are using their own physical appearance in terms of the social norms to provide indices about their understanding of their role, their social position and changes in these.

The Islamist groups and the orthodox Islamic establishment can always fairly claim that it is women as much as men who are demanding the implementation of the *shari'a* and are committed to the observance of Islamic principles and practice. For some women, an Islamic framework of reference is the only really viable means for change, since it would allow them to remain within the bounds accepted by society and which men cannot attack because it is based on Islam. However, it is precisely because of this, that Muslim women, however much they try to read liberal ideas into Islam, will come up against basic principles that differentiate between the role of men and women, and entail some differences in rights although they are considered equal in terms of spiritual status.[11] The Qur'an stresses that men and women who practice the principles of Islam will receive equal rewards for their efforts.

> Whosoever performs good deeds, whether male or female, and is a believer, we surely will make them live a good life and we will certainly reward them for the best of what they did. (XVI, 97)

Here, equality exists in the spiritual sphere and on the level of punishments, *hudud*, that must be identically enforced on men and women. The differences become explicit in relation, notably, to divorce, polygamy and inheritance.

Islam provides a legal framework for a social order within which not only women, but also men, are "constrained" or "liberated" by having what is permissible and what is forbidden made clear. This is particularly relevant in the area of sex and marriage. Different social orders have integrated the tensions between religion and sexuality in different ways.[12] In the Western Christian experience it was sexuality itself that was attacked and degraded, as the individual was split into antithetical selves, the spirit and the flesh. It was seen to be a constant struggle between the soul over flesh, of the controlled over the uncontrolled. In Islam there is a different emphasis: what is debased and attacked is not sexuality itself, but sexuality outside marriage and the limits set out by Islam.[13] Therefore, orthodox Muslims will argue that even polygamy as institutionalised sexual behaviour guarantees certain rights for women through marriage.

Islam is not a religion or a way of life for those who believe that men and women should have identical rights. They have different rights which make most sense within the context of an Islamic society that not only implements Islamic law as a matter of course, but is also imbued with the spirit of Islam, which views the law not only as the source of order and punishments but as the basis of social and cultural definition and identity.

The emphasis on the family, marriage and motherhood as among the important institutions of the *umma* offers women, within the context of an Islamic world-view, an enhanced position that demands that they be honoured as wives and mothers as an integral part of religious duty. Furthermore, by turning to Islam for legitimisation and to the legacy of learned women throughout Islamic history for inspiration, Muslim women today are attempting to authoritatively extend their roles beyond the home.

Despite the fact that Islam is seen as offering a clear moral direction, traditions and values are fluid and are constantly being remoulded. In the same way that Islamisation is affecting society, it is hard to deny that men and women committed to an Islamic alternative have not been influenced by changes this century, primarily in terms of the expansion of education and the increase in the number of working women.

Women in the context of these changes have adapted and formulated new ways of dealing with and shaping the world around them. Islam as an integral part of their civilisation and culture has throughout centuries of Islamic history contributed to their value-system and influenced their way of life. There is little reason why it should not do so in the present day, and why women should not unapologetically turn to religion as a means of managing their lives and as a route towards a degree of empowerment within an environment of increasing Islamisation.

NOTES

1 For a controversial reading of the gender and Islam issue see Leila Ahmed, *Women and Gender in Islam: Historical Roots of a Modern Debate* (New Haven: Yale University Press, 1992).

2 For a glimpse of the variety of regional and social contexts within which women function, see Camillia Fawzi el-Solh and Judith Mabro (eds.), *Muslim Women's Choices* (Oxford: Berg Publishers, 1994).

3 S. Pakzad, 'The legal status of women in the family' in M. Afkhami and E. Friedl (eds.), *In the Eye of the Storm: Women in Post-Revolutionary Iran* (London: I. B. Tauris, 1994), pp. 169–80.

4 R. Roded, *Women in Islamic Biographical Collections: From Ibn Sa'd to Who's Who* (Boulder and London: Lynne Rienner Publishers, 1994). Also see Bint al-Shati' ['Aisha Abd al-Rahman], *Tarajim sayyidat bayt al-nubuwwa* (Beirut: Dar al-Kitab al-Arabi, 1984). This is a collection of the author's previous publications on the Prophet's mother; the Prophet's wives; the Prophet's daughters; Lady Zaynab, daughter of Imam 'Ali; and Lady Sukayna, daughter of Imam Husayn.

5 Among the women who are prominent today in voicing Islamic principles and who represent different aspects of the Islamist assertion is 'Aisha Abd al-Rahman who is head of Islamic studies at a university in Morocco. She is recognised as a scholar of *tafsir* and contributes to a wide range of Islamic subjects in academic circles and official newspapers. Another prominent figure is Zaynab al-Ghazali who, as a member of the Muslim Brotherhood, suffered in Nasser's prisons and is known for her work with the women's groups of the movement and her various welfare work. Safinaz Kazem represents something of the more recent Islamist political fervour and is known for her journalistic contributions. These women in their different ways represent roles for women that are intellectually inspired by the Islamic tradition. They are allowed to voice their views within the existing institutions and organs of the state which cannot ignore Islam, while also being accepted by the Islamist trend as a whole.

6 See Mai Yamani, Chapter 12 in this volume.

7 For a thorough study on the Arab debate on women at work, see N. Hijab, *Womanpower: The Arab Debate on Women at Work* (Cambridge: Cambridge University Press, 1988).

8 Abu'l-A'la Mawdudi, *al-Hijab* (Jeddah, 1985). For a brief discussion of Mawdudi's view that the Qur'anic verses addressed to the Prophet's wives are binding on all Muslims and his understanding of hijab as a set of restrictions, see Barbara Stowasser, *Women in the Qur'an: Traditions, and Interpretation* (New York: Oxford University Press, 1994).

9 Arlene Elowe Macleod, *Accommodation Protest: Working Women, the New Veiling and Change in Cairo* (New York: Columbia University Press, 1991).

10 For a contemporary statement by an acknowledged '*alim* on the issue of '*halal*' and '*haram*', see Y. al-Qaradawi, *The Lawful and the Prohibited in Islam*, trans. K. El-Helbawy *et al.* (Indianapolis: American Trust Publications, 1976).

11 For an expanded version of this view see Hijab, *Womanpower*, pp. 60–1.

12 B. Musallam, *Sex and Society in Islam: Birth Control before the Nineteenth*

Century (Cambridge: Cambridge University Press, 1983).
13 F. Mernissi, *Beyond the Veil*: Male–Female Dynamics in a Modern Muslim Society (Cambridge, Mass.: Shenkman, 1975).

TEN

THE MYTHOLOGY OF MODERNITY: WOMEN AND DEMOCRACY IN LEBANON

Jean Said Makdisi

An astonishing dichotomy exists in Lebanon.[1] Perhaps nowhere in the Arab world, or at least in the Mashreq, do women appear to be freer. Even the most casual visitor must be struck by the visibility, force of character and self-assurance of women here, and of their conspicuous presence on the streets and on the beaches, where they show total and, some would say, daring, comfort with their exposed bodies. Lebanese women have had the vote since 1952. They form a large part of the population of artists; there are many women writers and academics; in the media women are very present, not just as beautiful and lavishly groomed "speakers" on television, but as serious journalists as well. In banks, schools, hospitals, shops and within the family structure, everywhere one goes, one is aware of this great female presence.

And yet always it seems, the female presence stops short of the top positions. Most significantly and alarmingly in a country claiming a tradition of democratic institutions and practice, women are almost entirely absent from politics, government, and public administration.

As of this writing, and unlike most other countries in the area, no woman has ever been included in a Lebanese government. Indeed, the inclusion of women has not even been raised as a serious issue, although some talk has occasionally taken place around the possibility of appointing a woman, always the wife or widow of an important man, to a cabinet post as a courtesy to his memory or his constituency.

Before the last elections, only one woman had ever been elected to Parliament and that was in an emotional by-election in the 1960s following the death of a Member of Parliament in a plane crash, when his daughter was elected to replace him. The last parliamentary elections, held in the summer of 1992 after almost eighteen years of civil war, brought drastic changes in the make-up of the Parliament, but not when it came to women. Of the 128 members, only three are women. One of those three was Nayla Mu'awwad, widow of the late President of the Republic who was assassinated in 1989 who was himself a Member of Parliament when he was elected President. The second, Bahiya al-Hariri, is the sister of the present Prime Minister, for whom she often acts as spokeswoman and personal representative. Though she was elected before his appointment as PM, his enormous influence and wealth had already made him a likely candidate and his power was already well-established by the time of the elections. The third woman, Maha al Khoury, picked up the family standard from her brother who was killed during the war. She was elected by forty votes, the only ones cast in the district she represents, the rest of the electorate having, with a large portion of the country, boycotted the elections entirely for reasons that had nothing to do with her candidacy.

It is worth noting here, that although at least the first two women have proved themselves to be vigorous and energetic members of Parliament, though there are dozens of similar wives, widows, and sisters of powerful men who are *not* engaged politically and there is a long tradition of family succession in politics, with sons, brothers or nephews succeeding fathers, brothers or uncles, these women are not given sufficient credit for their hard work or their personal initiatives, and are almost invariably perceived in the light of the manner in which they were brought to power. In other words, the fact of these women having been elected because of their male relations is held against them, and the validity of their political existence thus diminished. Aside from being unfair, this perception, announced as often by women as men, seems to me to be deleterious to the general advancement of women in politics. Other women, either as individuals or as a movement, have not taken advantage of the presence in the Parliament of these female members, nor have they shown themselves to be particularly anxious to be identified with the women's movement. Thus has an opportunity for women been lost.

A woman chairs the censorship board that oversees the showing of films and plays in the country. It was only very recently that for the first time in Lebanon, a woman, Ni'mat Kenaan, was appointed as *mudir 'amm* (general manager, the equivalent of permanent secretary) of a ministry, in this case the Ministry of Social Affairs. In other ministries, women are scarcely to be seen except as secretaries, file-clerks, and cleaning women, though occasionally a woman has been hired as a professional consultant.

This dearth of women in politics and in senior posts of the public administration is echoed by the situation in hospitals, banks, schools, universities, etc., where the presence of strong and efficient women is conspicuous, but where they are also often absent from the most senior decision-making positions. Not a single woman, for instance, sits on the Board of Deans, the highest decision-making body at the American University of Beirut, where women form roughly 30 per cent of the full-time teaching faculty.

Indeed, if we take the AUB as a random example of cultural reality, the figures for female participation in its hierarchy are startling, especially as it considers itself to be, and is popularly considered to be, the most "modern" and "advanced" of the foreign institutions – about which more later – in Lebanon.

As of this writing, of the 23 Full Professors in the Faculty of Arts and Sciences at the AUB, only one is a woman; of the 25 Associate Professors, only 2 are women. The figures change dramatically in the lower ranks: of the 56 Assistant Professors, 19 are women, and of the 59 Instructors, 37 are women. Most of the other faculties show similar asymmetry. In the Faculty of Medicine there are 32 Professors of whom none is a woman; of the 49 Associate Professors, only 4 are women, of the 71 Assistant Professors, 11 are women; of the 18 Instructors, 4 are women. In the Faculty of Engineering there is only one Associate Professor among 13; of the 5 Full Professors, not one is a woman, and there is only one Assistant Professor. In the Faculty of Agricultural and Food Sciences, again, of the 6 Full Professors, not one is a woman, and there is 1 Associate Professor among 5. Two of the 11 Assistant Professors are women, while there are 5 women among the 9 Instructors.[2]

Though the figures alone may be misleading, as they do not show the reasons for the discrepancies, such as age, application for teaching and for promotion, will, hard work, the extent of publications or contribution to the intellectual life of the institution, etc., the full impact of the figures in a cultural sense are what interests me here. In other words, what I wish to show is the reinforced impression that power, influence, and decision-making are, for whatever reasons, still male domains, even in such a bastion of "modernity" and "progress" as the American University.

The exceptions to the rule themselves confirm common cultural attitudes and are quite predictable: 100 per cent of the faculty of the School of Nursing in all ranks are women. The Faculty of Health Sciences comes next, where 1 of two Professors, 1 of 2 Associate Professors, 4 out of 6 Assistant Professors, and 11 out of 14 Instructors are women.

The gender proportions among students show an interesting echo to all this. Once again, though I am taking as a random example the graduating class of 1995, the figures reflect predictable cultural attitudes. Thus, for instance, almost 70 per cent of those who took BA degrees, and only 27 per cent of the BS students, were girls. About 32 per cent of the 76 graduating MDs, but only 12 per cent of the 200 graduating engineers were women. Again predictably, almost 87 per cent of those awarded a BS in Nursing were women.[3]

The figures carry through into professional life. Though women constituted 37 per cent of the labour force in the period 1990–2,[4] the figures issued by the syndicates of the liberal professions in 1993 show that only 14.3 per cent of registered physicians are women, 17.2 per cent of dentists, 26.8 per cent of pharmacists, 19.7 per cent of lawyers, 6.7 per cent of engineers.[5] (It is said that the relatively high percentage of women pharmacists is explained by the practice of renting or selling pharmacy licences in order to start a business: i.e. a woman pharmacist is not necessarily practising, but may rent her name and licence to someone else who will run a pharmacy in her name.) Though 19.7 per cent of lawyers may be women, a recent widely reported scandal occurred when women law students were barred from so much as sitting for the examinations which would have permitted them to qualify as judges.

Why all this is so is the question I am raising in this paper. It is my belief that (a) appearances to the contrary, women in Lebanon are in a far worse position socially, culturally and politically, than is widely recognised, even by women themselves, (b) that there is a large and growing gap between the situation of individual women, and the political movement, which in any case is now almost non-existent, demanding equal rights for women, (c) that the status of women as individuals peaked during the war and has gone into a sharp decline since the war ended, and that (d) this sorry state of affairs has to do with a general decline in democratic life and procedure, and with a persistent and damaging mythology based on cultural and historical misunderstanding.

The original impetus of the women's movement, fairly vigorous in the early days of national independence, as well as a long tradition of democratic life, an even longer tradition of female education, and a fairly prosperous national economy, had provided, historically, Lebanese women with the striking personal freedom and self-assurance which I have described, and which accounts for their general comportment.

It is precisely this legacy, however, that has lulled us into a kind of complacency and acquiescence which has done much damage to the situation of women, and to social justice and democracy in general. Professional women, those who normally would be expected to be in the forefront of the battle for democratic advancement, equal rights, and social improvement, are especially prone, I think, to this complacency. As they often belong to the privileged class, they seem unwilling to see their personal situation in the harsh terms of its economic and social reality, and are therefore less likely to identify with, let alone speak up for, women less fortunate than themselves. The urgency of the latter's situation surely fades as it is contemplated in the comfort of a privileged life. This aspect of class division seems to me to be one, but only one, of several reasons for the decline of the women's movement.

The situation of women everywhere reflects that of society in general; the same illusion of well-being and advancement that clouds the understanding of the status of women prevails as to the standing of democracy and human rights in Lebanon. It has seemed to me for many years that there exists in this country, especially since the war, a system of undemocratic privileges rather than of democratic rights. Thus, if one belongs to the privileged class, one is, for example, almost entirely liberated from the encumbrances of an often oppressive, corrupt, and capricious bureaucracy. An army of drivers, agents, employees, separate the upper classes from the obligation of dealing directly with the bureaucracy, and act as mediums between the two, carrying passports, filing necessary papers, retrieving documents etc. When necessary, members of the privileged classes can contact their personal acquaintances in the highest ranks of the bureaucracy, among members of Parliament, and in the cabinet, who will obligingly come to their assistance and provide them with whatever intermediation is required for the conclusion of their business. Rarely are members of the privileged classes required to do their own business with the government bureaucracy face-to-face, and they are therefore spared the frustration and humiliation which is the fate only of the poor and/or the unconnected. In almost all other aspects of social and civil life, from the observation of traffic laws to conscription to standing in queues, privilege supersedes order, and the well-connected are in effect often exempted from the letter of the law.

Being well-connected, however, is a social state which runs vertically as well as horizontally. Thus, a large number of poor and/or anxious sycophants attends every influential man (and his wife!) in the land. These hangers-on, whether actually employed or merely pressed into glowing service on occasion, cushion the system, and provide a most unrebellious and anti-revolutionary mood by disguising it with an acceptance which is often belied by their true feelings of anger and disgust. The hand-me-down privilege that comes from rubbing shoulders with the rich and the powerful is not easily surrendered, as the unprotected fall easy prey to a system which can, when it wishes, be merciless in its pursuit.

Women belonging to the wealthy class are even more liberated from social inconvenience than their men. They enjoy the privilege of by-passing the bureaucracy and the letter of the law even more than their husbands and fathers, as they often do not even have to deal with the intermediary functionaries, this unpleasant task left entirely to the men of the family. They are also freed of menial household tasks by the easy availability of cheap and unprotected domestic labourers, often these days imported from Sri Lanka or the Philippines, and by the lingering remnants of the extended family.

Many professional women, often attached to and protected by a powerful father or husband – or both – confuse the courteous and even sycophantic behaviour offered to them as members of the privileged class with the illusion that it is offered to them as *women*. This, they claim, is proof that there is no difference between men and women in this forward-looking society. For them, the class/gender distinction is better left unarticulated, as it is far more comfortable to enjoy the illusion of freedom and advancement than to recognise that one is in fact culling the fruit of an oppressive and corrupt system of society and government.

I have often heard women of my acquaintance arguing that in Lebanon "women can achieve anything", that "women can do anything men can", and that there is no distinction between the way men and women are treated. Often high-powered, highly educated, intelligent, sophisticated and cosmopolitan, and including some who participate in the "women's movement", they offer themselves as examples of this felicitous social state, and therefore seem to me to share precisely that complacency of which I spoke earlier.

There are, it is true, women who have for decades spoken up for women's legal rights, and who have argued for a definitive change in the oppressive personal status laws as they affect women. They have, indeed, concentrated the battle for female advancement on the issue of the personal status laws. These laws, however, it seems clear to me, will remain fixed and immutable as long as the present political and social make-up of the land continues, and as long as religious and clerical power, not to mention the new Islamist militancy, which hovers continually over the political landscape, persists, hampering free discussion, especially of personal issues, and blocking action towards change.

Many of these same women, furthermore, send out to society a clear message of non-aggression. They make their points in a polite and lady-like way, and thus appear to be part of the social system which such drastic changes as they apparently ask for would inevitably overthrow. Indeed, the very delicacy of their manner, their clear acceptance of social niceties, allows them to remain an essential part of the very system which they seem to be denouncing.

Thus has the women's movement become, over the decades, more and more part of the establishment, less and less rebel and adversary. Scarcely a symposium or lecture on women, within the academy, in the press, in the media, but a few familiar faces are present. Aside from proving the great energy and hard work of these ladies, and the esteem in which they are generally held, there can be no question that their ubiquity has provided the women's movement with a kind of stability and restraint, which is counter-productive to a rebellious and demanding movement: so commanding is the presence of some of these ladies, so much in charge are they, that other women are lulled into complacency, and therefore do not feel compelled to join in the struggle to achieve their own rights.

It has seemed to me for many years that, especially since the war, there is no effective women's movement in Lebanon precisely because I see no signs of a sweeping, democratic movement, aware of class dynamics and distinctions, and demanding of a just social system for all citizens. It seems clear to me that such a movement, with all its untidiness, is what is required, not only to liberate women from the many injustices implied or present in the laws, but also to help them free themselves from the cultural biases which inwardly and outwardly restrain them, and which lead to the political exclusion which undermines democratic life.

I have often thought of the contrast between the ladies in the women's movement here and the English and American suffragettes early in the century, and the noisy and unladylike demonstrations that took place in Europe and the United States in the 1960s and 1970s. These have to be seen in their wider social context: the 1960s and 1970s movement in the United States, for instance, was a direct descendant of the civil rights movement, and was unthinkable had that noble effort not been under way, and the anti-Vietnam War movement with it.

But here too there has been a tradition of women's demonstrations: a famous women's march, a photograph of which adorns school history textbooks, took place in 1943, demanding an end to the French mandate, and an independent Lebanon. This march has gone down into the oft-told story of the independence movement. Marches also took place in the early 1950s to demand the vote, which was indeed won, women proudly used to declare, long before women in France and Switzerland were allowed to vote. The tradition continued in universities, where strikes and demonstrations, protesting this and demanding that, involved women students along with their male classmates.

Such democratic manifestations, in which women of different classes, sects and educational levels rub shoulders and achieve solidarity, take the risk of offending the establishment and carry the attendant risk of possible arrest or even imprisonment – all of this is unthinkable in the context of the women's movement in Lebanon today. Thus has this movement been shorn of much of its power and potential, and remains, in my eyes at least, almost entirely formal in nature. At the same time, the sense of advancement, of freedom, and of "modernity" persists in the minds and in the language of those who discuss women in Lebanon.

To explain the dichotomy – and it is one which I have been observing and puzzling over for many years – one has to come to terms with another dichotomy, which I have also puzzled over and which I have finally rejected as invalid, misleading, and full of a clouding series of mythologies which have obscured historical vision and have utterly blotted out common sense. This false dichotomy is precisely the one which pits "modern" against "traditional" women. In this vision, a "modern" woman is usually and loosely, not to say carelessly, defined as one who is "educated", and/or "working", and/or "well-dressed". I use each of these words with self-conscious caution as they are, though apparently simple and naive, in fact loaded with hidden meanings and are responsible for half the falseness of the false dichotomy. The "traditional" woman, in this same view, is often but not necessarily wearing national costume, or, if she is a Muslim, even *hijab*; she looks after home and children, and is dependent on her husband for her livelihood. The variations in these formulae are endless; what remains constant is the fuzzy thinking and the governing mythology.

"Modern" women are loosely identified with Europe and America, as modernity itself surely and more directly is. And behind the word "traditional" looms the spectre of a rigorous application of Islamic *shari'a*, very often regarded by women outside Islamist circles, but by Muslims as well as Christians, as the final threat to "modernity" and freedom. As the Islamist position is so widely publicised these days, not only locally but internationally, few people, except those directly concerned, give much thought to Christian religious law, which, though it varies from sect to sect, is just as binding on Christians as *shari'a* is on Muslims here in Lebanon, where no civil law exists to govern personal status. Of the 16 officially recognised sects, the majority are Christian, and so a wide variety of laws govern, and further divide, women.

Some Christian sects, it is true, have intelligent and progressive laws governing such personal issues as divorce. The Protestant community to which I belong, for example, is governed by a very short legal text relating to marriage and divorce, which precisely because of its brevity is open wide to interpretation by the spiritual court. In its present composition today's court is extremely liberal, but it is not inconceivable that in another form it might be extremely conservative. In any case, the laws or regulations covering marriage, divorce, child custody, alimony, etc. are almost unknown to the community they govern. It was only in preparation for this paper, for instance, that I discovered with some consternation my rights under the law. Consciousness raising, it was confirmed to me by this little shock, remains one of the principal functions of an effective women's movement. Of what use, I asked myself, are rights if one does not know they exist? And why are the laws so little understood by the lay population?

The general social climate in this society takes family life very seriously, and frowns upon divorce, making it almost unthinkable to those who wish to maintain family ties. It is in Christian as much as, if not more than, in Muslim circles that a woman's family might respond to a request for help in seeking divorce that "We have no divorced women in our family," or "You married him, now you must live with him. Go back to your husband." Christians, I believe, more than Muslims, frown upon divorce, and Christian families, it has often seemed to me, are particularly sensitive to the approval of their peers, and vulnerable to disapproval. Thus even the unhappiest of women will probably find little support in her family, and will rarely go far enough in her personal rebellion to reach the point where she will have investigated the laws of her community. The divorce rate in the progressive and understanding Protestant community clearly reflects the general disapprobation surrounding divorce: the figures go down to 3 and 2 in the war years 1989 and 1990, rising to what the Chair of the spiritual court considered to be an alarming peak in 1994. During that year a total of 18 divorces took place in the entire Protestant community, numbering roughly 100,000 people.[6] Many unhappy marriages remain, one is inclined to conclude, hidden behind a thick curtain of propriety and disguised by the carrying on of accepted social functions.

Another reason so little is known, and so little time is spent in discussing the Christian personal status laws or other variables relating to
women, is the enormous emphasis, mentioned above, on Islamic law, and
the influence of the militant Islamist movements. Because of the sectarian system, the question of women inevitably requires some discussion
of *shari'a*. Fear of offending the militants by saying the wrong thing
leads many potential challengers of the system to be silent, or to utter, in
public at least, the most inoffensive and generalised thoughts on the subject. This diplomatic and gingerly avoidance of trouble leaves the field
to *sheikhs*, and thus puts the question of women into entirely theological
and therefore indisputable language. The *sheikhs* may safely argue
among themselves, but few are those who would today publicly dare to
argue with any of them. Silence, or at least a pleasant air of polite agreement, is chosen by those who do not wish to tangle with the militants.

Thus instead of the public discussion of women's problems as related not only to the personal status laws, but to secular issues, such as
poverty, sexual harassment and even crimes of honour and murder, health,
women's relation with the medical establishment, jobs, working conditions, promotions, the absence of democratic procedures, the exclusion
from the political process, and therefore from sharing in the economic
and social plans for the future, and, in short, to the real problems and
anxieties of real women, the tendency has been to discuss women in
idealised theological terms entirely. Too often have I seen television programmes, for instance, ostensibly devoted to the discussion of women's
issues, produce in a fair-minded but sterile tactic, a priest and a sheikh in
politic balance. Politely, though, I fear, not always sincerely, they pay
tribute to each other's traditions, while making their own laws sound
the most humane, rational, and egalitarian imaginable. In this kind of
atmosphere, it is difficult to have a serious or meaningful discussion, and
on the whole the old mythologies and divisions flourish.

In one area at least, and that is in matters having to do with inheritance, Christian and Muslim women are dealt with unequally by
Lebanese society. In 1959, the Christian sects relinquished to the state
the power granted to them by the constitution to legislate their own
policy on this subject. Thus, a civil law on inheritance, with a provision
that, unless otherwise specified, male and female descendants inherit
equal shares of a legacy, applies to only half the population, while *shari'a*
applies to the other. So is added to an already divided female society
another dramatic line. Property plays an inordinately important part in
the lives of people here, because personal security is directly linked to it

and not well enough legislated in this society. Thus inheritance forms a larger part of the public consciousness than would otherwise be the case.

In the murky sectarian waters of Lebanese politics, "modernism", partly as a result of the difference in inheritance laws, and of the fuzzy and un-thought-out clichés and myths, has become loosely and dangerously identified with Christian culture, and often with the West as well, and "tradition" with Islamic and local culture. Class considerations, which in my judgement do far more to explain divisions among women, are rarely referred to in this context.

The absurdity of this view of things becomes evident as soon as one begins to look at the social and class construction of the society. In the first place, it seems clear that religious law, whether Christian or Muslim, is tempered by the social status of the woman concerned: miracles can be accomplished by a rich and influential family in the protection – whether *de jure* or de facto – of their daughters.

Furthermore, however, the absurdity is illustrated by bizarre examples offered in everyday and un-thought-out conversation. Thus, a wealthy woman, whether Christian or Muslim, kept in luxury by an indulgent husband, might have little else to do in life but to oversee her toilette, her household, and her entertainments. In all of this she is assisted by a staff of servants, cooks, drivers, hairdressers, manicurists, etc. She may very well, if she knows French or English, or both – which she almost certainly would – and if she is dressed in a cosmopolitan, urban style, which she certainly would be – consider herself to be "educated" and "well-dressed", and therefore extremely "modern". This in spite of the fact that her situation requires her to behave in a manner totally subservient to the husband whose displeasure she dare not risk.

Her poorer counterpart, on the other hand, may be less fashionably dressed; she may belong to the class of urban or rural poor, and her costume might therefore include a head-covering *mandil* or even *hijab*, if she is a Muslim. This woman may be barely literate, or at least with no knowledge of languages other than Arabic. She might, however, be working in the fields or factories, or as a domestic worker, and therefore be facing the harsh world of economic competition. She may be required to surrender her hard-earned income to her husband, and may consequently rebel against this practice by lying about her salary, keeping part of it secret and hidden away: I have known several women who do this. She might be attending political meetings aimed at the poor masses and organised by any of a number of political parties. If she lives in the south, she might even be working underground with the resistance movement against Israeli occupation. Her political consciousness might therefore be far greater than the other's. Yet this same woman will, by the standards of everyday language, by virtue of her clothes and her class, not by her attitudes or mind-set, be considered "traditional" and less "modern" than the other.

This way of judging "modernity" by sect, dress, or language is patently ridiculous and unacceptable, and yet I am afraid it is more often than not an example of the context which defines the question of women these days. The problem has been fed by a Western academy (which inevitably influences the local one) and journalists obsessed with the exotic costume referred to as "the veil", which as part of the problem is never clearly defined: what, for instance, precisely is the veil? Can the traditional *mandil* be considered a veil? How about the ubiquitous *amta* (or *écharpe*, as it has interestingly come to be known) of rural costume? Are we not to differentiate between a woman covering her head because she intends some private religious meaning in doing so, or because it is merely traditional in her region and generation to do so, or because her father or brother has forced her to do so, or because all her friends are doing so, or because she has a political message to convey? Do we ever sufficiently differentiate between national and religious costume? The tendency has been to group all these kinds of costume together, and the personal histories of all who wear them as well, into one single, sweeping, symbol of something very vague but quite unsettling and even threatening.

The ultimate absurdity comes from viewing a theoretical set whose basis lies in the same mythology. If it is true, and perhaps it is, that the more covered a woman's body is, the more "conservative" the social circle she moves in, then the opposite of that is palpably *not* true, and therefore the entire argument is invalid or at least thoroughly irrelevant. For if it were true, we would have to argue that the *less* covered a woman's body, the more "liberal", "modern", "free", etc. her society. The logical conclusion of such an argument would be that the most uncovered woman, i.e. one wearing the flimsiest of bikinis, is by definition "freer" than her covered counterpart, though she may be lying on the beach for months at a time with the sole aim of improving her sun tan. In fairness, I can see a certain kind of freedom in such an aim, as in such a costume; but I cannot take it seriously as a political argument which is insidiously dividing a society and holding back the advancement of women.

The kind of futile and divisive conviction I have been describing forms a cultural viewpoint which must be understood in order to be exorcised. Furthermore, it seems to me quite clear that the kind of super-ficiality I have been describing is one of several reasons that the women's movement in Lebanon is bogged down, rendering it quite ineffectual, or, at best, making it in another way part of, instead of adversarial to, the existing political and class system.

A women's movement is required to call for an open and honest debate to examine the confusing and dangerous vocabulary used in discussing women, redefining and clarifying such words as "modern", "traditional", "free", "liberated" etc. These words have been too care-lessly bandied about with too little thought for too long.

The background to the historic misunderstandings which divide women lie, I believe, in the educational and cultural history of the last two hundred years. Beginning in the early nineteenth century, there occurred an influx of principally Catholic and Protestant missionary teachers, principally from Europe and the United States. These mission-aries established schools and universities which to this day dominate the educational landscape in Lebanon. While some of these have over the years lost their religious identity and became secular – the American University of Beirut, which, until 1920, was the Syrian Protestant College, is a good example of this – many of them have maintained their religious identity – the French Jesuit Université Saint-Joseph, with, until very recently, a French Jesuit rector, is only one example. In any case, these remain foreign schools, with a large percentage of foreign teachers on their staff, with foreign principals and boards making decisions regarding curricula, discipline and all other matters not directly subject to Lebanese law. National public schools, as well as the state university, on the other hand, limp along, far behind the foreign schools in power, status, money, grounds, laboratories, libraries, and over-all influence.

When the foreign schools were founded during the period of Ottoman rule, they brought in new ideas, new clothing, new languages, and new manners. The vigour and newness of the schools, their curricula and their methods, as well as, or perhaps because of, the growing power of their European and American sponsors, and the parallel decline in Ottoman power, naturally created around them an aura of authority and made them appear to be the appropriate models for the future. The Makassed Philanthropic and Islamic Association, which was to become, and remains to this day, an important cultural arm of the Beirut Sunni community, for instance, founded in 1878 the first of many schools in response to the invasion of foreign mission schools. Interestingly, this first school was for girls, and, but for its Muslim character, was meant to catch up with the mission schools, and thus regarded them as models. That the Makassed was self-consciously responding to the foreign cultural invasion is made clear by the moving, even distressing, statement contained in its First Annual Report.[7] A girls' school founded by another Beirut Muslim society named *jam'iyyat thamarat al-ihsan* (Society for the Fruits of Good Works) had as its first headmistress Alice Ydlbi, who was half English, had an English education, and spoke Arabic with an accent.[8]

Following the First World War, the collapse of the Ottoman Empire, and the establishment of French mandate over the newly created Lebanon, the foreign schools, especially the French, flourished even more than before. National independence in 1943 did not alter the general trend; in this, the Lebanese experience is quite unlike other countries in the area, including Syria, Iraq, and Egypt, where a similarly influential foreign school establishment went into eclipse, if it did not die out completely, after independence. The school I myself attended in Cairo, for instance, the English School, Cairo, was nationalised following the Suez crisis of 1956.

In Lebanon, the old reputation of the foreign schools as providing "modern" education, and being the model, precisely because of their foreignness, to be followed, survived, amazingly, the vicissitudes of colonialism as well as anti-colonialism, national independence and the wide awareness of cultural imperialism. Indeed, it seems to me that the signs or symbols of the presence, that is clothes, styles, manners, language, of the new and vital education, and the new power, as it came in the nineteenth century, became a sought-after end in themselves, often confused with that which they were originally merely symbols of, that is, modernity, the modern, the new, the vital, the vibrant and innovative, and the powerful.

It is perhaps most of all this last quality, power, before which all else bows in submission. Thus, in the face of this view of "modernity", a permanent state persists not only of division, but of self-doubt, impotence and therefore paralysis.

The growing influence and visibility of the Islamic movements in the area has, of course, been reflected in Lebanon as well, especially during the war years, and has led to a reinforcement of what I have called the false dichotomy. The appearance of strictly "Islamic dress", while often perceived as an aggressive sign of a militant movement, is nonetheless and surprisingly associated with "tradition" and the submission of women. I have repeatedly seen how women dressed in this fashion are gingerly treated by even the most impertinent of shopkeepers or taxi drivers, their dress clearly signifying a power, that of the militant Islam, not to be taken lightly. How these same women fare within the movement is another story, but as they face outward, they share the power of the movement which they represent. Thus does this simultaneous image of power and submission emerge to many people as a kind of threatening shadow over the future.

The Islamic movement in Lebanon differs from that in other countries in the region in that here the multi-sectarian structure of society opposes any single sect or group from imposing its vision on the country, whether as ruling party, as in Iran or Sudan, or as powerful opposition, such as in Egypt or Algeria.

Lebanon thus offers an interesting exception to the surrounding region, and is therefore like a social laboratory, in which some of these issues can be explored. Nowhere in the rest of the Arab world is there a Christian population as powerful or as influential as the Lebanese; and nowhere is there a population structure in which Shi'i and Sunni Muslims stand in almost equal, or at least in stand-off, numbers. Nowhere have western schools had the influence they do here. If the influence of Muslim law and attitudes, especially of the more recent militant sort, has been consistently, even obsessively, turned to in discussions on the status of Arab women, then an explanation must be found for the fact that in Lebanon women are legally and politically as badly off, if not worse off, than in other, more thoroughly Muslim, countries. An elected female Prime Minister, such as governs in Muslim countries like Pakistan, Turkey, or Bangladesh, is quite unthinkable in Lebanon, with its multi-sectarian population, and its "modern" mind-set and thousands of women university graduates.

Interestingly enough, the same neighbour countries which curtailed the foreign influence on education have regularly if not invariably included women in their governments. It is very tempting, therefore, to drive straight to the conclusion that there must be some connection between the Westernisation, past and present, so visible in Lebanon, and exerting so enormous an influence, and the absence of a truly democratic women's movement to demand, on the basis of democratic justice, an end to political exclusion. One must resist the temptation in order to look more carefully at the issue before arriving at any such conclusion.

Influences come and go with the military and political fortunes of their sponsors, but the divisions created by them can linger. The surrender to what was once perceived to be a superior cultural force; the desire of some to be associated with this superior force, and of others to react against it; the terrible and blinding fear in the hearts of the former, based on the sense of their own impotence in the face of that force, that to be torn away from it would mean weakness, decline and even a kind of cultural death; the equally terrible fear on the part of the latter that to continue to allow it would as certainly mean the death of our own native culture; in short, the incomplete process of decolonisation, which stopped short of a thorough and honest resolution of profoundly divisive cultural issues – these have resulted in the divisions that have prevented the solidarity of women in all their ranks.

But another experience shows that it is not only class division, sectarianism, and cultural mythology which is responsible for the situation of women and their feeble movement.

It seems to me that during the long war that began in 1975, as the state and most of its institutions were rendered impotent, the condition of women dramatically improved. The formalities associated with government, including political appointments, became almost meaningless; elections were suspended altogether; real power was in the hands of armed militias or of foreign governments. Daily civil life continued, however, on a parallel level with the war, though apparently thoroughly dissociated from it. Schools, universities, shops, etc., carried on a daily routine unconnected with the fighting, though governed by its schedules and the geography of boundaries which it created. Though government was effectively suspended, the militias did not interfere with the routine running of the affairs of non-combatants, and a kind of political/social vacuum existed in which people lived out their lives and solved their own problems.

In this strangely civilised and utterly anomalous situation, in this almost perfectly anarchical state, women, it seems to me, flourished. In domestic life, especially during the periods of heavy fighting and shelling, mothers and wives dominated the moment. Always providers of food, comfort, first aid, and so on, women became in those terrible days during which all other realities were suspended, the unquestioned pivot around which members of the family revolved. Husbands at times like these were almost invariably out of work, and their continuous and unusual presence at home was felt to be awkward and almost an invasion of territory. Especially in the shelters, all class distinctions, including those between husbands and wives, became meaningless, and humanity was face to face with itself.

Though men and women faced equal risks from shelling, and from the car bombs and street fighting which were so common an aspect of life during the war, at the barricades women were less threatened than men with kidnapping, assault, robbery, and death. The old taboos surrounding '*ard*, and the traditional respect for mothers, provided a kind of magical protection for women. Indeed, if a man landed at an enemy barricade, the chances of his meeting with misfortune were less if he was accompanied by a wife or mother. Thus did women sometimes become the protectors of their husbands, brothers, and sons. And thus too did women often show greater daring at a confrontation with armed men than their husbands or male colleagues, becoming consequently more outspoken at home and at work.

Of course, this was not always true. Women were raped and murdered with the usual wartime savagery on several occasions: the events at the Palestinian refugee camps of Sabra and Chatila were only the most notorious and perhaps ferocious of these. However, it does seem to me undeniable to claim that Arab and, more precisely, Islamic tradition contributed to the fact that women were generally routinely less badly treated here than in other combat areas around the world.

In addition, women had to deal with unusual circumstances at every turn, and to provide solutions for problems normally dealt with by husbands or by society at large. Indeed, many men were forced to seek employment abroad, leaving their wives in charge of the household. On a regular basis women faced terrifying dangers, and were able to measure their own courage, and taste the power of their own survival. All of this permitted the individual personalities of women to grow, and, unrestrained by the usual social restrictions, to flourish. Women, I think, tasted personal power during the war to a degree and in a way which was enormously exhilarating to them while unthreatening to anyone else.

When the war ended, however, and the state resumed its influence, when the old social forms were reinstated, and the old legal forms strengthened, this unscheduled and gratuitous strengthening of personality was undone, and women gradually retreated into their previous position. The modern nation-state itself, this form of political organisation imposed by the conquering mandate after World War I, brought with it the biases against women of the countries who imposed it. Indeed, the imperial countries themselves have long since outgrown those biases which continue to haunt the lives of those who inherited this once modern form. Thus, though Britain and France may have changed many of their laws concerning women, these same laws continue to flourish here. The most outrageous of these touches the most basic of civil rights:

the right to transmit citizenship to one's [non-Lebanese] husband and children is to this day still denied Lebanese women.

Democratic life in general suffered a terrible blow when the war began from which it has not yet recovered, though the forms of democracy remain visible and homage is paid to them continuously. Parliament is bustling, and the press can pretty much say what it pleases. Criticism of those in power is commonplace, and endless discussions go on publicly about everything from corruption to the public debt. Yet, as the former Prime Minister Selim al Hoss has repeatedly complained, though there be freedom, true democracy is absent, and accountability is almost never a serious threat to a wayward politician.

The problems that women face cannot be solved outside the framework of a truly representative and democratic system. The women's movement does not make any sense, nor can it be effective, if it is not plugged into a larger and more general movement to achieve the rights of all citizens, and to lessen the injustices in all aspects of life. That the true function of the women's movement is to be part of this larger one is not only clear, but necessary.

If this is true nationally, it is just as true on an international level. The Western feminist movement has won many admirers in Arab society for some of its accomplishments, especially the improvement in women's legal, economic, and personal standing. A heavy price, however, has been paid, and much useful territory has been lost, for itself and for other women's movements, because of its failures.

In particular, the alarming statistics on the breakdown of family life in Europe and especially the United States, the divorce rates, and the concomitant figures on juvenile crime, drug, and alcohol abuse, as well as what is perceived to be the alienation and depersonalisation of modern Western society, are repeatedly pointed to as the fruits of a movement led astray. Mothering, with all its domestic duties, including surveying the children; keeping them well fed, well behaved and well dressed; supervising school work, and helping them with it when necessary; providing them with comfort and discipline; seeing to their overall social and moral training and eventual success; all these are seen by thoughtful women here as an essential part of their role, retrieved from the ashes of family life put to the torch, as they see it, by the Western feminist movement.

That it is unfair to put the blame for the breakdown in Western family life only on women in general and the feminist movement in particular is something that can only become clear with consciousness raising, and the intelligent analysis of social ills which, as I have already pointed out, seems to me one of the primary functions of a women's movement.

The mothering role necessitates time and energy which otherwise might be relegated to a more aggressive attitude in professional life: it is this view which perhaps explains the absence of protest against the realities which I mentioned at the beginning of this paper. Many thoughtful professional women with whom I have spoken over the years have expressed what they see as the calmly sensible view that they could not realistically hope to accomplish everything; that they had chosen to expend their energies on raising their children while not sacrificing their careers, but merely curtailing the amount of energy devoted to the fight for professional advancement; that they considered this a necessary sacrifice, a sensible and inevitable management of resources; and that they did not in any way consider this choice to have constituted a diminution of their contribution to society's well-being, but quite the contrary, an important aspect of social development. In this conviction they were unshaken by the recognition that society had not rewarded them for this decision, or that they were left out of the political arena.

I do not know if it will be possible in the future to find a formula that will suit women's personal lives, allowing them to continue to fulfil the nurturing role which they value so deeply and take so seriously, and will at the same time allow them to participate more fully in the democratic process by achieving positions in which they can help to make decisions shaping the future. To help accomplish this double goal, it seems to me, a strong and popular feminist movement is required. Such a movement, to be effective, must first of all break down barriers between classes and sects by promoting, openly and courageously, a free and frank discussion of all issues.

NOTES

1 During the preparation of this paper, I had conversations with a number of women who kindly shared with me their thoughts on the subject and allowed me to test some of mine. Though the ideas expressed in this paper are mine and mine alone, and I take full responsibility for them, conversations with the following were of great value to me: Professors Najla Hamadeh and Hoda Zurayk of the American University of Beirut; Professor Bayan al Hout of the Lebanese University; Mrs Linda Matar of the Lijnat Huquq al-Mar'a al-Lubnaniah (the Committee for the Rights of Lebanese Women), and Mrs Ni'mat Kenaan, Director-General of the Ministry of Social Affairs. I am also indebted to the Revd Habib Badr, pastor of the National Evangelical Church of Beirut, who kindly shared with me his thoughts as well as his knowledge of the personal status laws as they apply to the Protestant community in Lebanon.

2 These figures are based on the lists of faculty members and their ranks in the American University of Beirut Catalogue, 1994–5.

3 Figures taken from the list of graduates as distributed at the Commencement Exercises on 12 July 1995.

4 UNDP, *Human Development Report 1994* (New York: Oxford University Press, 1994).

5 Figures quoted in an as yet unpublished study, *Strengthening Institutions for Enterprise Development for Women*, undertaken by Consultation and Research Institute, at the request of UNIFEM (Beirut, 1994), p. 38.

6 The figures of numbers of divorces in the Protestant community were given to me by the Revd Habib Badr, head of the spiritual court; the figure for the Protestant population is a very rough one, as there has been no census in Lebanon since 1932, nor has there been a certain count of the deaths or emigration during the war as these affected this or any other Lebanese community.

7 First Annual Report of the Makassed Philanthropic Association (Beirut: Thamarat al-Funun Printing Press, 1297 AH [1880 CE]). Translated into English as *The True Dawn* and printed as a pamphlet by the Makassed.

8 See Anbara Salam al Khalidi, *Jawla fi'l dhikrayat bayn Lubnan wa Filistin* (A Voyage through Memories, between Lebanon and Palestine) (Beirut: Dar an-Nahar, 1978), p.27.

ELEVEN

GULF WOMEN AND ISLAMIC LAW

Munira Fakhro

Revitalising Islamic Values

Is Islamic reform possible? This question has been raised by many reformists and scholars in the Muslim world. Since the early days of Islam, the *shari'a* developed from verses of the Qur'an and from the decisions of the Prophet Muhammad and his early companions into a complex system of legal opinions and judgements. It is often argued that the *shari'a* was not given in a finished form. The Prophet's method was a flexible dynamic adaptation of general principles to specific situations as they arose. In his study of Middle Eastern family law, Eric Mueller goes back to the early days of Islam and traces the events that have led to the present dilemma.[1] He argues that, after the death of the Prophet Muhammad in 632 AD, his first four successors carried on the tradition of flexibility. They believed that laws had to be understood and interpreted to remain true to their original purpose. During their time, laws were continually developed, and the successors to their secular authority were fully empowered to preside over and guide that process. Under Umayyad rule, the law became more rigid as it was employed by the rulers as a theoretical justification for state control. It was then that religious scholars collected and organised the various rulings of the Prophet and his first successors and created a legal system – from which all four Sunni schools of law emerged and the main collections of the Prophet's sayings, *hadith*, were compiled.

Parallel with the movement, other factions appeared in opposition to the State, including the Shi'is. Thus, the term "traditional Islamic law" stands for a whole variety of groups and opinions. The collapse of the 'Abbasid dynasty in the thirteenth century, at the hands of the Mongols, led the Muslims to withdrawal and conservatism and, in a widely received view, led to the alleged closing of the door of *ijtihad* – interpretation or self-exertion in understanding and interpreting the *shari'a* – which resulted in the relative stagnation of the Muslim community and its jurisprudence.[2]

By the twentieth century, the stage was set for the tide of reformist legislation that has modified or replaced traditional law in areas such as personal status, marriage and family laws.[3] All Arab and Muslim countries that have introduced reforms in family law, have incorporated major elements of the *shari'a* as well as modern legislation.

Since the turn of the century, several Muslim countries codified their laws in a way that increased women's rights significantly. Reforms in other Middle Eastern countries provide some perspective on the extent and possibilities for future reforms in Gulf states. For example, Syria introduced restrictions on the husband's unfettered right of repudiation. The Syrian Personal Status Law of 1953 included a stipulation requiring a Muslim man to obtain permission from the court before contracting another marriage. Court permission for a polygamous marriage has been adopted by other Muslim countries such as Morocco, Iran and Iraq.[4] In Egypt, modern Muslim law reform presented changes in marriage and divorce in 1979, such as the necessity for the husband to inform his wife before marrying another woman. The first wife has the right to seek a divorce if she disapproves of the marriage. Tunisia entirely outlawed polygamy in 1957, the only Muslim country to do so.

Despite the recent and on-going socio-economic changes, the conflict between the forces of conservatism and modernism has continued. The problem which has emerged can be described as one of *taqlid* (imitating tradition) versus *ijtihad*. Professor John Esposito suggests that the central task is to provide an Islamic methodology for Islamic reform, where the sources of legal reform, *ijtihad* and *ijma'* (the consensus of the community) can be rethought.[5]

There are a growing number of Islamic reformists who claim the right to *ijtihad* and reject a blind following of the past. These reformists seek to interpret and apply Islamic principles and requirements to modern life in order to develop appropriate Islamic responses for modern Muslim societies. This trend builds on a growing network of scholars and social scientists from all regions of the Arab Muslim world. We can think of Mernissi, Banani, Arkun and Jabri in North Africa; Ghazali, Abul-Majd and Abu Shaqqa in Egypt. In the Arab East one of the most famous reformists is Muhammad Shahrur.

In this paper, the ideas of two reformists, Muhammad Shahrur and Abdul-Halim Abu Shaqqa will be presented. These authors urge for reforms within the context of Islamic law and its impact on women.

Muhammad Shahrur's Reading of the Qur'an

With the help of linguist Ja'afar Daqq al-Bab, Muhammad Shahrur wrote *al-Kitab wal-Qur'an* (The Book and the Qur'an), which deals with the core of this issue.[6] It has become a best seller in Damascus, indicating the acute public need for explanations and solutions to these modern dilemmas.

Al-Bab studied the codes of the Arabic language, which he describes as being poor in synonyms, *muradafat*, but developing and excelling in a style parallel to human thought. He emphasised the parallel between language and thought and the function of connections from the beginning of human speech. His arguments are based on the structure and form of the language in its initial growth. He cites the example of recital, *tartil*, a form of chanting. He goes back to the etymology of the word, *rattala*, meaning to organise and discipline. Therefore, he argues, the Qur'an has been organised and classified into various subjects that appear in various chapters to be cast in one easily understood form. From this logic, the author has produced a collection of verses containing the word "Qur'an" and others that contain "The Book" and showed the clear difference between the two words. The author defines the *sunna* as all the Prophet's sayings or deeds that were recorded by religious scholars, *fuqaha*, according to their interpretations and not as the direct sayings of the Prophet himself, who insisted that the text of the Qur'an be recorded but not his own personal sayings.

Consequently, the author arrived at a contemporary understanding of the Prophet's Sunna, his sayings and deeds, in which the Prophet's role was to define the *shari'a* within the limits of divine tolerance, *hudud*. These need to be interpreted within the context of the seventh-century AD mentality in the Arabian peninsula, which means that the door to scholarly interpretation of *shari'a* is open. He thus developed a new approach in understanding the Qur'an and the Book and called it "the theory of limits" (*hudud*), for the modern understanding of Islam.

This new approach was also applied to the attitude of Islam towards women. The outcome of this research established a new set of guidelines following which he argued that women's emancipation, like that of slaves, began during the time of the Prophet, but was not completed then. Women's liberation became therefore subject to the historical evolution of humanity.

Shahrur collected verses related to women and tried to interpret them within the theory of limits (*hudud*):

a) Polygamy: The author considers the Qur'anic verse on polygamy to be a *hudud* verse, covering the highest and lowest limit in the number of wives setting the lowest at one and the highest at four.

b) *Sadaq* (dower): The *sadaq* is one of the marital *hudud* set in the nuptial agreement according to prevailing traditions and current economic considerations.

c) Attire of women: In order to avoid excesses, the attire of men and women and their social conduct have limits set by the Prophet in his known saying "The whole appearance of women is indiscreet save her face and hands." The Prophet in this interpretation sets the full covering of the body as an upper limit, but he did not allow women to cover their faces and hands, because identity is in a human face. Thus while a naked woman has exceeded God's limits, a totally covered woman has also exceeded the lower limit set by the Prophet.

d) The right of legislative representation and political activity: Political participation was the first right given directly to women by Islam. This was a milestone in the history of women's liberation. Women struggled with men on an equal footing, for their struggle was ideological. This can be seen in the cases of the sister of 'Umar, the second *Rashidi* Caliph and of Sumayya, the wife of Ammar ibn Yasir.

e) Marriage contract: In Islam this contract seeks to distribute authority evenly between man and wife by allowing extra clauses that state such things as which partner has the final say in dissolving the marriage. However, a woman may set whatever conditions she desires in the marriage contract, which are of course legally binding on both parties. Such conditions are among the *hudud* in Islam.

f) Divorce: Both husband and wife have equal rights to divorce and verbal divorce is not valid. Social misconceptions about marital relationships such as those regarding alimony, polygamy, impulsive divorce and other excessive behaviour by men towards their wives must be revised and studied more carefully, as the Qur'an does not encourage or even allow such misconceptions.

'Abdul-Halim Abu Shaqqa

The work of the Egyptian scholar Abu Shaqqa is considered by Muslim reformist scholars to be a comprehensive study of the Qur'anic texts and the Islamic interpretations of Bukhari and Muslim, who both recorded the most important collections of *hadith*.[7] He encourages the lifting from Muslim women of restrictions that have prevailed for many centuries in the Islamic world. Abu Shaqqa looked at the *hadith* for legislation governing the status of women, and he selected those *hadith* which highlight the prominence of many female personalities in Islam and their assumption of responsibilities in society in the days of the Prophet, such as their demands to be given more opportunities in education, to hold a general assembly in the mosque, to retain their right of selection of a husband and their right to end a relationship with a husband. His book is a socio-religious study of women in the days of the Prophet. It covers all aspects of public and private life of women in social relations and activities. The comprehensive study of six volumes can be summarised as follows:

a) The main features of women's personality: The Muslim woman in the days of the Prophet was fully aware of her status as set by the new religion. This is summarised by the Prophet himself as he established the rules of equality between men and women with a special reference to their specialised roles in society.

b) Attire and general appearance: No limits have been set on fashion except that the body must be decently covered in accordance with climate and society.

c) Participation in social life: The restriction of the veil was limited to the wives of the Prophet and did not include other women. Women share social life with men at both public and private levels in accordance with the needs of a serious and active life.

d) The family: A woman has the right to choose a husband and to part from him, provided she compensates him with what she has taken from him. The distribution of responsibilities of a married couple are those necessary for the achievement of a harmonious and co-operative family life. The *shari'a* has set the main guidelines for a happy married life by establishing the moral standards which must be adhered to.

The two books described above represent the growing literature of a reform movement within the context of Islamic teachings, which may result in a more positive acceptance of *ijtihad* and the rejection of a blind following of the past.

The Present Situation of Women in the Gulf States

Women constitute nearly half of the national indigenous population of the Gulf but less than one-third of the total population, including foreigners. Their status cannot be appraised under one classification; it varies according to the section of society to which they belong and the degree of education they acquire. However, whether they come from rich or poor families, conservative or modern, they confront the same restricting regulations under the *shari'a*, which ensure segregation of the sexes and discrimination against women in matters such as inheritance, divorce, child custody and other family issues. Separate societies for men and women have been fostered within a system that excludes women from public activities and confines them to their homes. Bahrain and Kuwait differ slightly from the rest of the Gulf states in that they have always been more open to the rest of the world and have been noted for their relatively enlightened attitudes.

Family law remains a key issue for women in the Gulf region. All the Gulf states, except Kuwait, still practise the old *shari'a* code. Even the Kuwaiti family law, which was issued in 1984, does not offer many rights for Kuwaiti women. As an example, women under the age of 25 cannot get married without the approval of a male relative as a guardian. Furthermore, those rights which do exist are often not respected. For example, a husband should not accommodate a second wife in the same household without the acceptance of the first wife but statistics indicate in 1985 that among 655 marriage cases there were 331 cases in which the husbands had more than one wife. Al-'Awadi argues that husbands continue to accommodate second wives, pretending to have obtained the approval of the first wives, without following the dictates of legislation.[8]

In the last four decades, Gulf societies felt the need to introduce some modifications in the laws, especially those concerning women and the family in general. However, whether under uncodified *shari'a* or under a "modern" statutory family law as in Kuwait, inequality is created among the sexes and females are deprived of their legal rights.

The condition of women in the Gulf differs from one state to the other depending on the degree of advancement in overall development and urbanisation. In education, for example, Bahrain pioneered public education for both sexes at the beginning of this century, followed by Kuwait, whereas the UAE and Oman only started such programmes in the 1950s and 1970s respectively. Kuwaiti women led the way in demanding political advancement; after the elections in 1984, some liberal members in the Kuwaiti parliament brought forward a bill to grant women the right to vote. The parliament's legal committee consulted with the Ministry of Islamic Affairs, which issued a ruling that "the nature of the electoral process befits men, who are endowed with ability and expertise; it is not permissible that women recommend or nominate other women or men".[9] Women were also prohibited from participating in the last elections which were held in October 1992 despite assurances given by the government during the Gulf War. As for Saudi women, they are the most deprived in the Gulf region. Saudi Arabia implements very strict rules concerning women and the family. It is the only state where women are not allowed to drive cars; this makes them totally dependent on a husband, a close male relative, or a hired driver. In November 1990, during the early days of the Gulf crisis, approximately fifty highly educated Saudi women attempted to gain the right to drive. They gathered on the busiest street in the capital, Riyadh, and drove their cars for nearly an hour. They were detained by the police for a few hours and they were later dismissed from their jobs.

Despite this strict segregation in Saudi society, women are employed to run women's schools as teachers and administrators. This segregation gives women a professional advantage because there is no competition with men within this field.[10]

Saudi females are required to wear a veil in public; they are not permitted to leave their country for any reason without the company of a male relative as a guardian, *muhrim*. In addition, they are not allowed to attend conferences or seminars even on an individual basis.

In the United Arab Emirates (UAE), traditional Islamic and tribal values are dominant in this society. In recent years, some changes have been occurring in marriage laws, but the *shari'a* remains the legal system governing all aspects of life. The spread of education has played a significant part in changing the role of women in the UAE. This has lowered the high level of illiteracy and increased educational opportunities.

In Qatar, the education of women, which started in 1955, has been met with great opposition from men. Qatari society is known as more conservative and tribal than those of the rest of the Gulf states. With the exception of a few working women, women are generally not allowed to drive cars. Additionally, with the exception of a branch of the Red Crescent Society, which has been established recently, women were prohibited from the formation of women's associations.

Although women's participation in the workforce started late in Oman, once it had begun female employment increased rapidly, especially in the public sector. Furthermore, Omani women now hold varied jobs, even as pilots and officers in the police force, and some hold high-ranking administrative positions as directors and under-secretaries. However, despite education and employment, Omani women are governed by classical *shari'a* rules in every aspect of their lives.

Prior to the discovery of oil in 1932, women in Bahrain were veiled and their role was mainly restricted to childbearing and the home. With the new economic order and the expansion of education, women's roles began to change. Such modification has been more visible in urban areas than in villages or in the poorer sectors of society, where women are still veiled and confined to their homes. Bahraini women constitute less than 10 per cent of the overall labour force. Most working women are employed at different government agencies, where few hold administrative positions; the majority work as teachers, secretaries and clerks.

The Need for a Reformed Family Law in the Gulf Region

Laws pertaining to marriage, divorce, inheritance and child custody in the Gulf region are governed by Islamic law. In the case of marriage, for example, the *shari'a* does not specify an age limit. Historically, boys and girls entered marriage at an early age, and a minimum age for marriage has never been introduced in the Gulf, except for Kuwait where it is set at 15 years for both sexes. In the remaining Gulf states, it is left to the father or the nearest male relative to decide when to sign the marriage contract. In Qatar, the 1991 census recorded that the number of married women aged 15 to 19 years was 387 cases or 33.3 per cent of the total married women in that year.[11] In Bahrain, the 1991 census showed that the number of married women aged 15 years and under reached 11,085 or 17.3 per cent of the total married female population. However, such statistics are not reliable because child marriage is more common in villages and remote areas where girls get married at an early stage of their lives. This practice is still recognised as legally valid because of the absence of the minimum age for marriage. Early marriage can be seen as a main cause of the high birth rate in the Gulf.

Polygamy continues to arouse strong resentment among women at all social levels. Islamic law allows men to have up to four wives at any one time. In Bahrain, those who were married to more than one wife account for 5.6 per cent of the total married Bahraini women in 1991; higher than a decade ago when it was 5.4 per cent. In Qatar, the percentage of men who are married to more than one wife reached 5.5 per cent of the total in 1991, while in Kuwait it exceeded 50.5 per cent in 1985. However, whether the percentage is high or low the threat of polygamy affects all women.

As for divorce, women's right to dissolve their marriage is denied to them in most Muslim countries. The power of divorce lies completely in the hands of the husband. It is left to his will and conscience to decide on divorce. Divorce procedures can be conducted orally; a husband can be divorced from his wife if he utters three times in succession, "You are divorced", and he compensates his wife with whatever remains unpaid on the dowry. At present, divorce rates are high in the majority of the Gulf states. In Bahrain it was 18.3 per cent in 1992, a slight decrease from a decade ago when it reached 20 per cent. In Qatar divorce rate is considered very high at 29.1 per cent although the rate has not changed since 1984. Paradoxically, some scholars in Qatar relate such high rates to government policy towards divorced women; each divorcee receives a monthly allowance in addition to the grant of a house. These figures are considered relatively high for traditional Muslim countries, though they may be moderate by Western standards, where divorce rates exceed 60 per cent in some European states.

The custody of children is also an area in need of reform. Divorced or widowed mothers retain the custody of their children for a limited period, then custody passes to the father or the nearest male relative on the father's side. However, during the mother's period of custody which lasts until a daughter is nine years old and a son is seven, the father remains a guardian of the child. In addition, the mother loses her right of custody as soon as she is remarried. Such laws do not allow much consideration for a divorced woman whose role as wife and mother may be taken away, although she is given no say in the divorce action.[12]

The need for a progressive family law which would regulate marital patterns and relations; view marriage as a partnership with shared duties and obligations; and in the event of a divorce grant full parental rights and duties to the parent who is responsible for the care and rearing of the child, is pressing.

Perspectives on the Future

The Gulf states, have undergone drastic social and economic changes in the last few decades. The most evident of these changes, especially in the education sector, has taken place in the last two decades after the sharp increase in oil revenues. Women form the majority of students in most Gulf universities where a significant number of them are pursuing post-graduate degrees. This trend will most likely have an effect on conservative Gulf societies, but their full impact still lies some time away.

The voice of pressure groups in the Gulf region is not strong enough to force the ruling elites to make concessions. The efforts of women's associations in reforming Islamic laws governing women are very limited. Moreover, labour unions and formal political parties are banned in most of the Gulf states. Therefore, political activities are taking place in religious centres, cultural societies, sports clubs and women's voluntary and professional associations. It is only indirectly through the medium of non-political organisations and institutions that political change can be channelled.

Organisations play an important role normally performed by political parties in other democratic societies. They reflect the social and political changes that have taken place in the Gulf region and represent a new social force that might bring about changes in the future. The number of those organisations exceeds 80 with 32,000 active members of both sexes (see the table below). The role of such organisations is expanding, which may lead to more involvement in the political and social events in the future. The governments of the Gulf states are aware that such pressure groups might form a threat to their authority, and they are trying to minimise their power by different means. In Bahrain, for example, the government recently issued legislation limiting the role of all associations. The new legislation grants absolute power to the Ministry of Labour and Social Affairs to dissolve any association without even giving a justification. In addition, professional societies are banned in most Gulf states, only charitable ones are allowed to exist.

In conclusion, one can say that the pace of change in the areas of education, social change and political consciousness will eventually lead to a modernisation in the political sector and to a broadening of the base of decision-making to include women. At the same time, democracy alone will not lead to reforms in Islamic law: when the Islamic groups won the majority seats in the parliament in Jordan and Kuwait recently, their priority was to amend the constitution so that the *shari'a* becomes the sole basis of legislation. Any reform in Islamic law in the region cannot be achieved without the effort and willingness of all Muslim countries to work together to find a formula that combines modernity and the essence of Islamic teachings. Islamic reform within the context of Islam and the implementation of *ijtihad* and *ijma'* which will, hopefully, resolve the conflict between Islam and modernity.

Estimated Numbers of Associations and Members in the Gulf States

State	No. of Associations				Members			
	Professional	Charitable	Women	Total	Professional	Charities	Women	Total
UAE	11	8	6	26	2281	6666	3485	5766
Bahrain	7	6	5	18	–	2163	684	5420
Oman	–	–	7	7	–	–	1500	1500
Qatar	–	1	–	1	–	500	–	500
Kuwait	16	9	4	29	15,332	2177	1304	8813
Saudi Arabia	–	68	19	87	–	22,073	3084	25,156
Total	34	77	42	168	–	–	–	57,156

Source: Derived from Table 2, p. 60, Annajjar Baqir, *Voluntary Social Work in the Gulf States* (1988).

NOTES

1 See Eric Mueller, 'Revitalizing Old Ideas: Development in Middle Eastern Family Law' in Elizabeth W. Fernea (ed.), *Women and the Family in The Middle East* (Austin: University of Texas Press, 1985), p. 226.

2 John L. Esposito, *Women in Muslim Family Law* (Syracuse, N.Y.: Syracuse University Press, 1982), p. 2. On the alleged closure of the gates of *ijtihad*, see however W. Hallaq, 'Was the Gate of Ijtihad Closed ?' *International Journal of Middle Eastern Studies (IJMES)*, 16 (1984), pp. 3–41.

3 *Ibid.*, p. 93.

4 *Ibid.*, p. 131.

5 Esposito, *Women in Muslim Family Law*, p. 133.

6 Muhammad Shahrur, *al-Kitab wal-Qur'an: Qira'ah mu'asirah* (The Book and the Qur'an: A Contemporary Interpretation) (Damascus: al-Ahali lil-Tib'ah wa-al-Nashr wa-al-Tawzi', 1990).

7 'Abdul-Halim Abu Shaqqa, *Tahrir al-mar'a fi 'asr al-risala* (The Liberation of Woman at the Time of the Prophesy) (Kuwait, 1990).

8 Badriya al-'Awadi, *al-Mar'a wal qanun* (Woman and the Law) (Kuwait, 1990).

9 *The Middle East Magazine* (October 1985), p. 7.

10 Nesta Ramazani, 'Arab Women in The Gulf', *The Middle East Journal*, Vol. 39, No. 2 (Spring, 1985), p. 7.

11 Mueller, 'Revitalizing Old Ideas', p. 244.

12 Esposito, *Women in Muslim Family Law*, p. 11.

TWELVE

SOME OBSERVATIONS ON WOMEN IN SAUDI ARABIA

Mai Yamani

The twentieth-century phenomenon of feminism has found great variety of expression in different cultures and at different times. In the Kingdom of Saudi Arabia the current social circumstances of the country have caused an identifiable strand of Saudi women to make of Islam the vehicle for expression of feminist tendencies. They have, in an alluring way, sought their sense of power, their sense of identity, their freedom, and their equality with men through the basic precepts of Islam. It could even be argued that some Saudi women have manipulated these concepts to their advantage, rather than having recourse to stratagems more familiar in the experience of what may be crudely defined as Western feminism. This is partly because those who have tried to move forward along a Western-style liberal strategy, mostly in the shape of acts of defiance against the Saudi authorities, have not seemed to achieve any serious practical results.

And yet it is no longer possible for any Arab or Muslim community or country to live and develop in isolation from the influence of neighbours or "the global village". It is trite to say that barriers have broken down through the influence of the mass media, but this is none the less true for being so. It is important in this context to bear in mind the standardising influence of an agreed national curriculum in schools. Nor must it be forgotten that, to take the Arab countries alone, the use of classical Arabic as a medium in education has also acted as an instrument for a wider exchange of ideas.

After defining the wider setting in which women find themselves in the Kingdom, this chapter will briefly examine the expression of a form of feminism observed in Saudi Arabia during the 1980s among women who are using the existing framework of Islamic law to challenge or even question their own status in Saudi society. These women act, not in an overtly political way, but more subtly, from "behind the veil".

A feminist movement based on the use of fundamental Islamic concepts is not restricted to Saudi Arabia and can be found elsewhere in the Arab and Muslim world. For these women, the only legitimate example or aspiration comes from a representation of archetypal models derived from early Islamic history and built around the figures of the *ummahat al-mu'minin* (literally the "mothers of the believers").[1]

These are leading role models in the history of Islam, in particular of Arab Islam, who can be seen to encourage a range of activities legitimately open to good Muslim women. A *hadith* is often quoted in this context: "Learn half of your religion from that red-headed one!" By this is meant the example of the Prophet's wife, 'A'isha, the daughter of the future Caliph, Abu-Bakr. The earliest Arabic texts acknowledge 'A'isha as the favourite wife of Muhammad and collections of *hadith* are known which quote her opinion on matters of religion. Indeed, it has been calculated that one-sixth of the *hadith* record her as being part of the chain of transmission of the Traditions of the Prophet. The most famous incident in her life as a prominent Muslim woman was her participation in 656 AD in the "Battle of the Camel", a decisive moment in the first civil war. Such a strikingly obvious political role for a woman could of course be seen as creating a problematical role model.[2]

Preceding 'A'isha was another highly significant figure in the context of feminine role models among the *ummahat al-mu'minin*, namely Khadija, the first wife of the Prophet. Before and after her marriage to the Prophet she was a successful businesswoman. Her activities in the economic sphere have often served as an example encouraging women's participation and the exercise of power in society through money. Indeed Khadija not only continued her business activities after marrying the Prophet, but actually employed him in her business.

Regional Distinctiveness

An important reference must be made to regionalism within Saudi Arabia.[3] A distinguishing feature of women in the Hijaz is that they come from a region which has a more heterogeneous character than other regions of the Kingdom. Furthermore, the cities from which they come have historically been known for their distinctive economic activities, and for certain specialised occupations. The region is also marked by a relatively high level of development, by heterogeneous education and by social and cultural values which can be differentiated from those of the other major regions. Hijazi women are more "used to going outdoors" and expressing themselves publicly, a phenomenon more reserved for men in other regions of the Kingdom, especially Najd. The result is that while in the

Najd a fundamentalist tendency is found principally among men, in the Hijaz it is the women who are going back to religious basics. While the leaders of the movement, however, are women from the upper strata of society, this feature seems to be increasingly moving down to reach other sections of society.

That said, whether upper or middle class, the role of women in the Kingdom of Saudi Arabia can only be seen in the context of their patronymic group and of the national purpose and not as one section of society struggling for its rights in isolation from men.[4]

General Historical and Political Setting

The study of women's roles in Saudi Arabia must take into account social and political events in relatively recent times: the Kingdom was formally proclaimed only sixty-three years ago and, since that proclamation, changes have taken place which are perhaps unique in modern history. There has been the impact of previously unimaginable wealth on society in an extremely compressed period of time, while a quite conscious effort has been made to preserve a system of religious and social values, frequently at odds with the values of the outside influences affecting Saudi society. The period from 1932 to the present day can be usefully divided into three stages.

The first stage began with the slow unification of the Kingdom, during which the impact of change was manageable. Then from the early 1950s to the end of the 1970s, a period of increasing oil wealth and contact with the West followed. This period could be described as one of relative and rapid changes. Foreign migrant labour accounted for 43 per cent of the total workforce in the mid-1970s.[5] An economic upheaval due to the increased income from oil led a trend towards education abroad, and changes in lifestyle, which affected the whole structure of society.

The third stage, beginning in the 1980s, was marked by religious revival, which corresponds to a period of consolidation. The state and people have seemed relatively less receptive to Western influences and have become preoccupied with defining their identity and sharpening their sense of belonging and, for the government, its legitimacy.

The aftermath of the Gulf War may have ushered in a new period marked by an increase in fundamentalist tendencies and attempts at political reforms by the government as well as, for the first time, the emergence of an open Islamic opposition at war with the system; but some distance is needed to appreciate the possible distinctiveness of the period.

Amidst such social changes, political power has remained remarkably stable for the area. Since 1932, power in Saudi Arabia has been wielded by the Al Saud family, in close connection with that of the current Wahhabi[6] religious elite, with the two powers serving to legitimise one another.

In fact, the alliance between the current political and religious establishments, which started in 1745 with a pact between Muhammad ibn 'Abdul Wahhab and Amir Muhammad ibn Saud, underpinned the foundation of the state of Saudi Arabia in 1932. In practice, the power of the religious elite has fluctuated according to the personal determination of the ruler, and, to a lesser extent, to the prevalent internal and external circumstances.

An example of this fluctuation can be seen during the 1960s when King Faisal appointed the chief *'alim* from outside the ranks of the Al Sheikh extended family. Since the 1930s the *'ulama* had been appointed exclusively from this family. Not only was this person not from the Al Sheikh family, he was a Najdi, not of "pure" blood, a *khadiri*. By this act, King Faisal reduced the influence of the *'ulama* in general and the Al Sheikh group in particular. Faisal was in a good position to control the *'ulama*, not only because of his strong personality, a reputation for piety and Islamic austerity, but also because his mother was from the Al Sheikh family. Incidentally, whilst women have always been excluded from the circles of *'ulama*, the prestige associated with their descent, and the continued reality of the Prophetic *hadith* about "the *'ulama* being the heirs of the Prophets", has succeeded in making the daughters of *'ulama* influential as derivative successors to *ummahat al-mu'minin*.

During the 1960s the leading political influence in the region was the secular pan-Arabism of Nasser which, for a while, threatened Saudi Arabia politically and indeed militarily, but left largely unchallenged its claim to religious pre-eminence in the Islamic world. The position and role of Saudi women in work and public life has therefore remained determined by the established religious authorities. Women were to remain in a marginal position, although much progress in education has been made; this, together with a mounting interest in joining professional life on the part of women, is marking the scene for change – within religious boundaries.

In the 1980s, with Khomeini leading an Islamic government in Iran, Saudi Arabian leaders had to show themselves worthy of their position in the heartland of Islam. Saudi Arabian religious influence was strengthened as a reaction to the Shi'a Islamic revolution in neighbouring Iran. The danger from Iran lay in that it appeared to offer an alternative to the Sunni Wahhabi doctrine and to question the legitimacy of the Al Sa'ud as the custodians of the Holy Places. This was the time for a new type of more radical challenge to the state. During the 1980s, Saudi Arabian elites became increasingly concerned with promoting an image of piety. The desire (or the pressure for some) for greater religious involvement was felt by everyone in Saudi Arabia, including members of the political elite. Radio, television and newspapers carried more religious instruction than they did in the 1960s and 1970s.

With the increased tension across the Arab world, repercussions inside Saudi Arabia took the form of a challenge to the state from both the Islamic movements and those more timid circles demanding liberalisation, who naturally curried more favour in the West. In response to the first group, King Fahd reinstated the position of Grand Mufti in 1993 in order to control the issuing of fatwas by unreliable self-appointed quarters. The King also founded a Ministry of Islamic Affairs. This is in addition to the Ministry of Hajj and to the Committee of the Ordering of the Good and the Forbidding of Evil (*mutaw'a*).

Most importantly, and in response to both liberal and Islamist pressures, and seemingly as a response to a memorandum sent to the King by a number of influential citizens, the government of Saudi Arabia established in 1991 the Majlis al-Shura, an appointed consultative council to allow more participation of the people in the running of their country's affairs.

The Majlis, which marks the first acknowledgement of a separation of powers in the Kingdom, was established by a Basic Law. Article 40 states: "The Majlis is comprised of a head and sixty members appointed by the King for their knowledge, experience and expertise." Among the sixty "knowledgeable" persons, as defined by the government, there are no women, even though one could see in neighbouring Arab countries, including in relatively conservative states of the Peninsula such as Oman, women in the local Majlis al-Shura and in other ministerial and parliamentary positions. (There have been two women participants in the Majlis al-Shura of Oman since October 1994.)

Credentials and restraining limits for those sitting on the Majlis include the age of the individual participants being limited to thirty years of age or over, and a four-year duration of appointment; however, there is no mention of women in any capacity or form. The background in Saudi public law to this omission is obviously the understanding that there is no role for women at any level in public officialdom, whether as an ambassador or a council member or a minister or a judge, or now as a member of the Majlis. Total omission, however, is interesting because it opens, in theory, the way to the possibility of women's access to these positions if the political and cultural circumstances evolve in the right direction. There is no doubt, however, that the mental horizon of the present rulers, as well as public opinion at large, does not as yet entertain such thoughts. The only relevant mention in the text of the Basic Law (and even there the word woman does not appear) relates to the home: "The family is the basic unit of Saudi society and the guardian [male head] should be obeyed." (Article 40)

In parallel to these politically muted overtures, which leave women at the margin of public participation, the last years have seen the emergence of an Islamic opposition, for the first time in the history of the state since the early challenges of the Ikhwan to King Saud in the 1920s. Perhaps not surprisingly, the place of women does not rank high on the otherwise revolutionary agenda of these groups.

The unofficial opposition of Saudi Arabia has emerged as a self-appointed champion for legitimate rights. A group of fundamentalists formed the Committee for the Defence of Legitimate Rights (CDLR) in the capital, Riyadh, in 1993, and is headed by a professor of physics, 'Abdallah al-Mas'ari, who has been living in exile in London since 1994. The CDLR claims to protect human rights in the context of the *shari'a* and urges the government to be more concerned about the rights and freedoms of citizens. In their manifesto, they call for more freedom of expression and freedom of movement (notably going abroad). They express concern about the victims of various incidents during the pilgrimage in Mecca, and they complain about corruption of the rich and the maltreatment of foreign workers, especially Asians.

Nevertheless, in the whole of their manifesto there is no mention of rights or any public role for women. When women are referred to, they are wives or relatives of "significant" men. The CDLR further stresses that the government should be less liberal and should give more power to the all-powerful Committee for the Ordering of the Good and the Prohibition of Evil in order to fight corruption. However, affiliates of the latter, known as the *mutaw'a*, are the same people who impose restrictions on women's movements and dress in public. Thus, if one goes by their published programme, the Islamic opposition's general language excludes women altogether from any civic role.

Thus, in the higher political sphere, women remain outside the horizon for the search for wider participation, whether by the government or the oppositional Islamic force. This has not prevented them from taking advantage of any area where room for manoeuvre for greater freedom and effectiveness was allowed. We will examine these public areas in the remainder of the chapter, starting with the education system.

The Education System

The education system in Saudi Arabia has undergone changes but it has always remained separate for men and women. Prior to 1932 there were already a number of secular elementary schools in Mecca and Jeddah for men.[7]

Education for men took place in the circles of the *'ulama* in the mosques, especially in the Great Mosque of Mecca. The first school in Jeddah of a more secular nature, named Falah (Success), opened in 1903, and two years later in Mecca under the same name.[8] These schools were only for men. Women during that period received the traditional forms of education at home or at the *kuttab* schools for the memorisation of the Qur'an. Their education consisted solely of reading and memorising the Holy Book as well as some of the *hadith*. It is noteworthy that at the *kuttab*, women taught other women, and women were well-versed in religious texts. This is consistent with the general philosophy of education in Islam, with well-known *hadith* such as "Seek knowledge from the cradle to the grave", and "Seek knowledge even from China", often cited by women to back up their desire to learn.

The first schools of a secular nature for women opened in Jeddah only at the beginning of the 1960s. The first was Dar al-Hanan (House of Tenderness) sponsored by 'Iffat, the wife of the late King Faisal. The objectives of Dar al-Hanan were described as producing better mothers and homemakers through Islamic-based instructions. The saying "The mother can be a school in herself if you prepare her well", became a motto and is reproduced in school books. Then, from the end of the 1950s until the end of the 1970s the trend among the more wealthy families was to send their children (both sons and daughters) to study abroad – mostly to other Arab countries and to Europe or the United States. This was possible because of the great wealth acquired in the boom conditions of the times. Women belonging to the wealthier social strata during that period pursued higher education and several women obtained university degrees from foreign schools.

However, the trend in the later 1980s was for education at home rather than abroad in accordance with the prevailing moods of "piety" and "tradition". A contributory factor was the need to reduce expenditure in the new, less favourable economic climate. Parents also became more reluctant to educate their children in the West as schools in Saudi Arabia started having higher standards, offering subjects like computing and modern languages. Furthermore, towards the end of the 1970s the government strongly discouraged Saudi women from studying abroad unless they were accompanied by their families, i.e. their husbands or parents. Large numbers of women now attend universities in the main cities of Saudi Arabia. Nevertheless, not all subjects are open for women to study and they are barred from such fields as geology, petroleum, engineering and law. Three of Saudi Arabia's seven universities – Imam Muhammad ibn Saud Islamic University in Riyadh, the University of Petroleum and Minerals, and the Islamic University in Medicine – do not accept women.

Most women under 40 have some experience of modern schooling, many including university education in Saudi Arabia or abroad. Since the 1980s, as education became more widespread, it fell under stricter *'ulama* control, even at university level. Although women read widely and keep in touch with international developments, many claim in conversation to read the Qur'an more than any other written work. This is generally to comply with the mood of "piety". Whilst older women remained imbued with the traditional social roles expected of them since they were socialised so as to accept a role as "housewife", the younger generation faces a disjunction between their educational preparation and the roles ascribed to them, which have not changed. This has resulted in younger women trying to take active roles in redefining their social identity. Before giving some examples of the language used in this exercise in redefinition, other aspects of women's rights in the kingdom need to be explained.

The Veil, Segregation and other Social Norms

The veil

If seen in terms of the UN Women's Convention, the situation of Saudi Arabian women exhibits specific and consistent discrimination.[9] The reality is more nuanced, at least in the perception of those women themselves.

Social norms in Saudi Arabia treat women differently from men. The veil – including covering the face – is compulsory whenever in public. Traditionally, all women are veiled when in contact with male strangers, i.e. non-family. The veil is compulsory in Saudi Arabia. The rule is that when a woman steps out of the gate of her family home, she wears the veil, which in Saudi Arabia consists of two pieces of black/ opaque silk materials. One covers her body and is worn like a cape, the other covers her head and is wrapped around the head and carefully tied to the side.

Whilst there was a period in recent Hijaz history when upper-class women generally did not cover their faces, present attitudes towards the veil are ambiguous. Even some of those women who were educated abroad during the 1960s and 1970s generally view the veil not as a restriction, but as a normal feature of everyday life. The veil, they explain, has been there for themselves, their mothers and grandmothers, without the interruption that occurred under colonialism in other Muslim societies. They further argue that the veil is a garment that must only be worn outdoors. At any place or occasion, women leave their veils at the door with the cloakroom attendant. Hence, it is compared to a coat and a hat in Europe in bygone days.

The wearing of the veil for some of the wealthy groups has been not an expression of female timidity, but a means of maintaining social distance, placing a barrier between the woman who wears it and the men and women she is in contact with. Some women explain that they veil in their country to maintain the honour of their patronymic group, and not to unnecessarily offend the authorities. If a woman is not veiled in public the authorities will contact her male guardian whose honour ('*ird*) is considered to be at stake. When abroad many do not veil since, as they put it, "it would attract more attention than modesty". If many Saudi women wear the veil to strengthen their sense of identity and belonging, they may also do so to avoid getting into confrontations with members of The Committee for the Order of Good and the Forbidding of Evil. Indeed, the *mutaw'a* have authority to impose the social restriction on women, while male family members are expected to enforce women's compliance with social restrictions.

Freedom of movement

Regardless of the veil issue, women have minimum freedom of movement inside the country. They are never to walk on the streets unaccompanied by a male relative known as *mahram*. Travel outside the country requires a written consent by the guardian, generally husband or father.

Women are, by law, forbidden to drive cars. The prohibition was customary until the driving demonstration in November 1990 when forty-seven veiled Saudi women drove their cars on King Abdul Aziz Highway in Riyadh. These women, all professionals belonging to prominent Saudi families, were arrested, taken for a few hours to jail, and lost their jobs. Their passports were taken away and they were forbidden to travel abroad for a year. This incident gained political significance partly because of the timing, in the middle of the Gulf War. It also received negative reactions from the people whose attitudes and beliefs are sometimes more conservative than those of the government. Yet it remains the single most daring act of defiance by Saudi women.

Public segregation

Most positions in both the public and the private sectors are still held by men in Saudi Arabia. Women are only encouraged by the government to join certain professions and are not allowed to practise others. Jobs that require minimum interaction with men are permitted while those that would lead to mixed public contact are forbidden. The social disapproval of women working with men is a phenomenon widespread in other Muslim countries, but Saudi Arabia is specially strict on this issue, with elaborate arrangements to keep the sexes apart, even to the extent of providing separate elevators in all buildings.

The separation of the sexes in Saudi Arabia follows a government policy and is strictly applied in all public spheres. Medicine is an exception to this rule. Female doctors are respected for practising what is considered an honourable task. However, whether at a hospital or at her private clinic she is required – when in front of men – to dress according to a strict code.

At restaurants in Saudi Arabia there is a separate section for "families", i.e. women. In all mosques there are separate sections for women. This separation also applies in professional areas. Women are separated at universities. They are also separated in professions which they are increasingly practising, such as teaching both at girls' schools and in women's sections at the universities. They are separated in some ministries where they work as social researchers and planners. The separation of the sexes is seen in separate branches of banks, and in women's shops. In all the big malls and commercial centres there are shops exclusively owned, run, patronised and staffed by women. These have very visible signs at the entrance reading: "For women only: men are forbidden to enter!"

Legal Aspects

In the following general overview, the perspective will not so much be a purely legal one as one focusing on the point of view of women themselves, their knowledge or ignorance of the law, their concerns and aspirations, and the more general economic and social context of the law in which historical changes operate.

When one examines women's perception of themselves, the separation of the sexes, the concept of the veil, the type of jobs they are allowed to take or even the fact that they cannot drive, one must view and understand their role within the total social structure.

I shall concentrate on two aspects of the law which are of great relevance to Saudi women, family law and commercial law.

Family law

Unlike other fields such as company and tax regulations, where an effort of codification and simplification has taken place over the years, fiqh texts still regulate issues of marriage and divorce in Saudi Arabia. These matters must, therefore, be assessed by means of the texts of tradition, together with the practice of the courts and social usage. There is consequently an element of uncertainty, but also of flexibility that can work both to the advantage and to the disadvantage of women.

Family disputes in Saudi Arabia fall under the jurisdiction of *al-mahakim al-shar'iyya* (the general *shari'a* courts), under a Grand *Shari'a* Court which has a bench of three judges, "and is competent in all cases which are not within the jurisdiction of the summary courts (*al-mahakim al-musta'jala)*". The texts used in Saudi courts today are treatises from the Hanbali school, and include Ibn Qudama's encyclopaedic work *al-Mughni*, as well as other texts such as Hijawi's *Zad* and al-Bahuti's *Kashshaf al-qina'*. These appear as obscure and complex documents to lawyers, let alone to the lay person.

Women in Saudi Arabia rarely appear in court, not even in cases of divorce. A woman, if she chooses to litigate, is represented by one of her male kin, her father, uncle or brother. A woman is given in marriage by her male guardian (this is with her consent and in front of two male witnesses) and similarly she is helped out of marriage by her guardian. In other words, she seldom has to deal with a lawyer or the court directly since her male guardian "protects" her and acts in her financial, moral and social interest. Saudi women explain that standing in court is considered shameful, *'ayb*, to the family. Many women do not fight for their rights (even if they are aware of them) because of family reputation. There are cases of foreign women married to Saudi men who have gone to court upon divorce. There they stand, all veiled with a lawyer alongside, but Saudi women rarely deal with lawyers – those who do so do not go to their offices, they either meet them privately in their houses or just consult with them over the telephone.

A method for understanding women and their legal and social status in Saudi Arabian society is by examining their ties to their patrilineal kin. In Saudi Arabia, the family (*'a'ila*) is held to be the basic unit of friendship, obligation, loyalty, moral support, socialisation and economic help. Kinship remains the prime means of social organisation and associations. The identity based on the patronymic group is used to define a person's worth, as well as to define legal and social status. This identity for men and women is not altered by marriage: women do not change their family name by adopting their husband's name. As the motto goes, "Whom you are born to is for life while whom you marry can be changed by separation or divorce."

Marriage, a social and religious contract, is threatened by the possibility of separation or polygamy. These practices are perceived differently in different parts of Saudi Arabia. The country is vast and culturally heterogeneous, with customs prevailing among the tribal inhabitants which differ from those of urban dwellers, and which differ, within the same region, in accordance with the socio-economic position of the family.

It has been generally observed that tribal Bedouin men and women alike are more "relaxed" about divorce and polygamy, while city inhabitants in Jeddah and Mecca attach more stigma to such practices. From my observations, rarely does a Saudi woman accept or tolerate the possibility of her husband remarrying another while she is still his wife. The exceptional cases here are women who belong to fundamentalist groups emerging today (those who claim to accept polygamy as defined in the Qur'an), and women who have little emotional or financial attachment to their husbands.

Women today are increasingly aware of their right to attach a series of conditions, *shurut*, to the marriage contract. A woman can ask for the marriage to be dissolved if her husband takes another wife, and she can ask for the right to continue her education or for the right to run her own business. These conditions are particularly distinctive of Hanbali *fiqh*. More importantly, under Hanbali law, a woman can stipulate in her marriage contract that she has her '*ismat* in her hand, that is the freedom to dissolve the marriage. Saudi men are however often reluctant to accept granting the '*ismat* clause in the marriage contract.

When a marriage is entered into in Islamic law, the rule is that property bought by the spouses always remain separate. This is particularly important for the woman who, in case of divorce, cannot rely on alimony or compensation. Any maintenance or compensation would only be connected with the maintenance of children so long as she remains their guardian. The law of custody allows the mother to keep her son until the age of seven and her daughter until the age of nine, after which the children must reside with their father or his patrilineal family.

The separation of property is viewed as a vital protection for women. The husband, who must provide for maintenance (*nafaqa*) throughout the marriage, cannot lay claim on his wife's material possessions. Women in Saudi Arabia retain control over their money, many being given or inheriting bank accounts held at home or abroad through their fathers or guardians before marriage. Even after marriage, the husband has no authority over his wife's possessions. Women consider the idea of joint property a disadvantage. The husband is expected to support his wife, even if she is wealthy in her own right. Saudi women hold on to this legal rule. Furthermore, there is the concept of *kafa'a* in marriage, which requires the husband to support his wife in accordance with her social status and style of life prior to marriage.

This financial independence is also a central feature of the woman as a business protagonist in Saudi Arabia.

Commercial law

Whether under the *shari'a* or under the Kingdom's statutory *qanuns* and *nizams*, there is no distinction between men and women over the control and use of their money. A woman can own property, buy and sell with no control from her husband or from anyone else for that matter.

From the age of 16 women have equal financial rights and equal economic capacity to men. However, there are subtle distinctions in this area between men and women based on custom and tradition. For example, a woman never goes to the Ministry of Commerce to comply with legal and administrative formalities for her business: instead she sends a *wakil shar'i*, a male with power of attorney to do the job on her behalf. Men also often send a *wakil shar'i* but this is for practical reasons – to smooth the workings of the bureaucracy. Men are free to attend themselves to these matters at the Ministry of Commerce.

Although there is no law that forbids women from entering government buildings or banks, such an act is unusual and is tied to concepts of family shame. It is the rule of honour and tradition that prevents women from doing so. Another typical illustration of this dichotomy is that driving a car was, until recently, simply not done, because of custom and practice rather than law. Women did not drive because they were not given driving licences and indeed none would have ever thought of applying for one. However, following the driving demonstration that some Saudi women staged in Riyadh in 1990 the Saudi authorities have passed a law forbidding women to drive in Saudi Arabia. Three specific restrictive aspects on women's work are worth mentioning.

First, the separation of the sexes, which, as mentioned earlier, is strictly applied in all public spheres. The implications are manifold. A man can own and run a shop that deals with both women and men while a woman can only run a shop which caters only for women. But when a woman owns a shop that caters for both sexes, the rule is she is not allowed to work on the premises. However, these women like other minorities in other times and countries have been pushed into a solidarity which greatly benefits their business.

This leads to a clear distinction between ownership and management. Thus a woman can be a major shareholder in a company, but is not allowed to attend a board of directors' meeting. She must instead be represented by a male of her choice, that is a proxy with power of attorney. A woman usually chooses a brother, another relative or just a person she considers trustworthy. This is again not so much an express rule of the *shari'a* as social practice. The reason given for the strict separation of the sexes is, under classical law, the fear of the *khulwa*, that is, the presence of a man and woman in a room on their own without legitimate family or kin (*mahram*) attending the meeting. The prohibition of the *khulwa* is substantiated in a well-known saying: "If a man and a woman are alone in a room the devil is always the third." But so long as a woman works with other women or with men who are her *mahram*, such practical impediments are lifted.

Secondly, the legal–social concept of *iltizam* poses an obstacle to women's work in some cases. *Iltizam* is the fact that men of the extended family are financially responsible for female members of the extended family. Whether she is married, divorced, or widowed, one of the male kin is legally responsible for her financial security. Hence, many men find it an expression of male honour and pride to undertake the maintenance of women in the family, which entails the woman staying at home. Nevertheless, in the words of an educated Saudi man, "Things are changing nowadays. With the recession, husbands encourage their wives to work for economic reasons. Since the mid-1980s additional income is considered welcome to protect the standard of life for the family."[10]

Thirdly, Saudi law prohibits women from leaving the country unless they are accompanied by a legal guardian (husband or father). Many women manage to get around this law with a letter from the guardian, which alone is not sufficient, but does the trick when presented by a relative or a person of influence and responsibility. However, this does not mean that a woman travels alone! A woman travelling on business is usually accompanied by another woman, either a female relative or a woman hired for the job. This is because a woman of "good reputation" should never be seen "alone" in public whether in Saudi Arabia or abroad.

Despite all these restrictions, there are an increasing number of women in business (2,000 women were on the Jeddah commercial register in January 1994). These women are not necessarily women with higher education but they have basic schooling (about eleven years). The sort of businesses Saudi women own or manage are mostly geared or related to women's needs: boutiques selling women's clothes and accessories, beauty salons, etc. However, some enterprising Saudi women are venturing outside this field, engaging in import/export businesses or even manufacturing. One woman owns and leases shipping containers, another has started a lime and gravel business in Yanbu in collaboration with a French company. On the lighter side, others own and manage book stores, stationery shops, perfumeries, art galleries, antiques and carpet shops and even own department stores.

The New "Islamic Feminists"

It is against this complex picture that the recent phenomenon of Saudi Islamic feminists has grown. In a way, the history of women since the establishment of the Kingdom can be broadly made to corresponds to the three stages presented at the beginning of the paper. In a first stage, women's roles during the early period from 1932 to about 1950 can be defined as having been more socialised toward the traditional roles of mothers, daughters or wives – the centre of the family and home-makers.

During the more secular period of the 1960s and 1970s – or that of openness to change, especially under King Faisal – there were more opportunities for women to expand their activities, including having a more liberal education, especially abroad, more job opportunities, less restricting religious pressure, with few religious fatwas affecting women's physical and social mobility. In short, women could develop more liberal thinking and enjoy less constrained ways of life.

The third stage saw women's roles suffering a set-back resulting from the puritanical atmosphere, which was ushered in by the Iranian Revolution in the early 1980s and continued through the two wars in the Gulf region.

Paradoxical as it may seem, the second Gulf War has resulted in an increase in the Islamic fundamentalist tendency among some young women, while at the same time others have been encouraged to embrace a bolder attitude towards reform, as best typified in the driving demonstration.

The new breed of female fundamentalists believe that their mission is to fight corruption and Westernisation in Saudi Arabia. To emphasise their distinctiveness from those who wear only a limited veil, they dress severely in black from head to toe when appearing at every traditional formal gathering – birth, marriage and death – reprimanding others for their "indulgence" and threatening them with the fires of hell.

Unlike other Saudi women, these women wear their veil both indoors and outdoors. Those who travel to the West, insist on wearing the veil there irrespective of the suitability to the milieu, for example, whether at a beach with bathers or at restaurants in a Western capital. The dresses they wear under the veil are of basic colours: brown, grey, beige and black. Bright colours and make-up that had become widespread among Saudi women from all regions and sections of society, are considered "seductive" and hence works of the devil. Furthermore, this new breed of women fundamentalists reject "worldly tools of corruption" like satellite television, music, dancing, Western cosmetics and per-fumes. The Islamic code of dress for these women is parallel to that among fundamentalist men who wear shorter robes (not covering the ankles as is customary) and long beards to express their strict Islamic beliefs.

When questioned, women who recently adopted the new type of veil, which is a modification of the traditional veil, explain "*Allah hadani*" (Allah has blessed me with His guidance). In a Saudi Arabian environment, this needs no further explanation. These women appear to believe strongly that they are guided by God. Because they are "properly" dressed, their mission is not restricted to indoor activities. They reprimand other women in the mosques and in the market-place and can be sometimes seen intimidating the male *mutaw'a*. Some among them have even acquired the title "female *mutaw'a*". Often, these women's great religious culture enables them to enter into quite erudite and serious disputations, which can infuriate religious as well as liberal groups.

These emerging female fundamentalists do not claim the right to vote or to drive or to work alongside men. Instead, they condemn these supposedly Western practices. However, they go to university, work in women's branches of banks, work as teachers and in business, as Khadija did. They aim to go back to the basics of the *shari'a*. They choose to gather in large numbers, reaching sometimes up to 500. These gatherings are unusual in that they cut across class, economic and social barriers. The majority among these women are young, in their twenties and thirties, while their leaders are usually older – with wisdom of age backed up by wealth.

Gatherings are conducted under the leadership of charismatic, wealthy women, knowledgeable in religion and *shari'a*. The best known leaders are university educated, lecturers and writers. They select and distribute "suitable" religious literature for the instruction of those join-ing the movement. The theme of the congregations varies from day to day. *Fiqh, tajwid* (rules of recitation of the Holy Qur'an) or *tafsir* (inter-pretations of the Qur'an), will be allotted certain days. Meetings last for two or three hours and then remain the topic of conversation and guidance for weeks.

This is a new phenomenon that has emerged at the women's sections of the universities in the 1980s, and intensified following the most recent Gulf War. It should be noted that in Saudi Arabia there have not been any women's religious gatherings since the unification of the country in 1932.

Even such religious celebrations as the birth of the Prophet, *mawlid*, which were particular to the Hijaz region, had been strictly discouraged by the authorities upon the unification of the country.

Whether consciously or unconsciously these women are seeking a sense of purpose or recognition, or simply seeking a type of power to legitimise their actions in society. By going back to the basics of the *shari'a* they seem to derive a liberating force. They are creating a forum with a cultural context or idiom with which they are able to negotiate power. Since the 1980s religion has become the platform on which the power game is played. This is not only for men, women are also caught in the complexity of factors arising from the Iranian revolution and further complicated by the Gulf War and its aftermath.

NOTES

1 This paper has mostly benefited from observations in the Hijaz over a period of years of women who are distinguished mainly by their wealth and lifestyle and are one of several elite circles in the Kingdom of Saudi Arabia who are competing for control, for resources, for status, and for recognition. The feminist trend based on the knowledge of the shari'a is rooted among this circle and spreads from it.

2 D. Spellberg, 'Political Action and Public Example: 'A'isha and the Battle of the Camel' in Nikkie Keddie and Beth Baron (eds.),*Women in Middle Eastern History: Shifting Boundaries in Sex and Gender* (New Haven: Yale University Press, 1991), p. 45.

3 The peninsula (today's Saudi Arabia) comprised the following provinces until 1932: (1) the Hijaz extending along the Western Coast of Arabia on the Red Sea, (2) 'Asir – between the Hijaz and the Yemen, (3) Najd in the Central part, (4) the Ahsa along the Gulf between Kuwait and the Trucial Coast.

4 See generally Mai Yamani, 'Fasting and Feasting: Some Social Aspects of the Observance of Ramadan in Saudi Arabia' in Ahmed al-Shahi (ed.), *The Diversity of the Muslim Community: Anthropological Essays in Memory of Peter Lienhardt* (London: Ithaca Press, 1987).

5 See A. al-Yassini, *Religion and State in the Kingdom of Saudi Arabia* (Boulder, Colorado: Westview Press, 1985), p. 115.

6 Wahhabism is an interpretation of the Hanbali Islamic School of Law by Muhammad ibn 'Abdul Wahhab (1703–87). Wahhabis, who preferred the term Muwahhidun, are strict monotheists. The aim of the founder of the movement was to do away with all innovations, *bida'*, after the third century of Islam. Anything that departs from the religion's rules pointed out by 'Abdul Wahhab is idolatry, *shirk*. The Hijaz, however, followed three Schools of Law: the Shafi'i, the Hanafi and the Maliki, the first two being predominant; but there are officially no longer differing schools of law in Saudi Arabia, even if Hanbalism is practically dominant.

7 See M. Field, *The Merchants: The Big Business Families of Arabia* (London: John Murray, 1984), p. 23.

8 al-Yassini, *Religion and State in the Kingdom of Saudi Arabia*, p. 61.

9 See Connors in this book, Chapter 16.

10 A Saudi man belonging to one of the families studied complained that "The problem is that our wives are wealthier than us because we lost our money on the stock exchange but we still have to spend on them."

Part Four

The Confines
of Law

THIRTEEN

STRETCHING THE LIMITS:
A FEMINIST READING OF THE
Shari'a IN POST-KHOMEINI IRAN

Ziba Mir-Hosseini

Women's issues are now an integral part of modern Islamic discourses, as evidenced in the plethora of "Women in Islam" titles in religious publishing projects all over the Muslim world.[1] In practice, this has entailed re-readings of the old texts in search of solutions – or more precisely, Islamic alternatives – for a very modern problem, which has to do with the changed status of women and the need to accommodate their aspirations for equality and to define and control their increasing participation in the politics of the Muslim world. Despite their variety and diverse cultural origins, what these re-readings have in common is an oppositional stance and a defensive or apologetic tone. Oppositional, because their agenda is to resist the advance of "Western" values and lifestyles which were espoused by states and adopted by secular elites earlier this century. Apologetic, because they are attempting to explain the gender biases which are inadvertently revealed by going back to the *shari'a* texts.

A question that arises is whether these solutions can be "feminist", in the sense of representing women's perspectives as well as redressing their oppression at work, in the home, and in society. In other words, to what extent and by what means can limitations imposed on women by *shari'a* texts be renegotiated? In this paper I argue that a "feminist" re-reading of the *shari'a* is possible – even becomes inevitable – when Islam is no longer part of the oppositional discourse in national politics. This is so because once the custodians of the *shari'a* are in power, they have to deal with the contradictory aims set by their own agenda and discourse, which are to uphold the family and restore women to their "true and high" status in Islam, and at the same time to uphold men's *shari'a* prerogatives. The resulting tension – which is an inherent element in the practice of the *shari'a* itself, but is intensified by its identification with a modern state – opens room for novel interpretations of the *shari'a* rules on a scale that has no precedent in the history of Islamic law.[2]

Iran is a case in point. Now fifteen years into an Islamic Republic, there are clear signs of the emergence of a feminist re-reading of the *shari'a* texts. This is manifest in two opposing currents. The first reflects the official Shi'a discourse adopted by the Islamic Republic, and is most evident in the 1992 Divorce Amendments. These amendments represent a radical, and if you like feminist, interpretation of *shari'a* divorce provisions. They not only curtail men's right to repudiation, *talaq*, but place a monetary value on women's housework and entitle them to *ujrat al-mithl*, "domestic wages", for the work they have done during marriage. The second current reflects the recent non-establishment Shi'a discourse and is most manifest in legal articles published in *Zanan*, a women's magazine launched in February 1992. These put forward a novel interpretation of *shari'a* provisions on women; they neither cover up nor rationalise the gender inequalities that are embedded in many aspects of the *shari'a*, but propose to recast them within the limits of the *shari'a*. Both currents, in their different ways, can pave the way for an unprecedented reinterpretation of the *shari'a* rules which is indeed gender sensitive, if not "feminist" in the Western sense.

By tracing the evolution of the *shari'a*-based discourses in Iran, I aim to show how and why such "feminist" re-readings of the old texts have come about. The paper is divided into two main parts. The first part is an attempt to place the contemporary Shi'a discourses, as they emerged in the last decades before the revolution, in their proper context. Such contextualisation is in order because they continue to be read in an essentialist and anachronistic way. The second part first explores their impact on other post-revolutionary discourses on women and then examines the emergence of a "feminist" discourse, as articulated in *Zanan*.

Pre-Revolutionary *Shari'a* Discourses on Women

With the establishment of an Islamic Republic in Iran came a wave of popular and scholarly Western publications on Shi'ism. Two topics have predominated: Shi'ism as a religion of protest, and Shi'a attitudes to women. While the first is a scholarly response to the Revolution,[3] which caught students of Islam and Iran by surprise, the second is motivated by a feminist concern to safeguard women's rights in an Islamic Republic.[4]

Two events early in the revolution validated such a concern. The first was the dismantling of the Family Protection Law, which had come into effect in 1967 and had restricted polygamy and made divorce easier for women; and the second was the imposition of Islamic dress (coat and head-scarf).

It was in such a climate that a large portion of the literature on Shi'a attitude to women was produced. Attention was focused on two writers, Dr 'Ali Shari'ati and Ayatollah Mortaza Motahhari: they were not only the most prominent contemporary Islamic thinkers (in Iran) whose writings dealt with women's issues, but both men were dead, which gave their views an aura of immutability. Their writings soon came to shape the contours of the contemporary Shi'a discourses on women, in short, they became "texts". In this way not only were they decontextualised but they were read and examined anachronistically, that is in the light of events in the early years of the Revolution. In focusing on their gender assumptions, the literature on both texts tends to trivialise the specific circumstances which gave rise to each.[5]

In what follows my aim is not to offer a critique of this literature, nor of the two texts themselves, rather it is to describe the circumstances in which the texts were produced. First it should be noted that both texts were written in the context of gender debates and legal reforms of the late Pahlavi era.

'Ali Shari'ati's text: Fatima is Fatima

'Ali Shari'ati was a lay Islamic thinker who enjoyed enormous popularity in the Iran of the 1970s. He came from a clerical family, read sociology at the University of Paris and became a vocal critic of the Pahlavis. Upon his return to Iran in 1964, he was imprisoned for his anti-regime activities but he was released after six months and became Professor of Sociology in Mashhad University. However, he was soon dismissed and continued to be persecuted. In 1977, shortly after his latest release, he died in England where he had gone for medical treatment. His ideas formed the intellectual backbone of a modern Shi'a opposition to the Pahlavi regime and its policy of blind Westernisation. He used his public lectures in the Hosseinieh Ershad, a celebrated religious institution, to air his views.[6]

His seminal text on women has its origin in one of these lectures, delivered in April 1971. The text of this lecture was later published in an extended form as *Fatemeh Fatemeh ast* (Fatima is Fatima), which came to be regarded as an Islamist treatise on women, though it can best be read as a critique of Iranian society and its values in the early 1970s, rather than a treatise on women in Islam. Its rhetorical style and revolutionary tone arouse emotions without ever entering on any kind of serious examination of women in the *shari'a*. In fact its preface reveals the extent to which Shari'ati improvised during the lecture.

> I first wanted to talk about Professor Louis Massignon's research on the complex life of Fatima, especially its impact on Muslim societies . . . But when I entered the room and saw many others in addition to my own students, I realised that the gathering called for a more urgent topic. So I decided to provide an answer to this "destined question" which today intensely occupies our society. Women who endure their traditional mould have no problem, and women who accept their new imported mould have the problem solved for them. In between these two types of "moulded" women, there are those women who can neither tolerate the inherited mould nor can surrender to the imposed new one; what should they do? These women want to choose for themselves, want to "make" themselves; they need a "model", an "ideal type". For them the question is "how to become". Fatima by "being" herself is the answer to this question.[7]

The text, which could be divided into two parts, sets out to answer this question. In the first part (pp. 1–90), Shari'ati attempts to define the "women's question" and the dilemmas that Muslim women are facing in this century. He is critical of both those Muslim women who unquestioningly accept their "traditional" role, and those modern, Westernised women who, by aping the West, are becoming mindless consumers. He sees the latter as a new addition to the human species: "a creature who shops"[8], for which he blames the colonial policies of the West. Having understood women's pivotal role in maintaining the fabric of Islamic societies, the West set out to alienate them from Islam so that Muslims could be dominated. But Muslim men and the narrow-minded clergy, who continued to misrepresent Islam, are equally to blame: they also conspired to deny Muslim women their truly Islamic rights. By being denied their humanity, educated women were left with little option but to look to the West for an alternative.

In the second part (pp. 91–189), Shari'ati discusses the solution, which is to be found in the person of Fatima, the Prophet's daughter,

'Ali's wife, and mother of Hassan and Husain. The picture that he draws of Fatima's life is romanticised but rather gloomy. More than offering a clear and tangible model to be emulated, it epitomises the Shi'a ideals of silent suffering and covert defiance. As he has it, Fatima died of grief at the injustice that followed her father's death, in which 'Ali was denied his right to the Caliphate, at having her inherited land (*fadak*) taken away from her, and at the failure of her attempts to enlist support for 'Ali's claim.

The text ends without providing a coherent answer to the crucial question that Shari'ati considered was facing Iranian women of the 1970s. In fact the question is often by-passed; out of 189 pages, less than ten deal with the question of women in Islam. Even in these pages Shari'ati neither elaborates on women's position in the *shari'a*, nor does he engage with the proponents of the *shari'a* discourse on women. Instead he uses the occasion to elaborate on his own interpretation of Shi'a history, to condemn those in power for distorting it, to denounce Iranian society as one of pseudo-Muslims, whose ways have little resemblance to true Islam, to blame the clergy and intellectuals alike for not enlightening people on true Islam. Although he is critical of narrow interpretations of Qur'anic rules, he remains imprecise and evasive. On the other hand, he is both explicit and direct when he criticises the secularising policies of the Pahlavis.

In short, what he had to say on "women in Islam" was vague, contradictory and at best inconclusive. He did not offer a concrete solution but a romanticised revolutionary vision, which was soon eclipsed with the establishment of the Islamic Republic.

Mortaza Motahhari's text: The System of Women's Rights in Islam

The thinker whose writings on women survived into the post-revolutionary era, and became identified with the view of the Islamic Republic, was a clergyman, Ayatollah Mortaza Motahhari. Motahhari was both a theologian and an academic, teaching both at religious schools in Qom and at secular universities in Tehran. He became a member of the Revolutionary Council in February 1979, but was assassinated in May of that year. Motahhari was one of the few Shi'a clergy to have written lucidly and extensively on the issue of women's rights in Islam, and the only one who has entered a debate with secular thinkers on the issue.

The debate, which was conducted in a glossy women's magazine, *Zan-e Ruz*, was predicated on the enactment of the Family Protection

Law in 1967, which introduced radical changes in divorce provisions. In 1966 *Zan-e Ruz* was airing the views of those who were arguing for changing the family provisions of the Iranian Civil Code, which reflect the dominant opinions within Shi'a *fiqh*. The most prominent among the reformers was a secular judge, Mahdavi Zanjani, who had prepared a 40-article proposal to replace some of the articles of Book Seven of the Code, which deals with marriage and divorce. This had alarmed the religious authorities, and Motahhari was approached by a leading Tehran clergyman to prepare a response in defence of the Code. Motahhari agreed to do so, provided that his replies were printed intact. His condition was accepted and *Zan-e Ruz*, as a good-will gesture, even printed his original letter which contained his proviso. Motahhari's first reply appeared in November 1966 as a direct response to the first of the 40 articles proposed by Judge Mahdavi. Although the sudden death of Mahdavi meant that the debate ended after six issues, Motahhari continued his discussion, which by then had attracted a large readership, for another 27 issues. In 1974, he compiled these articles into a book, *The System of Women's Rights in Islam*.[9]

The book is divided into 15 sections, each dealing with a cluster of rights and obligations arising from marriage. It starts with marriage proposal and engagement, the subject-matter of the first articles of Book Seven of the Civil Code, which was also the starting-point of Judge Mahdavi's 40-article proposal. In the following chapters Motahhari deals with temporary marriage, women and social independence, Islam and modernity, women's human status according to the Qur'an, the natural basis of family laws, differences between men and women, *mahr* and maintenance, the question of inheritance, the right to divorce, and polygyny. In each section, Motahhari is selective in choosing his facts and sources, especially when he invokes Western scholarship to justify the necessity for the different treatment of women in Islam.

Evidently, Motahhari's text cannot be separated from the debates and legal reforms of the Pahlavi era; it was written to offset the harsh criticisms of the *shari'a* position on women, embodied in Book Seven of the Iranian Civil Code. To defend the *shari'a* Motahhari not only painted a rosy picture of its treatment of women but glorified gender inequality by arguing that it is in harmony with the law of nature. He dismissed equal rights for men and women as a Western concept and alien to the Islamic world-view. He argued that, if properly understood, the *shari'a* laws are the very essence of divine justice, as they embody God's design for men, women and society. While he admitted the injustices done in the name of the *shari'a* – the plight of divorced and abandoned women was widely highlighted by *Zan-e Ruz* – he blamed this state of affairs on un-Islamic society and men who abandoned Islam. In so doing, he not only detached the *shari'a* from social reality but also left little room for debate and changes in line with the demands of the time.

Post-Revolutionary Discourses

With the triumph of the Islamists early in the Revolution, Shari'ati's text with its idealistic and vaguely reformist vision soon faded into obscurity, while Motahhari's text with its legalistic approach became the Islamic Republic's official discourse on women. In 1981 his book was translated into English, and by 1989 it had been reprinted in Persian over fifteen times. His arguments are the most eloquent and refined among those which hold the concept of gender equality to be contrary to the *shari'a*. They were successfully invoked to stifle any opposition to the dismantling of the Family Protection Law in the early years of the Revolution, and later to validate the gender policies of the Islamic Republic.[10]

For over a decade Motahhari's text remained uncontested, at least at the public and official level. The larger part of the vast post-revolutionary literature, especially that produced by the Islamic Propaganda Organisation, not only embodies his position but simply reproduces his arguments verbatim. However, this hegemony is now losing ground to a different discourse which, although located in the *shari'a*, argues for gender equality on all fronts.

The new discourse combines the legalistic style and tone of Motahhari with Shari'ati's egalitarian vision, but it differs from them both in two fundamental ways. First, it no longer defines itself in opposition to the West, but in opposition to patriarchal interpretations of the *shari'a*. Secondly, it challenges the hegemony of the orthodox interpretative process, paving the way for tackling the "women's question" from an entirely novel perspective within the *fiqh*.

As far as context and medium of expression are concerned, there are two striking parallels between this discourse and that developed by Motahhari. Both were grounded in debates generated by state initiatives in changing the divorce laws; and in both cases a women's magazine became the forum for their articulation and development. Let me elaborate.

In December 1992, more than a decade after dismantling the Family Protection Law (FPL), which curtailed men's right to divorce and polygamy, the Majlis (Parliament) ratified a law with similar goals. The new law, entitled Amendments to Divorce Law, outlaws registration of all divorces without a court certificate called Impossibility of Reconciliation – incidentally the same name as that required by FPL. A divorce can now be effected and registered only when the husband pays his wife, in cash, all her dues (*mahr*, past *nafaqa* and maintenance, '*idda*) unless it is of *khul'* type, that is, when she forgoes all her dues in return for her release. These amendments also require that every divorcing couple go through the process of arbitration; and allow the appointment of women judges as advisers to the main judge. More importantly, they enable the court to place a monetary value on women's housework and entitle her to *ujrat al-mithl* (literally wages in kind) for the work she has done during marriage, provided that divorce is not initiated by her or is not caused by any fault of hers. All these amount not only to the resurrection of the rejected provisions of the pre-revolutionary law of divorce, but to taking them a step further, in short a complete U-turn.

But this U-turn proved to be neither smooth nor complete. It caused a rift between two of the highest law-making bodies. The first draft of these amendments passed by Majlis in March 1991 was twice rejected by the Council of Guardians, whose task is to ensure that all laws passed are in line with the *shari'a*. The Council objected to the concept of *ujrat al-mithl*, as formulated by the Majlis. The dispute between these two bodies was not resolved until November 1992, and then only through the intervention of the highest constitutional authority.[11] In December 1992, the new law came into effect, but it soon became evident that, rather than protecting women against an undesired divorce, by requiring all cases to go through arbitration the new amendments are creating problems not only for the court but for those couples who have reached mutual consent.[12]

All this suggests that debates over women's position in law, which were so harshly stifled early in the revolution, are resurfacing. Interestingly, they centre on divorce provisions, as these have come to embody the essence of the injustices to which women are subjected in law. But this time debates are conducted in an Islamic Republic, whose claim to uphold the *shari'a* makes it directly responsible for such injustices. It is in this context that the journal *Zanan* makes its first appearance, opening a new chapter in an old debate. The magazine itself is the fruit of the Revolution, an outgrowth of "Islam in power" for over a decade. Its editor and founder, Shahla Sherkat, was among those who helped to Islamise *Zan-e Ruz*, the glossy pre-revolutionary women's magazine which featured Motahhari's articles in the 1960s. She was invited to join *Zan-e Ruz* in 1982 and remained its chief editor until 1991 when she was dismissed because of unresolved disagreements over the ways in which gender issues were being addressed. Seven months later, in February 1992, the first Number of *Zanan* appears, to coincide with the 13th anniversary of the revolution. Referring to a decade of fighting against the centuries-old oppression of women in Iran, and hinting at obstacles faced, Sherkat writes:

> We believe that the key to the solution of women's problems lies in four realms: religion, culture, law and education. If the way is paved in these four principal domains then we can be hopeful of women's development and society's advancement.[13]

At the end of 1994, 19 Numbers of *Zanan* have appeared. With a few exceptions, every issue contains articles classified under "Law/Rights", *Huquq*, where aspects of gender inequality in the *shari'a* are discussed and new interpretations are attempted. So far, the following three themes have been addressed: women in family law (*Zanan* 1, 2, 9, 18, 19); women as judges, arbitrators, and *mujtahids* (*Zanan* 4, 5, 6, 7, 8, 17); women in penal law, *qissas* (*Zanan* 11, 13, 14, 15, 16).

It is in these articles that one can find the contours of a different Shi'a discourse. In what follows I attempt to convey something of the evolution of ideas and interpretations of the sacred texts in these articles, especially the ways in which *Zanan* manages to reinterpret them to accommodate women's aspiration for equality and to introduce notions such as the legitimacy of women's choices and their demands for equal treatment at home and in society.

The beginning: A hesitant voice

Legal sections of the first three Numbers, written by lay women, are similar to Shari'ati's writings, where the mode of argumentation is more sociological than legal. Like him, the authors shy away from engaging with *fiqh* sources, instead they focus on Civil Code provisions and hold them responsible for making women subordinate in marriage. In support of their position, which is that of partnership in marriage, they resort to the Qur'an and appeal to its patent message of equality and justice. The end result is that the authors do not challenge on their own grounds *fiqh* concepts such as *tamkin* (woman's duty to submit to her husband's will) and *nushuz* (her refusal to submit, rebellion), which legitimate women's subordination in marriage, but instead they add two qualifiers. First, *tamkin* as it is interpreted by the Civil Code is faulty: "in a mutual human relationship, shaped by modes and characters of those involved, one cannot consider the woman as a (sexual) object ready to be manipulated and used." Secondly, *tamkin* and *nushuz* must be reciprocal, that is, it is necessary to take into consideration women's sexual needs and to subject men's defiance of their duties to legal sanctions.

To illustrate the tone and mode of argumentation in these articles, let us take a closer look at two of them, representing *Zanan's* earlier stance. The first article, co-authored by Shokufeh Shekari and Sahereh Labriz, is entitled "Tamkin" and opens with the text of Article 1105 of the Civil Code, stating: "headship of the family is among men's attributes, *khasa'es.*" The authors note that this article raises a number of critical questions for women in our society. For instance, "According to what logic and on what grounds is the man head of the family? Does such a headship imply his absolute rule? Does the mandate of *tamkin* in conjugal life equally apply to men? If not, why not? Should a woman be beaten if she is unwilling or is not ready – psychologically and physically – to fulfil her husband's (sexual) wishes?"

In search of answers the authors go through a wide body of legal opinions in Shi'a *fiqh* and in legal text-books in which Civil Code articles are expounded on. Although overtly critical of the Code, they remain hesitant to challenge its gender premise and other assumptions which are all derived from the Shi'a *fiqh*. Instead they tend to reinterpret them in a more liberal light, to play them against each other, or against other articles of the Civil Code. For instance, as regards men's headship, they write:

> this headship does not imply that a man has an absolute and despotic rule in the family according to which the wife is required to slavishly follow him; but it entails a certain authority defined by law and custom. A woman is not her husband's mere subordinate but his partner, companion and aide.

Likewise, as regards *tamkin*, the authors cite a passage from Ayatollah Khomeini's treatise in which *tamkin* is limited to a woman's submission to her husband's sexual demands. To this the authors add a modifier: "the emphasis placed on meeting the husband's sexual demands should not be taken as his wife's ever-readiness for sexual intercourse." Without questioning the prime assumption of the passage, which, in line with the fiqh position, sees sexual submission as a woman's duty in marriage, they make two deductions from it. First, in the non-sexual aspects of marital duties – which they term "ordinary duties" – a woman is not required to obey her husband and can even demand wages for what she does in the house. Secondly, whereas in *fiqh, nushuz* (rebellion, non-fulfilment of marital duties) pertains to the conduct of both spouses in marriage, in the Civil Code it merely pertains to the wife's. When a man neglects his marital duties, there is no legal recourse open to his wife apart from asking for a divorce. "Such a solution is not befitting of an Islamic state, given the degree to which Islam abhors divorce."[14]

The second article, entitled "Man, Partner or Boss?", places the question of headship and power relations in the family in an evolutionary framework. Drawing on anthropological theories of the evolution of societies from matriarchy to patriarchy, the authors note that "in the Islamic world view we encounter a new anthropology and a fresh perspective in which men and women are declared equal before God, and that they are created from the same substance in order to console, to complete and to fulfil each other." Referring to Verse 13 of Sura Hujurat (see below), they contend that "this verse on its own suffices to convince us that, despite other existing evidence, Islam is not a sexist and racist school of thought."

This becomes a prelude to defying the conventional understanding of other verses, notably verse 34 of Sura Nisa (see below), which the authors believe is mistakenly invoked to perpetuate the belief that "in essence, in attributes and in conception, men are superior to women; this is so deep-rooted that even some women came to believe that they are defective, *naqis*." The reader is reminded that such beliefs have little to do with Islam but are products of historical processes that not only pre-date Islam but gained momentum after the Prophet's death due to socio-political realities of the time. Today there are other realities: women are now highly educated and skilled, they actively participate in society at large – even take part in wars. There is now more than ever an acute need to redefine their *shari'a* rights. The authors end their discussion by demanding total equality in marriage: "in our view, in a healthy relationship there is no need to have a superordinate and subordinate"; and "in many cases women are more to be trusted with the headship of the family."[15]

Gaining legitimacy: A fiqh *voice*

With *Zanan* 4, not only is there a discernible shift in tone, style and mode of argumentation but the focus changes from gender biases in the Civil Code to those introduced soon after the revolution. Articles in five consecutive Numbers, which appeared between May and December 1992, discuss the question of women's right to serve as judges and arbiters in marital disputes in courts, and as *mujtahids*. Interestingly – but perhaps not unexpectedly – the author of these five articles is a male cleric in Qom using a female pseudonym, Mina Yadegar Azadi. He takes issue with the very premise on which the official Shi'a discourse on the position of women is based, laying bare its inherent gender bias. His mastery of the shari'a art of argumentation, coupled with his command of the sacred sources, not only ensures that the debate remains within acceptable boundaries but gives a different edge to these arguments.

To appreciate the nuances of these arguments, we should take a closer look at the mode of argumentation, the juristic and logical devices the writer employs to obtain different interpretations of those Qur'anic verses on which *shari'a* rules on women are based. Two of these articles, entitled "Women in Judgement" (*Zanan* 4 and 5), discuss the sensitive issue of forbidding women since 1979 to serve as judges on the grounds that it is against the explicit rule of *shari'a*. The author says that those who see women as unfit to serve as judges resort to two kinds of reasoning. The first is that women have delicate constitutions, are ruled by emotions, and are, thus, unable to deliver justice. The second is that Islam forbids them to do so, and "in support of this assertion they invoke the Qur'an; *sunna*, practice of the Prophet; *ijma'*, consensus of the jurists; and '*aql*, reason." It is those who use the latter argument that the author considers it more important to tackle first, especially since some of them are opposed to women's work outside the home. They ground their arguments in three Qur'anic verses (4 (Nisa): 34, 2 (Baqara): 228, and 59 (Ahzab): 33); and so the writer commences by discussing these.[16]

He opens the discussion by interpreting the first part of verse 34 of Sura Nisa as follows:[17]

> According to God's way, *sunnat*, which has caused some to excel over others, men, because they give from their own property, have an advantage over women, thus honourable and respectful women guard their husband's interest covertly, as this right has been reserved for them (men) by God.

He then adds that those who oppose women serving as judges say that,

> according to this verse, men have dominion over women and God
> has made men maintainers of women; thus how can women judge
> men and decide their fate? Whereas this verse as translated does not
> indicate that men are superior to women, it merely recalls the place
> of married men and women and reveals an external fact; and dis-
> cusses the status of men in conjugal life. Beside, this verse does
> not embrace single or widowed men and women.

In order to confine men's supremacy to the realm of the family, and more importantly to define it as a condition arising from the contract of marriage, the writer performs an etymological analysis of two key words of the verse which are taken as Qur'anic evidence for men's superiority and women as their wards: *fadl*, to excel, and *qawwam*, to maintain. He starts by reviewing the usage of each word in other verses to establish that *fadl* does not denote a natural/intrinsic advantage but an achieved/ earned one, which in most cases relates to material and welfare matters. He then deliberates on the meaning of *fadl*, which, as he has it, is a kind of "excess from equilibriant" which can have either a positive or a negative sense. In a positive sense – referred to as *fadl-i mamduh* – it can be one of the following three: (a) *fadl* by variety, jins, such as superiority of animal kind over plant kind; or (b) *fadl* by species, *nou'*, such as superiority of human species over horse species; and (c) *fadl* by essence, *zat*, such as advantage of one person over another which is commonly measured by some determined criteria, such as wealth.

> Therefore, men's *fadl* to women is the superiority of one person
> over another among the equal species of human, and in the hon-
> oured verse, man in his capacity of being married and managing
> the family has an advantage, not that all men are superior to all
> women.

The same goes for *qawwam*, which speaks of a convention, a custom, a contract according to which men voluntarily undertake to run the affairs of the family. This in no sense signifies that they are superior, but merely that they protect and maintain their wives.

Seen from this perspective, the verse is indeed not about men's dominion over and guardianship of women but is about married women, who are called to fulfil their share of duties in the family.

The two other verses are subjected to the same treatment. As regards verse 228 of Baqara – which is again taken as evidence of men's superiority, as it says men are a degree higher than women – Azadi argues that, given the entire text of the verse, this supremacy again has to do with men's and women's different marital rights and duties.[18]

> Difference in rights and duties, which is both relative and a matter of convention, cannot be taken as men's intrinsic (natural) superiority over women. Both are human, thus equal.

As regards Verse 33 of Ahzab, which is invoked by those who disapprove of women's work outside the home because in it they are enjoined to stay home and not to display their ornaments, Azadi has the following to offer.[19] First, as the preceding verse (32) reveals, it is addressed to women of the Prophet's household, thus it is not incumbent on all Muslim women, who certainly are not on the same level. Secondly, even if it were addressed to all women, its command, *hukm*, is a guiding, *irshadi*, not a binding, *ilzami*, one. On this all jurists agree, in his words: "We have not yet heard a single *faqih* decree as a binding and obligatory command of God that women be house-bound."

He concludes his discussion of the Qur'anic verses by reiterating that the three verses in no way oppose women's right to serve as judges; and that they are but a pretext for those whose real intention is to keep women in a state of depravity, restrict the scope of their activities, and in short confine them to the home.

Having dealt with the Qur'anic verses, the *Zanan* writer turns his attention to the Traditions that opponents of women judges invoke in support of their position. He finds these to be of three kinds. First, those sayings, *rawayat*, in which there is a specific ban on women from assuming certain offices, such as a judge or public prayer leader. Secondly, those from which a ban can be inferred because of the repercussions on women's work outside home, such as the preference, *istihab*, for their segregation, or the abhorrence, *ikrah*, of their presence in Friday prayers. Thirdly, those traditions that the author classifies as dealing with general themes and banning women as a result of their own internal logic. He starts with the first kind and focuses on three sayings. The first is a saying by Imam Baqir (the fifth Shi'a *Imam*), who is reputed to have said "do not leave judgement to women." The second is the Prophet's last will addressed to 'Ali, in which, among a long list of prohibitions placed on women, two are: "women are not to be in charge of the task of judging, and they are not to be consulted." The third is the *wilayat hadith* whereby the Prophet said that "the people, the *wilayat* (running) of whose affairs is entrusted to a woman, will not be saved."

To set the record straight, and more importantly to show why and how these three sayings do not constitute a ban on women's right to serve as judges, the writer puts forward altogether 20 arguments, 13 relating to the first two sayings, and seven relating to the third one. These arguments are varied: some are rooted in *fiqh*, others in linguistics, sociology, logic, reason and common sense. They range from discussing their chain of transmitters to etymological and logical arguments, with the aim of placing them in context by drawing attention to the fact that each pertains to a specific set of events and reflects the dictates of its time, which are not necessarily the same as ours. For instance, as to the third *hadith*, in a long passage he argues that the Prophet was specifically referring to events in Persia, where a female monarch had just assumed the throne. The *hadith* is a political commentary on the affairs of Sassanid Persia, where in the course of four years twelve monarchs had been enthroned.[20]

> It reveals an external fact about the Persians, that this time too the Sassanid throne cannot be saved, not that if women rule, people will not be saved in *akhirat* (the last day).
>
> Suppose in a given society, all men are afflicted with the disease of feeble-mindedness, and there is one wise and learned woman, in that case is her *wilayat* still invalid? What happens if we assign this *wilayat* to imbecile men?! Or let's suppose that in other planets, women are stronger and more learned than men, do we accept their custom or do we reject it totally?

In the next Number (*Zanan* 5, June–July 1992) the writer turns his attention to *ijma'* (consensus of jurists on an issue). He starts the discussion by defining the nature, scope and function of *ijma'* in Shi'a *fiqh*, clarifying its place in the process of *ijtihad*. The gist of his argument is as follows. *Ijma'*, strictly speaking, entails gathering the opinions of Islamic scholars and jurists on a certain issue, and on its own is not a source of law but merely a tool for deriving a law from the primary sources. In practice, since there is no requirement as to the minimum number of these opinions, it has become customary to claim that *ijma'* has been achieved for some legal rulings whose essence is not strictly in line with the primary sources. There are two kinds of *ijma'*: *ijma'-i muhassil* (obtained consensus), whereby one needs to collect the views of contemporary jurists on an issue; and *ijma'-i manqul* (narrated *ijma'*), whereby a *faqih* or *mujtahid*, in support of his own opinion, makes a claim of other jurists' consensus, without any thorough research. Since obtaining the first type of *ijma'* is difficult, and even impossible, when-ever jurists invoke *ijma'*, they are talking of the second type. In that case its function is that of affirming the *sunna* and has little validity on its own, otherwise the jurists' opinion could replace the Book and the Tradition.

With this background, Azadi concludes that, with regard to male-ness as a prerequisite for judgement, there is no *ijma'* of the first kind; and he then lists arguments that some jurists have put forward that the *ijma'* (which is of course the second kind, *manqul*) requires a judge to be of male sex. He points out that the whole issue of maleness as pre-requisite for judgement is in fact a Sunni debate which entered Shi'a *fiqh* in the sixth century AH under the influence of Shaikh Tusi, mainly in order to gain acceptability and avoid further criticism by his Sunni counterparts.

In the last part of the discussion, which is entitled "Women's Judgement from the Perspective of Reason", Azadi notes:

> Probing the reasons put forward by those Islamic jurists who deny women the right to be a judge, proves that their offensive on woman focuses on her incapacity and inability. It is the question of women's gender shortcomings and men's natural superiority. They regard men as powerful beings and women as weak and worthless. It is of course evident to us that such perceptions arise from centuries of confinement, living behind closed doors, in inner quarters, *andarun*, of homes separated from the society . . . Nevertheless, to prove women's inadequacy they have brought up other arguments.

He then discusses three arguments that are put forward by jurists in support of the doctrine that women are innately flawed. First, there has never been a woman prophet or Imam, which proves that God has not entrusted women with the task of judging men. Secondly, the primary postulate is that of everyone's *'adam-i wilayat*, i.e. that no one has the right of *wilayat*, authority or jurisdiction, over anyone else; therefore, those who oppose this postulate must provide convincing evidence. Thirdly, women are defective in nature and thus cannot be entrusted with tasks such as *wilayat* or judgement.

The way Azadi tackles each of these sets of reasoning is both skilful and provocative, laying bare their circular nature, inner contradictions and misogynous roots. For instance, as to the first, he states:

> 1) It is obvious that not having become a prophet or *Imam* is different from not being able to become one; as we learned in philosophy and logic, not finding something does not prove that it does not exist.

> 2) That women have not taken the mantle of Prophethood – which requires intense social activity – cannot be taken as an evidence for women's depravity so as to deny them other offices. This (women not becoming prophets) did not happen for numerous factors that the Divine Law-Maker willed.

> 3) That women have not been appointed as prophets is after all a report; perhaps there were women prophets whose missions were denied by men.

> 4) According to the explicit text of the Qur'an, revelation, which is one of the attributes of prophecy, was received by women, such as the mother of Moses, and particularly Mary mother of Jesus.

As to the second set of arguments, the *'adam-i wilayat* postulate, Azadi states that if we are to take this postulate literally then no one, including men, can judge or rule, thus there can be no rule or government. He then expresses a view that goes against the very grain of establishment clerical opinion:

> The Divine Law-Maker (*Shar'-i Islam*) has left ordinary affairs to people themselves and only guides them in this respect; whether people are going to vote for this or that person is something which belongs to the realm of the ordinary; religion is neither for nor against it, unless the actions of the voters or candidates contradict a principle of the faith.

As to the third argument, women's defectiveness (*naqs*), he focuses on Imam 'Ali's Sermon (*khutba*) 79 in *Nahj al-balagha*,[21] in which the Imam registers women's deficiencies in clear and strong terms, leaving no room for modification.[22] Here Azadi is clearly at pains to qualify the Imam's saying, or cast doubts on its authenticity; what he does is to place the *khutba* in context and argue that one cannot generalise from it. It was delivered soon after the Battle of the Camel and it specifically addresses 'A'isha's ill-judgement and action, not all women.

Finally, he turns to tackle those who argue that because of their delicate and emotional nature, women are incapable of correct judgement.

> Rather than criticising women, they are willy-nilly implicating the Creator, and if they believe that there is no defect in the Creation, then they cannot claim that women's emotionality makes them defective, and if they believe otherwise, then we need to enter a discussion on the fundamentals (*usul*) with them; their views on women are attributable to other belief systems than Islam and knowledge of God.

He ends the whole discussion on women and judgement by going back to the Qur'an, and cites verse 13 of Hujurat,[23] to prove that men and women are equal in the eyes of God; what invests either with privilege is their action; and verses 21 to 42 of Sura Naml, to prove the wise judgement and good rule of a woman through the Qur'anic account of the encounter between Solomon and the Queen of Sheba.[24]

In the next three Numbers (*Zanan* 6–8, which appeared between July and December 1992), Azadi turns his attention to two themes: women as arbitrators in family courts and as religious leaders (*marja'*). Given the subject-matter of the preceding articles, his first theme seem repetitious, if not incongruous. But as his argument progresses it becomes evident that they are an implicit critique of the post-revolutionary divorce laws and the Majlis debates concerning the disputed divorce amendments which were rejected by the Council of Guardians. In these articles Azadi offers an extended commentary on Verse 35 of Nisa, which recommends that if separation between spouses is feared, an arbiter from each side should be appointed to deal with the dispute. This verse became the basis for the establishment of *shari'a* courts in 1979 to replace the Family Protection Courts as well as the first modification in *shari'a* divorce provisions effected in the Islamic Republic.[25] Azadi first takes issue with "some of the graduates of *Howzeh*" (centres of religious learn-ing in Qom) who contend that the Verse is addressed to the judge and, thus, "it is up to him to choose to settle the dispute by appointing the arbiters." Before offering his own view, Azadi discusses diverse com-mentaries on this verse, and then concludes that,

> the choice of the arbiters must be left to the disputing couple; it is allowed, even preferable, that one of them should be a woman; they should be empowered to settle the dispute by bringing about either a reconcilation or a negotiated divorce.[26]

In the second part, he discusses the limits to the powers of arbiters as understood from the above verse. He then turns to an examination of arbitration in the modern legal systems of three Muslim countries: Iran, Iraq and Lebanon. He uses the occasion to point out that, apart from two minor details, the provisions of the dismantled Family Protection Law correspond with the *shari'a* mandates, and its dismantling has resulted in a number of problems which need urgent attention.[27]

In his last contributions, entitled "Women's *Ijtihad* and *Marji'at*", Azadi follows his usual format and grounds the question in sacred texts and rational debates. However, both the thrust of his argument and the tone of his writings are more forceful and less implicit. He draws a clearer line between primary (the Qur'an and *sunna*) and secondary (*fiqh* texts) sources of Islamic law. He then points out that there is no evidence in the primary sources to support the contention of the secondary sources which bans women from issuing decrees and becoming religious leaders. According to him, the secondary sources reflect views and conceptions of Muslim thinkers not Islam. They should not be accepted at face value and need to be questioned in the light of the primordial principles inher-ent in the primary sources. In refuting the views of some Muslim thinkers, Azadi takes his arguments, refined in the course of the last four issues, to their logical conclusion and calls for absolute gender equality in all spheres of the *shari'a*. This is done under the heading of "Rational Principles" (*Usul-i 'Uqala'i*), in which he elaborates on six principles amounting to a declaration of a *shari'a*-based bill of rights for women. All entail equal rights in (1) following education, (2) choosing an occupation, (3) administering justice, (4) attaining spiritual perfec-tion, (5) receiving rewards and punishments, and finally (6) developing a healthy society and fulfilling other social and human needs.[28]

Debating the sacred and the legal: A challenging voice

A year after its launch, in a review of Ayatollah Javadi Amoli's book, *Women in the Looking Glass of Majesty and Beauty, Zanan* starts to take issue with the official Shi'a discourse on women.[29] The book is important not only because it is the first substantial publication by an eminent Ayatollah since the Revolution but it also encapsulates the latest, state-of-the-art, official Shi'a discourse on women produced under the Islamic Republic, as evidenced in three ventures in which the book is rooted.[30] The first is a course of lectures that Ayatollah Amoli delivered in Qom in 1989–90 to female students of the al-Zahra seminary. These students, who were all at the advanced level of religious studies, also helped in "elucidating certain ambivalences of *fiqh* texts and Qur'anic commentaries". The second is a seminar organised by the Iranian National Radio and Television in which Amoli prepared a special text to fit the seminar's theme, "The high status of women in Islam, protecting their honour by amicable means in the society, and combating the Western cultural invasion." The third is a set of "scientific questions with regard to specific Qur'anic exegesis", asked by the director of the Centre for Women's Studies.[31]

Ayatollah Amoli's stance on gender is identical to that taken by Ayatollah Motahhari three decades earlier, although his mode of argumentation is different. While concurring with Motahhari's thesis of the complementarity of gender rights and duties, Amoli places the whole issue of gender inequalities in the *shari'a* on a spiritual plane, justifying them through a series of mystical inferences. In so doing, he aims to relegate gender disparity in the *shari'a* to the mundane material realm and refers the reader to the spiritual realm, where the real destinies of men and women lie. For instance, as far as family matters are concerned, he writes that "The endurance of hardship (for women) might on the surface appear an evil (*sharr*) but its immense goodness (*khair*) is to strengthen the family and protect its essence."[32] The book's title, on which Amoli dwells at length in the introduction, aims to underline the eternal duality in the mundane and spiritual destinies of men and women. In Amoli's words:

> In short a woman must offer the subtleties of wisdom (*zara'if-e hikmat*) in the subtleties of art (*zara'if-e honar*) and man must display subtleties of art in subtleties of wisdom, that is to say that a woman's majesty (*jalal*) is hidden in her beauty (*jamal*) and a

man's beauty is reflected in his majesty and this division of labour is neither a blame for women nor a praise for men. But it is the guide-line for each, each (sex) is assigned to its proper tasks and deserves praise for compliance with this order, and blame for defiance.[33]

Zanan's review, entitled "Women in the Perspective of Reason and Perfection", marks the beginning of a new phase in *shari'a*-based discourse in post-revolutionary Iran. Its author, Mohsen Sa'idzadeh, is a cleric teaching in Qom who takes a totally different position from Amoli's.[34] Drawing upon arguments developed in previous Numbers, Sa'idzadeh rejects the very premise of Amoli's arguments and denounces the notion of "complementarity of rights" – developed by Motahhari and on which Amoli's arguments rest – as a pretext to deny women their Islamic rights. In a set of inter-connected arguments, Sa'idzadeh contends that Islam grants women the same rights as men in all matters, including the right to become leaders, both religious and political, and to serve as judges. Islam regards the material and the spiritual as two sides of the same coin, and it is sheer folly to expect that we can continue to subjugate women in this material world through an illusory promise of spiritual reward. The following extracts give an idea of the nature and force of his arguments, which are both challenging and novel.

Money is the root of all good as much as it can be the root of absolute corruption. If a woman were an (economically) independent legal person (in marriage) and did not have to depend on her husband for *nafaqa* (maintenance), she would not put up with the indignity of an unjust *tamkin* (obedience) and a thousand and one other hardships; this is what frightens men. If humanity ruled, irrespective of being wealthy or not, a woman would be her husband's partner and aide. Did Khadija not spend her large wealth for the Prophet? Was she not wealthy and powerful? Why did she follow him and remain loyal to him?

It is time to ameliorate men's level of awareness in society, to make them understand that the criterion for good conjugal relations is no longer domination, paying for women's maintenance and ruling them, but the reason for a woman obeying a man is his humanity. Indeed we do not have any strata in this country more oppressed and sacrificing than women.

It is not evident why, instead of being realistic, some of our religious leaders resort to fanciful, and sometimes distorted, justifications and interpretations. Why do they not want to accept women's God-given and intrinsic demands, which are in no way threatening to society? Why in the sphere of Islamic law, which claims universal application, should these matters be missing?

We believe that the problem is not with Islam but with Islamic thinkers' understanding of Islam, which is tinted with political and patriarchal notions. Why, as soon as an enlightened *mujtahid* or an aware Islamic scholar tries to correct these, is he faced with all sorts of accusations? If our logic is strong then we should not be frightened and if it is weak we should find ways to remedy it.[35]

With two gaps, the legal sections of the next five Numbers (*Zanan* 11–16, which appeared between June 1993 and February 1994) extend the debate to an examination of the gender basis of current penal laws. The debate started with *Zanan*'s decision to publish an article by a secular woman lawyer, Mehrangiz Kar, delivered at the "First Seminar of Women's Social Participation". The seminar, organised by the Tehran Governor's Office, was part of an official campaign to promote women's status in society by highlighting their "high status" in Islam. Kar's paper is a factual analysis of the gendered basis of the Islamic Punishment Law as codified in 1991, in which she merely lists – without one single comment – the instances in which men and women receive different punishments for the same crime.

Zanan's decision to publish a paper by a secular feminist, whose primary assumption is that "gender equality even in punishment" is a principle to which the legislator should adhere, marks another phase in the development of *Zanan*'s stance. *Zanan*'s willingness to join forces with secular feminists to protest against the gender biases of a law which is derived from the *shari'a* is indeed novel in post-revolutionary politics. Capitalising on recent pro-women slogans, *Zanan* introduces Kar's article with an explicit call for *ijtihad*:

In recent years Iranian women have been subjected to especial praise and honours, naturally raising their expectations. They now expect the thinkers and policy-makers to re-examine the inequalities that exist in penal laws of the country and prescribe a fundamental revision. In other words: "It is time for *ijtihad*." [36]

To defuse an eventual riposte, the introductory passage to Kar's paper contains two other points: first, that

> Islam is a collection of Qur'anic Verses, *sunna* and opinions of the Islamic jurists, and we know that jurists differed in their perspectives and opinions. Some refute others and it is exactly here that we can be hopeful for progressive *ijtihads*.

Secondly, that when the author refers to "legislator", *qanungozar*, she means "law-making authorities and apparatus of the country", not the "Divine Law-Maker", *Shar'i-e Islam*. This distinction is also made in the title of Kar's article: "The position of Women in Penal Laws of Iran".

Zanan 13 continues the debate, but this time from the *fiqh* perspective. This is done in a three-part article entitled "Position of Women in Penal Laws of Islam", written under the name of Zinat al-Sadat Kermanshahi. The approach and the style of argumentation in these articles are exactly the same as in those written by Azadi. However, they have a stronger tone and the arguments are further refined, giving them a more forceful thrust. Before starting the discussion, the author carves out a framework with two objectives: to ground and contain the discussion within the *fiqh* tradition with the aim of pre-empting any charge of heresy; and to promote *shari'a*-based arguments for reforming the present penal laws which are themselves based on the *shari'a*. To expand the scope of debate as developed in earlier issues of *Zanan*, and to free the author from previous constraints, five points are stressed at the outset. These are:

> 1) In arguing for gender equality in the penal laws of Islam we start with the postulate of *takafu* (equality) in religion, then we proceed to examine the postulates of gender, freedom and slavery – all within the *fiqh* framework.

> 2) After the Prophet's death, the need for new laws and re-interpretations of the old ones gave rise to the emergence of various schools of law and thought whose founders used their own judgements in an endeavour to find solutions for legal problems. Thus their views and deductions cannot unequivocally be attributed to Islam, as they are the views and commands of Muslims not Islam.

3) It is evident from the arguments and views of Islamic jurists, *hadith* experts, and commentators that the penal laws of Islam are more ratifactory (*imza'i*) than foundationary (*ta'sisi*); and that Islam largely accepted past customs and introduced certain modifications, including the removal of discrimination. Thus well versed in the rules of *fiqh* and *usul*, the present writer does not find it necessary to confine him/herself to current idioms.

4) The requirements of the age, of place and politics have undeniably shaped Islamic laws, *fiqh* and its commands, as confirmed by a number of *hadith*. Therefore, a review of these laws does not diminish their value and sanctity but enhances their power. The "Divine Law-Maker of Islam" had foreseen and allowed for such changes.

5) This article is a critique to assist the legislator (*qanungozar*) in reforming (penal) laws; its aim is neither to be a decree (fatwa) nor to innovate (*ibda'*).[37]

Within this framework, the author proceeds to examine the place of gender in *shari'a* penal laws under five headings: retribution in case of murder, *qissas-i nafs*, retribution in case of the loss of a bodily organ, *qissas-i 'uzw*, money compensation paid in lieu of *qissas* (*diya*), fixed punishment, *hudud*, and punishment defined by the Islamic judge, *ta'zirat*, For each of these forms of punishment, the author scrutinises the diverse opinions of the jurists and divides them into three groups: advocates of the "theory of difference", who maintain that men and women should be subjected to different punishments for committing the same crime; proponents of the "theory of equality", who hold that men and women should receive the same punishment for committing the same crime; and supporters of the "theory of inequality", who argue that a man should not be subjected to *qissas* for murdering a woman.

These articles are interrupted in *Zanan* 14 (October–September 1993) by a harsh critique of Kar's paper, to which *Zanan* duly replies in the same Number. The critique, apparently written by a seminary-educated woman, Muzhgan Kiyani Sabet,[38] is in fact a pretext to rebut the earlier articles in the legal sections of *Zanan*, written by Azadi. However, its author chooses to single out Kar's article as the culprit. This is so not only because Kar, as a secular feminist, is a safer target to attack, but also because the author probably found it difficult to challenge Azadi's articles which are all argued within acceptable *fiqh* boundaries.

The critique, and *Zanan*'s reply, written by Sa'idzadeh, encapsulate the conflict between *Zanan* and those who see gender differences in the *shari'a* as reflecting the divine design for mankind. Space does not allow a full treatment here; I can give only an intimation.[39]

Following the style set by *Zanan*, "Kiyani Sabet" starts her critique with an introductory section, establishing the framework and the position taken. This section makes seven points, whose primary aims seem to be twofold: to close the debate on gender inequality in the *shari'a*, and to reaffirm the official Shi'a position. These are conveyed in a set of seven arguments in which the author contends that (1) as penal laws in Iran are now derived from the *shari'a*, any discussion of them involves the *shari'a*, i.e. the sacred; (2) to object to them is to object to the *shari'a*, which is not permissible as the believer is required to follow its provisions without any probing. The following four arguments simply reiterate that Islamic law is divinely ordained, based on the laws of nature; women are treated differently because their natures are different and this is indeed the very essence of justice. Here the author simply reproduces the arguments put forward by Ayatollah Motahhari and more recently by Amoli, quoting from their books. The final argument is theological, whereby the author states that "prior to entering a discussion of *fiqh* one needs to enter a discussion on fundamental and doctrinal issues of Islam," which is followed by a discussion of two of the fundamentals of religion, *usul-i din*: Unity of Attributes, *Towhid-i Sefati*, and Divine Justice, *'Adl-i Elahi*.[40]

Zanan's reply, entitled "But Our Response", written by Sa'idzadeh, is not only daring and erudite but carves out another space for *Zanan*'s position within the *fiqh*-grounded debates. It tackles the critique on its own terms, responds to each of its arguments within the *fiqh* context, shows how its author commits the very sin that s/he forbids others, and points out the instances in which the author deviates from the *fiqh* and the fundamentals of the religion by issuing a number of groundless fatwas. In so doing, *Zanan* highlights the ways in which the critique misunderstood and misrepresented *fiqh* fundamentals, the Iranian legal system, and Kar's article, laying bare its implicit gender biases.[41]

Debating the legal and moral: An emerging feminist voice

Zanan 18 (June–July 1994) marks another important phase in its progression towards a *shari'a*-based feminist discourse. Here *Zanan* questions the classic divide in *shari'a* marriage rules between the moral and the legal and holds it responsible for the injustices in marriage to which women have been subjected. This is done in two ways. First, *Zanan* takes issue with assertions made about *nafaqa* (maintenance) by the head of the judiciary, Ayatollah Yazdi. Reflecting the dominant opinion within the Shi'a *fiqh*, Ayatollah Yazdi, in a Friday Prayer sermon (3 June) said that, legally speaking, the wife's right to maintenance does not include the expenses of major medical treatments.[42] *Zanan*'s critique of the Ayatollah's position, again written by Sa'idzadeh, took the form of an extended article, entitled: "According to What Law Is a Husband Not Responsible for his Wife's Major Medical Expenses?" The Ayatollah felt compelled to reply to these challenges not merely to his credentials as an advocate of justice, but to his competence as a jurist/scholar.[43] Secondly, *Zanan* adopts a different approach in discussing issues which were examined in the first two Numbers, such as the wife's obedience and the husband's right to headship of the household, dealing now with the sociological, legal and *fiqh* aspects separately, and highlighting their interconnections.

The sociological aspects are examined in a section labelled "Report", which like the "Legal" is a feature in most Numbers. In Number 18, the "Report" is devoted to women's actual experiences of marital violence, under the title: "Sir, Have You Ever Beaten Your Wife?" It consists of a number of interviews with men, women and children from different walks of life, seemingly innocent, but sharply pointed. These interviews reveal the extent to which women are at the mercy of their husbands, who see it as within their right to beat them if they object to or ignore their demands. In other words, the Report shows what the *shari'a* concepts such as *tamkin* and *nushuz* entail in practice, and how humiliating and disturbing is their impact on women and children.

The "Report" is followed by an interview with a female lawyer (Mehrangiz Kar), discussing the legal rights of a wife who is trapped in a violent marriage. Only in case of extreme physical violence can a woman have recourse to law, either to claim compensation or to obtain a divorce. But since the concept of "maltreatment" (of a wife) is not clearly defined by the Civil Code articles, the outcome of many cases depends on the outlook of the judges, who are all male and *shari'a* trained. Some consider that a man has the right to punish his wife, while others consider beating as a violation of her rights. The whole legal procedure is complex and a woman must provide medical reports or bring witnesses in support of her claim, and only those whose injuries are severe, such as loss of a limb, can get any kind of compensation. Since this is not always the case, women often end up giving their consent to abandon the case against their husbands.[44]

The *fiqh* dimensions are discussed in a two-part article (*Zanan* 18 and 19, June–September 1994), under the title: "Wife-beating: Another Consequence of Men's Headship". In contrast with the first two Numbers, *Zanan* not only now engages with *fiqh* texts but tackles Qur'anic verses which are commonly used to legitimate women's subordination. The author of this article is a man well-versed in sacred traditions; although he uses the name Mohsen Qa'eni, he is rumoured to be the same cleric who has contributed many earlier articles. Like the contributors to Numbers 1 and 2, he starts the discussion with Article 1105 of the Civil Code and verse 34 of Sura Nisa, but unlike them he sets out to prove that Article 1105 has no *shari'a* justification, and that its content cannot be attributed to the divine Law-Maker of Islam. He challenges dominant interpretations of the above verse and the underlying assumptions behind them before offering his own reading, which reflects *Zanan*'s position: that men's headship of the household is a male construct, and, like other male privileges which are attributed to *shari'a* laws, actually has its roots in the culture and customs of the time of revelation. In these sections the author introduces a number of ingenious ideas and opens the way for a feminist reading of some of the Qur'anic verses. To understand how this is done, we should take a closer look at these two articles.

After a lengthy critique of the prevailing conceptions of marriage and marital relations in the works of Islamic jurists, Mohsen Qa'eni asserts that, in the sphere of the family as elsewhere, the Qur'an's aim was to introduce change gradually. For instance, at the time when women had no inheritance rights, the Qur'an entitled them to half the share of a man; had the economic and social conditions been favourable, most probably they would have been given equal shares then and there. The absolute authority of men, and the maltreatment of women, were among the customs of Arabs; the Qur'an, however, modified them to a large extent. For instance, the wealthier or more powerful a man, the more wives he took; what the Qur'an did was to limit the number to four and make women a party to the contract; if the situation had arisen, it would have limited the number to one, as there is a clear indication of this in several places in the Qur'an itself.

To show the extent to which verse 34 of Sura Nisa is predicated on the customs and conventions of its time, Qa'eni urges the reader to follow the practice of the Prophet, reminding the believer that s/he is required to do so by the Qur'an itself. He then goes through 15 Traditions to argue that the Prophet himself never acted according to the dictates of the verse: not only did he never raise his hand to strike any of his wives, but he condemned wife-beating. However, he tolerated it as it was a part of the patriarchal culture of the time, which he intended to abolish gradually through reforms. To separate the ideas and views of Islamic thinkers further from those of the Prophet, the author makes six logical deductions, the gist of which is as follows.

1. Islam intends to resolve disputes primarily through persuasion, *mu'izeh*, and advice, *nasihat*, and by logical means, then through indirect means, such as avoidance, *qahr*, and it is only after these that out of necessity a warning or a threat is issued. The same holds true for marital disputes: the permission, *ibaheh*, to beat is merely a gesture, a caution, aiming to create awe. Seen from this perspective, Islam empowers both spouses to prevent each other from straying from the correct path of marital life. Each (sex) may resort to different measures.

2. To improve social relations, Islam has endorsed some of the existing rules – and probably added some, that is to say that, since certain customs and beliefs were so deep-rooted among Arabs, Islam did not see it expedient to fight them overtly. Among them were beating of wives and *talaq*, but the fact is that Islam abhors men who beat their wives or divorce them at will.

3. In Islam, "command", *amr*, has different functions – depending on the context. Whenever a command is inferred from the Qur'an, compliance is not required. For instance, Verse 3 of Nisa cannot be taken as commanding men to take four wives.[45]

4. According to the view of some commentators, beating is to be resorted to only in case of the husband's inability to achieve the desired result in a conciliatory manner, i.e. in case of extreme duress, *iztirar*. Evidently, any *iztirar* is blameworthy, *makruh*; the preferred command of Islam for a man is to establish a loving relationship with his wife and not to hurt her. Those who take this verse at its face value and criticise the Qur'an for sanctioning wife-beating either have other motives or lack knowledge of its essence.

5. Positively, the content of the verse is a report on the people of that age. To extend its relevance to all times, we need other proofs, *dalil*. One issue in theoretical bases of Islamic law, *usul al-fiqh*, is the question of the extent to which Qur'anic commands can be extended validly to those who were not its face-to-face addressees, *ghair-imushafihan*. According to the perspective of the non-extension, *'adam-i shumul*, it is up to those who hold that the Qur'an sanctions the beating of a wife to provide proofs that the command extends to people of all ages. The same is true of those verses which were used to legitimate men's dominance over women. The Qur'an states that men have a privilege over women, which is that granted to them as their maintainers, but it does not say whether this (being their maintainers) is good or bad. The rest of the verse merely states that "good women are obedient" but does not tell them to be obedient. If the Qur'an wanted them to be obedient, it would have said so directly. Why has it not ordered them to be so, as in other instances when men and women are ordered to obey God and his Prophet, and to do their prayers five time a day and to fast during the Ramadan? This means that the Qur'an simply endorsed the conduct and custom of the time – as it did with other marriage rules – but it does not mean that the Qur'an held them as just and unchangeable.

6. If we accept the view of some of Islamic jurisprudents, *ulama-yi 'ilm-i usul*, a Qur'anic command can be revoked, *naskh*, by means of visible proofs. In the case of the above verse we are facing a kind of *naskh*. The order to strike, *daraba*, in its conventional interpretation is removed because of the interest of the situation, *mashli-hat-i waz'*, of wisdom, *hikmat*, and of other interests. In light of the traditions, *ahadith*, discussed above – transmitted by both Sunnis and Shi'as – and given other principles of the Qur'an and Sunna which oppose any kind of aggression and seek to promote peace and harmony in all matters, the revocation, *naskh*, of the word *daraba* (in its conventional meaning) is then certain.[46]

Having put forward the above logical reasoning, the author then surveys the *fiqh* literature to show the diversity of jurists' opinions on the subject. A minority, who share the author's point of view, hold that men are not permitted to beat their wives under any condition. The majority, who think otherwise, are divided into two groups: those who consider this treatment applicable to all women; and those who make a distinction according to the wife's status, which suggests that the command has always had its social side. In subtle ways the discussion reveals the complexity and yet the absurdity of the whole issue, especially in the modern legal context when the wife can successfully challenge any charge of disobedience. It is argued that beating a wife has no religious legitimacy and is a matter that the legal system must deal with. Men who beat their wives must be brought to justice.

Finally, in *Zanan* 19, the writer goes back to the verse and offers an alternative interpretation, which is indeed novel. Under the title "But Our Stand-point", Qa'eni argues that, first, we need to understand the real sense of the verse, and its underlying message. The verse, more than telling men how to punish their wives, tells them how to understand the psychology of women and the reasons for their disobeying. It is indeed about marital disharmony and how a man should respond if he fears that his wife might enter the state of *nushuz*. There are many underlying reasons for *nushuz* (itself a vague term, which can mean rebellion in general, or a denial of sexual access in particular). As some commentators remark, some women become rebellious in order to seek further attention, some want to test their husband's love, and there are many other reasons. Qa'eni then examines the root radicals for three key words in the verse: *wa'aza*, to exhort, *hajara*, to abandon, and *daraba*, to strike. He argues that, in the verse concerned, the first word enjoins the husband to reason with her, the second to give her space, and the third to strike her with fondness. To arrive at this, the author engages in a linguistic analysis whose gist is that in the Qur'an the word *daraba* has different senses whose meaning becomes clear in association with others (it means "striking with awareness" in verses 75 and 76 of Nahl, "travel" and "speed in flight" in verse 156 of 'Umran, etc.). "Whenever *daraba* is used in the sense of beating it is in association with another word, for example in verse 27 of Muhammad and verse 44 of Suad." This is not the case in verse 34 of Sura Nisa where, he argues,

> *daraba* when read in *bab al-af'al*, and when taken in association with *wa'aza*, no longer denotes beating. Therefore, the meaning of the verse could be that "disobedient" women are of three kinds: those who need to be reasoned with; those who need to be left alone for a while; and those who need to be caressed, and taken to bed, rather than abandoned.[47]

Conclusion

In the course of 19 Numbers, the legal sections of *Zanan* have not only refined a mode of argumentation, but taken it to its logical conclusion by using it to tackle some hoary issues in the *shari'a*. As is evident, the approach is that of *fiqh* texts: first, by reviewing the divergent positions of the Muslim jurists, the issue is introduced and placed in context; then diverse opinions of the jurists are scrutinised in the light of the Qur'an, *hadith, ijma'*, reason and the practice of their time; finally, those which are contrary to the writer/s' position are refuted and those which are not are elaborated. Among the juristic and logical devices that *Zanan's* writer/s use/s, the following can be singled out: distinctions between the divine Law Giver (*Shar'-i Islam*) and the mundane law maker (the Islamic Republic), and between primary and secondary sources of *shari'a*. While primary sources are subjected to innovative interpretations, the secondary sources are debated and at times refuted by the aid of the former. It is argued that time and politics are among the decisive factors in upholding or modifying any *shari'a* rule, even if it is rooted in explicit Qur'anic injunctions, which are in turn divided into two categories: *ilzami*, binding, and *irshadi*, guiding. At the same time the classical divide in the *fiqh* rules between moral and legal is challenged, and jurists are urged to give legal force to the former; finally they are reminded that the time for radical *ijtihad* has come. In this way, *Zanan's* writer/s is/are gradually but surely turning the classical texts on their head, using their own style of reasoning and argumentation.

The process is still unfolding; so is our understanding of it. However, some tentative conclusions can be offered at this stage.

Zanan's shari'a discourse is not isolated, but is part and parcel of a new tendency within the centre of the religio-political establishment. This tendency, which can perhaps be best termed "post-fundamentalist", represents the latest faction in post-war and post-Khomeini Iran. It is changing the very terms of not only the *shari'a* discourse on women but that of the Islamic Republic, by arguing for a kind of demarcation between state and religion. Ironically, its most outspoken advocates were part of the early political leadership which defined the Republic's polity. This tendency has its intellectual core in Tehran, gathered around Dr Abdul Karim Sorush, the guiding inspiration of the Kiyan Cultural Institute, which publishes a monthly *Kiyan – Zanan's* brother paper – in which these views are aired.[48]

This tendency advocates a brand of feminism which takes Islam, not the West, as its source of legitimacy. What is significant about this "feminism", and especially its line of argument, is that it is grounded in a Shi'a discourse which is radically different from the official one – still closely identified with the position taken by Ayatollah Motahhari as part of the discourse of opposition to the Shah's reforms. Whereas Motahhari used Western scholarship to explain the reasons and the necessity for the different treatment of women in Islam, the new "feminists" use Shi'a scholarship to argue that old texts should be re-read in line with changed conditions. They take for granted gender equality on all fronts, including the rights accorded by the *shari'a*, unlike Motahhari, who rationalised gender difference in terms of complementarity of rights. Again, in contrast to Motahhari and other *shari'a*-based discourses, the new tendency sees women's sexuality as defined and regulated by their familial and social circumstances, not by nature and divine will. By diverting the focus of *fiqh* away from women as sexual beings to women as social beings, the new discourse has opened a door which can no longer be closed. It has given a new lease of life to the old question of "Women in Islam" and by asking suppressed questions it has brought about a shift in the very premises of the debate on women's role at home and in society. What made such a shift possible is the Islamic Republic's ideological understanding of Islam, which opens the way to challenging the hegemony of the orthodox interpretative process.

Finally one should note parallels in the emerging conditions of the pre- and post-revolutionary *shari'a*-based discourses. What gave rise to both were debates that preceded changes in family laws, especially those pertaining to divorce. In both cases, a women's magazine became the forum for this debate: *Zan-e Ruz* in the pre-revolutionary era, and now *Zanan*. Despite their differences, both discourses have provided an "Islamic" alternative to the state-sponsored feminism of their time. What separates them is that, while in the 1960s such an "Islamic" alternative was defined in opposition to the Shah's gender policies, now it is defined in opposition to those promoted by the Islamic Republic.

NOTES

1 I make a distinction between *shari'a*-based writings on women, whose writers are mostly Muslim/Islamist men and with which I am concerned here, and feminist writings on Muslim women, whose writers are mostly Muslim feminist women who locate their feminism in Islam. For examples of the first type see B. Stowasser, 'Women's Issues in Modern Islamic Thought' in J. E. Tucker (ed.), *Arab Women: Old Boundaries, New Frontiers* (Bloomington: Indiana University Press, 1993); and for recent examples of the second, see L. Ahmed, *Women and Gender in Islam: The Roots of a Modern Debate* (New Haven: Yale University Press, 1992), F. Mernissi, *Women and Islam: An Historical and Theological Enquiry* (Oxford: Blackwell, 1991).

2 See Z. Mir-Hosseini, 'Divorce, Veiling and Feminism in Post-Khomeini Iran' in H. Afshar (ed.), *Women and Politics in the Third World* (London: Routledge, 1996).

3 For example, see J. R. I. Cole and N. R. Keddie (eds.), *Shi'ism and Social Protest* (New Haven: Yale University Press, 1986); B. Lewis, 'The Shi'a', *New York Review of Books*, Vol. 32, pp. 7–10.

4 For example, see G. Nashat (ed.), *Women and Revolution in Iran* (Boulder, Colorado: Westview Press, 1983); F. Azari (ed.), *Women of Iran* (London: Ithaca Press, 1983); A. Tabari and N. Yeganeh (eds.), *In the Shadow of Islam* (London: Zed Books, 1982); K. Millet, *Going to Iran* (New York: Coward, McCann & Geochegan, 1982).

5 Both texts are treated extensively in the literature on women in post-revolutionary Iran. For example, A. K. Ferdows, 'The Status and Rights of Women in Ithna 'Ashari Shi'i Islam' in A. Fathi (ed.), *Women and the Family in Iran* (Leiden: E. J. Brill, 1985); M. K. Hermansen, 'Fatimeh as a Role Model in the Works of Ali Shar'iati' in G. Nashat (ed.), *Women and Revolution*; G. Nashat, 'Women in the Ideology of the Islamic Republic' in G. Nashat, *Women and Revolution*; S. Mahdavi, 'The Position of Women in Shi'a Iran: Views of the Ulama' in E. Fernea (ed.), *Women and the Family in the Middle East: New Voices of Change* (Austin: University of Texas Press, 1985); F. Azari, 'Islam's Appeal to Women in Iran: Illusions and Reality' in F. Azari, *Women of Iran*; Tabari and Yeganeh, *In the Shadow of Islam*; N. Yeganeh and N. R. Keddie, 'Sexuality and Shi'i Social Protest in Iran' in Cole and Keddie, *Shi'ism and Social Protest*. With the exception of the latter, the rest largely deal with the gender premises of both texts.

6 For a bibliographical sketch and a sample of his lectures in English, see A. Shar'iati, *On the Sociology of Islam*, trans. H. Algar (Berkeley: Mizan Press, 1979).

7 A. Shari'ati, *Fatemeh Fatemeh ast* (Tehran: Shabdiz Press, 1978), pp. i–ii. His other text, based on another lecture 'The Expectation of the Present Era from the Muslim Woman' (Tehran: n.d.), expresses similar views.

8 A. Shari'ati, *Fatemeh Fatemeh ast*, p. 88

9 M. Motahhari, *The Rights of Women in Islam* (Tehran: World Organization for Islamic Services, 1981), pp. xxxvii–xl. In this English translation, the word "system" (*nezam*) was omitted from the title.

10 For the dismantling of the Family Protection Law and its post-revolutionary counterpart, see Z. Mir-Hosseini, *Marriage on Trial: A Study of Islamic Family Law*

(London: I. B. Tauris, 1993).

11 The Assembly for Ascertaining the Regime's Interest (*Majma'-e Tashkhis-e Maslehat-e Nezam*).

12 For an extended discussion of these changes in law, see Mir-Hosseini, 'Divorce, Veiling and Feminism in Post-Khomeini Iran'.

13 *Zanan* 1 (February 1992/1370), p. 2.

14 *Zanan* 1 (February 1992/1370), pp. 58–63.

15 *Zanan* 2 (March 1992/1370), pp. 26–33.

16 *Zanan* 4 (April 1992/1371), pp. 20–6.

17 The verse reads: "Men are the maintainers of women because Allah has made some of them to excel others and because they spend out of their property; the good women are therefore obedient, guarding the unseen as Allah has guarded; and (as to) those on whose part you fear desertion, admonish them, and leave them alone in the sleeping-places and beat them; then if they obey you, do not seek a way against them, surely Allah is High, Great." This and other translations are taken from Holy Qur'an, translated by M. H. Sakir (Qom: Anasariyan Publications, n.d), which is distributed abroad by the Islamic Republic.

18 The verse reads: "And the divorced women should keep themselves in waiting for three courses; and it is not lawful for them that they should conceal what Allah has created in their womb, if they believe in Allah and the last day; and their husbands have a better right to take them back in the meanwhile if they wish for reconciliation; and they have rights similar to those against them in a just manner, and the men are a degree above them, and Allah is Mighty, Wise."

19 The verse reads: "And you stay in your houses and do not display your finery like the displaying of the ignorance of yore; and keep up prayer, and pay the poor-rate, and obey Allah and His Apostle. Allah only desires to keep away the uncleanness from you, O people of the House! and to purify you a (thorough) purifying."

20 Compare Fatima Mernissi's account in *Women and Islam*.

21 *Nahj al-balagha* is the most reputed collection of the sayings of 'Ali, the first Shi'i Imam.

22 The *khutb* reads: "O people, women are deficient in belief, inheritance and wisdom. Their deficiency in belief is due to not praying and fasting during menses; their deficiency in wisdom is that witness of two women equals one man and in inheritance is that their share is half of men's. Therefore, avoid bad women and beware good ones; do not follow their good advice and actions so as not to encourage them to spread bad advice and actions (i.e. impel you to follow them)."

23 The verse reads: "We have created you of a male and a female, and made you tribes and families that you may know each other; surely the most honourable of you with Allah is the one among you most careful (of his duty)."

24 *Zanan* 5 (June–July 1992), pp. 17–26.

25 See Mir-Hosseini, *Marriage on Trial*, pp. 55–6.

26 *Zanan* 6 (August 1992/1371), pp. 22–9.

27 *Zanan* 7 (September–October 1992/1371), pp. 25–9.

28 *Zanan* 8 (November–December 1992/1371), pp. 24–32.

29 *Zanan* 9 (January–February 1993).

30 Ayatollah Javadi Amoli, *Zan dar A'ineh-ye Jalal va Jamal* (Tehran: Reja' Cultural Press, 1371/1992).

31 Amoli, *Zan*, pp. 17–18.

32 Amoli, *Zan*, p. 22.

33 Amoli, *Zan*, p. 28.

34 Sa'idzadeh is believed to be the author of *Zanan*'s previous legal sections, writing under the pseudonym Azadi. The fact that he chooses to use his own name when taking issue with Amoli can be interpreted as an indication not only of his confidence, due to the acceptability and erudition of his earlier contributions, but also of the appeal of *Zanan*'s line of argument among some clerics. The debates among these clerics, the issue of male authorship of *Zanan*'s legal articles and the use of female pseudonyms are among the topics that I discuss in a larger project of which the present paper is a part.

35 *Zanan* 9 (December–January 1992–3/1371), pp. 29–34.

36 *Zanan* 11 (June–July 1993/1372), p. 16.

37 *Zanan* 13 (September 1993/1372), pp. 56–60.

38 It is rumoured that the article was written by her husband, himself a cleric.

39 I am dealing with these two perspectives in a forthcoming book.

40 *Zanan* 14 (October–November 1993/1372), pp. 42–9.

41 *Ibid.*, pp. 50–7.

42 *Zanan* 18 (June–July 1994/1373), pp. 34–7.

43 *Zanan* 19 (August–September 1994), pp. 7–8. Ayatollah Yazdi starts his reply by expressing his delight that among women there are those who are apparently capable of such scientific and analytical, i.e. *fiqh*-based, discussion, but chooses on the one hand to ignore that the critique of his own speech was written by a man (Sa'idzadeh), while insinuating that *Zanan*'s articles were written by men. This again raises the issue of male authorship and the ways in which women's issues have become a main debating ground among male clerics.

44 As my own study of divorce cases shows, maltreatment is the most difficult ground to establish, although it is the most commonly claimed, constituting 34 per cent of all cases. For an extended discussion, see Mir-Hosseini, *Marriage*, pp. 67–71.

45 The verse reads: "And if you fear that you cannot act equitably towards orphans, then marry such women as seem good to you, two and three and four; but if you fear that you will not do justice (between them), then (marry) only one or what your right hands possess; this is more proper, that you may not deviate from the right course."

46 *Zanan* 18 (June–July 1994/1373), pp. 55–9.

47 *Zanan*, 19 (August–September 1994/1373), pp. 68–70.

48 For a journalist's account of Sorush's ideas, see R. Wright, 'An Iranian Luther Shakes the Foundations of Islam', the *Guardian*, 1 February 1995. It is rumoured that this tendency has a clerical core in Qom, of which little is reported.

FOURTEEN

STATUTORY DISCRIMINATION IN LEBANON: A LAWYER'S VIEW

Souad Mokbel-Wensley

The Lebanese Constitution of 1926 established the principle of equality among all Lebanese. Article 7 provides that:

> All Lebanese are equal under the law; they all equally benefit from the same civil and political rights, and they all have the same obligations and duties, with no distinction.

As the principle of equality is established in such a comprehensive manner, the Lebanese legislator did not see the necessity to include an article dealing specifically with equality between men and women, unlike other Arab constitutions such as those of Kuwait, Algeria, Iraq, Qatar, Sudan, Egypt or Yemen. All these constitutions are more recent than the Lebanese one, and even the UN treaty abolishing discrimination between men and women did not come into being until 1979. For much the same historical reasons, the Lebanese constitution did not mention the more "modern" social, economic, or cultural rights, let alone gender equality.

No law in Lebanon specifically addresses the legal capacity of women (unlike French law, for instance, where the principle was, originally, the non-capacity of married women as a consequence of their marital status). According to the Code of Obligations and Contracts (the Lebanese Civil Code of 1932), the principle is that every person of 18 years of age enjoys full legal capacity, unless the law provides otherwise. Both women and men are deemed to have attained the legal age of capacity at 18. In terms of property acquisition and ownership, marriage does not affect the assets of either spouse, as the principle of community of property has never existed in Lebanon (unlike in some Western systems). Therefore, the Lebanese woman, married or not, has the right to acquire property and assets, manage them, and dispose of them, whether she acquires them before or during marriage.

As a result women appear to be on constitutional par with men; they attain the same legal capacity at 18, and their rights regarding their assets and property are not affected by their marriage. We should, therefore, not find in the Lebanese legislation laws which discriminate against women, since they would contravene the principle of equality provided by the Constitution, and be unconstitutional. This is however not the case.

A number of discriminatory laws remain on the books, and women lawyers have been understandably concerned at their detrimental effect on women. These antiquated statutes operate against the background of a modern legal system, particularly with regard to equal rights under the law. These statutes have in the main survived from other legislation – old French law and Ottoman law: in the Law of Property of 1926, women's testimony cannot be received (as in the Ottoman Majalla), although in practise such discrimination is not operational.

More seriously, many infringements upon the principle of equality between men and women as enshrined in the Constitution can be found in statutes which are still effective. Some of the most glaring cases are discussed in this paper.

Nationality Law

According to the Lebanese Nationality Law of 1925 (amended in 1960), the marriage of a Lebanese woman does not have any effect on her nationality. She can keep her nationality if she marries a non-Lebanese, even though she may acquire the nationality of the husband. Dual nationality is accepted by Lebanon, whether acquired by marriage or otherwise. Nevertheless, a wife's Lebanese nationality cannot be passed on to her husband; nor can it be passed on to her children even if they are born in Lebanon.

In contrast, in the case of a Lebanese man who marries a non-Lebanese woman, his wife can acquire Lebanese nationality a year after the registration of her marriage in Lebanon. (Before the law of 1960 she could acquire the nationality at any time after the marriage, and the children of this marriage are considered Lebanese at birth, even when born outside Lebanon.)

This difference is explained by the fact that Lebanese nationality is acquired either by *jus sanguinis* (blood relation of the father) or by *jus soli* (when children are born in Lebanon with no other nationality). There are only two exceptional situations where the Lebanese nationality can be acquired through the mother. In the case of an illegitimate child (defined as non-adulterous natural child), where the identity of the father is not known, the child of a Lebanese mother is Lebanese. In the case of a widowed non-Lebanese woman, who later acquires Lebanese nationality, her minor children from the previous marriage can acquire Lebanese nationality. This is usually justified by the legislator's wish to protect the unity of nationality of the family. Can the minor children of a Lebanese mother acquire Lebanese nationality after the death of the non-Lebanese husband? The answer is negative, as the courts have decided otherwise.

It seems illogical that a woman who is not Lebanese by birth should receive better treatment than a Lebanese woman married to a non-Lebanese. Here the justification of the unity of nationality of the family is completely disregarded. There is, therefore, a need for new legislation on nationality giving men and women similar rights in passing their Lebanese nationality on to their spouses and children.

Life Insurance

Another infringement on the legal capacity of women which requires new legislation is found in the provisions on life insurance in the Code of Obligations and Contracts. Lebanon's Code of Obligations and Contracts of 1932 copied the law from the old French Insurance Law of 1930, which was passed eight years before French women acquired full legal capacity in France.

The law requires that an insured person, who is the subject of a life insurance policy taken out by a third party, give his, or her, written consent; otherwise the insurance is considered null and void. This is the reason why the subject of a life insurance policy cannot be a Lebanese minor of less than 15 years, or one who is mentally insane, or one who is deprived of his civil rights (Articles 995 and 996).

In the case of a married woman who is the subject of a life insurance policy, the law requires express authorisation of the husband, exactly as in the case where the subject has been placed under guardianship. The law adds that such authorisation does not exempt the person with no legal capacity from giving consent, thus implicitly placing the woman in a position of having no legal capacity at all (Article 997).

Trading and the Married Woman

A further instance where the authorisation of the husband is required is found in the Code of Commerce (Articles 11–14) and concerns trading carried out by married women. Article 11 states:

> A married woman, whatever the provisions of her personal status, is legally qualified for trading only insofar as she obtains her husband's express or tacit consent.

> Tacit consent is presumed granted where trade is publicly carried out and manifest, and is carried out without the husband's opposition.

Consequently, the married woman who by law has full legal capacity becomes legally incapable of practising commerce or trading unless she obtains her husband's consent. If we bear in mind, as mentioned above, that the marriage of a woman, according to the Lebanese law, has no consequences upon her legal capacity, and that the system of community of property between husband and wife does not exist in Lebanon, the wife's trading activities should normally be of no consequence to her husband's property.

It becomes harder to understand why a woman who, before her marriage, had full legal capacity to carry out commercial activities should lose the capacity upon marriage, and regain it if the marriage ends.

Once the husband grants consent, the married woman enjoys unrestricted legal capacity to carry on her business, unfettered (Article 13). However, Article 12 provides that consent may be revoked by the husband, for "just motives", subject to "judicial control" if need be. The woman can object by taking her case to court, which can examine the alleged "just motives" and take a decision.

We should note here that the law mentions "just motives" and "judicial control" in the case of the revocation of the husband's consent, but not in the case of his refusal at the time of the initial request for his agreement. Two reasons are usually given to justify this differentiation. Firstly, at the time of the revocation of consent an enterprise may be in existence, and an abrupt cessation of business would affect the rights of third parties involved. Secondly, where there is ongoing commercial activity, the courts can study the facts of the case and take a decision, while in the case of initial refusal the judge would have no facts to consider. The husband in the latter case is deemed to be better qualified than the judge (or the wife) to decide on his wife's ability to run a business.

Lebanese courts have ruled that there are "just motives" when the family of the married woman trader lives in a house that she owns, as the possible losses of her commercial activities could jeopardise the safety of the house and the security of the family; "just motive" was also found where a married woman is likely to be subject to criminal sanctions as a consequence of her trading.

There are two cases were the consent of the husband cannot be retracted: if the married woman is a partner in a partnership or if the married woman is a financial partner in a limited partnership (Article 13). In these two cases, the married woman must first have the specific authorisation of her husband, and such an authorisation, once given, cannot be retracted. It is argued that the partners must be protected from the sudden moods of the husband, as they would be personally, jointly and severally responsible for the liability of the company.

In their authoritative Annotated Code of Commerce, Professors Fabia and Safa explain the principle of the husband's consent for his wife to practise commerce as being rooted in social and moral considerations of the husband as the *Pater Familias*, who must be in a position to decide that the activity of his wife as a trader might jeopardise the interests of the family. As well as the odd equation of married women with the insane and minors, this explanation is difficult to sustain in view of the fact that a married woman can undertake to work in any other lucrative profession, without the permission of her husband, and can also carry out individual commercial acts without his permission (i.e. sell, buy, mortgage, etc.).

A draft legislation which was to do away with those articles of the Commercial Code suggests replacing Article 11 with the following provisions:

> A married woman can practise commerce freely, unless her husband objects in writing. In such a case the married woman can take her case to Court within 30 days of being notified of the objection. Failure to do so within the 30-day period will cause her to lose the right.

This is similar to the old French law of 1942, which was itself replaced by the law of 1960. It clearly remains insufficient.[1]

Criminal Law

The most striking statutory discrimination against women is found in the Lebanese Criminal Law (Code Pénal) with regard to adultery and crimes of "honour".[2]

Adultery

Under Lebanese law the concept of adultery operates differently according to gender. Three elements define adultery in the case of a woman: (i) sexual intercourse with someone other than her spouse; (ii) existence of marriage; (iii) criminal intention.

For a man there are two different elements: Sexual intercourse with someone other than the spouse *in the conjugal house*; or openly taking a concubine. Thus, if a married man commits adultery with a married woman *outside the conjugal house*, then he is not legally considered to have committed adultery, whereas the woman involved would have done so. The man is therefore not liable for his act, while the woman is.

If a married man has committed adultery outside his conjugal home, he is only criminally liable if there is an element of repetition, which results from his taking a concubine, and if such adultery is publicly known. A married woman, in contrast, is considered to have committed adultery even if this is done in secret, outside the conjugal home, and only once. Another result of the law is that there is no adultery if the man has sexual relations with various and numerous women; or repeatedly with the same woman, unless it is publicly known.

The penalty for adultery also varies depending on gender: For the wife who commits adultery, the penalty is imprisonment from 3 months to 2 years. For the husband who commits adultery, the penalty is imprisonment from 1 month to 1 year. Furthermore, the man who is the accomplice of an adulterous woman incurs a lesser penalty if he is not himself married; in contrast the woman accomplice of an adulterous man incurs the same penalty whether she is married or not.

There are obvious problems with this legislation, and it is interesting to note that Kuwait is the only Arab jurisdiction which does not distinguish between men and women with regard to adultery.

Crimes of honour (Article 562 Code Pénal)

If a man surprises his spouse, one of his female ascendants, his daughter or other female descendants, or his sister, in *flagrante delicto* with a third person, and then commits an unpremeditated homicide or deals an injury to any of the persons involved in the act, he can claim a defence and be acquitted.

If he surprises one of the above mentioned in an "ambiguous situation" with a third party, and he commits homicide or deals an injury to any of these persons, then he can profit from an attenuating excuse. In this case, however, the set penalty is greatly reduced. If the penalty is capital punishment then it is reduced to imprisonment of at least a year.

Such "excuses" are mandatory upon the court, unlike normal mitigating circumstances which are left to the discretion of the judge. The beneficiaries of such defences are husbands, male ascendants, male descendants and brothers.

Three elements trigger the application of Article 562 of the Code Pénal: (i) Surprise (i.e. previous unawareness of the relationship); (ii) *flagrante delicto* or ambiguous situation (both described restrictively in order to excuse the reaction of the offender); (3) committing the crime on the spot as a consequence of surprise and "loss of control". Once the three elements are fulfilled, a legal presumption arises on the temporary inability of the offender to distinguish between right and wrong.

It is interesting to note in this field that, except for Syria and Jordan, most Arab legislation include attenuating excuses, but not "excuses" involving acquittal; and most refer to adultery, and not to "ambiguous situations" , and then restrict the beneficiaries to direct relatives.

Conclusion

Antiquated Lebanese laws openly flout women's equal rights. But new laws, although essential as a first step, will not offer a miraculous solution. There is a deep social reluctance to accept the equality of men and women in many fields.

A common example is found in the inheritance process. According to the Muslim laws of inheritance, the share of a woman with a similar relationship to the deceased is often half that of a man. But even for non-Muslim Lebanese, whose inheritance laws establish in principle that women inherit equally to men, one finds in practice many cases where fathers go to any length to avoid their daughters inheriting equally with their sons.

The same incapacitating philosophy can be found in employment law, in which there are many restrictions to the work that women can undertake (such as mining, foundry work, brewing and distilling, driving heavy equipment, tarmac work, etc.); not surprisingly, the same restrictions apply to children, as the law tends to treat women like persons with no legal capacity, while the protection of their rights where it really matters (i.e. maternity leave, etc.), remains insufficient and backward.

Fortunately women lawyers have been practising freely for generations in Lebanon, and are aware, from within, of the shortcomings of the law. That is not to say that they do not occasionally encounter discrimination from their male colleagues: we have yet to see the election of a woman Bâtonnier at the head of the Beirut and Tripoli bars.

NOTES

1 Editor's note: Since this chapter was completed, the legislator has amended all three articles by bringing total equality between genders in commercial life. Article 11 now states that "the married woman possesses entire capacity to conduct commercial activities." (Law 380 of 4 Nov. 1994, Official Journal Add. to 45, 10 Nov. 1994, 3).

2 See generally the comparative analysis of Lama Abu-Odeh in Chapter 7 of this book.

FIFTEEN

ISLAMIC FAMILY LEGISLATION: THE AUTHORITARIAN DISCOURSE OF SILENCE

Najla Hamadeh

The concurrence of religious and political powers in the Islamic world in waging a relentless war against democracy and freedom of expression awaken suspicions that they share similar aims. When political authorities impose silence and threaten those who break it, the subjects resent but understand this as an ancient strategy of those in power to exclude anyone else from it. When such political powers formulate ideologies that attempt to justify their tactics, people easily see through them recognising them as hypocritical and flimsy coverings for the apparent greed and self-serving manoeuvres. But how do people react to religious authorities when they follow the same policy, wearing similar transparent ideological garments, especially when the doctrine of the religion in whose name they rule happens to be, like that of Islam, one that encourages and insists upon the pursuit of learning, thinking and dialogue, the very activities that these authorities try to pre-empt or fight.

The status that Islamic family law assigns to women and the deterioration of this status with the passage of time, encourages the suspicion that those who pose as representatives of the schools of law (*madhaheb*) often chose to overlook the morally egalitarian and sensibly moderate spirit of the sources of Islamic law, namely the Qur'an and the *sunna*. They appear to espouse the cause of patriarchal power by magnifying the advantages that these sources confer on men while ignoring the advantages and rights that the same sources bestour on women. One indication of the representatives of the *madhaheb* being moved by thirst for power, rather than a genuine desire to uphold God's *shari'a*, is the fact that, while pretending to guard matters as they are, behind the closed doors of *ijtihad*, they actually slipped, gradually, in the direction that privileged oppressors often take, i.e. that of giving themselves, their gender in this case, more and more privileges and taking more and more of the rights that Islam and its early practice gave to women.[1]

It is true that Islam permits and encourages people in general, and those better versed in religion in particular, to be involved in political life. But certainly the aim of such encouragement is to temper political activity by giving it spiritual content that counters the forces of self-interest, not to use religion for self-interest, which is the hallmark of *realpolitik*. An appropriate test of whether or not those who speak in the name of religion are doing their religious duty in the political field is to observe whether they take the side of the people, especially those with less rights than religion allocates to them, or the side of political power. Such a test would show that the predominant trend in the Islamic world is for men of religion to espouse the cause of political power. For, instead of promoting discussion and genuine involvement in religious matters they join forces with the totalitarian regimes, to make sure that the power they hold at present should persist across successive generations. In trying to secure their authority over the Muslim multitudes, both endeavour to shut the door firmly on discussion, criticism and possible dissent.

This paper limits itself to discussion of the two laws by means of which women are prevented from getting a divorce or annulments of their marriage contracts, when they so wish, and are denied custody of their children, beyond a certain age (between two and nine years, depending on the gender of the child and the *madhhab* of the family). The paper deals with the general trend in Islamic family law rather than with specific details that vary between schools of law. I argue that the two laws in question have been imposed on people and protected by enforced silence that allows authoritarian regimes to rule at their pleasure, unchecked either by common sense or by realities. I shall point out that while purporting to derive these laws from the Qur'an and *sunna*, religious jurists (all of them men) twist the sacred sources in directions that suit their own purposes while silencing the voices of dissent. I shall start my discussion with an example about the relationship between silence and untruths.

A Conspiracy of Silence

To illustrate the difference in attitudes and beliefs that stem from the imposition of silence on people or allowing them self-expression, one may cite the different views held about the question of whether or not a mother makes a contribution to the traits of her child. In ancient democratic Athens, notwithstanding that society's regard for freedom of speech and argumentation, the imposition of silence on women and their exclusion from democratic life permitted Aristotle to claim that the mother contributes only matter, but no form, to the foetus in her womb.[2] In contrast, the ancient Arabs, pre-Islamic and early Muslims, whose community at that time enjoyed a more universal access to self-expression than that of Aristotle's Athens, acknowledged the mother's contribution to traits inherited by their offspring.[3] Thus, even the great Aristotle, famous for seeking rational as well as empirical truth, argued against clearly observable evidence, that is of the resemblance between mother and child. Women's enforced silence enabled him to glorify his own gender at the expense of the "other" gender. It is interesting to note, in this connection, that at later, indeed recent, periods in Arab history, when women were silenced and stripped of their rights, public opinion reverted to a position similar to that of Aristotle. This is apparent in the popular sayings that compare women to closets and storage spaces out of which the husband gets what he has deposited. The "Aristotelian" view became influential in some Islamic schools of legislation, leading to the stipulation that as a woman is like a field owned by the husband any child she bears, even by another man, belongs to him. The fact that the science of genetics confirms the woman's contribution to (and thus right over) the child she brings into the world, is not a guarantee that her right be recognised. A more reliable basis for acknowledging her right would be her contribution to the discourse that affects her society.

History abounds with examples that indicate that whenever silence was imposed on women, or any other group for that matter, it has led to erroneous and self-contradictory views about them, which in turn has led to the build-up of traditions as well as laws detrimental to them.[4] Similarly, Islamic legislators have opted for an interpretation of Islam that gives a capricious and unrealistic portrayal of the female nature and diminishes the rights Islam allocates to women, ignoring not only the dictates of common sense, but also the spirit, and sometimes the explicit sense, of the Qur'anic text as well as the generally accepted facts about the life of the Prophet. In order to perpetuate such an interpretation, the voices of women jurists, and those who engage in dialogue about Islam, were progressively silenced.[5] Thus, at the time of the Prophet and the caliphs who followed his example, women could speak up and could influence public opinion and religious interpretation; but nowadays women's contribution to the legal and religious life of the Islamic community is being blocked and pre-empted by various techniques and strategies, not least of which is the claim that the woman's voice is a *'awrah* to be hidden from the ears of the public just as her body must be hidden from public view.

A Woman's Right to Divorce

It is clear that the issue of whether women possess human souls or not does not arise in the Qur'an. Indeed, the Qur'an gives women political and social rights and duties and subjects them, like men, to judgement, promising them reward or punishment.[6] All this implies that women have rationality and discrimination and that they are capable of pleasure and pain and that therefore they naturally seek the former and avoid the latter, in this life and in the next. Yet, Islamic family law treats the wife as a creature of undiscerning needs, whose feelings and preference can be totally ignored, and whose judgement is, in many ways, suspended or disregarded.

For most Sunni groups the actual state of the law where divorce is concerned, is that a man can divorce his wife by simply saying: "I divorce thee" and inform the authorities later. But, even if he doesn't inform anyone, the wife is considered to be divorced by virtue of this statement.[7] For most Muslim groups, a husband may take back his wife without her consent or that of her guardian during the legal *'iddah* (period that must lapse before divorce becomes absolute).[8]

The wife has a mediated right to annul the marriage through a civil court (or a family court), only if her husband suffers from one of the few major specified defects. Her right is a silent and passive one, mediated through a judge and subject to his ruling. In Jaafari (Shi'a) communities, freeing a wife from an unwilling husband, no matter what her reasons are, is almost impossible. Under almost all forms of Islamic family law, there is no way out of a marriage for a woman whose husband refuses to let her go; she and her family are often found trying to bribe the husband with money and property to coax him into divorcing his wife.

Islamic family laws make divorce extremely easy for men, regardless of the Prophet's *hadith* that describes divorce as "abhorrent" to God. They make it extremely difficult for women, disregarding the Qur'anic stipulation, "Women have such honourable rights as obligations"[9] (II, 229), and the Qur'anic command, "Do not retain them [your wives] by force, to transgress [against their rights]" (II, 228). Strangely, the Qur'anic stipulation and command seem to be read to mean that the wife has no practical, moral or emotional rights beyond the right to food to sustain her, a roof over her head and a "right" to have sex with her husband, one which is severely circumscribed by the fact that she is duty-bound to acquiesce, whenever the fancy takes him, regardless of her wishes. (Can one call this a right?) Her other explicit rights, such as the right to work and to dispose of her property as she sees fit, are impeded or rendered void by the husband's right to total obedience on her part. Even her political and social duties, doing what is right and forbidding what is wrong (see Qur'an IX, 71) are rendered meaningless by the claim that her obedience to her husband should almost be total, and will only be suspended if he demands of her to disobey God!

The understanding of the marriage contract, as implied by the laws governing divorce, is that it is a contract that turns a free woman, whose consent is required for her marriage, into one, not just bound to the husband, but living in bondage that she can never revoke by her own will. This being so, common sense and moral responsibility should prevent any woman from agreeing to get married. For just as a living person transgresses when he/she commits suicide, a free person must be considered a transgressor when he/she accepts bondage.[10] The state of Islamic family law frightens women by allowing them no escape from a marriage that does not work. It puts them totally at the mercy of their husbands, who, as experience shows, may be good and gentle men (rulers) who grant their wives divorce when they so wish, or tyrants who elect to keep them on precisely because they want to be liberated. Thus, when Muslim wives are not experiencing their marriage as a reign of terror, this is certainly not because of the protection the law accords them, but because of other factors such as the husband's temperament or rationality, but above all, because of his observance of the moral codes of Islam, that are often found to be at odds with the family legal codes.

Moreover, the Islamic family laws governing divorce are not in harmony with what is generally known about the life of the Prophet. The Prophet considered a wife's disinclination to be his wife as tantamount to breaking the marriage contract, as happened with Amrah bint Yazeid al-Kilabiyyah, on their wedding night. Moreover these laws are not in line with the principle implicit in the Prophet's acceptance of the marriage proposal made to him by Khadija. The implied principle here is that women can initiate marriage by their independent will, and, as a corollary, it may be argued that women can end the marriage on their own initiative. The fact that Sukainah, the Prophet's great-granddaughter, stipulated in her marriage contract that she retain the titular right of divorce, together with the precedent of Khadija and Amrah, offers Muslim society enough leeway to revise the existing family laws. In fact, these precedents impose on it the duty to recognise the wife's will and her right to decide her own fate in this most crucial and most intimate aspect of her life, especially since the Qur'an, though giving the husband the right to divorce his wife, nowhere denies such a right to the wife.

Modern writers who want to keep things as they are in family laws, romanticise Muslim family life by depicting Muslim men as enamoured husbands who energetically seek their wives' favours, sacrificing money and comfort in the process.[11] Other writers, with similar aims, claim that harmony pervades Muslim family life, unlike the situation prevailing in families in the West.[12] Even if such portrayals were true about the prevalent state of affairs, it is to be kept in mind that the function of the law is to deter, not nice people and doting husbands, but transgressors and criminals. The law is there to protect the weak from the tyranny of the strong, when the latter choose to use their power to oppress the former. By putting powerful legal weapons in the hands of *every* husband, no matter what his mental or moral qualities happen to be, the wife is left at the mercy of her luck; and family law which is supposed to protect the weaker member in the marriage, does the opposite, leaving her in a precarious position.

Those who argue that women should not have the right to divorce, or otherwise end the marriage, base their arguments on two claims:

1. The claim that divorce is both acceptable and in harmony with nature when willed by husbands, but wrong and unnatural and even irrational when willed by wives.

2. The claim that women are more likely to rush into divorce, when they have the right to do so, than are men, because of women's emotional (irrational) nature.

The fallacy of female incompetency to divorce

Some authors decry divorce, often pointing to family instability in the West as a living proof of the soundness of their position.[13] Yet, if divorce is not desirable, why is it made so easy for men? Western societies have a religious background that prohibits divorce; but because they have judged the misery caused by divorce to be a lesser evil than the misery caused by having to persevere in an unwanted marriage, they have decided to make divorce available, albeit with some difficulty, for those who want it. In this, the stance of Western societies is similar to that of Islam which permits divorce while describing it as "abhorrent" to God. By allowing men very easy access to divorce, Islamic family law departs from this reasonable stance shared by sources of Islam and by Western legal systems. It also departs from the two converging lines of reasoning, but in the opposite direction, by denying women access to getting out of a marriage they no longer want. Thus, the wisdom of God and of human legislation in democratic, and hence reasonable societies, see divorce as a necessary evil, that becomes acceptable only if the alternative is marital misery; and Islamic jurisprudence stands alone in making divorce sometimes too easy and sometimes too difficult.

In order to justify this double standard, Mutahhari claims that the nature of men and women and of the relationship between them dictates that divorce should conform to Islamic jurisprudence.[14] Since a woman's love is natural only when it comes about as a consequence of a man's love but unnatural when she initiates it, a "natural" divorce is one initiated by a man, and "unnatural" when it is initiated by a woman. One may say, faced with such reasoning, that if it is unnatural for women to initiate marriage or end it they need not be stopped from doing so. Moreover, it is a reasoning that is reminiscent of, for example, white Americans claiming that Afro-Americans are incapable of learning, when there is no schooling for the latter.

The fallacy of female inadequacy to divorce

The other argument used to justify denying the woman's right to end her marriage is that women's nature with its stronger emotionality (and weaker rationality) would multiply the divorce rate as women would resort to divorce at the simplest provocation. Thus, al-Asfi fears that if women were allowed access to divorce, it would be occurring over disagreements about trivial issues like the colour of a dress.[15] Mutahhari fears that if given this right a women would, as happens in America and Europe, divorce a husband on the ground that he did not kiss the dog or did not like the movie she liked.[16] Bin Murad says: "*Shari'a*'s putting divorce in the hand of the man, and his divorcing his wife a thousand times a day, is better than what happens in America."[17] And al-Ibsheehi advises his daughter, equally without rational grounds, that even if her husband was to be as ruthless and cruel as the Pharaohs of Egypt she should bear and accept her burden.[18]

The "rationality" of the above arguments together with the hundreds of examples in Muslim society's memory of men who use the divorce oath, for example, to pressure a friend to have dinner with them ("If you don't come to dinner, my wife will be divorced") makes such claims to the rationality of men versus the emotionality of women empty and groundless. It is ironic that while claiming that women are more emotional and men more rational, our Muslim societies allow men to indulge in gratifying emotional and sensual desires and exact from women the utmost of rational self-restraint and self-denial. Moreover, the so-called "emotionality" of women, as in her love for her children, may prove to be a powerful deterrent against the break-up of the family, as this would harm her children. Furthermore, those who claim that when both partners in a marriage have legal access to divorce, women's initiation of the procedure will be the more frequent, do not support their claim by any statistics from societies which practise this type of legal equality. Leila Ahmed maintains in her research that divorce occurs more frequently at the instigation of men rather than women.[19] But, apologists for Islamic family law say whatever they please, confident that whatever they say will pass unchallenged, because of the imposition of silence on voices of genuine discussion which might serve the cause of equity and justice.

If allowed to be heard, the voices of fairness and common sense would hardly fail to tell us that some men and some women, in any society, may initiate divorce, when they have it within their power to do so, for good reasons or for trivial reasons. The claim that Muslim men are above divorcing their wives for trivial reasons, and that Muslim women are "beneath" seeking divorce for good reasons, is neither reasonable nor empirically justified.

The Buyer and his Acquisition

In order to justify treating women as owned objects, Islamic family law emphasises the man's obligation to support his wife financially, twisting this stipulation of the Qur'an in such a way as to render the man's other obligations much less important than the right that accrues from it. In this way, a husband's obligation to support his wife becomes his *only* obligation and her *only* right, rather than merely *one* of his obligations and *one* of her rights.

In line with the spirit of God's Law in the Qur'an, the rationale behind the stipulation that the wife is to be financially supported by her husband is to protect the family from insecurity and disruption when the mother, who is more crucially needed in the home, has to leave her children in order to earn a living. (The provision explicitly defines the male and female roles.) Bride price, *mahr*,[20] is another insurance against the abuse of women who have no other means of support or may be incapable of earning their living during pregnancy or the early years of child care. Financial support and *mahr* are rights of women which help to protect them and their children. But emphasis on materialistic values, while ignoring the other values that women contribute to the marriage, degrade the exchange between husband and wife, from an exchange of roles that complement one another, to a commercial transaction in which the man pays and the woman delivers, and by so doing, the woman forfeits her freedom, her rights, her worth and the dignity that the Qur'an and the Prophet bestowed on her.

Treating the marital relationship as one between buyer and his acquisition, as well as the contradictions inherent in the laws governing the rights and status of women, is reflected in the attitude to female sexuality. All schools of Islamic law acknowledge women's right to sexual pleasure, so much so that her permission is required for coitus interruptus so that her pleasure is not interrupted without warning.[21] Yet, legislators rule as though sexual relations are (a) a mechanical activity in which the woman's right to pleasure is a right to intercourse, where her will and inclination are not to be taken into consideration, (b) as though the relationship is a kind of commercial transaction, whereby the husband pays and the wife delivers. In both attitudes to sexual relations, women are not treated as free beings with specific inclinations and desires. In the former case, women are recipients of a right, but a right of an animalistic rather than a human nature; in the latter case, they are perceived as having an obligation to perform a service. Those who speak in that vein, make sexual pleasure the husband's right (not only in this life but also in Paradise) and its provision the wife's duty, thus contradicting the legal prescription that a wife has a right to sexual pleasure. Indeed, they assert that the wife's primary duty is to give pleasure to her husband, for which she is kept by him.[22] Family laws in Islam stipulate that disobeying the husband in providing him with sexual gratification is the primary reason for considering the wife disobedient (*nashiz*), a state for which she may incur various and progressive forms of chastisement.

Some writers apportion arbitrary characterisations to female sexuality and nature and offer unconvincing arguments for why such characteristics should lead to the conclusion that family laws should be
preserved as they are. For example, when Mutahhari says that women
have sexual drives greater than men's, but that they are endowed with a
greater ability to control them, he aims, not at granting what (according
to him) women's nature requires, but at depriving them from getting
gratification on the grounds of their superior self-control.[23]

Motherhood and its Muted Rights

It is remarkable how little is written about mothers and mothering in
books about the position or the rights of women in Islam. There are
volumes about the husband's dominance and the justification for it, about
the nature of the woman that justifies her subjugation, and even about
what part of her body she has to cover to ward off the damage that may
result from her *fitna* (seduction) but very little about her role of mothering. This is a strange oversight, an omission that can hardly be an innocent one, given the obvious fact that mothering is by far the dominant
preoccupation of most women, during most of their lives, compared
to which, their relationships with their husbands are almost always
secondary; and compared to mothering, *fitna*, the seductive allure, possessed by some women for a limited period of their lives, is a very minor
issue.

The value of mothering and the rights derived from it are far from
being ignored by the Qur'an or by the Prophet. The Qur'an emphasises in
several verses the rights of both parents over their children (IV, 35 and
XVII, 23–4 and XXXI, 14) and, in so doing, mothers' pains in carrying
the child to term and in nursing and rearing are particularly emphasised
(Qur'an XLVI, 15 and XXXI, 14). Moreover, the Tradition (*hadith*) of
the Prophet gives motherhood three times the recognition as fatherhood
as regards companionship and good treatment.[24] It gives priority in
custody to mothers, and relatives on the mother's side.[25] Indeed, the
Prophet himself was raised, after his father's death, by his mother (among
her own family) until her death.

Islamic family law, purporting to derive guidance from such sources,
gives custody to mothers for the first few years of the child's life (sometimes until the child is only two years old), after which the right of
custody belongs to the fathers, while all the recognition that the Qur'an

and Tradition give to motherhood is overlooked. As a result, mothers suffer deeply, and are often driven to sneak in to their children's schools to catch a glimpse of their young, who nature and Islam intended them to be close to their mothers. It is for the sake of depriving motherhood of its rights that books about women's rights in Islam are so silent about motherhood; and women are made to appear in books that support the present state of Islamic jurisprudence, to be continuously possessing *fitna* and always getting married or divorced, but rarely becoming mothers and growing to maturity.

Islamic family law's ruling that after the early years of a child's life custody should go to the father, purports to derive from the principle that the man's duty of spending on the family, gives the man precedence in everything, including child custody, even if the man is not actually supporting the child. Jurists argue whether custody is a right of the child or of the parent. They agree that in the early years it is a right of the child, and rule that during these years the child should stay with its mother. Some rule that after early childhood, custody becomes the right of the parents and accordingly, the right transfers automatically to the father, since men have dominance over women. Some claim that when the child's needs are more for education and moral cultivation, it is more in need of a father than a mother.[26] This is one of the many instances when insult is added to injury as far as women are concerned. For, the implication here is that the mother's role ends with nursing and physical care because women are incapable of moral and mental nurturing. Probably this was partially true about mothers who were deprived of education or even of learning about the world through experience since they were made to live as prisoners. But nowadays, when a high proportion of educators are women, and when women are exploring and experiencing life as men do, such a justification makes little sense.

In situations where parents are no longer together, it is best that the children stay with their mother and be protected by the father – should the need arise. It is a fact that fathers rarely spend much time with their children anyway, and to give custody to the father would result in the children being deprived of both parents.

The ruling of Islamic family law which gives custody to fathers stems from a misplaced and exaggerated emphasis on the general patriarchy of Muslim society which is recommended in the Qur'an, as in the passage: "Men have the right of dominance over women by the advantages that God has conferred on some of you more than on others and by what they spend" (IV, 134), and the passage: "Their men have a degree above them" (II, 228). Family law may also justify its ruling by the fact that the Islamic family is patrilinear, calling children after their fathers.

Male Spending and Female Rights

Giving total pre-eminence to the one responsible for financial support is not what is implied by the above-quoted Qur'anic statements. The verse (IV, 134), often used to justify not only men's dominance over women (patriarchy) in every domain, but also robbing women of most of their rights, places other criteria ("the advantages that God has conferred on some of you more than others") for dominance above the criterion of spending. A thoughtful reading of this verse should tell us that intelligence, moral uprightness, character, wisdom, education or works are also criteria that ought to lead to dominance. All these attributes[27], cannot be realistically claimed to be found in greater measure in every man than in every woman. Even if one is to make such an unreasonable claim (a claim which is constantly being challenged), it is impossible to claim that God prefers fatherhood to motherhood, which contradicts what the Prophet said on this subject, and does not agree with what is in the Qur'an. Indeed, the sources of Islam clearly designate parenting as the one area in which women are at least equal to men. Yet, Islamic family law makes of motherhood the area of women's greatest aggravation and vulnerability, causing every mother to feel threatened that her children may be taken away from her, and allowing this threat sometimes to become a reality.

Even where the criterion of spending is concerned, there exists variations between husband and wife, such as who spends on whom. This criterion may also be affected by factors like position in work or in society or lineage, all of which are conditions whose variation confers on the less advantaged spouse benefits that accrue from the association with the more advantaged spouse. Islam, as indeed does other codes of family law, makes the husband responsible for earning the family's living for convenience and not in order to dehumanise and denigrate the wife. That the right to be financially supported by the husband is one that women may claim, or may choose to forgo, is illustrated by the fact that the daughter of the Prophet, Fatima, accepted only a token of two silver pennies for her *mahr*; and his wife, Khadija, who was far better off than he, did not depend on him financially. If earning the family's bread gives all those advantages to husbands, why should such advantages persist when both husband and wife are earning, or when she is spending on him or even if she happens to have most of "the advantages that God has conferred on some of us more than others"?

Islamic family law does not concern itself with specific variations that may happen to benefit women. But, the wisdom of the Qur'an (as in IV, 34) and of the *sunna*, as indicated above, and other[28] examples from the life of the Prophet, allow scope for individual variations, and consequently, for variations in the conditions which govern society. Islam as it is practised, could then evolve to become compatible with logic and common sense and bring about moral equity, while continuing to obey and be inspired by the two basic sources of inspiration to which the Muslim community subscribes.

Patriarchy and Patrilinearity

Where the second verse commanding patriarchy is concerned, "Their men have a degree above them" (II, 228), Islamic family law seems to have multiplied the "degree" a hundred-fold. For, without disputing that Islam, like other monotheistic religions, is patriarchal, one can still ask why should "a degree" relegate women to a state of abject dependence on the husbands' goodwill and cost them all their rights, including the maternal ones that the Qur'an and the *hadith* honour and glorify? The men in charge of Islamic jurisprudence seem to have seized the opportunity afforded by the "degree" to stretch it to infinity; whereas if women had a chance to express themselves in open discussion, Islamic patriarchy would be the mildest in the world, with only one "degree" separating the status of wives from that of husbands.

The patrilinearity of families is a policy that, not only Islamic society, but most of the civilised societies in the world, have adopted. The wisdom backing this policy is not one that aims at relegating motherhood to second place, but one that aims at giving a role to fatherhood. Since nature has already secured the closest possible bond between mother and child, no heavenly emphasis and commands are required to bring it about. This is not the case in the relationship between father and child. The wisdom of the Qur'an, which is in tune with modern psychoanalysis and with the study of cultures, ensures the father's inclusion in the life of the family and commands him to take responsibility in raising his children. This inclusion has indisputable benefits. The husband's contribution remains beneficial provided it does not impinge on the more basic and indispensable relationship of mother and child. In fact, since the father's primary duty is financial, and since the duty of the child towards the father is originally symbolic (i.e. taking the father's name),[29] the father–child relationship does not necessarily depend on a continuous physical proximity as the child is growing up. This is not the case with the role of mothering, which cannot be carried out without the cohabitation of mother and child.

In the matter of custody, as well as in several other matters, actual practice and popular traditional and moral codes show much more wisdom than Islamic family law does. For, in reality most men realise that their children are better off living with their mothers; and public opinion is much harsher on a mother who leaves her children than when a father does. Thus, in practice the children of a broken marriage stay with their mothers, but the ruling of man-made Islamic law places a powerful weapon in the hands of the worst of men, the ones who are vindictive towards their ex-wives and negligent towards the welfare of their children. Such men are given the opportunity to wrench the children from their mothers, an act of cruelty and vengeance made legitimate and easy by the "wisdom" of family law.

It may be argued, within the Islamic context, that in their ruling about custody, the men who happened to be in a position to legislate did not take cognisance of the fact that by preventing a relationship much commended by religion – as conferring benefits in the afterlife on the mother for her care of the child, and on the child for showing respect and appreciation to its mother – they were blocking a way to Paradise that God has made available for mankind. Indeed the status that their legislation gives to women often encourages children, especially sons, to be disrespectful to their mothers, thus forfeiting the benefits religion promises the children when they are dutiful.[30] By putting all men in a position of dominance over all women, Islamic family law creates a serious conflict in the mother–son relationship. For the son – commanded by God to obey, honour and humble himself before his mother – when elevated by family law to become his own mother's guardian, who makes decisions on her behalf, and may in doing so oppose her will,[31] may find himself in a position where he is torn in opposite directions. Thus, the man-made laws make it difficult for the son to obey God's laws in his treatment of his mother. Indeed, since sons cannot split their personalities between dominance over and humility towards their mothers, there is a risk that they may disobey them, bully them and even beat them. By giving too much to the male, and taking too much away from the female, family law is morally responsible for all these woes.

Conclusion

By imposing an oppressive silence on the multitudes of Muslims, Islamic jurists have chosen to espouse the cause of totalitarian rule, which is contrary to the Prophet's practice and to characteristics commended by the Qur'an as belonging to those who "believe and put their trust in their Lord" (Qur'an XLII, 36). If this is a price that the men in charge of Islamic family law have consciously accepted to pay in order to preserve for their gender more privileges than God has already bestowed on them, then it is time that their authority be questioned. The fact that their actions have political consequences that encourage and reinforce totalitarian political systems, makes their actions doubly blameworthy in its departure from the ways recommended by God at the political and social levels.

Those of the Islamic community who genuinely wish to apply God's Law ought to restore Islamic family law to its true sources (the Qur'an and the *hadith*) and to initiate deliberation and discourse concerning the best procedures that will enable God's word to permeate and command human society. It is the duty of true Muslims to do this, not only in order to restore to Muslim women their rights, but also in order to remove blemishes on the image of Islam in the world caused by deviations, mis-interpretations, complacency and stagnant thought of some so-called jurists who think they are the sole defenders of God's Law and have mastery of its meaning.

Only God's word and God's wisdom are eternal and unchanging, appropriate for all time and all places. No human interpretation of God's Word can claim to attain the status of eternal wisdom. Indeed, if works of religious interpretation should come to an end on the pretence that the task is complete, the answer is that the task of interpreting God's wisdom could never cease.

Any discourse that closes upon itself is bound to ossify or die, for two reasons: (1) the continuous effort injected into a living discourse refines and enriches it by the ideas of numerous generations, while a closed discourse cannot benefit from the efforts and intelligence of more than one generation; (2) by arresting discourse and intimidating those who can effectively contribute to it, leaving the floor only for those who merely reiterate the age-old arguments, Islamic jurisprudence will fail to cope with changing conditions in a changing world. In fact, the im-position of silence ends up creating a greater need for silence, and those who have closed the discourse for their own benefit, feel more vulnerable as time wears on; as a result, they will oppose any criticism or attempts to reopen the debate, with even greater ferocity, using intimidation and fear. Just as political despots surround themselves with syncophants – who cause them to degenerate even further – religious oppressors attract mediocre supporters to fight off opposition, and by so doing, render the juridical monologue even more sterile. Probably one of the factors that brings oppressive religious authorities and political despots together is their realisation that people who are open to discussion and fervently seek it are too perspicacious to silence or to appease. So they shut them out and elect to converse amongst themselves.

When the Qur'an is silent about certain issues, such as women's rights to initiate divorce or to have custody of their children, the silence is unintended and so allows room for thought and choice of what is appropriate for different times. But when writers about Islamic family law maintain silence regarding women's rights and roles as mothers, when they disregard Qur'anic passages and the Traditions of the Prophet that protect women from husbands who hurt them by keeping them in a marriage they no longer want, these writers serve the cause of political oppression and the interest of those who appoint themselves, and their gender, the sole guardians of God's Law.

NOTES

1 See Hasan al-Turabi, *al-Mar'a bayna ta'alim al-deen wa taqaleed al-mujtama'* (Jeddah: Dar al-Saudiyyah, 1984) and Joseph Schacht, *Origins of Muhammadan Jurisprudence* (Oxford: Clarendon Press, 1950), pp. 182–3.

2 See Aristotle, *Generation of Animals*, trans. D. M. Balme (Oxford: Clarendon Aristotle Series, 1972), Book I, Chapter 21.

3 The Arabs, whose women had access to the community's discourse, unlike Athenian women, as is evidenced by their having included poets (al-Khansa'), queens (Arwah al-Sulaihiyah) and business women (Khadija, the Prophet's first wife) recognised that mothers contribute forming traits to their offspring. This is indicated by the many instances in Arabic poetry where self-aggrandisement includes pride in the poet's matrilinear as well as patrilinear descent. Moreover, in the famous love and war epic of Antar bin Shaddad the hero is said to have been denied marriage to his paternal cousin, Ablah, because his mother was a slave.

4 Popular opinion and prejudice has claimed that women are sexually insatiable and deficient in sexual desire; that they are less intelligent than men but more cunning; that they are emotional and deficient in rationality, yet more capable of self-control, while men are said to be more rational and less capable of controlling their lust. Moreover, while intelligent women were discouraged from expressing themselves (by burning them at the stake for being witches) they were said to be intellectually deficienct. The political silencing of women was coupled by the twentieth-century claim of psychoanalysis that female desire cannot be self-determined or object-directed because desire is formed through language, and female desire is naturally mute. Other such political theorising about blacks and other disadvantaged groups is quite common.

5 In al-Madaini, 'al-Murdifat min Quraish' in Abdul-Salam Haroun (ed.), *Nawadir al-makhtoutat* (2 Vols., Beirut: Dar al-Jeel, 1991), a number of vocal and influential women of the time of the Prophet are mentioned, and in Vol. 12 of Abdul-Rahman al-Sakhawi's *al-Daw' al-lami' fi a'yan al-qarn al-tasi'* (original manuscript 1497 AD), a large number of women who were learned and influential in matters of religious and religious-based legislation are acknowledged. Nowadays, such women do not exist; and the new Islamic revival is only teaching some women to be apologetic, justifying the way things are; and even this is done in closed circles. Real access for women to openly discuss matters of religion is totally denied. Indeed, even men who have platforms for such discussion, are barred from engaging in real debate about Islamic legislation by intimidation and fear, while those who have managed to gain a claim to "immutable religious authority" hide behind such persecution in complete safety.

6 See Qur'an (XVI, 97), (XXXIII, 35), (II, 195), (LVII, 11–12) and (IX, 71).

7 See Lois Beck and Nikkie Keddie (eds.), *Women in the Muslim World* (New Haven: Yale University Press, 1978), p. 57.

8 Ibn Taimiyah's *Fiqh al-nisa'*, was explained and commented upon by al-Sayyid

al-Jamili (Beirut: Dar al-Fiqr, 1989), p. 171.

9 This and all subsequent citations are from Arthur Arberry's interpretation of the Qur'an (London: Oxford University Press, 1964).

10 The option to make choices that one cannot go back on is discussed in Jean Paul Sartre's *Critique of Dialectical Reason*, where it is found to be an option that inevitably leads to a "reign of terror". The Islamic marriage contract terrorises only women, since men can revoke the contract at will, and very easily.

11 Murtada Mutahhari, *Nizam huquq al-mar'a fi al-Islam*, trans. Haidar al-Haidar, 2nd edn (Beirut: al-Dar al-Islamiyya, 1991), pp. 182–4.

12 Muhammad al-Salih bin Murad, *al-Hidad 'ala imra'at al-Haddad* (Tunis, 1931), pp. 186–7.

13 See Muhammad Mahdi al-Asfi, *al-'Ilaqat al-jinsiyah fi al-Qur'an al-Kareem* (Najaf: No'man, 1968) and Bin Murad, *al-Hidad 'ala imra'at al-Haddad* and Muhammad Muhammad Ali al-Ibsheehi, *Rasa'il ila ibnati* (Beirut: Mu'assaset al-Risalah, 1981).

14 Mutahhari, *Nizam,* pp. 182–4.

15 al-Asfi, *al-'Ilaqat*, pp. 218–20.

16 Mutahhari, *Nizam*, p. 273.

17 Bin Murad, *al-Hidad*, pp. 186–7.

18 al-Ibsheehi, *Rasa'il*, pp. 112–13.

19 Leila Ahmed, *Women and Gender in Islam* (New Haven: Yale University Press, 1992), p. 106

20 The English term "bride-price" implies the sale of the wife; whereas the Arabic term "*mahr*" has a wider meaning that varies between "token" and "compensation".

21 See Basim Musallam, *Sex and Society in Islam* (Cambridge: Cambridge University Press, 1983), pp. 31–4.

22 Shahla Haeri, *Law of Desire: Temporary Marriage in Shi'i Iran* (Syracuse, N.Y.: Syracuse University Press, 1989), p. 38.

23 Mutahhari, *Nizam*, p. 183.

24 In al-Bukhari, *Kitab al-adab* (Cairo: Matba'at al-Sha'b), in the chapter on who has the first right of good companionship, he tells that a man asked the Prophet, "Who among people is the most deserving of my good companionship?" The Prophet answered: "Your mother." The man asked "And who deserves it next?" The Prophet said: "Your mother." The man inquired: "And who after that?" Muhammad answered: "Your mother". The man asked: "And after that?" Muhammad answered: "Your father." This *hadith* is also recorded in Muslim, *Sahih Muslim*, Vol. 8 (10 Vols., Beirut: Dar al-Fikr, 1972), p. 102.

25 See Abu al-Yakzan Atiyah al-Jabbouri, *al-Hadith al-sharif wa ahkamah* (Cairo: Dar al-Ansar, 1978), p. 89.

26 al-Jabbouri, *al-Hadith al-sharif*, p. 89.

27 Aside from the most important criterion, according to which God in Islam prefers one person to another, namely the fear of God (*taqwah*).

28 The fact that the Prophet, while recommending the payment of *mahr* and the husband's spending on his wife, and while permitting polygyny, did not necessarily stick to these practices in his own life (the *mahr* of Fatima was nominal, Khadija was initially the Prophet's employer, and he did not allow his son-in-law 'Ali to marry other wives than his own daughter Fatima) indicate: (1) That family laws are

stipulations that allow variation in implementation and include forms that can be improved upon; (2) that the spirit of Islamic law is to serve mankind, as Jesus' saying suggests: "The sabbath is made for man and not man for the sabbath." This line of thinking would lead to the conclusion that human happiness and virtuous living are, to God, more sacred than laws, made originally for man's convenience. Such laws lose their value when they stop promoting happiness and virtue in the life of human society.

29 There is a Qur'anic command concerning this (XXXIII, 5). In the modern context, Jacques Lacan explains the crucial role that psychoanalysis assigns to the name of the father in structuring the personality of the child so that it is equipped to live in society. Lacan talks of the importance of according respect for "the name of the father". (See, for example, Wilfried Ver Eecke, 'Phenomenology and Paternal Metaphor', *Phenomenology and Psychoanalysis*, 1988.

30 In the *hadith* of the Prophet recorded in *Sahih Muslim*, Vol. 8, pp. 104–6, sons whose parents are alive are advised to stay with them so as to reap more benefits in God's eyes than they would if they were to fight for the cause of Islam.

31 Lebanese law exonerates or greatly reduces the blame of a son who kills his mother for her sexual misbehaviour. "The man who finds his wife or one of his roots or descendants or sister in a situation of adultery . . . is a beneficiary of the exonerating excuse." See Laure Mughayzil, *al-Mar'a fi al-tashri' al-lubnani* (Beirut: Mu'assaset Nawfal, 1985).

Sixteen

The Women's Convention in the Muslim World

Jane Connors

Introduction

The Convention on the Elimination of All Forms of Discrimination Against Women[1] (The Women's Convention), which entered into force on 3 September 1981, was drafted by the Commission on the Status of Women in the early years of the United Nations Decade for Women. Its origins lay in the perception that despite the efforts of the United Nations to promote equality of rights between women and men through both the legal norm of non-discrimination[2] and specific treaties concerning women,[3] extensive discrimination against women continued to exist. Such discrimination it was believed, as the Convention's Preamble States, "violates the principles of equality of rights and respect for human dignity, is an obstacle to the participation of women, on equal terms with men, in the political, social, economic and cultural life of their countries, hampers the growth of the prosperity of society and the family, and makes more difficult the full development of the potentialities of women in the service of their countries and humanity".

In essence, the Women's Convention constitutes an elaboration of the legal norm of non-discrimination on the basis of sex, with specific provisions concerning matters where gender discrimination is most marked. It obliges States parties to eliminate discrimination in the enjoyment of all civil, polit-ical, economic, social and cultural rights, not only in public, but in private life. Obligations imposed extend beyond the elimination of discrim-ination, however, and require the establishment of the means to eliminate discrimination. States parties agree, thus, to initiate constitutional, legislat-ive, administrative and other measures, while, most importantly, States con-tract not only to address discrimination entrenched de jure, but also de facto.[4]

Despite the comprehensive obligations imposed on States parties by its terms, the Women's Convention has experienced little difficulty in attracting ratifications. It entered into force less than two years after its adoption by the General Assembly, faster than any previous human rights convention had come into force. At 18 January 1995, 139 countries had deposited instruments of ratification or accession with the Secretary-General of the United Nations. While the speed and rate of commitment of States to the Women's Convention have been pleasing, such commitment has been more apparent than real, as this treaty, more than any other, has been plagued by reservations. As of January 1995, 42 States parties had made reservations or declarations on ratification, accession or signature. Some of these are essentially procedural, generally concerning article 29, which provides for the jurisdiction of the International Court of Justice for the settlement of disputes arising out of the Convention. A significant number are, however, substantive and, as one commentator has suggested, go "to the heart of both values of universality and integrity"[5] in international human rights law generally and in that relating to women in particular.

A number of scholars have devoted attention to the general content of the reservations to the Women's Convention and their legality in international law.[6] Despite the fact that the most notorious reservations to the Women's Convention have been made by countries who apply, to a greater or lesser extent, the Islamic *shari'a*, there has been little analysis of the participation of those countries in the preparation and elaboration of the treaty and the meaning of their reservations. Further, very few commentators have examined the question of whether the reservations made by these countries are, in fact, required by the *shari'a*.

What follows thus seeks to review the participation of these countries in the Women's Convention generally. It will commence with an account of the attitude of these countries in the preparation of the treaty in order to set the context for subsequent reservations by them. It will go on to consider how countries who apply the *shari'a* and who are States parties to the Women's Convention have approached their obligations with respect to it. Finally, it will seek to assess how far reservations by countries who apply the *shari'a* are required by Islamic law and how far such reservations are a product of ideology.

Participation of "Islamic" Countries in the Preparation of the Treaty

The Women's Convention was preceded by a Declaration on the Elimination of Discrimination Against Women. This had been drafted following the unanimous adoption of a resolution in November 1963 calling for its preparation which had been sponsored by 22 developing and Eastern European States.[7] It is of interest to note that the sponsors of this resolution included Afghanistan, Algeria, Indonesia, Morocco and Pakistan, all predominantly Muslim countries. Thirty-three governments, fifteen non-governmental organisations and four UN specialised agencies responded to the resolution's request to send comments and proposals to the Secretary-General. Of the government respondents seven – Afghanistan, Iraq, Morocco, Sudan, Syria, Turkey and the United Arab Republic (Egypt) – were comprised of predominantly Muslim inhabitants.[8]

Afghanistan's response indicated that overcoming discrimination required "combating of traditions, customs and usages which thwart the advancement of women", recommended that "intense educational efforts" to enlighten public opinion should be initiated and suggested that "amends must be made to women by granting them certain privileges".[9] The United Arab Republic's response stressed equality in nationality and domicile, aid to widows and divorcees and educational campaigns to overcome discriminatory customs and traditions. Drafting of the Declaration, by a committee selected from within the Commission on the Status of Women,[10] began in 1965, with the Declaration ultimately adopted by the General Assembly in November 1967.[11]

Areas of controversy that emerged during this process was whether the Declaration should call for the *abolition* of customs and laws perpetuating discrimination or for the modification or change of those customs or laws and the approach to be taken with respect to women's legal capacity. As the instrument was a declaration – a statement of moral and political intent, with no contractual force – and its implementation mechanism consisted merely of country reports to the Commission on the Status of Women – unanimity, even on article 2, which called for all appropriate means to be deployed to abolish existing discriminatory laws, customs, regulations and practices, was achieved.

The preparation of the Convention was an entirely different matter, with seven years elapsing between the initial proposal from the Commission on the Status of Women,[12] to its final adoption by the General Assembly. The text was prepared by working groups within the Commission on the Status of Women and then considered in what Roberta Jacobson[13] describes as "long and painful" deliberations by a working group of the Third Committee from 1977 to 1979. Much time was spent on the preamble which has been described by one commentator as "diverging further from the central issue – the elimination of discrimination against women – than does the preamble to any other human rights treaty",[14] while a full week was spent debating articles 15 and 16 which give women equal capacity and equality under marriage and family law.

In the event, the final Third Committee vote on the resolution sending the Convention to the General Assembly was 112 to 1 (Mexico). Thirteen States, including Morocco, Saudi Arabia and Yemen abstained.[15] The voting pattern on the draft Convention in the General Assembly the next day, however, is perhaps more instructive and, to a great extent, predictive of reservations. Paragraph 2 of article 9 granting women equal rights to convey nationality to their children was carried by a vote of 92 to 13, with 28 abstentions, those voting against the article predominantly constituting countries of the Middle East and those abstaining including other Muslim countries, such as Afghanistan. Paragraph 1(c) of article 16 covering equal rights and responsibilities during marriage and at its dissolution was passed by a vote of 104 to 0, with 32 abstentions, primarily drawn from the Muslim world. The final vote, however, was 130 – 0 with 11 abstentions. These included Bangladesh, Djibouti, Mauritania, Morocco and Saudi Arabia.[16]

Pattern of Ratification and Reservation

As at 18 January 1995, those countries with predominantly Muslim populations who had ratified or acceded to the Women's Convention were – in order of ratification – Egypt (18 September 1981), Yemen (30 May 1984, such ratification being made by the former Democratic People's Republic of Yemen), Indonesia (13 September 1984), Bangladesh (6 November 1984), Tunisia (20 September 1985), Turkey (20 December 1985), Iraq (13 August 1986), Libyan Arab Jamahiriya (16 May 1989), Jordan (20 June 1992), Maldives (1 June 1993), Morocco (21 June 1993), Tajikistan (26 October 1993) and Kuwait (2 September 1994).[17] Of these, all, except Tajikistan, have entered reservations to the treaty.[18]

Although framed variously, the reservations of all, except Indonesia (the most populous Muslim nation in the world) Turkey and Yemen, relate to the preservation of Islamic law, the *shari'a*, to a greater or lesser degree in matters of personal law, including the law of succession, in those countries. Before examining those reservations based on the preservation of Islamic law, it is convenient to consider the reservations of Indonesia, Turkey and Yemen.

The reservations of both Indonesia and Yemen concern article 29(1) of the Convention which allows reference of any dispute concerning the interpretation or application of the Convention to the International Court of Justice. Both these States indicate that they do not consider themselves bound by the article, with Indonesia taking the position that any dispute relating to the interpretation or application of the Convention may only be submitted to arbitration or to the International Court of Justice with the agreement of all the parties to the dispute. These reservations are compatible with article 29(2) which allows a State party to declare that it does not consider itself bound by article 29(1).

Turkey's reservations relate to article 29(1) and also to various paragraphs of articles 15 and 16 which it considers incompatible with the provisions of the Turkish Civil Code. In particular, it reserves with respect to paragraphs 2 and 4 of article 15, the former obliging States parties to accord to women, in civil matters, a legal capacity identical to that of men and the same opportunities to exercise that capacity, specifically in the context of the conclusion of contracts and the administration of property and the latter requiring States parties to accord men and women the same rights in relation to the movement of persons and the freedom to choose residence and domicile. It reserves, further, with respect to paragraphs 1(c), (d), (f) and (g) of article 16, which oblige States parties to take measures to eliminate discrimination in family life and, in particular, to ensure that men and women have the same right to enter into marriage, the same rights and responsibilities as parents, irrespective of their marital status in matters relating to their children, the same rights and responsibilities with regard to guardianship, wardship, trusteeship and adoption of children and the same personal rights as husband and wife, including the right to choose a family name, a profession and an occupation. Turkey has also entered an interpretative "declaration" seeking to preserve articles 15 and 17 of the Turkish Law on Nationality, which it interprets as consistent with articles 9(1) and 5(1) of the Women's Convention,[19] its view being that the intent of the domestic nationality provisions which regulate the acquisition of citizenship through marriage is not to discriminate on the basis of sex, but to prevent statelessness.

Bangladesh, Tunisia, Iraq, the Libyan Arab Jamahiriya, Jordan, Maldives, Morocco and Kuwait[20] have each entered reservations which are justified on the basis of the *shari'a*. The reservations are, however, different and vary importantly in their specificity. The widest has been entered by the Maldives. This indicates that "the Government of the Republic of the Maldives will comply with the provisions of the

Convention, except those which the government may consider contradictory to the principles of the Islamic Shariah upon which the laws and traditions of the Maldives are founded." It adds that the Republic of the Maldives does not see itself bound by any provision of the Convention which obliges it to change its constitution and laws in any manner. The Libyan Arab Jamahiriya, similarly, indicates that its accession is subject to the general reservation that such accession cannot conflict with the laws on personal status derived from the Islamic *shari'a*. Tunisia, again, has filed a "general declaration" stating that "it shall not take any organisational or legislative decision in conformity with the requirements of this Convention where such a decision would conflict with provisions of Chapter 1 of the Tunisian Constitution". The first article of this Chapter declares Islam to be the official religion of the state, while article 6 guarantees equal treatment before the law.

The remaining States are more specific, but no less sweeping, in their reservations. A number enter specific reservations to article 2,[21] the core of the treaty, obliging States parties to combat sex discrimination by taking specific legislative action, either in its entirety or to some of its aspects. Bangladesh indicates that it does not consider itself bound by the provisions of article 2, as it is of the view that it conflicts with Islamic law. Although framed differently, Egypt enters a similar reservation, expressing its willingness to comply with article 2, "provided that such compliance does not run counter to the Islamic Sharia". Morocco, in an interpretative declaration, asserts that it is also ready to apply the provisions of article 2, except insofar as they may impact on the rules of succession to the Moroccan throne and as long as they do not conflict with the Islamic *shari'a*. As a matter of explanation, Morocco adds that "certain of the provisions contained in the Moroccan Code of Personal Status according women rights that differ from the rights conferred on men may not be infringed upon or abrogated because they derive primarily from the Islamic *shari'a*, which strives, among its other objectives, to strike a balance between the spouses in order to preserve the coherence of family life". Again, Iraq, as well as reserving its position on the state of Israel, enters reservations with respect to article 2, but it confines its objections to article 2(f), which requires States parties to "take all appropriate measures including legislation to modify or abolish existing laws, regulations, customs and practices which constitute discrimination against women" and article 2(g) requiring repeal of penal laws that discriminate on the basis of sex. No explanation is given for these reservations.

Specific objection is raised by a majority of Islamic States to article 9 which requires States parties to grant women equal rights with respect to their nationality and to the nationality of their children. Egypt reserves with respect to this article, explaining that it does so to prevent a child acquiring two nationalities, which it considers may be prejudicial to its future. Egypt goes on to explain that the most suitable approach in the context of nationality is for a child to acquire its father's nationality, both because this does not infringe the principle of equality and because it is customary for a woman to agree on marrying an alien that the children shall be of the father's nationality. Iraq, Jordan, Morocco, Tunisia and Kuwait also reserve with respect to article 9. Morocco reserves here on the basis that the Law of Moroccan Nationality permits a child to bear the nationality of its mother only in those cases where it is born, irrespective of place of birth, to an unknown father, or, if born in Morocco, to a stateless father. In these cases, the nationality of the mother devolves on the child so as to guarantee each child the right to a nationality. Morocco adds that a child born in Morocco of a Moroccan mother and a foreign father may acquire the nationality of its mother by declaration on attaining majority, provided that his or her customary and regular residence is in Morocco. Similarly, Tunisia and Kuwait reserve on the basis that the provisions of, respectively, the Tunisian Nationality Code and the Kuwaiti Nationality Act should be preserved.

Except for the reservations of Bangladesh to article 13(a) which obliges contracting States to accord women the same rights as men to family benefits and of Kuwait to article 7(a) which preserves the privilege of electoral voting to males, the remaining reservations entered by States parties with predominantly Muslim populations relate to articles 15 and 16.

Article 15 provides that women will be accorded equality with men before the law, identical legal capacity to that of men in civil matters and the same opportunities to exercise that capacity, in particular, to conclude contracts and to administer property, and will be treated equally in all stages of procedure in courts and tribunals. It goes on to provide that all contracts and all other private instruments of any kind which seek to restrict the legal capacity of women shall be deemed null and void and that men and women will be accorded the same rights with regard to the law relating to the movement of persons and the freedom to choose their residence and domicile.

Jordan's reservation with respect to this article explains baldly, in brackets, that a woman's residence and domicile are with her husband.

Morocco and Tunisia indicate that article 15, particularly where it relates to a woman's independent residence and domicile, is subject to compatibility with the Code of Personal Status, as, it will be remembered, does Turkey. It should be noted that reservations of this nature could be predicted from the discussion in the Commission on the Status of Women at the time of the preparation of the treaty, during which the Egyptian delegate explained that according to the Qur'an, the husband must choose the site of the matrimonial home and the wife has the same domicile as her husband, a position agreed with by the Indonesian and Iranian delegates. Because their domestic law had been reformed and was consistent with its terms,[22] both the representatives of Egypt and Indonesia were nonetheless able to accept the terms of the article as it now appears.

Article 16[23] is the principal provision of the Women's Convention requiring States parties to eliminate discrimination against women in matters affecting marriage and family relations. In particular, it accords women the same rights as men to enter into marriage; freely to choose a spouse and to enter into marriage only with their free and full consent; the same rights and responsibilities during marriage and at its dissolution; the same rights and responsibilities as parents, irrespective of their marital status, in matters relating to their children; the same rights to decide freely and responsibly on the number and spacing of their children and to have access to the information and means to enable them to exercise these rights; the same rights and responsibilities with regard to guardianship, wardship, trusteeship and adoption of children, or similar institutions where these concepts exist in national legislation; the same personal rights as husband and wife, including the right to choose a family name, a profession and an occupation; the same rights for both spouses in respect of the ownership, acquisition, management, administration, enjoyment and disposition of property, whether free of charge or for a valuable consideration. The article also provides that the betrothal and marriage of a child shall have no legal effect, and all necessary action, including legislation, shall be taken to specify a minimum age for marriage and to make the registration of marriages in an official registry compulsory. This article, along with article 2, constitutes the crucial core of the Convention, with article 16 addressing the private sphere and family life, the fundamental site of discrimination against women which, effectively, sets the framework and opportunity for discrimination in public life. Like article 15, article 16 proved controversial during the preparation of the treaty,[24] with States with predominantly Muslim populations attempting, even in the discussions in the Third Committee of the General Assembly, to amend the draft Convention so as to conform with the principles of Islamic law.[25] Thus, for example, the representative of Morocco argued that the roles of men and women "were not "traditional", but had arisen in the deep consciousness of the human race" and that to provide for equality of rights for men and women would affect the "psychic and moral balance of children".[26] In the event, the article was not amended to conform to Islamic law and, accordingly most states, parties with predominantly Muslim populations have entered reservations to its terms.

Thus, Bangladesh, Egypt, Iraq, Jordan, Morocco, Tunisia and Kuwait have all entered reservations to article 16. Tunisia states, without explanation, that it does not consider itself bound by article 16.1(c), (d) and (f) and that paragraphs (g) and (h) must be consistent with the provisions of its Personal Status Code relating to succession and the granting of family names to children. Bangladesh is content to state that it does not consider itself bound by article 16.1(c) and (f) as they conflict with the *shari'a*, while Kuwait similarly declares that it does not consider itself to be bound by article 16(f) "in as much as it conflicts with the Islamic *shari'a*, Islam being the official religion of the state."

Egypt, Iraq, Jordan and Morocco seek to explain their reservations in terms which suggest that women are, in fact, advantaged by the domestic regime. Thus, Iraq indicates that its reservation is based on the view that the *shari'a* accords women rights equivalent to the rights of their spouses so as to ensure a just balance between them. The reservations of both Egypt and Morocco, which are in similar terms, provide further explanation. Both indicate that the *shari'a* grants women rights relating to marriage and family relations equivalent to those of their husbands so as to ensure a "just balance between them", which Morocco's reservation states serves to "preserve the sacred bond of matrimony" and "the coherence of family life". Egypt's reservation pursues this philosophy further, indicating that the basis of spousal relations is an "equivalency of rights and duties so as to ensure complementarity which guarantees true equality between spouses, not a quasi-equality that renders the marriage a burden on the wife." The reservations of Egypt and Morocco go on to point out that the provisions of the *shari'a* lay down that the husband has an obligation to pay a financial sum to the wife on marriage, maintain her fully during marriage and pay a lump sum on divorce. At the same time, Islamic law provides that the wife retains full rights over her property and is not obliged to contribute to her own maintenance while the marriage subsists. These rights in the Muslim wife, the reservations further explain, are the reason for the apparent inequality between husband and wife where divorce is concerned, the wife requiring a judge's ruling and the husband being able to informally divorce.

Activity to Address Reservations to the Women's Convention

Reservations generally, and particularly those entered by Islamic States, have attracted objections by other States parties to the Women's Convention.[27] Here, the most active States have been Mexico, Germany and Nordic States, particularly Sweden,[28] who argue that the wide and often vague and indeterminate reservations of particularly those States who reserve on the basis of Islamic law are incompatible with the terms of the treaty, which in article 28(2) precludes reservations incompatible with its object and purpose.

By the terms of their objections, both Mexico and Germany indicate that their objections should not be interpreted as impediments to the entry into force of the Women's Convention between Mexico and the reserving party or Germany and the reserving party. Sweden, however, has made uncompromising objections, explaining that to accept reservations that it considers incompatible:

> [Reservations] would render a basic international obligation of a contractual nature meaningless. Incompatible reservations . . . not only cast doubts on the commitments of the reserving States to the object and purpose of the Convention, but also contribute to undermine the basis of international contractual law.

Sweden, moreover, observes that "it is in the common interest of States that treaties to which they have chosen to become parties are also respected, as to object and purpose, by other parties."

In no case, however, has an objecting State stated that its objection precludes the entry into force of the Convention between it and the reserving State.

State objections have not been the only response to the large number of imprecise and far-reaching reservations to the Women's Convention. At the instigation of a number of experts of the Committee on the Elimination of Discrimination against Women (CEDAW) which had considered this issue at its fifth meeting,[29] Canada placed the question of reservations on the agenda of the third meeting of States parties to the Convention, at which a resolution was adopted urging full respect for article 28(2) of the Convention, and requesting the Secretary-General to seek States parties' views on reservations that would be considered to come within article 28(2) and to report those views to the following (41st session) of the General Assembly.[30] The meeting also decided to place the question on the agenda of the next meeting of States parties in 1988.

Despite the fact that the resolution had been adopted by consensus, it caused controversy[31] when the Women's Convention and CEDAW was discussed at the 1986 session of the Economic and Social Council. The Council was not required to take any action on the States parties' decision, but Sweden and the other sponsors of the traditional ECOSOC resolution on the status of Women's Convention, decided to recall the decision with respect to reservations in the text of the resolution. At that time, the widest-reaching reservations had been entered by Bangladesh and Egypt and sought to subject the terms of the Convention to the *shari'a*. A number of delegations thus, considered the draft resolution was anti-Islamic, notwithstanding the fact that there had been objections to reservations which had been made by non-Muslim countries and which were unconcerned with Islamic law. The draft resolution and the issue of the Women's Convention reservations generally were quickly translated into an attack by the West on, first, the Islamic world and, by extension, the whole of the Third World.

Only seventeen States responded to the Secretary-General's request for views, less than 20 per cent of the then States parties and only one of them, Turkey, a States party with a Muslim population. No responses were received from States who had reserved on the basis of the *shari'a*.[32] Although all responses reflected different approaches, Belinda Clark, in her analysis of the responses, concludes that their small number, plus their poor quality is reflective of a view that Women's Convention is somehow separate and distinct from other multilateral treaties, afforded a lesser status than other treaties because of its culturally-sensitive content and perceived more in the nature of statement of intent or rhetoric, rather than a codification of internationally binding obligations.[33]

Consideration of the Secretary-General's report at the Third Committee at the General Assembly's 41st session in 1986 was conducted in a hostile and politicised atmosphere. Muslim countries alleged cultural insensitivity and interference with their sovereign right to make reservations. The resolution adopted by the Committee and, in turn, by the Plenary made no specific reference to reservations, but "recalled the decision of the States parties" and "emphasised the importance of strict compliance with the Convention".[34]

Notwithstanding this clear example of the dangers of wading into deep religious waters, CEDAW was not content to give up on the issue of reservations. At its sixth meeting, held shortly after the events above, amongst the reports to be considered was the initial report of Bangladesh. No doubt to some extent influenced by Bangladesh's report, CEDAW formulated General Recommendation 4 which expresses concern at "the significant number of reservations that appeared to be incompatible with the object and purpose of the Convention", welcomes the decision of the States parties to consider the issue of reservations at its coming meeting in 1988 and suggests States parties "reconsider these reservations with a view to withdrawing them."[35] More controversially, and clearly linked to the consideration of Bangladesh's report, during which experts had expressed concern about the effects of Islamic law on the rights of women in Bangladesh, CEDAW also requested the United Nations "to promote or undertake studies on the status of women under Islamic laws and customs and in particular on the status and equality of women in the family . . . taking into consideration the principle of El Ijtihad in Islam".[36]

CEDAW's General Recommendation and its request for studies on the status of women in Islam, proved divisive. Some weeks later, Bangladesh's delegate to the Economic and Social Council urged "the greatest caution in using the Convention as a pretext for doctrinaire attacks on Islam."[37] Allegations by the delegations of Bangladesh and Egypt that CEDAW was indulging in cultural imperialism and religious intolerance attracted widespread support at the Economic and Social Council, which recommended in its Resolution 1987/3 to the General Assembly that no further action be taken on CEDAW's request for studies on Islam,[38] a suggestion accepted by the General Assembly at its 42nd session. Inevitably and unfortunately, the whole question of reservations was perceived to be bound up with Islam. Reservations were not included in the resolution on the Women's Convention adopted by the Economic and Social Council in 1987, while discussion in the General Assembly was brief and resulted in a bland resolution urging strict compliance by States parties with their obligations under the Convention.[39]

The question of reservations was included on the agenda of the 4th meeting of States parties in March 1988, albeit Egypt reserved its position on the inclusion of the item. In the event, a two-clause decision was adopted, recalling the decision taken at the third meeting of States parties, noting the reports to the General Assembly and the various views expressed at meetings of the General Assembly, the Economic and Social Council and States parties during 1986 and 1988.[40]

Despite rebuffs with regard to the reservations question generally and the position of women in Islamic law, CEDAW has been persistent. In 1988, it again made clear that given the references by States parties to Islamic law and practices in their reservations, it would be useful for CEDAW to have material on the subject.[41] The Committee, further, has not been discouraged from closely questioning States on the issue of their reservations and has continued in its pursuit of what some States still perceive as cultural imperialism and religious intolerance where Islam is concerned. A further General Recommendation concerning reservations was formulated in 1992, while at its meeting in 1994, encouraged by helpful text within the Vienna Declaration and Programme of Action,[42] the Committee amended the Guidelines[43] for the preparation of initial and periodic reports required by the Women's Convention[44] to include guidance for States who have entered substantive reservations. Such States should report specifically with regard to their reservations, why they consider them to be necessary, their precise effect on national law and policy and whether they have entered similar reservations to other human rights treaties which guarantee similar rights. Such States are also required to indicate plans they might have to limit the effect of the reservations or withdraw them and, where possible, specify a time-table for withdrawing them. The Committee made particular reference to those States who have entered general reservations, who would include countries such as the Maldives, or to articles 2 and 3, for example, Egypt and the Libyan Arab Jamahiriya, indicating that the Committee considers such reservations to be incompatible with the object and purpose of the Convention and requiring a special effort from such countries who are directed to report on the effect and interpretation of their reservations.[45] It remains to be seen whether affected States will follow CEDAW's new guidelines and whether States parties with predominantly Muslim populations will take exception to their terms.

The Reservations and Islamic Law

Two issues arise in the context of the reservations to the Women's Convention by States parties with predominantly Muslim populations. The first, and one which has been dealt with elsewhere, is the permissibility of these reservations within the framework of international law.[46] The second, and less examined question, is whether such reservations, particularly where they are wide-sweeping and unexplained, are required by the prescriptions of the *shari'a*.

Historically, Islamic law advanced the position of women by guaranteeing them rights which had not been recognised in the pre-Islamic cultures of the Middle East, wherein women had no say in the initiation and termination of their marriages, lost all rights to inheritance on marriage, were "sold" by their families to their husbands and where men were entitled to an unlimited number of wives.[47] With the advent of Islam, women no longer lost their rights to family property on marriage, they were entitled to be heard on the contractual provisions of their marriage and their husbands were required to pay money directly to them, rather than their families, in consideration of the marriage. Although the pre-Islamic practice of polygamy was not entirely eliminated, Muslim husbands could only take four wives at one time, but only where such husbands could treat all wives equally in all ways.[48]

The four primary sources of Islamic law are traditionally seen as the Qur'an, believed by Muslims to be the living word of God revealed to His Prophet, the Sunna, the deeds and sayings of the Prophet Muhammed, recorded in what are described as the *hadith, ijma* or consensus, which is the unanimous agreement of jurists on a specific issue and *qiyas* or reasoning by analogy.[49] The prescriptions of the Qur'an are conclusive, binding, infallible and beyond question, the *hadith* of the Prophet is binding and attributed to divine revelation, but *ijma* and *qiyas* are less immutable.

Although Islam is effectively a way of life, Islamic law as established in the Qur'an and the *hadith* of the Prophet, regulates, in the main, matters of personal law, such as marriage, divorce, maintenance, the custody and guardianship of children and succession. It does not touch on matters such as, for example, employment, political participation, education and economic life, which are all areas in which the Women's Convention guarantees women equality with men. As the fundamental prescriptions of Islamic law established in the Qur'an and the hadith do not touch upon these areas, States parties who enter general reservations or those that concern these spheres cannot explain their reservations by incompatibility with Islam. Again, the basic prescriptions of Islamic law do not regulate citizenship, thus it is questionable whether reservations with respect to article 9 of the Women's Convention can be explained as contradicting Islamic law. It is similarly questionable whether Islamic law requires a general and widely drawn reservation to article 2 of the treaty. States parties who reserve generally and to the whole of article 2, effectively rendering their treaty commitment meaningless, should be pressed to explain why it is their view that all parts of the treaty or all parts of article 2 are incompatible with the *shari'a*. States parties who have such widely drawn reservations may, on examination, decide that their reservations could be drawn far more narrowly so as to truly reflect the prescriptions of the *shari'a*. An example in this context is the Libyan Arab Jamahiriya, whose initial report required by the Women's Convention was considered by CEDAW during its 13th session in 1994. As we have seen, the Libyan Arab Jamahiriya subjects its obligations under the Women's Convention to a general reservation that its accession cannot conflict with the laws of personal status derived from the Islamic *shari'a*, but, as its initial report revealed, the domestic situation of women in the Libyan Arab Jamahiriya in terms of equality with men de jure and de facto is such that this general reservation is not required. In these circumstances, CEDAW suggested that the reservation be drawn more precisely to reflect the position the States party required.

Although the prescriptions of the *shari'a* may not require reservations of the reach that some States parties have entered, it is certainly the case that Islamic personal law stands in the way of formal equality between women and men in a number of areas. These include inheritance, where the Qur'an prescribes that the male heir inherits the portion of two females and where husbands inherit a greater share of their wives' property than do wives of that of their husbands,[50] marriage and divorce,[51] including custody of children and on matters of evidence.[52] Islamic personal law, thus, stands in the way of unreserved acceptance of article 16.

Nonetheless, even in these areas some modification has been introduced which does serve to advance the status of women in a number of States with significant Muslim populations, including Iraq,[53] Egypt,[54] Tunisia,[55] Morocco[56] and Jordan.[57]

All of these are States parties to the Women's Convention.

Conclusion

It is undeniable that a number of provisions of the Women's Convention, particularly those relating to inheritance and responsibilities in marriage, which are enshrined in the Holy Qur'an, are in contradistinction to Islam and cannot be contracted to by States which apply Islamic law. Most of the guarantees enshrined in the Women's Convention are not precluded by Islamic law. It is incumbent on the human rights community to encourage Islamic States to draw reservations as narrowly as possible, and to demand the removal of vague and general objections outside the prescriptions of the religion. Support should be given to the approach of CEDAW in its review of the initial report of the Libyan Arab Jamahirya where the Committee requested the state to frame its reservations as narrowly as possible.

In the event, however, that the prescriptions of Islamic law do, in reality, conflict with the requirements of the Women's Convention, one can only encourage those scholars who are seeking to discern norms of non-discrimination and equality in the Holy Qur'an, the Sunna and the early commentaries and challenge the traditional view that Islamic law is incapable of evolution.

NOTES

1 GA Res 34/180, 34 UN GAOR Supp. (No 710.46) at 193, UN Doc. A/34/46 (1979) (entered into force Sept. 3, 1981).

2 Articles 2(2) and 3, International Covenant on Economic, Social and Cultural Rights, GA Res 2200, UN GAOR, 21st Sess., Supp. No. 16, at 49, UN Doc A/6316 (1966); articles 2(1) and 3, International Covenant on Civil and Political Rights, GA Res 2200 UN GAOR, 21st Sess., Supp. No. 16 at 52, UN Doc A/6316 (1966).

3 *Compendium of International Conventions Concerning the Status of Women*, United Nations Publication, Sales No. E.88.IV.3, New York, 1988.

4 There is now a large literature on the Women's Convention. A useful bibliography of this literature has been compiled by Rebecca J. Cook, 'Women's International Human Rights: A Bibliography', *New York Journal of International Law and Politics*, Vol. 24, No. 2, 1992, pp. 857–88.

5 Rebecca J. Cook, 'Reservations to the Convention on the Elimination of All Forms of Discrimination Against Women', *Virginia Journal of International Law*, Vol. 30 (1990), p. 644.

6 See, for example, *ibid.* and Belinda Clark, 'The Vienna Convention Reservations Regime and the Convention on Discrimination Against Women', *American Journal of International Law*, 85 (1991), pp. 281–321.

7 United Nations, *Report of the Economic and Social Council* A/5606, 15 November 1963, p. 26. The sponsors of the resolution were: Afghanistan, Algeria, Argentina, Austria, Cameroon, Chile, Colombia, Czechoslavakia, Gabon, Guinea, Indonesia, Iran, Mali, Mexico, Mongolia, Morocco, Pakistan, Panama, the Philippines, Poland, Togo and Venezuela.

8 United Nations, *Draft Declaration on the Elimination of Discrimination Against Women, Memorandum by the Secretary-General* (E/CN.6/426) 30 October 1964.

9 *Ibid.*, p. 5.

10 ECOSOC, *Official Records*, 39th Session Supplement No. 7; CSW *Report on the 18th Session*, 3/1– 3/10, 1965, p. 23.

11 For an account of the drafting process, see Arvonne Fraser, 'The Convention on the Elimination of All Forms of Discrimination Against Women', unpublished paper, 1991.

12 UN Doc. E/CN.6/591.

13 Roberta Jacobson, 'The Committee on the Elimination of Discrimination Against Women' in P. Alston (ed.), *The United Nations and Human Rights: A Critical Appraisal* (Oxford: Clarendon, 1992), pp. 444–72, 446.

14 Noreen Burrows, 'The 1979 Convention on the Elimination of All Forms of Discrimination Against Women', *Netherlands International Law Review*, 32 (1985), 419–60 at 423.

15 GAOR 34th Session, Agenda Item 75 (A/34/PV.107), 18 December 1979. Other countries who abstained were Brazil, Burma, China, Dominiecan Republic, Malawi, Mali, Senegal, Sri Lanka, Upper Volta and Venezuela.

16 GAOR A/34/PV.107.

17 The Republic of India which has a substantial Muslim population, ratified the Convention on 9 July 1993. At ratification, it confirmed the interpretative

declarations and the reservation it made upon signature. The declarations relate to articles 5 (a) and 16(1) and (2) of the treaty and note that the Government of the Republic of India will abide by these provisions in conformity with its policy of non-interference with the personal affairs of any community without its initiative and consent and that, while it fully supports the principle of compulsory registration of marriages, this is not a practical aim in a country as vast and various as India. India also reserves with respect to article 29(1) of the convention.

18 Text of the declarations and reservations to the Women's Convention, as well as objections and notifications of withdrawal of reservations, are collected in *Declarations, reservations, objections and notifications of withdrawal of reservations relating to the Convention on the Elimination of All Forms of Discrimination against Women*, Note by the Secretary-General, CEDAW/SP/1994/2, 26 October 1993.

19 Article 9(1) provides that "States Parties shall grant women equal rights with men to acquire, change or retain their nationality. They shall ensure in particular that neither marriage to an alien nor change of nationailty by the husband during marriage shall automatically change the nationality of the wife, render her stateless or force upon her the nationality of the husband", while article 5(1) obliges States Parties to take all appropriate measures to "modify the social and cultural patterns of conduct of men and women, with a view to achieving the elimination of prejudices and customary and all other practices which are based on the idea of the inferiority of either of the sexes or on stereotyped roles for men and women."

20 Morocco and Kuwait also reserve with respect to article 29(1).

21 Article 2: "States Parties condemn discrimination against women in all its forms, agree to pursue by all appropriate means and without delay a policy of eliminating discrimination against women and, to this end, undertake:

a. to embody the principle of equality of men and women in their national constitutions or other appropriate legislative and other measures, including sanctions where appropriate, prohibiting all discrimination against women;

b. to establish legal protection of the rights of women on an equal basis with men and to ensure through competent national tribunals and other public institutions the effective protection of women against any act of discrimination;

c. to establish legal protection of the rights of women on an equal basis with men and to ensure through competent national tribunals and other public institutions the effective protection of women against any act of discrimination;

d. to refrain from engaging in any act or practice of discrimination against women and to ensure that public authorities and institutions shall act in conformity with this obligation;

e. to take all appropriate measures to eliminate discrimination against women by any organisation or enterprise;

f. to take all appropriate measures, including legislation, to modify or abolish existing laws, regulations, customs and practices which consitute discrimination against women;

g. to repeal all national penal provisions which constitute discrimination against women.

22 UN Doc. E/CN.6/SR.650.

23 Article 16:

1. States parties shall take all appropriate measures to eliminate discrimination

against women in all matters relating to marriage and family relations and in particular shall ensure, on a basis of equality of men and women:

a. the same right to enter into marriage;

b. the same right freely to choose a spouse and to enter into marriage only with their free and full consent;

c. the same rights and responsibilities during marriage and at its dissolution;

d. the same rights and responsibilities as parents, irrespective of their marital status, in matters relating to their children; in all cases the interests of children shall be paramount;

e. the same rights to decide freely and responsibly on the number and spacing of their children and to have access to the information, education and means to enable them to exercise these rights;

f. the same rights and responsiblities with regard to guardianship, wardship, trusteeship or adoption of children, or similar institutions where these concepts exist in national legislation; in all cases the interests of the children shall be paramount;

g. the same personal rights as husband and wife, including the right to choose a family name, a profession and an occupation;

h. the same rights for both spouses in respect of the onwership, acquisition, management, administration, enjoyment and disposition of property, whether free of charge or for a valuable consideration.

2. The betrothal and the marriage of a child shall have no legal effect, and all necessary action, including legislation, shall be taken to specify a minimum age for marriage and to make the registration of marriages in an official registry compulsory.

24 UN Doc. E/5909.

25 UN Soc. A/C 3/34. SR 70–3.

26 Noreen Burrows, 'The 1979 Convention on the Elimination of All Forms of Discrimination Against Women', p. 450.

27 See Rebecca Cook, 'Reservations to the Convention on the Elimination of All Forms of Discrimination Against Women'; and Belinda Clark, 'The Vienna Convention'.

28 CEDAW/SP/1994/2. On 5 May 1994 the UN Secretary-General received objections from the Government of Finland to the reservations of the Maldives, while on 14 July 1994 he received objections from the Government of The Netherlands to the reservations of the Maldives and the reservations and declarations of Morocco and India.

29 Report of the Committee on the Elimination of Discrimination against Women on its Fifth Session, 41 UN GAOR Supp (No 45) at 46, UN Doc. A/41/45 (1986).

30 CEDAW/SP/10(1986).

31 Belinda Clark, 'The Vienna Convention', pp. 283–9.

32 UN Docs. A/41/608 and Add. 1(1986).

33 Belinda Clark, 'The Vienna Convention', pp. 284–7.

34 GA Res. 41/108 (4 December 1986).

35 General Recommendation 4, Report of the Committee on the Elimination of Discrimination against Women, Sixth Session, 42 UNGAOR Supp (No. 38), para. 579, UN Doc. A/42/38 (1987).

36 *Ibid.*, para. 583.

37 UN Doc. E/1987/SR. 11, p. 13.

38 ESC Res 1987/3 (26 May 1987).

39 Andrew Byrnes, 'The "Other" Human Rights Treaty Body: The Work of the Committee on the Elimination of Discrimination Against Women', 14 *Yale Journal of International Law* (1989), pp. 52–5.

40 Report of the Fourth Meeting of the States Parties to the Convention on the Elimination of All Forms of Discrimination Against Women, UN Doc. CEDAW/SP/14 (1988), p. 2.

41 Report of the Committee on the Elimination of Discrimination Against Women (Seventh Session), 43 UNGAOR Supp (No. 38) UN Doc A/43/38(1988), para. 61.

42 United Nations World Conference on Human Rights: Vienna Declaration and Programme of Action, 25 June 1993, 32 ILM 1661 (1993), para. 39 states: "Ways and means of addressing the particularly large number of reservations to the Convention should be encouraged. Inter alia, the Committee on the Elimination of Discrimination against Women should continue its review of reservations to the Convention. States are urged to withdraw reservations that are contrary to the object and purpose of the Convention or which are otherwise incompatible with international treaty law."

43 The Chairpersons of the supervisory committees established under the International Covenants on Civil and Political Rights, Economic, Social and the Cultural Rights, the Conventions on the Elimination of All Forms of Racial Discrimination, Suppression and Punishment of the Crime of Apartheid, Against Torture and Other Cruel, Inhuman or Degrading Treatment or Punishment and on the Elimination of All Forms of Discrimination against Women agreed consolidated guidelines for reporting in 1991 (HRI/1991/1). CEDAW has itself adopted general guidelines for the form and content of initial and periodic reports. These are described in Zagorka Ilic, 'The Convention on the Elimination of All Forms of Discrimination against Women', *Manual on Human Rights reporting*, United Nations, HR/Pub, 91/1, 1991, pp. 153–75.

44 Article 18.

45 Committee on the Elimination of Discrimination against Women, 13th session, New York, 17 January–4 February 1994, Report of Working Group 1, CEDAW/C/1994/WG.1/WP.1/Rev.1, 31 January 1994. The Committee also requested that a special letter be sent by the Secretary-General, drawing attention to the Committee's concern, to those States parties that have entered substantive reservations to the Convention and recommended that the programme of advisory services of the Centre for Human Rights and the Division for the Advancement of Women be available to provide advice to States parties on the withdrawal of reservations. Consolidated guidelines including these amendments were issued by the Committee during its 14th session in 1995.

46 Rebecca Cook,.'Reservations to the Convention on the Elimination of All Forms of Discrimination Against Women' and Belinda Clark, 'The Vienna Convention'.

47 John L. Esposito, *Women in Islamic Family Law* (Syracuse, N.Y.: Syracuse University Press, 1982), p. 20.

48 Qur'an IV, 3: "And if you are apprehensive that you shall not deal fairly with orphans, then, of other women who seem good in your eyes, marry but two, or three or four; and if you still fear that you shall not act equitably, then one only; or the

slaves whom ye have acquired: this will make justice on your part easier",
Muhammad Valibhai Merchant, *A Book of Qur'anic Laws* (Lahore: Law Publishing
Co., 1947), p. 136.

49 Jamal J. Nasir, *The Islamic Law of Personal Status* (London: Graham & Trotman,
1986), pp. 18–22.

50 Qur'an IV, 12, 13, 14.

51 Qur'an II, 234; IV, 38; II, 228; II, 229. See Aftab Hussain, *Status of Women in Islam*
(Lahore: Law Publishing Co., 1987).

52 Qur'an II, 282.

53 Norman Anderson, 'A Law of Personal Status for Iraq', *International and Comparative Law Quarterly*, 1960, pp. 542–64.

54 Law No. 100 of 1985.

55 Norman Anderson, 'The Tunisian Law of Personal Status', *International and
Comparative Law Quarterly*, 1958, pp. 262–79.

56 Norman Anderson, 'Reforms of Family Law in Morocco', *Journal of African Law*,
1958, pp. 146–59.

57 L. Welchman, 'The Development of Islamic Family Law in the Legal System
of Jordan', *International and Comparative Law Quarterly*, 1988, pp. 868–86.

SELECT BIBLIOGRAPHY

Accad, Evelyne, *Sexuality and War: Literary Masks of the Middle East* (New York: New York University Press, 1990).

Afshar, Haleh, (ed.), *Women in the Middle East: Perceptions, Realities, and Struggles for Liberation* (London: Macmillan, 1993).

Afshar, Haleh and Carolyne Dennis (eds.), *Women and Adjustment Policies in the Third World* (London: Macmillan, 1992).

Ahmed, Leila, *Women and Gender in Islam* (New Haven: Yale University Press, 1991).

Altorki, Soraya, *Women in Saudi Arabia: Ideology and Behavior Among the Elite* (New York: Columbia University Press, 1986).

Arberry, A. J., *The Koran Interpreted* (2 vols., London: Allen and Unwin, 1955).

Aziz, Ahmad, *Islamic Law in Theory and Practice* (London: Punjab Educational Press, 1956).

Badran, Margot, *Feminists, Islam and Nation: Gender and the Making of Modern Egypt* (Princeton: Princeton University Press, 1995).

Badran, Margot and Miriam Cook (eds.), *Opening the Gates: A Century of Arab Feminist Writing* (London: Virago, 1990).

Benallecue, Nora, 'Algerian Women in the Struggle for Independence and Reconstruction', *Social Science Journal*, 1983.

Best, Geoffrey, 'Justice, International Relations and Human Rights', *International Affairs*, October, 1995.

Bouiidiba, A., *Sexuality in Islam* (London: Routledge & Kegan Paul, 1975).

Buonaventura, Wendy, *Serpent of the Nile: Women and Dance in the Arab World* (London: Saqi, 1989).

Butler, Judith, *Gender Trouble: Feminism and the Subversion of Identity* (New York: Routledge, 1990).

Chehata, C., *Etudes de Droit Musulman* (Paris: Faculty of Law, University of Paris, 1971).

Chhachhi, A., *Women, Islam and the State* (London: Macmillan, 1991).

Cole, J. R. I. and N. R. Keddie (eds.), *Shi'ism and Social Protest* (New Haven: Yale University Press, 1986).

Cooke, Miriam, *Wars' Other Voices: Women Writers on the Lebanese Civil War* (Cambridge: Cambridge University Press, 1988).

De Bellefonds, Linant Y., *Traité de droit musulman comparé* (Paris: Mouton, 1965).
Doi, Abdur Rahman I., *Women in Shari'a* (London: Ta-Ha Publishers, 1989).

Esposito, John L., *Women in Muslim Family Law* (Syracuse, N.Y.: Syracuse University Press, 1982).

Fakhro, Munira A., *Women at Work in the Gulf* (London and New York: Kegan Paul International, 1990).
Fathi, A., (ed.), *Women and the Family in Iran* (Leiden: E. J. Brill, 1985).
Fernea, Elizabeth Warnock (ed.), *Women and the Family in the Middle East: New Voices of Change* (Austin: University of Texas Press, 1985).
Fernea, Elizabeth Warnock and Basima Qattan Bezirgan (eds.), *Middle Eastern Muslim Women Speak* (Austin: University of Texas Press, 1977).

Haeri, S., *Law of Desire: Temporary Marriage in Islam* (London: I. B. Tauris, 1989).
Hafez, Sabry, *The Genesis of Arabic Narrative Discourse: A Study in the Sociology of Modern Arabic Literature* (London: Saqi, 1993).
Hijab, Nadia, *Womanpower: The Arab Debate on Women at Work* (Cambridge: Cambridge University Press, 1988).
Hourani, Albert, *A History of the Arab Peoples* (London: Faber and Faber, 1991).

Ingrams, D., *The Awakened: Women in Iraq* (London: Third World Centre for Research and Publishing Ltd., 1983)
Iqbal, M., *The Reconstruction of Religious Thought in Islam* (Lahore, Pakistan, 1971).

al-Khayyat, Sana, *Honour and Shame: Women in Modern Iraq* (London: Saqi Books, 1990).
Keddie, Nikkie and Beth Baron, (eds.), *Women in Middle Eastern History: Shifting Boundaries in Sex and Gender* (Oxford: Blackwell, 1991).
Kocturk, Tahirc, *A Matter of Honour: Experiences of Turkish Women Immigrants* (London: Zed Books, 1992).

Marsot, Afaf Lutfi al-Sayyid, *Women and Men in Late Eighteenth-Century Egypt* (Austin: University of Texas Press, 1995).

MacLeod, Arlene Elowe, *Accommodation Protest: Working Women, the New Veiling and Change in Cairo* (New York: Colombia University Press, 1991).

Mallat, Chibli and Jane Connors, (eds.), *Islamic Family Law* (London: Graham and Trotman, 1990).

Malti-Douglas, F., *Women's Body, Women's World: Gender and Discourse in Arabo-Islamic Writing* (Princeton: Princeton University Press, 1992).

Mernissi, Fatima, *Beyond the Veil: Male–Female Dynamics in a Modern Muslim Society* (Cambridge, Mass.: Schenkman Publishing Company, 1975).

—— *The Veil and the Male Elites: A Feminist Interpretation of Women's Rights in Islam* (Massachusetts: Addison-Wesley, 1991).

—— *Women and Islam: An Historical and Theological Enquiry* (Oxford: Blackwell, 1991).

Minai, N., *Women in Islam* (London: John Murray, 1981).

Mir-Hosseini, Ziba, *Marriage on Trial: A Study of Islamic Family Law* (London: I. B. Tauris, 1993).

Moi, Toril, *Sexual/Textual Politics: Feminist Literary Theory* (London: Methuen, 1985).

Motahhari, M., *The Rights of Women in Islam* (Tehran: World Organization for Islamic Services, 1981).

Musallam, B., *Sex and Society in Islam: Birth Control before the Nineteenth Century* (Cambridge: Cambridge University Press, 1983).

Nashat, G., (ed.), *Women and Revolution in Iran* (Boulder, Colorado: Westview Press, 1983).

Nasir, Jamal J., *The Islamic Law of Personal Status* (London: Graham and Trotman, 1986).

Pakzad, S., *In the Eye of the Storm: Women in Post-revolutionary Iran* (London: I. B. Tauris, 1994).

Rahman, Fazlur, *Role of Muslim Women in Society* (London: Seerah Foundation, 1986).

Saadawi, Nawal, *The Hidden Face of Eve: Women in the Arab World* (London: Zed Books, 1980).

al-Samman, Ghadah, *'al-Matlub tahrir al-mar'a min al-taharrur'*

(Beirut: Manshurat Ghadah al-Samman, 1980).

Shabaan, Bouthaina, *Both Right- and Left-Handed: Arab Women Talk about their Lives* (London: Women's Press, 1991).

al-Shahi, Ahmed, (ed.), *The Diversity of the Muslim Community: Anthropological Essays in Memory of Peter Lienhardt* (London: Ithaca Press, 1987).

Smith, W. Robertson, *Kinship and Marriage in Early Arabia* (London: Adam and Charles Black, 1907).

Shar'iati, A., *Fatemeh Fatemeh ast* (Tehran: Shabdiz Press, 1978).

—— *On the Sociology of Islam* (Berkeley: Mizan Press, 1979).

Siddiqui, Mazharuddin, *Women in Islam* (Delhi: Adam Publishers and Distributors, 1987).

Stowasser, Barbara, *Women in the Qur'an: Traditions and Interpretations* (New York: Oxford University Press, 1994).

Tabari A., and N. Yeganeh (eds.), *In the Shadow of Islam* (London: Zed Books, 1982).

Tucker, Judith (ed.), *Arab Women: Old Boundaries, New Frontiers* (Bloomington: Indiana University Press, 1993).

UN Compendium of International Conventions Concerning the Status of Women (United Nations Publications, Sales No. E. 88. IV, 3, New York, 1988).

Weiseberg, Kelly, (ed.), *Feminists Legal Theory Foundations* (Philadelphia: Temple University Press, 1993).

al-Yassini, A., *Religion and State in the Kingdom of Saudi Arabia* (Boulder, Colorado: Westview Press, 1985).

Ziadeh, F. J., 'Equality in the Muslim Law of Marriage', *American Journal of Comparative Law*, 1957.

INDEX